Aquinas and the Theology of the Body

Aquinas and the Theology of the Body

The Thomistic Foundations of
John Paul II's Anthropology

THOMAS PETRI, OP

The Catholic University of America Press
Washington, D.C.

The paper used in this publication meets the minimum requirements of
American National Standards for Information Science—Permanence of Paper
for Printed Library Materials, ANSI z39.48-1984.

∞

Library of Congress Cataloging-in-Publication Data
Names: Petri, Thomas
Title: Aquinas and the theology of the body : the Thomistic foundations
of John Paul II's anthropology / Thomas Petri, OP.
Description: Washington, D.C. : The Catholic University of America Press, 2016. |
Series: Thomistic ressourcement series ; Volume 7 | Includes bibliographical
references and index.
Identifiers: LCCN 2015048888 | ISBN 9780813231501 (cloth : alk. paper)
Subjects: LCSH: Human body—Religious aspects—Catholic Church. |
John PaulII, Pope, 1920–2005. Theology of the body. | Thomas, Aquinas, Saint,
1225?–1274. | Sex—Religious aspects—Catholic Church. |
Theological anthropology—Catholic Church.
Classification: LCC BX1795.B63 P48 2016 | DDC 233/.5—dc23
LC record available at http://lccn.loc.gov/2015048888

Nihil Obstat:
Reverend Christopher Begg, STD, PhD
Censor Deputatus

Imprimatur:
Most Reverend Barry C. Knestout
Auxiliary Bishop of Washington

Archdiocese of Washington
March 26, 2015
The nihil obstat and imprimatur are official declarations that a book or
pamphlet is free of doctrinal or moral error. There is no implication that those
who have granted the nihil obstat and the imprimatur agree with the content,
opinions, or statements expressed therein.

Nihil Obstat:
Reverend John Corbett, OP, STL, PhD
Censor Deputatus

Imprimi Potest:
Very Reverend Kenneth Letoile, OP, STL
Prior Provincial

Dominican Province of Saint Joseph
April 8, 2015
The nihil obstat and imprimi potest are official declarations that a book or pamphlet
is free of doctrinal or moral error and that the author has been given permission
by his major superior to publish the work. There is no implication that those who
have granted the nihil obstat and the imprimi potest agree with the content,
opinions, or statements expressed therein.

In loving memory of my parents, Jack and
Mary. Dedicated to my Dominican brethren
with fraternal affection and gratitude

Contents

Abbreviations

AAS	*Acta Apostolicae Sedis*
AS	*Acta Synodalia Sacrosancti Concilii Oecumenici Vaticani II*
CC	*Casti Connubii* (encyclical of Pope Pius XI)
FC	*Familiaris Consortio* (apostolic exhortation of Pope John Paul II)
GS	*Gaudium et Spes* (document of Second Vatican Council)
HV	*Humanae Vitae* (encyclical of Pope Paul VI)
MD	*Mulieris Dignitatem* (apostolic letter of Pope John Paul II)
PG	*Patrologiae cursus completus. Series graeca*, ed. Migne
PL	*Patrologiae cursus completus. Series latina*, ed. Migne
SCG	*Summa contra Gentiles* (Thomas Aquinas)
ST	*Summa Theologiae* (Thomas Aquinas)
TOB	*Theology of the Body* (Pope John Paul II)

Preface

As a Catholic priest born in 1978, the year of three popes, I lived much of my young life during the pontificate of Pope John Paul II. Like many priests my age, John Paul became for me a shepherd larger than life and a model for my own priesthood. Only after I entered seminary studies and later the Order of Preachers did I come to realize the significance of his pontificate for so many people in the church and in the world. How could one not grow in admiration of him? Thomas Aquinas, on the other hand, was perennially present in my home growing up, since my mother had a devotion to him (for reasons I still do not quite know). But when I began to study Aquinas in seminary and later as one of his brother Dominicans, my devotion both to him and to his teaching grew. This book grew out of a genuine affection for these two great saints and a real conviction that their thought is more connected than is often suggested.

For various reasons, some of which were beyond my control, this book has taken many years to produce and there are several people who must be acknowledged as assisting and supporting its publication along the way. First among those deserving thanks is John Grabowski, who directed the writing of an earlier version of this manuscript during my doctoral work at the Catholic University of America and later insisted repeatedly that it should be published immediately. John Corbett, OP, and William Mattison were also crucial reviewers in the early days of the manuscript. I am also grateful for the CUA Press peer reviewers: Jarosław Kupczak, OP, and Deborah Savage. The feedback of these great scholars strengthened this book and I trust the reader will not hold them responsible for any error they might find herein.

Every book needs editors. Eleanor Nicholson performed above and beyond all expectation when she agreed to edit this manuscript in the months just prior to giving birth to her second child, Veronica Eve. Through the intercession of saints Thomas Aquinas and John Paul, may Veronica find happiness in this life and know it perfectly in the next. Bianca Czaderna pored over the manuscript to check the spelling of every Polish word. James Kruggel, John Martino, Paul Higgins, and the editorial staff at CUA Press were not only constant supporters of this project, but worked tirelessly to bring it to fruition. This book would never have seen the light of day without the invaluable assistance of its editors.

I am honored that Matthew Levering and Thomas Joseph White, OP, invited this book to be included in the Thomistic Ressourcement Series. The series has published some of the best scholars in Thomism, and I am grateful to have my small contribution stand next to theirs since, like them, I believe Thomas Aquinas has much to contribute to present-day conversations and debates.

Dominic always sent his brethren out two by two; Dominicans do not engage the world alone, but always together. This book would also not have been possible without the support of my Dominican brethren. Fr. Dominic Izzo, OP, and Fr. Brian Mulcahy, OP, as successive Prior Provincials during my doctoral studies and the writing of this book allowed me the time and space necessary to complete this work. Fr. Kenneth Letoile, OP, and Fr. John Langlois, OP, were also instrumental in encouraging and promoting my studies. Various houses throughout the Order welcomed and supported me as I wrote this book throughout the years: the Dominican House of Studies in Washington, D.C.; St. Pius V Parish in Providence, Rhode Island; and St. Thomas Aquinas Priory at Providence College. Their patience with me and support for this work has been a constant witness of the fraternal charity that so characterizes Dominican life. This is why I am dedicating this book, in part, to my Dominican brothers.

The cloistered Dominican nuns at St. Dominic's Monastery in Linden, Virginia, welcomed me monthly over the last year as I completed this book. Dominic founded communities of cloistered women to support the active mission of the friars. The good fruit that Dominican friars bear to the world is due, in large part, to their intercession for us. Finally, the Dominican Sisters of Mary Mother of the Eucharist in Ann Arbor, Michigan, provided me the necessary seclusion in the home stretch of this manuscript's completion. We Dominican friars are always grateful to be co-workers with our active sisters for the evangelization of the world.

Finally, this book is in memory of my parents, Jack and Mary, with gratitude for the life they gave me and with a prayer that one day we will see each other again in the life to come.

REV. THOMAS PETRI, OP
Nativity of the Blessed Virgin Mary
September 8, 2015

Aquinas and the Theology
of the Body

Introduction

On September 5, 1979, Pope John Paul II began a series of catechetical talks on man, woman, love, marriage, and sexuality during his Wednesday general audience. These weekly catecheses concluded on November 28, 1984. They were interrupted only during the pope's recovery from an assassination attempt in 1981, during a Holy Year (1983–84), and for various other intermittent topics. Collectively, these catecheses have been referred to as a "theology of the body." Delivered during a time of exceptional confusion on these matters in the church and in society, the content of these addresses has become the focus of a cottage industry of commentaries and popular works. Papal biographer George Weigel suggested that "these 130 catechetical addresses, taken together, constitute a kind of theological time bomb set to go off, with dramatic consequences, sometime in the third millennium of the Church."[1] Only time will prove the veracity of this claim.

Given the richness of these catechetical talks and the dynamic way John Paul practiced theology in their composition, it is an understandable temptation to interpret this work solely on its own terms. But my proposition is that an authentic understanding of this "theology of the body" relies on an appreciation of the intersection of the thought of John Paul II and Thomas Aquinas. The reason for this is to be found in one of the central concepts of the catecheses: "the spousal meaning of the body." According to John Paul, the body necessarily expresses the gift of self, that is, of the person. This spousal meaning is rooted in

1. George Weigel, *Witness to Hope: The Biography of Pope John Paul II* (New York: Harper Collins, 1999), 343.

man's very being and nature. The spousal meaning of the body is most apparent in the conjugal act of spouses and is at the heart of many of the pope's assertions about man's existence in the world. This meaning is not limited to marriage. Rather, it is fulfilled in the communion of persons, in which even celibates and virgins can participate, and is perfected in the beatific vision of God. Still, throughout these catechetical talks, the spousal relationship between man and woman is the prime reference for the spousal meaning of the body.

As the opening chapters of this book will show, Pope John Paul II was a priest very much concerned with the struggles of the faithful to live the moral teachings of the church. He was particularly convinced that the objectivistic tendencies that characterized the moral theology and philosophy he had learned during his priestly formation were no longer suitable in communicating and defending these teachings to the modern world. The scholasticism he had inherited needed to be supplemented in his view by a more subjective approach.

This is where Thomas Aquinas (d. 1274) traditionally makes his appearance in a narrative that considers the work of Pope John Paul II. The scholastic movement that began in the twelfth century had a tremendous impact on the theology and practice of the universal church.[2] Though not uninterrupted, Aquinas's influence has endured through the centuries. His intellectual progeny often refer to themselves as Thomists.[3] Scholasticism itself experienced a revival of sorts in the

---

2. "Scholasticism" is here understood to be the movement founded on a particular method of theological instruction developed at the universities of Paris and Oxford in the twelfth century. The father of the movement, Peter Abelard (d. 1142), employed the custom already use at the time by canon lawyers of "grouping opposed authorities on either side of a clearly established 'either-or' question" and settling the matter through disputation. Gerald A. McCool, *The Neo-Thomists* (Milwaukee, Wis.: Marquette University Press, 1994), 11.

3. The word "Thomism" refers to a species of scholasticism. The definition of Thomism has been in dispute for a number of years. Fundamentally, it refers to a movement that is in relation, somehow, to the thought of Thomas Aquinas. However, specifically delineating who qualifies as a Thomist and who does not has been an area of contention. See Romanus Cessario, OP, *A Short History of Thomism* (Washington, D.C.: The Catholic University of America Press, 2005), 11–28. James Weisheipl has offered a good working definition. For him, Thomism is "a theological and philosophical movement that begins in the thirteenth century, and embodies the systematic attempt to understand and develop the basic principles and conclusions of St. Thomas Aquinas in order to relate them to the problems and needs of each generation." James A. Weisheipl,

mid-nineteenth and early twentieth centuries. This new scholasticism, or neo-scholasticism, was situated in opposition to the secularism of the Enlightenment, which emphasized reason over faith.[4] Neo-scholasticism was a broad movement comprising many different strands of Thomism (hence "neo-Thomism") as well as the devotees of other medieval theologians and philosophers. In contradistinction to the Enlightenment's subjectivism, they argued that objective moral norms were sustainable.

Influenced by neo-scholasticism, and neo-Thomism in particular, moral theologians began to identify objective criteria to evaluate human action in order to discern the rightness or wrongness of particular human choices. The impact of their work was significant due to the importance of the moral theology manuals being used to train priests at the time. Catholic moral theology and practice was thus dominated from the seventeenth century to the mid-twentieth century by an emphasis on objective moral norms and the evaluation of human actions by their physical structure. That is to say, the manualist tradition into the twentieth century tended to describe human action as it could be observed exteriorly, and without reference to the interior workings or movements of the person. Additionally, following the scholastic emphasis on the absolute authority of nature, the manualists tended to identify the ends (telê) of human nature with the physical structures of the body.

Practically, this meant that the moral good in the sexual arena was synonymous with the finality of the procreative organs. The purpose or goal (the telos) of these organs is to procreate. Therefore, the manualists held, any act which frustrated this use was intrinsically immoral. And so this emphasis on physical structure of the act and its relationship to nature was easily associated with human biology and its purposes. In time, this exclusive focus on biology would be referred to somewhat pejoratively as "physicalism" or "biologism."[5] This fo-

---

"Thomism," in *The New Catholic Encyclopedia*, ed. Bernard L. Marthaler (New York: McGraw-Hill, 1967), 14:126.

4. "Neo-scholasticism" was a broad movement in the nineteenth and early twentieth centuries that included not only a renewed interest in Thomas, although this was substantial, but also an interest in the scholastic method generally.

5. Charles E. Curran was among the first to use the word "physicalism" when, in 1969, he wrote an article responding to Pope Paul VI's encyclical on birth control,

cus on biology was most evident in sexual and medical ethics. Masturbation, for example, was thought to be intrinsically evil because it confounded the natural finality of the generative organ. Similarly, the manualists explained that contraception is intrinsically immoral because it also circumvents of the physical or biological *telos* of the procreative organs.

The limitations of this approach were felt well before the introduction of the birth control pill. The pill uses the hormone progesterone, which is natural to a woman's body. It also imitates the natural infertility a woman experiences during her menstrual cycle. Thus, the pill seemingly worked with the biological structures of the body rather than against them. Additionally, its use would not constitute a physical barrier in the conjugal act itself.[6]

In the twentieth century, another philosophical and theological movement arose, which would directly respond to physicalism. Though it is as varied and as multifaceted as scholasticism, personalism is a school of thought that emphasizes the person, rather than nature, as the primary object of moral discourse.[7] In the Catholic

---

Humanae Vitae. He wrote that physicalism is "a natural law methodology which tends to identify the moral action with the physical and biological structure of the act." Charles E. Curran, "Natural Law and Contemporary Moral Theology," in Curran, ed., *Contraception: Authority and Dissent* (New York: Herder and Herder, 1969), 159; see also 160–67.

6. While I will be offering a detailed history of the debate surrounding the birth control pill, John S. Grabowski offers a succinct analysis of these issues and their relation to the manuals of theology. See John S. Grabowski, *Sex and Virtue* (Washington, D.C.: The Catholic University of America Press, 2003), 1–22.

7. A movement as broad as personalism with so many varied scholars eludes simple definition. The definition I have offered here is provided only in brief to assist the reader in categorizing the thinkers who will be presented in the first two chapters of the book. As J. A. Mann has noted, "any philosophy that insists upon the reality of the person—human, angelic, or divine—may legitimately be classified as personalist, the name personalism more commonly designates a movement of some significance ... [that] is usually theistic in orientation, and places great stress on personality as a supreme value and as a key notion that gives meaning to all of reality." J. A. Mann, "Personalism," in *The New Catholic Encyclopedia*, ed. Marthaler, 11:172. Not all personalists were so for the same reasons. Some were responding to the philosophical materialism of the nineteenth century, others to evolutionism, and still others to idealism. As will be seen in chapter 2, many Catholic personalists were responding to what they perceived to be an exclusive emphasis on human nature at the expense of the human person. What the movements all have in common is this concern for the human person and the attempt to shift discourse to the importance of the human person. Personalism took root in both America

church, personalism grew within the larger discussion, which began in the early 1920s, on the nature of marriage, conjugal love, and procreation. As Catholic theologians and the laity explored new and dynamic presentations of the church's teaching on marriage, the inadequacy of the traditional (and somewhat physicalist) presentation of marriage was apparent.

Perceiving the imbalance of the Catholic teaching on marriage at the time, some personalists, like Dietrich von Hildebrand, sought to reemphasize the category of the person in moral discourse. Other personalists wanted to revise church teaching on marriage, some in more extreme ways than others, and thus they may be labeled as revisionists. As we will see in chapter 2, Herbert Doms would advocate a moderate revision of church teaching by insisting that the traditional teaching on the hierarchy of the ends of marriage (procreative and unitive) should be reversed, making the unitive aspect of marriage primary. But he was not a wholesale revisionist as Louis Janssens—and later, Charles Curran and Bernard Häring—would prove to be. These theologians would argue that the human person has complete authority over nature and therefore the church's ban on contraception should be lifted. This was a position to which Herbert Doms never subscribed.

Initially, the debate in the mid-twentieth century surrounding the birth control pill began as a debate between the physicalist and personalist schools. However, as the church gradually adopted a more personalist approach (as in *Gaudium et Spes* and *Humanae Vitae*), the debate shifted to the more fundamental issue: the relationship between person and nature. This is the context in which we will consider Karol Wojtyła (d. 2005). Not only was he committed to the subjectivist tendencies of personalism, he in fact relied upon the objective ontology of Thomism. His unique personalism was apparent in his early books, *Love and Responsibility* and *The Acting Person*, the latter being an edited form of his 1953 dissertation.[8] Wojtyła's Christian per-

---

and Europe. For brief histories of personalism, see Mann, "Personalism," 172–74; John Cowburn, *Personalism and Scholasticism* (Milwaukee, Wis.: Marquette University Press, 2005), 47–84.

8. See Karol Wojtyła, *Miłość i Odpowiedzialność. Studium etyczne* (Lublin: KUL, 1960). English translation: Karol Wojtyła, *Love and Responsibility*, trans. H. T. Willets (San Francisco, Calif.: Ignatius Press, 1991), and Karol Wojtyła, *The Acting Person*, trans. Andrzej Potocki (Boston: D. Reidel, 1979).

sonalism is especially dominant in these catechetical talks. Although many scholars and catechists have read and commented on these talks, there has been little scholarship on the pope's Thomistic pedigree in this teaching—a critical point that this book seeks to remedy.

One of the concerns of this book is to show that in the 1960s and early 1970s Karol Wojtyła often incorporated references to Thomas Aquinas and was seldom critical of Aquinas's theological positions. Nevertheless, he was searching for a way to move beyond Thomistic philosophy and theology in order to include human experience as a theological category. His study of John of the Cross and Max Scheler helped him to do this. The philosophical fruit of that quest was *The Acting Person*.

In his articles after the publication of *The Acting Person*, Wojtyła was more likely to be respectfully critical of the Angelic Doctor, even noting, as we will see, that Aquinas's presuppositions were not suitable for a major discussion of human experience and consciousness. Throughout the 1970s, Wojtyła's philosophical and theological writings were more concerned with elaborating the subjective aspect of the human person. This emphasis was brought to bear in his many defenses of *Humanae Vitae*, the culmination of which is the theology of the body catecheses. According to John Paul, *Humanae Vitae* was the catalyst for these catecheses.[9] Thus, these talks are best read as a continuation of Wojtyła's work on sexual ethics from the 1960s and 1970s. We will study this development in chapter 4.

The pope never renounced metaphysical or ontological categories. On the contrary, as will be shown in chapter 3, he insisted upon their absolute necessity, even at the end of his life. Still, because he presumes ontological conclusions already established in the tradition, he spends little time, for example, arguing for the stability of human nature or describing the nature of human action. And this is apparent in his catechesis. So while he argues that man must be true to the natural spousal attribute of the human body and must convey the

---

9. See John Paul II, *Man and Woman He Created Them: A Theology of the Body*, trans. Michael Waldstein (Boston: Pauline Books and Media, 2006), no. 133 [hereafter, *TOB*]. Note that I have adopted Waldstein's citation system. He has numbered the catecheses consecutively and numbered each paragraph in each catechesis. Thus, "*TOB*, no. 12:5" refers to catechesis 12, paragraph 5.

meaning of the body, he does not explain exactly how the body has an intrinsic meaning.

This is the point at which a deeper consideration of the work of Thomas Aquinas will prove particularly fruitful. During the time of Pope John Paul's pontificate, there was a renewed interest in the recovery of the thought of Aquinas as distinct from his commentators and the interpretations of neo-Thomists. This renewal is characterized by a focus on the works of Aquinas and on the sources he himself used.[10] Though he lived in a different historical era than Pope John Paul and was responding to different issues, Aquinas formulated a variety of concepts concerning the relationship between person and nature, of love, of marriage, and of the body. These came to fruition in his final work, the *Summa Theologiae*, in which he provides a thorough analysis of key theological ideas.

Pope John Paul had good reason to emphasize consciousness and experience in the twentieth century. During the twenty-first century many of the ontological and metaphysical categories in which Wojtyła was trained, and which are in the background of the theology of the body, have faded from the discussion of marriage and sex, even in the excitement over the pope's theology. Such is the purpose of this study. A mutual interaction between Aquinas and John Paul's *Theology of the Body* would be beneficial to the thought of both; even further, it is critical for the full understanding of the pope's thought.

This study will proceed as follows. Since I am suggesting that John Paul's theology of the body is a work of personalism developed in response to the manualist tradition rather than to Aquinas's theology, the first chapter follows the analysis of several reputable contemporary scholars and historians who have successively shown the shift of manualist theology away from the work of Aquinas himself. The second chapter then turns to the development of personalism within the

10. An example of this renewal is certainly the work of Servais Pinckaers, OP, and Jean-Pierre Torrell, OP. See, for example, Servais Pinckaers, OP, *The Sources of Christian Ethics*, trans. Mary Thomas Noble (Washington, D.C.: The Catholic University of America Press, 1995); Servais Pinckaers, OP, *The Pinckaers Reader: Renewing Thomistic Moral Theology*, eds. John Berkman and Craig Steven Titus (Washington, D.C.: The Catholic University of America Press, 2005); and Jean-Pierre Torrell, OP, *Saint Thomas Aquinas*, 2 vols. (Washington, D.C.: The Catholic University of America Press, 1996–2003).

larger ecclesial discussion on marriage and the debate on birth control. This chapter traces the development of personalism in the twentieth century as a reaction to the perceived physicalism of the Catholic manuals of moral theology. Chapter 3 surveys Karol Wojtyła's moral theory as it exists in his published works before his election to the pontificate. Chapter 4 then turns to his ethics of sex and marriage, while chapter 5 offers an exegesis of the spousal meaning of the body in John Paul's theology of the body catechesis.

Beginning in chapter 6, the study turns to Thomas Aquinas with an exegesis of his anthropology by focusing on his treatment of nature, person, and the body in the *Summa Theologiae.* Chapter 7 then focuses on Aquinas's notion of love—principally the various forms of love—and his teaching that love must be rightly ordered. Finally, chapter 8 offers an exegesis of the Angelic Doctor's teaching on marriage and the conjugal act. In this concluding chapter, we see how his anthropology has ramifications for his view of the relationship between husband and wife. These chapters, for which the general conclusion provides a synthesis, unite to present a reading of the spousal meaning of the body according to the *Summa Theologiae:* a Thomistic spousal meaning of the body, if you will.

Some brief words about organization and methodology are in order. We will not proceed with a straight chronological approach (which might have been expected by some readers). In fact, our chosen roadmap will progress through history to the work of Karol Wojtyła before reflecting back in greater depth upon Aquinas. In fact, this book can serve as a template for what it will, hopefully, inspire— that is, a theology of the body which is illuminated by and itself illumines elements of Aquinas's thought.

The first two chapters of this study are essential historical narratives. The chapters concerning my two subjects, Karol Wojtyła and Thomas Aquinas, are primarily exegetical. Since much of Wojtyła's published work addresses a wide variety of topics, I have limited myself to those works necessary for our study.[11] The *corpus* of Thomas's

---

11. Not all of Wojtyła's works have been translated into English. The rare times this book cites a work of his that is not in English, a translation from Polish into another language is offered to the reader. References to original Polish works are also offered in the notes.

work is massive. Therefore, I have limited myself to the *Summa Theologiae* with the presumption that, as his final work, it represents his settled convictions.

I have referred to his other works only inasmuch as they elaborate what he writes in the *Summa Theologiae*. These other sources are especially needed since Aquinas did not finish the *Summa Theologiae* and his treatment on marriage was relegated to a *supplementum* added to that work posthumously by his students. I have presumed that Aquinas's opinion on topics he treats in the *supplementum* remained unchanged during his life unless he specifically makes a new argument in a later work, which he does in regard to indissolubility and monogamy in the *Summa contra Gentiles*. When his later works further elaborate or modify his opinion in the *supplementum*, I offer an exegesis of those texts in this study.

The theology of the body catechetical talks were translated into various languages by the Vatican newspaper, *L'Osservatore Romano*. Pauline Books and Media later published the collection of these 130 catecheses in four volumes.[12] Later, the same publishing company combined these four volumes into one, entitled *Theology of the Body: Human Love in the Divine Plan*.[13] The primary difficulty with the *L'Osservatore Romano* translations is that different translators translated different catecheses. As a result, key terms such as the "spousal meaning of the body" are translated differently throughout the text.[14]

Michael Waldstein discovered in the Vatican archives the original Polish manuscript on which *Theology of the Body* was based. Waldstein surmises that the original manuscript had been ready for pub-

---

12. John Paul II, *Original Unity of Man and Woman: Catechesis on the Book of Genesis* (Boston: Pauline Books and Media, 1981); *Blessed Are the Pure of Heart: Catechesis on the Sermon on the Mount and the Writings of St. Paul* (Boston: Pauline Books and Media, 1983); *The Theology of Marriage and Celibacy: Catechesis on Marriage and Celibacy in Light of the Resurrection of the Body* (Boston: Pauline Books and Media, 1986); *Reflections on Humanae Vitae: Conjugal Morality and Spirituality* (Boston: Pauline Books and Media, 1984).

13. John Paul II, *The Theology of the Body: Human Life in the Divine Plan* (Boston: Pauline Books and Media, 1997).

14. For a summation of the difficulties with the translation of *Theology of the Body*, see Michael Waldstein, introduction to John Paul II, *Man and Woman He Created Them*, 11–14, and M. Waldstein, "The Project of a New English Translation of John Paul II's *Theology of the Body* on its 20th and 25th Anniversary," *Communio* 31 (2004): 345–51.

lication before Wojtyła's election to the pontificate. Wojtyła brought the manuscript to Rome when he began his pontifical ministry.[15] This manuscript included headings for the text that were previously unknown, as well as additional sections that were never publicly delivered. In 2006, Michael Waldstein published his own translation of *Theology of the Body*. He gave it the title that appeared on the manuscript, *Man and Woman He Created Them*.[16]

This new edition has several benefits over the previous editions. First, it is translated by a single translator and thus it is translated consistently. Second, Waldstein has included the headings from the original manuscript and these reveal the structure of Wojtyła's argument, allowing the work to be read systematically rather than disjointedly as a series of talks. Finally, in some instances the pope modified the text before delivering it and in some cases he omitted substantial portions. When they differ, Waldstein has included both the original text and the delivered text, using a side-by-side layout so the reader can easily identify the changes. In my opinion, Waldstein's translation is the best critical edition of these important catecheses now available in any language.[17]

This then is our situation and our goal. John Paul II wrote *Theology of the Body* from a Thomistic perspective and so he did not elaborate its ontological and metaphysical foundations explicitly. Aquinas, on the other hand, did not explore consciousness or human experience in the same way that John Paul did. Thomas's anthropology, with its rich metaphysical foundation, can not only support the concept of the spousal meaning of the body articulated by the pope in these catecheses but can benefit from it. There is a continuity between Thomas Aquinas and John Paul II. Indeed, this exegesis will show that their thought is mutually enriching.

15. See Waldstein, Introduction, 6–11.
16. See John Paul II, *Man and Woman He Created Them*.
17. While Waldstein has changed the title of the work, throughout this book I will continue to refer to the pope's talks as *Theology of the Body* rather than *Man and Woman He Created Them* to avoid confusion, since the former title is more commonly known.

1

From Thomas Aquinas to the Manualists

We begin our study with an outline of the historical discontinuity between Aquinas's moral theology and that of the manualist tradition.[1] The manualists and the theologians upon whom they depended (the neo-Thomists of the late nineteenth and early twentieth century) claimed Aquinas as their mentor, though, in fact, as the work of scholars such as Servais Pinckaers has clearly shown, the manualists are the intellectual descendants not of Aquinas but of the nominalism introduced by the Franciscan philosopher William of Ockham. This is a critical point for our study for two reasons: first, it is against the background of the manualist tradition that the birth control de-

1. This chapter is only a survey of the history; more thorough studies of Catholic moral theology are available. See John Mahoney, *The Making of Moral Theology: A Study of the Roman Catholic Tradition* (Oxford: Clarendon Press, 1987), 1–71; Pinckaers, *Sources*, 104–33, 195–215; and Servais Pinckaers, OP, "A Historical Perspective on Intrinsically Evil Acts," translated by Mary Thomas Noble, OP, and Craig Steven Titus, in *The Pinckaers Reader: Renewing Thomistic Moral Theology*, eds. John Berkman and Craig Steven Titus (Washington, D.C.: The Catholic University of America Press, 2005), 185–235. See also John A. Gallagher, *Time Past, Time Future: An Historical Study of Catholic Moral Theology* (New York: Paulist Press, 1990), 5–28; Albert R. Jonsen and Stephen Toulmin, *The Abuse of Casuistry: A History of Moral Reasoning* (Berkeley: University of California Press, 1988), 21–136; and Michael Bertram Crowe, *The Changing Profile of the Natural Law* (The Hague: Nijhoff, 1977), 52–135.

bate developed; second, this is precisely the environment in which Karol Wojtyła's thought arose.

The current chapter has two sections. In the first, we will briefly trace the transition from the theological synthesis offered by Aquinas to the nominalism of William of Ockham. The second section will then identify significant developments in moral theology after Ockham with the development of the confessional manuals during the Reformation and the birth of neo-Thomism in the late nineteenth century. We will conclude the chapter with a modest critique of this tradition.[2] This conclusion serves as preparation for a consideration of the rise of the birth control debate, which lays the foundation for Wojtyła's early work on marriage and the family.

FROM THOMAS AQUINAS TO NOMINALISM

The Early Penitentials and Confessionals

The history of Catholic moral theology, and of the manualist tradition in particular, is intrinsically connected to the development of the sacrament of penance and auricular confession, which precedes both Aquinas and Ockham by several centuries. John Mahoney provides a detailed history of the sacrament's influence along with a thorough bibliography.[3] The Celtic penitential movement, which flourished between the sixth and tenth centuries, was the catalyst for the development of casuistry and the modern manualist tradition. The practice of repeated individual and private confession between a confessor

---

2. It is good to recall the words offered by Michael Sherwin before his own historical survey of the manuals: "It is perilous to speak in generalities about the manuals of moral theology. There was not one monolithic type of moral manual. The Church contains within it various different traditions of moral reflection and the manuals, as the product of these traditions, reflect their differences. Also, the perspectives of these traditions developed over time and the manuals were shaped by these developments. Nevertheless, there was a dominant perspective and this perspective shaped the most influential manuals." Michael P. Sherwin, OP, *By Knowledge and By Love: Charity and Knowledge in the Moral Theology of St. Thomas Aquinas* (Washington, D.C.: The Catholic University of America Press, 2005), 1n1.

3. See Mahoney, *Making of Moral Theology*, 1–36.

and a penitent developed in Ireland and was exported to continental Europe in various ways from the sixth to the ninth centuries.[4]

With the increased popularity of private confession, a desire for universal standards of penance grew among the clergy. This led to the development of what became known as penitential books or, simply, the "penitentials." Given the absence of diocesan or episcopal guidance in this early period of the sacrament, the penitentials were generally produced by monks.[5] The penitentials' "primary function was to provide priests with a tariff of penances to be enjoined for various sins."[6] They contained definitions of specific sins and listed specific penances to be imposed for said sins.[7] As the penitentials developed, they would include precise formulas for celebrating the sacrament.

Because of their purpose, the penitentials were more concerned with sin and vice than with beatitude. Still, Mahoney's criticism seems excessively hyperbolic when he complains that the penitentials "constitute at best an unsuccessful attempt to apply with some degree of humanity an appallingly rigid systematized approach to sin, and no one ever appears to have asked the serious theological question to what end (other than social order) all this suffering was really being imposed."[8] This is a classic temptation for any historian: to judge the past according to a modern standard. John Gallagher, on the other hand, has observed that the Celtic monastic movement, like Celtic Christianity, is more distinctively influenced by the pre-Christian Celtic culture than it is by Roman Christianity. In this pre-Christian Celtic society we find confession, austere repentance, and hymnody: "The religious dimension of the culture also provided for spiritual guides who required persons to perform penances proportionate to their sins. The primitive legal system provided for compensations by which restitution could be made to injured parties."[9] The peniten-

---

4. See ibid., 5. Cf. Gallagher, *Time Past, Time Future*, 7, and Jonsen and Toulmin, *Abuse of Casuistry*, 96–100.

5. See Mahoney, *Making of Moral Theology*, 5.

6. Ibid., 6.

7. A catalog of medieval penitential books has been gathered in *Medieval Handbooks of Penance: A Translation of the Principal Libri Poenitentiales and Selections from Related Documents*, ed. John T. McNeil and Helena M. Gamer (New York: Columbia University Press, 1938).

8. Mahoney, *Making of Moral Theology*, 7.

9. Gallagher, *Time Past, Time Future*, 9.

tial movement incorporated these elements with the best of Christian monasticism. In fact, Harold Berman has argued that the penitentials were understood to be primarily concerned with healing the soul, with reconciliation within society, and with holding all things in harmony—a basic if unarticulated understanding of virtue.[10]

The codification of church law, which began with the reforms of Pope Gregory VII in 1027, provides a background for the second major development in Catholic moral theology: the publication of the *Summae Confessorum*, or the confessional books.[11] The codification of canon law was accomplished by collecting and synthesizing the mass of curial decrees that had accrued over the centuries, many of which were case-specific and thus listed the circumstances that gave rise to particular legislation and legislative interpretation. The collection of these cases would directly impinge upon the practice of confession, especially since "clergy needed to be instructed how to match the complexities of the new canon law to the cases their penitents presented to them."[12]

One of the most influential of such works was authored by the Dominican Raymond of Peñafort in 1221. His *Summa de Poenitentia* focused on sins against God, sins against neighbor, and the duties attached to various states of life. As Jonsen and Toulmin point out, "each section of Peñafort's *Summa* begins with a proposal about how the matter will be presented, followed by definitions of the principal terms, such as lying or simony. He then relates the 'true and certain opinions' on the question under discussion, drawn from earlier writers, followed by those questions and cases about which the received answers are more doubtful."[13] Raymond's method of presentation would be adopted by most of the canonists of his generation and was the method to which Aquinas will eventually respond by attempting to situate morality within the broader context of dogmatic theology and beatitude.

10. See Harold J. Berman, *Law and Revolution: The Formation of the Western Legal Tradition* (Cambridge, Mass.: Harvard University Press, 1983), 68–78.

11. For a history of Gregory's reforms and their historical development and impact, see Gallagher, *Time Past, Time Future*, 11–17; Jonsen and Toulmin, *Abuse of Casuistry*, 101–17; and Berman, *Law and Revolution*, 199–224.

12. Jonsen and Toulmin, *Abuse of Casuistry*, 118.

13. Ibid., 120.

Peñafort was attempting to implement the reforms established by the Fourth Lateran Council in 1215. The council, convened by Pope Innocent III (d. 1216), produced an astonishing seventy constitutions in under one month and legislated that individuals go to confession at least annually.[14] That particular decree goes on to insist that the confessor "shall be discerning and prudent, so that like a skilled doctor he may pour wine and oil over the wounds of the injured one. Let him carefully inquire about the circumstances of both the sinner and the sin, so that he may prudently discern what sort of advice he ought to give and what remedy to apply, using various means to heal the sick person."[15] The council also mandated that provincial councils be established to monitor the observance of its decrees.[16] Bishops were to ensure that priests were well trained in the practice of caring for souls.[17] With this legislation, the council initiated a series of provincial diocesan synods as well as chapters in various religious orders to address the implementation of its decrees. This, combined with the growing maturation of speculative theology within the newly established universities, provided the stage for the influence that Aquinas would have on theology, and, after him, William of Ockham.

The Synthesis of Thomas Aquinas

Born in 1224, Tommaso d'Aquino entered the Order of St. Dominic when he was twenty years old. He quickly ascended in the intellectual life of the Order, initially studying at the University of Paris and then teaching there as a bachelor on the *Sentences* of Peter Lombard in 1252. He would become a master of sacred theology four years later in 1256. Throughout his life, he would teach in Paris, Naples, Orvieto, and Rome. Nearly a decade before his death, Aquinas was appointed master of friars in formation.[18]

14. Fourth Lateran Council, *De Confessione Facienda*, November 30, 1215, in Norman P. Tanner, ed., *Decrees of the Ecumenical Councils* (Washington, D.C.: Georgetown University Press, 1990), 1:245 (canon 21).

15. Ibid.

16. Fourth Lateran Council, *De Conciliis Provincialibus*, November 30, 1215, in Tanner, *Decrees*, 1:236–37 (canon 6).

17. Fourth Lateran Council, *De Instructione Ordinandorum*, November 30, 1215, in Tanner, *Decrees*, 1:248 (canon 27).

18. Aquinas had been critical of his province's lack of zeal for study and his posi-

Aquinas's work in Rome with his student friars can only rightly be understood in the context of his work as a master of sacred theology. A master was, first and foremost, a *magister in Sacra Pagina*. A master of the sacred page had three functions: *legere, disputare,* and *praedicare*.[19] The first, *legere*, was to read the sacred scripture and to comment on it verse by verse. This was the work that Thomas concerned himself with when he began teaching in Paris in 1256. Many of Aquinas's scripture commentaries were written during this period. The *disputatio* was a form of instruction in which opposing positions were set against each other and the *magister* would offer his answer. Finally, having read and commented on scripture, having considered subtle and disputed points of theology, the master was ready to preach the truth. Theological study thus lent itself to pastoral practice.

It was precisely this lack of a connection between pastoral practice, theology, and scripture that Aquinas sought to remedy in the Roman province. His task in Rome was to form friars in moral theology and the practice of sacramental confession. Jean-Pierre Torrell notes that Aquinas "had at his disposal the manuals published by the first generations of Dominicans; but that predominance of practical theology in the formation of friars ... gave them only a partial and narrow view of theology; this resulted in a marked imbalance, to the detriment of dogmatic theology, which could not help but leave Thomas dissatisfied."[20] While wanting to maintain the tradition of providing manuals for the friars, Thomas nonetheless attempted to present moral theology within a larger theological framework. The *Summa Theologiae* is the result of that project.

The *Summa* is divided into three parts. The first part concerns the nature of God, the persons of the Trinity, the angels, the work of cre-

---

tion as a permanent voting member at provincial chapters probably influenced his appointment. Aquinas was effectively given his own *studium* in Rome to train the best of the friars in formation from all over the province. He retained the right to return them to their priories if they performed less than expected. See Torrell, *Saint Thomas Aquinas*, 1:142; Thomas Käppelli, OP, and Antione Dondaine, OP, eds., *Monumenta Ordinis Fratrum Praedicatorum Historica*, vol. 20, *Capitulorum Provincialium Provinciae Romanae* (1243–1344) (Rome, Institutum Historicum Fratrum Praedicatorum, 1941), 20:32; and Leonard Boyle, *The Setting of the* Summa theologiae *of Saint Thomas*, Etienne Gilson Series (Toronto: Pontifical Institute of Mediaeval Studies, 1982), 5:15.

19. See Torrell, *Saint Thomas Aquinas*, 1:54.

20. Ibid., 1:144.

ation, the nature of man and original sin, and, finally, divine providence. The first half of the second part begins by discussing the end
(*telos*) of man, and specifically the beatific vision. Only then does the
prima secundae discuss human action, the passions, *habitus*, virtue,
law, and grace. The second half of the second part, the *secunda secundae*, further specifies the work of the first half by devoting particular attention to the three theological virtues and the four cardinal virtues, along with their corresponding vices and gifts of the Holy Spirit.
The *secunda secundae* concludes with a treatment of the counsels and
consecrated life. The third part of the *Summa*, finally, concerns the incarnation and person of Jesus Christ, his suffering, death, and resurrection, along with the establishment of the church, the seven sacraments, and, ultimately, the last judgment.

The *Summa* follows the biblical structure of salvation history.
Aquinas brings the student from considering God in himself before
turning to creation and the fall of man to considering man's destiny
and human action. From there, the Angelic Doctor leads us to consider virtue, law, and grace. But to achieve our goal (*telos*), the beatific vision, we need Christ incarnate and the life of grace offered in the
church. Thomas then presents the path to the final consummation of
all things in Jesus Christ.

It is not surprising, therefore, that the very first question of the
secunda pars is on man's last end, and the first article is "Whether it
belongs to man to act for an end?" It is only after this treatise on beatitude that Aquinas addresses human action and the goodness of human acts, and only upon finishing that discussion does he begin to
speak of passion, *habitus*, virtue, and vice. Everything that follows in
the *secunda pars* is, in fact, dependent on the worldview established in
those first few questions. Thomas posits two aspects of human happiness or beatitude: the objective and the subjective.[21] Objectively, the
telos or beatitude of man consists in a good.[22] Subjectively, there are

21. Throughout this book, I will be using the words "beatitude" and "happiness"
interchangeably for the state Aquinas describes with the word *beatitudo*. Of course, we
can distinguish between perfect and imperfect happiness, the former only possible in
the beatific vision of God.

22. See Thomas Aquinas, *Summa Theologiae* (Turin: Edizioni San Paolo, 1999), I-II,
q. 2 [hereafter, *ST*]. Unless otherwise noted, English translations are from Aquinas,
Summa Theologica (New York: Benzinger Brothers, 1948).

specific actions that will make a person blessed.[23] The final two questions of the treatise on happiness concern first those subjective elements of beatitude and then the powers that a person uses to attain beatitude.[24] Servais Pinckaers observes: "Beatitude is both objective and subjective. It is objective, because it is caused by a good reality, one which renders [the] person good and blessed. It is subjective, because it corresponds to the desire of man, which carries him toward the good and beatitude."[25]

The foundation for Thomas's theory of beatitude rests with his understanding of human nature. In the *tertia pars*, when he explains the relationship between the person of Jesus and his two natures, Aquinas offers an explanation of the word "nature."[26] Following Aristotle, he distinguishes between four uses of the word: (1) it can signify the act of generation of living things (since it comes from the word "nativity"); (2) later it came to signify the source of this generation; (3) since generation stems from a principle within the generator, it came to signify an interior principle of movement; and (4) finally, since the end or *telos* of a thing is implicated in its generation, the word "nature" can also signify the thing's essence. The third and fourth uses of this term are essential for Thomas. Pinckaers observes that for Aquinas, "What characterizes 'natural' action is that it proceeds from inner principles or sources.... Because of this, nature is linked with the person in view of all the external causalities that may affect him. At the core of the person it forms an essential component of human interiority. This interiority is not only biological or psychological; it is dynamic."[27] For Thomas, it is precisely those interior principles at the core of human nature that both guide human action and direct the human person to goodness and truth.[28]

The line running from these interior principles of human nature to beatitude is a line directed toward finality. For Thomas, all human

23. See *ST* I-II, q. 3.

24. See *ST* I-II, qq. 4–5.

25. Servais Pinckaers, OP, "Beatitude and the Beatitudes in Aquinas's *Summa theologiae*," in *Pinckaers Reader*, 119.

26. See *ST* III, q. 2, a. 1.

27. Servais Pinckaers, OP, "Aquinas on Nature and the Supernatural," trans. Mary Thomas Noble, OP, in *Pinckaers Reader*, 361.

28. See *ST* I-II, q. 63, a. 1.

action is directed by the agent toward a goal or end, which the agent understands to be good.[29] Aquinas characterizes all objects of desire under the rubric of "the good" and "perfection." For Thomas, the essence of goodness is desirability: to be good is to be desirable, and to be desirable is to be perfect and, therefore, perfecting of another.[30] By emphasizing the equivalence of being, goodness/desirability, and action, Aquinas is placing agency squarely within a metaphysical and ontological conception of the universe. Daniel Westberg notes the boldness of the claim, "[Aquinas] is speaking not just of persons or animals, but in the broadest way possible, of all substances and potency to act.... The basis for agency in the universe is that beings cannot simply exist, nor are they merely the subjects of events and forces which cause change; they desire their perfection."[31] This desire for perfection is synonymous with a thing's nature.

Everything but God lacks some perfection. All contingent being is in a state of becoming.[32] The nature of a thing directs it to perfection, to act in accordance with its abilities—for a plant to grow, for an animal to hunt and eat, or for a human person to think and to love, etc.—and in so doing, fulfilling its nature. Aquinas, like Aristotle, calls this desire for perfection "appetite." Everything has an appetite toward the fullness of its own natural form:

Now everything has this aptitude towards its natural form, that when it has it not it tends toward it; and when it has it, it is at rest therein. It is the same with every natural perfection, which is a natural good. This aptitude to good in things without knowledge is called natural appetite. Whence also an intellectual nature has a like aptitude [to the good] as apprehended through its intelligible form; so as to rest therein when possessed, and when not possessed to seek to possess it, both of which pertain to the will.[33]

Thus, Thomas is quite clear that all created beings have fundamental inclinations that are commensurate with what they are. Everything acts with a purpose—the fulfillment of its nature—in either a direct-

29. See *ST* I-II, q. 1, a. 1.
30. See *ST* I, q. 5, a. 1.
31. Daniel Westberg, *Right Practical Reason: Aristotle, Action, and Prudence in Aquinas* (Oxford: Clarendon Press, 1994), 45.
32. See *ST* I-II, q. 18, a. 1.
33. *ST* I, q. 19, a. 1.

ed or self-directed manner, as the case may be. The mere fact that everything seeks perfection means that no one thing (except God) is completely perfect in itself. Everything must, therefore, come out of itself in search of that which perfects it.[34]

The human person has a rational appetite, the will, and so is able consciously to direct himself in freedom to his final perfection. In other words, the human person can understand the relationship of human action to a final goal. "The difference between the human will and animal appetite," Westberg writes, "lies not primarily in a wider range of objects open for consideration, but in the ability of the human agent to see actions in relationship to a goal."[35] A human being, may, in fact, choose something that causes immediate pain (surgery, for example) for an end which is good (healing). An animal's action, on the other hand, is automatically activated by its desires. An animal will necessarily flee from pain, even if a certain amount of pain would bring about a good. "A human being, however, is not immediately moved into action in response to the activation of the sensitive appetite [the passions] (whether to pursue or avoid), but awaits the command of the superior appetite [the will]."[36] Aquinas confirms that "the lower appetite [the sensitive appetite] is not sufficient to cause movement [in us], unless the higher appetite [the will] consents."[37] The human person is directed to his goal, to his good, not through the attainment of immediate goods but through deliberate actions of mediate goods directing him to his final perfection.

The fundamental interior principles at work here are those defining powers of the human nature, the powers that separate us from brute animals: reason and will. The powers of the soul, Aquinas says, are distinguished by their objects, the goals which they each seek.[38] As has already been seen, the will, as an appetite, has the good as its object. The object of the reason is truth and universal being.[39] Thomas further divides reason into the speculative intellect and the practical intellect. The former concerns knowledge of truth as such while

34. This movement figures prominently not only in the work of Thomas but also in the anthropology of Karol Wojtyła.

35. Westberg, *Right Practical Reason*, 74.

36. Ibid., 80.

37. *ST* I, q. 81, a. 3.

38. See *ST* I, q. 77, a. 3.

39. See *ST* I, q. 16, a. 1.

the latter concerns action.[40] Since the will is not merely a natural appetite but a *rational* appetite it is always in relationship with the intellect. The will tends toward the good as apprehended by the intellect.[41]

Aquinas holds that "self-evident first principles" in both the speculative and practical intellects govern all things concerning human action and morality. In the speculative intellect, he designates the first principle as *intellectus*. *Intellectus* is the aptitude that all persons have to understand basic theoretical principles without having to prove them. They are simply given and understood "at once by the intellect [*statim ab intellectu*]."[42] These principles are encapsulated in such maxims as "the whole is greater than its part" and "things equal to the same thing are equal to one another." The principle of non-contradiction is also a maxim of *intellectus*. These speculative first principles are the foundation of all scientific reasoning, which progresses from them. A person simply could not make rational judgments without these first principles. Think of the absurdity of asserting that something is both above you and below you at the same time. It violates the principle of non-contradiction.

Similarly, *synderesis* is the knowledge of first principles in practical matters. Thomas writes, "*synderesis* is said to incite to good, and to murmur at evil, inasmuch as through first principles we proceed to discover, and judge what we have discovered."[43] *Synderesis* is the capacity to measure our actions as for or against the good of our nature. As such, it is the catalyst of moral action, directing action according to the primary principle of practical reason: "do good and avoid evil."[44] The importance of *synderesis* cannot be overestimated in Aquinas. Pamela Hall rightly notes that *synderesis* ensures that "an agent cannot completely lack guidance in the moral life. He or she has even initially some root, an inerrant apprehension of a good with

---

40. See *ST* I, q. 79, a. 11.

41. See *ST* I, q. 82, a. 3. The fascinating relationship between the intellect and the will in human action is not of immediate concern to us here, though it is essential for understanding Thomas's moral theory. We are concerned here with the fundamental or first principles of each of these powers.

42. *ST* I-II, q. 57, a. 2. Cf. Sherwin, *By Knowledge and By Love*, 55.

43. *ST* I, q. 79, a. 12.

44. See *ST* I-II, q. 94, a. 2. Cf. *ST* I, q. 79, a. 12; II-II, q. 47, a. 6.

which to begin the moral life and moral deliberation. We begin with
at least the necessary conceptual equipment."[45] Thus, as Aquinas sees
it, the human person is built to desire the good and to seek truth, and
is hardwired with the basic faculties for fulfillment of these desires.

Subjectively, however, the spiritual faculties of the human person can be and are mistaken about concrete goods. The "conceptual
equipment" to do good and avoid evil is not always fully or properly developed in a particular person. The will can be led to seek only
what is an apparent good. Original sin also plays a role in the operation of the faculties. We are no longer sure of our final end.[46] Still,
Thomas asserts that original sin does not destroy the fundamental inclinations of human nature, without which human nature could no
longer be defined as such.[47]

One can glean two important observations from this survey of
Thomas's position. First, goodness is, for Thomas, something that everyone desires. That which is truly good is that which fulfills human
nature. As Pinckaers notes, "for Thomas, as for Augustine, the term
bonum combines inseparably the ideas of the good and of beatitude:
what is good is what makes one blessed."[48] Second, since a nature is
defined by its proper inclinations, and since the inclinations proper
to the human being are the inclinations of reason and will, the moral
life is deeply embedded in a person's interior life. It is less about the
exterior activity and obligations of the person than it is about the fulfillment and perfection of the person himself. A brief word about this
last observation is necessary.

---

45. Pamela Hall, *Narrative and Natural Law: An Interpretation of Thomistic Ethics*
(Notre Dame, Ind.: University of Notre Dame Press, 1994), 31.

46. Thomas held that in original justice, Adam and Eve lived with their "reason being subject to God, the lower powers to reason, and the body to the soul" (*ST* I, q. 95,
a. 1). This original state was a unique gift of grace and a good of nature. In the *Quaestiones disputatae de malo*, written at the same time as the *Summa Theologiae*, Aquinas goes
on the say that because man is a composite being of body and spirit, his intellect could
identify several "final ends" when it is hindered by the desires of the flesh. But this is the
case only after original sin (see Aquinas, *De malo*, q. 5, a. 1, co.). In original justice, Adam
and Eve were completely in harmony with their bodies through the unique gift of grace
in which they were created. The rupture in the relationship with God introduces dishar-
mony into their lives. Men and women now find themselves pursuing many different
ends as if these were their true and ultimate good.

47. See *ST* I-II, q. 85, a. 1.

48. Pinckaers, "Beatitude and the Beatitudes," 119.

Servais Pinckaers notes that the term *"intrinsece malum"* did not occur in Christian moral theory until the sixteenth century.[49] Though the debate surrounding contraception centered on whether it was to be counted among "intrinsically evil acts," Pinckaers argues that prior to the sixteenth century, theologians were more concerned with the beatitude of man than with categorized lists of actions. This is not to say that the early Christians were not concerned with evil actions. Rather, as Pinckaers has effectively argued, they were concerned with delineating actions which were conducive either to beatitude or to wickedness.

Servais Pinckaers summarizes the point:

> For St. Thomas, reason (or intelligence) and will precede and engender free will and its act, choice. The source of freedom lies in the natural inclinations to truth and to goodness or beatitude, which constitute our spiritual nature and confer on us an opening onto infinite truth and goodness, rendering us free in regard to all limited good. We are free, *not in spite of, but because of* our natural inclination to truth and beatitude. The attraction of the true and the good are the foundation of our freedom and orientate it. We can therefore call it freedom for excellence.[50]

In this view, the role of the law, natural or otherwise, is to serve as "the expression of God's wisdom and benevolence, revealing to us our spiritual nature orientated to truth and beatitude and prescribing the paths leading thereto."[51] All of this, however, is on the subjective side of beatitude—discerning which human actions and principles contribute to human happiness. On the objective side, only God himself can fully satisfy the human person. But God is infinitely beyond us and therefore we cannot achieve a relationship with God by our own efforts. That God deigns to offer the grace of communion with him is utterly gratuitous and cannot be forced.[52]

As capacities for growth in freedom and perfection, the basic inclinations of human nature constitute a *capax Dei*, a "passive capacity

---

49. See Pinckaers, "Historical Perspective," 186.

50. Ibid., 212 (emphasis added).

51. Ibid.

52. See *ST* I, q. 19, a. 4; I-II, q. 112, aa. 3 and 5. Cf. Matthew Levering, *Predestination: Biblical and Theological Paths* (Oxford: Oxford University Press, 2011), and Daria Spezzano, *The Glory of God's Grace: Deification According to St. Thomas Aquinas* (Washington, D.C.: The Catholic University of America Press, 2015).

to receive the vision of God."[53] Our desire for the universal good and the universal truth, this "natural desire to see God" provides the paradox of grace: "the human person is both capable and incapable of God. We are capable of receiving the vision of God, and absolutely incapable of attaining it by ourselves."[54] Grace builds on nature. And the structure of the *Summa* itself reveals that the virtues and gifts of the Holy Spirit give our natural inclinations, and especially *synderesis*, a new source for action at the very core of our being to effect union with God by God's own gift.

The second half of this book will explore more closely the importance of these facts for Aquinas's theology of love, marriage, and the relationship of the body to the soul. For now, we turn our attention to the subsequent breakdown of Thomas's synthesis with the rise of Ockham and nominalism.

William of Ockham and Nominalism

At the risk of oversimplifying the dispute between the Franciscans and the Dominicans, one can observe that the Franciscans of the medieval era were generally devoted to Augustine's theology and Plato's philosophy. The difference between Plato and Augustine, on the one hand, and Aristotle, on the other, led to an overarching disagreement. "Where St. Thomas affirmed the primacy of the intellect, defining the first and formal element of beatitude in terms of this faculty, as the vision of God, the Franciscans maintained the primacy of the will and made love the essential element of beatitude."[55] In the thirteenth century, these "neo-Augustinians" were considered the institutional "conservatives" at the University of Paris; the Aristotelians were the "radical liberals." For all intents and purposes, Aristotelianism was regarded as heterodox.

Not long after Aquinas's death, the bishop of Paris condemned several of Thomas's theses. If not for the defense offered by his then aged-teacher, Albert the Great, the interregnum following the death of Pope John XXI, and the fact that the college of cardinals forbade

53. Servais Pinckaers, OP, "Aquinas on Nature and Supernature," in *Pinckaers Reader*, 362.
54. Ibid., 363.
55. Pinckaers, *Sources*, 240.

the bishop of Paris from proceeding further, Thomas's work might have been formally and universally censured in 1277.[56] In response, the Dominican Order decreed that no Dominican was to speak ill of Thomas and that his works were to be held in high honor. Political and theological struggles ensued until the Dominican Order made "Thomism" its official doctrine in 1309. Thomas's reputation was finally restored in 1323 when he was canonized by Pope John XXII, who praised the saint's teaching. In 1325, a new bishop of Paris withdrew the condemnations issued in 1277.[57]

William of Ockham was born in 1288, joined the Franciscan Order at a young age and studied at Oxford, probably from 1309 to 1321, although (perhaps reflecting the disposition of the chancellor of the university) he never attained the degree master of sacred theology, hence his honorific title as the "Venerable Inceptor."[58] Ockham came to prominence at approximately the same time that Aquinas's reputation was being rehabilitated. Just a year after Thomas's canonization, Ockham was summoned to Rome by Pope John XXII to defend some of his questionable teachings. Knowing that the pope espoused Thomas's theology, Ockham knew his case was compromised and fled to Germany where he entered the service of the emperor, Louis of Bavaria, who was having his own political struggles with the pope.[59]

Ockham is widely credited for initiating the movement eventually called "nominalism," although his Franciscan elder brother John Duns Scotus (1266–1308) has been labeled a moderate nominalist by some.[60] Nominalism takes its name from Ockham's denial of the existence of universal forms independent of human reason. In classical Aristotelian philosophy, reason was the contact-point between the knower and the known, between the person and reality. Ockham, however, maintained that there was no such thing as universal nature existing outside of the mind. In his commentary on Peter Lombard's

---

56. For an analysis of these condemnations, see John F. Wippel, "Thomas Aquinas and the Condemnation of 1277," *Modern Schoolman* 72 (1995): 233–72.

57. For a more detailed history of this period, see Simon Tugwell, OP, "Introduction to the Life and Work of Thomas Aquinas," in Simon Tugwell, OP, ed., *Albert and Thomas: Selected Writings* (New York: Paulist Press, 1988), 234–44; Torrell, *Saint Thomas Aquinas*, 1:298–326.

58. See Pinckaers, *Sources*, 241.   59. Ibid.

60. Crowe, *Changing Profile*, 192–201.

Sentences, he writes: "No universal is anything existing in any way outside the soul; but everything which is predicable of many things is of its nature in the mind, whether subjectively or objectively; and no universal belongs to the essence or quiddity of any substance whatever."[61] This text is part of a larger argument in Ockham's system in which he argues that the distinctive qualities we ascribe to existing things do not adhere to the things themselves but exist only in the mind. Therefore, according to Ockham, our identification of common natures in reality is a contradiction.[62]

For Ockham and those that followed him, freedom became the primary category of import for the human person. Freedom here is "conceived as the will's power to choose between contraries, between the yes and the no, at each instant—at least in theory."[63] The Venerable Inceptor defines freedom as the power "by which I can indifferently and contingently produce an effect in such a way that I can cause or not cause that effect, without any difference in that power having been made."[64] Whereas for Aquinas freedom stems from the mutual interaction between reason and will, for Ockham, the will became the center of the human person and absolute freedom of the will became the locus of morality. Pinckaers has called this concept of freedom a "freedom of indifference," which is exercised "independently of all other causes except freedom, or the will itself."[65] Ockham thus interpreted Lombard's dictum, "Free choice is the faculty of reason and will [*Liberum arbitrium est facultas rationis et voluntatis*]" in a way radically opposed to Aquinas and his predecessors.[66] Ockham understood freedom as the power to reason and to will, and therefore understood freedom as *preceding* those two important spiritual faculties of the human person.

61. William of Ockham, *Super quattuor libros sententiarium subtilissimae quaestiones* I, dist. 2, q. 8 (author's translation).

62. Some have insisted that Ockham's position is much more subtle than this. See the noted Ockhamist, Marylin McCord Adams, *William Ockham* (Notre Dame, Ind.: University of Notre Dame Press), 1:3–69, 109–41. She argues for the logical consistency of Ockham's objection against Aristotelian realism.

63. Servais Pinckaers, OP, "Conscience and the Christian Tradition," trans. Mary Thomas Noble, OP, in *Pinckaers Reader*, 335.

64. William of Ockham, *Quodlibeta*, q. 1, a. 16 (author's translation).

65. Pinckaers, *Sources*, 242.

66. Peter Lombard, *Sententiae in IV Libris Distinctae* II, dist. 25, a. 1, q. 2.

Since freedom precedes the two characterizing faculties of the human person, the intellect and the will, and since he has already denied the existence of extramental universal natures, it is not surprising to learn that Ockham insisted that the person can choose to disregard any sort of natural inclination. Whereas Aquinas grounded the morality of human action in the natural inclinations of the intellect to truth and the will to goodness as well as in the human desire for beatitude and happiness, Ockham insists that the will is free even in regard to these:

I say that the will in this state is able to refuse the ultimate end, whether the end is presented in a general sense or in a particular sense. This can be proved thus. The will is able to reject that which the intellect says ought to be rejected. (This is obvious.) But the intellect can believe that nothing is the ultimate end or happiness, and as a consequence, can dictate that an ultimate end or happiness is to be rejected. Secondly, anyone who can reject the antecedent can reject the consequent. A person is able to desire not to be. Therefore, he is able to reject the happiness that he believes follows upon his existence. Furthermore, I say that the intellect can judge a certain thing to be the ultimate end, but the will can reject that end. This is so because a free power [*potential libera*] is capable of contrary acts. It can order itself in one way or another. The will, as a free power, is capable of rejecting or choosing any object. Therefore, it can choose God, but for the same reason, it can reject God.[67]

This was William of Ockham's decisive claim, effectively reorienting his moral theology away from human nature and toward human freedom absolutely. The majority of the tradition before him measured the goodness or wickedness of human action in reference to that action's appropriation of the good sought by the agent, on the subjective side, and the true good of the human person, communion with God, on the objective side. Ockham theorized that persons are free, in fact, not to desire their own good.

This creates an immediate problem when discussing human action. The finality of the human person and the relationship of an action's immediate end to that finality were central to Aquinas's theory of morality. By eliminating the influence of the natural inclinations and the importance of the interaction between intellect and will, action for Ockham neither stems from interior principles at the core of

---

67. Ockham, *Super quattuor libros sententiarium* IV, q. 15 (author's translation).

the human being nor leads to a goal. There is no other cause of human action than self-determination. In Pinckaers's words, "From this it followed that each of our voluntary acts becomes a single reality, isolated in time by the very power that enables us to choose between contraries. We could not be bound by a past action or obliged to a future one without losing the radical freedom that is ours at each moment."[68] Human conduct is nothing but "a succession of individual actions."[69] Considering human action only in isolated moments with no connection between one action and the next is the immediate precursor for casuistry and the manualist tradition, which emphasized the study of isolated cases of conscience.

Assessing the intrinsic morality of particular actions once freedom is separated from human nature and its inclination to perfection is a contradiction. When our natural inclinations no longer provide the *telos* of human action, only some extrinsic principle can determine the morality of action. Hence, Ockham turns to law and obligation, where law is understood not as stemming from nature but from the will of the divine legislator, God. He writes, "Evil is nothing else than to do something when one is under an obligation to do the opposite. Obligation does not fall on God, since he is not under any obligation to do anything."[70] And, like the human will, the unbounded power of the divine will precedes divine reason. On the contrary, God can impose seemingly irrational obligations upon us. For example, Ockham insists: "Every will can conform itself to divine precept, but God can command that the created will hate him, and the created will can do this. Therefore, that which can be a right act in this life, can be so in the next [*in patria*], thus just as to hate God can be a right act in this life, if it be commanded by God, so can it be a right act in the next life [*in patria*]."[71] Ockham thus establishes the two primal realities of morality: the divine will and the human will. Pinckaers writes: "The origin of morality resides in the law, the expression of the free and sovereign will of God the Creator, which is imposed upon man under the form and with the force of obligation. Human

---

68. Pinckaers, *Sources*, 243.
69. Ibid.
70. Ockham, *Super quattor libros sententiarum* II, dist. 5 (author's translation).
71. Ibid., IV, dist. 15 (author's translation)

acts, indifferent in themselves, become moral through their connection with legal obligations."[72] The divine law of God is here considered to be antagonistic to a person's freedom. We are not permitted to choose what God forbids simply because he forbids it, even if he forbids it for seemingly irrational reasons.

If human freedom, on the one hand, and law and the divine will, on the other, stand at the polar extremes of absolute freedom, conscience for Ockham is the median between the two. Moral discernment "revolves around assessing the relation of each free act with the law, and this is done primarily through a consideration of the object of the act which harmonizes best with the law as it is verbally expressed."[73] The relationship between law and freedom will thus be marked by a certain tension which is at the heart of Ockham's freedom of indifference and his obligation-based morality: "Freedom and law are opposed to each other, like two landowners, disputing over the territory of human acts.... The principal task of conscience, as of moralists, will therefore be to mark off the limits between the domain of the law and the domain of freedom. It is a question of what is allowed, what is forbidden; what is obligatory, what remains free."[74] The primary virtue in such a system is the virtue of right action in accordance with law. It is merely "a habit of obeying the law."[75]

Due to this perpetual tension with the law and the clash of wills, human freedom is unable and unwilling to be obedient to the divine will at all times. Since it is both objective (dictating the law) and subjective (within the person), conscience inevitably "fluctuate[s] between zeal for the law, capable of turning into rigorism, and excessive concern for the subject, which can lead to laxity."[76] By definition, the human will is prone to sin if only to affirm occasionally its own self-determination.

To be fair, a more sympathetic reading of Ockham is possible, especially when his political writings are considered; they hint of an un-

---

72. Pinckaers, "Conscience," 336; cf. Pinckaers, "Aquinas on Nature," 365; Pinckaers, *Sources*, 247.

73. Pinckaers, "Historical Perspective," 213.

74. Pinckaers, "Conscience," 336; cf. Pinckaers, "Historical Perspective," 213.

75. Pinckaers, "Morality and the Movement of the Holy Spirit," trans. Craig Steven Titus, in *Pinckaers Reader*, 392.

76. Pinckaers, "Conscience," 344.

derstanding of natural law.[77] Some authors argue that, for Ockham, God's divine will is manifest in right reason and that when the will chooses to follow right reason, it chooses to follow God's will. God has thus established the structures of right reason and nature according to his will, but, they argue, this does not mean that God is merely arbitrary. Rather, in order to find some logic to God's action, one "would have to be able to point to some external standard according to which the will of God is bound to operate."[78] Otherwise, we run the risk of imposing upon God our own limited human understanding. Those who sympathize with Ockham simply insist that we cannot impose our own logic upon God.

Yet, even those who are trying to rehabilitate Ockham's thought admit not only that Ockham argues that there is no external standard known to us with which we can measure God's will, but also that he believes there is no such standard in fact. God's freedom is not bound by even his own reason. Thus, they admit that while God has willed creation to exist in the way it does, he could just as easily willed a world in which it was righteous to hate him.[79]

We can agree, therefore, with Pinckaers that there are three long-lasting effects of Ockham's nominalism on the history of moral theology.[80] First, since for Ockham every human act is the movement of a freedom that can always and everywhere choose equally between contraries, human action is atomized and no longer considered within a larger trajectory stemming from interior principles to finality. "This is the logical origin of casuistry, of moral theology viewed as a study of cases."[81] Second, morality has come to be considered primarily as an obligation determined by the relation between freedom and law. This necessarily focuses on the exterior principles of action, which, in turn, leads to physicalism. Pinckaers writes: "Because he is watching the tra-

---

77. See Crowe, *Changing Profile*, 202; Kevin McDonnell, "Does William of Ockham Have a Theory of Natural Law?" *Franciscan Studies* 34 (1974): 383–92; and Marilyn McCord Adams, "The Structure of Ockham's Moral Theory," in *Context of Casuistry*, ed. James F. Keenan, SJ, and Thomas A. Shannon (Washington, D.C.: Georgetown University Press, 1995), 25–52.

78. McDonnell, "Does William of Ockham Have a Theory of Natural Law," 387.

79. See ibid., 392; Adams, "Structure of Ockham's Moral Theory," 43.

80. See Pinckaers, "Historical Perspective," 216–17.

81. Ibid., 216.

jectory of the legal obligation, the moralist will in fact fix his attention on what St. Thomas called the external act in its relation to its matter or object, insofar as it can be directly touched by the law in its imperative or prohibitive expression."[82]

Finally, as Thomists react against nominalism they will, nonetheless, be influenced by it as they attempt to argue for acts which are intrinsically evil based on an understanding of natural law. Unable to escape the influence of this freedom of indifference, "they will not be able to escape the irreducible opposition it establishes between the subject on the one hand, with its radical demand for freedom, and on the other hand the object, law, nature, other subjects as well, and society, which oppose the subject by restricting its freedom."[83] In attempting to establish hard boundaries on freedom, moralists will focus less on the human person and interiority, and more on exteriority, law, and nature as the objective norms of morality.

AFTER WILLIAM OF OCKHAM

The Development of Casuistry after the Thirteenth Century

The work of both Aquinas and Ockham would influence the confessionals and the manuals down to the twentieth century. Confessional *summas* were not sufficient to implement fully the reforms of the Fourth Lateran Council. A true renewal of the priesthood through systematic training and formation of the clergy was needed.[84] However, the formation of the clergy would not be formalized until the Council of Trent in the sixteenth century. At the same time, scholasticism experienced its own renewal. Since the sacrament of penance was administered by a semi-literate and ill-formed clergy, Martin Luther's "double charge of perverse laxity in penance and oppressive rigidity in the hearing of confessions" was not unwarranted.[85]

---

82. Ibid.

83. Ibid., 217.

84. Both John Mahoney and William Pantin make this point. See Mahoney, *Making of Moral Theology*, 21, and William A. Pantin, *The English Church in the Fourteenth Century* (Cambridge: Cambridge University Press, 1955), 218.

85. Mahoney, *Making of Moral Theology*, 22, citing John T. McNeil, *A History of the*

The fifteenth and sixteenth centuries saw no improvement in the practice of confession. The growth of speculative scholastic theology in the universities, while beneficial in many ways, would prove even more alienating to the pastoral work of ordinary clergy. "Theology developed in the universities along the lines of an intensification of the rational procedures of scholasticism: a wider use of dialectic and logic, a stress on speculative orientation, and a proliferation of distinctions, questions, and arguments. A technical vocabulary and specialized terminology developed, along with a penchant for abstraction and a growing complexity of problems and discussions."[86] Theology was thus relegated to the universities and was the field of specialized clerics who had pursued higher studies.

While speculative theology flourished in the realms of higher education, spiritual or mystical theology concerned "the experience of the life of faith [and] attempted to disclose the divine realities perceived in the interior life and the growth of the believing soul."[87] The spiritual authors of the period spoke concretely rather than abstractly, and appealed to all Christians, not just to clergy and academics. Pinckaers believes that the separation between moral theology and mystical theology was crystallized with the separation between precepts of the law and the counsels. "Moral theory dealt essentially with precepts, which determined obligations in various sectors of human activity and were imposed on all without distinction. The counsels were supplementary and dealt with supererogatory actions let to each individual's free initiative. By this very fact, they were reserved to the chosen few who sought perfection; this was the terrain of asceticism and mysticism."[88] This division between the ordinary and obligatory, on the one hand, and the extraordinary and the phenomenal, on the other, contributed to the neglect of the universal call to holiness so prevalent in the church before the Second Vatican Council.

The Protestant Reformation in the sixteenth century prompted the Council of Trent to legislate the establishment of the seminary

---

Care of Souls (New York: Harper, 1951), 165–66. See Mahoney, *Making of Moral Theology*, 22n89, for his interesting observations on Aquinas's defense of the friars' work in confession as markedly superior to that of the secular clergy.

86. Pinckaers, *Sources*, 255.   87. Ibid.

88. Ibid., 256.

system to train young men to become priests. The men, the council decreed, were to "study grammar, singing, keeping church accounts and other useful skills; and they should be versed in holy scripture, church writers, homilies of the saints, and the practice of rites and ceremonies, and of administering the sacraments, particularly all that seems appropriate to hearing confessions."[89] The necessity of textbooks and manuals for new seminary classes on confession emphasized the need for moral theology manuals and confessionals.

A second significant development during the Reformation was the flourishing of the Society of Jesus in the latter half of the sixteenth century, and, with it, the renewal of scholasticism.[90] The Jesuits wanted to meet the needs of the time by preparing men to engage in pastoral work, and especially in spiritual direction and confession. To that end, a *ratio studiorum* for the Jesuit Order was drawn up and implemented at the end of the sixteenth century. A commission was established in 1586 to discuss what the *ratio* should contain. Thirteen years later, in 1599, a draft was implemented. Albert Jonsen and Stephen Toulmin report that the long debate centered on the relationship between cases of conscience and speculative theology. "Some commentators felt that the rigid separation of practical casuistry from speculative moral theology, as taught from the *Summa Theologiae*, was to the detriment of both. The final *Ratio* struck a balance, requiring both an explanation of principles and a study of casuistry for students in the long and short courses alike."[91]

Jonsen and Toulmin go on to explain the pedagogy employed by the Jesuits of this milieu: "The rules of the professor of cases established the format: avoidance of speculative questions, succinct presentation of principles, acceptance of probable opinions, and resolution by solid argument. Every member of the Society became familiar with this technique; practiced it in case conferences as a student; heard it weekly for his entire career in the Society and made use of it in his ministry."[92] Pinckaers observes that on the speculative side of

---

89. Council of Trent, *Decreta Super Refromatione*, July 15, 1563, in Tanner, *Decrees*, 2:751 (canon 18).

90. See Pinckaers, *Sources*, 259; Jonsen and Toulmin, *Abuse of Casuistry*, 146–51.

91. Jonsen and Toulmin, *Abuse of Casuistry*, 150.

92. Ibid.

the *ratio* only those elements that were necessary for moral theology were taught, and these became known as "fundamental moral theology." Thus, those areas of theology that were deemed too speculative were dropped from the curriculum. The treatises on beatitude and the end of man, grace, and the gifts of the Holy Spirit were among the topics dropped.[93] The more concrete treatises on human action, *habitus*, virtue, law, conscience, and sin were retained, of course. In addition, the commandments and the precepts of the church were studied and, eventually, the curriculum included the obligations necessary for each state of life.

The Spanish Jesuit and professor Juan Azor (1536–1603) was a singularly important influence in this tradition.[94] From 1600 to 1611, Azor's massive *Institutionum Moralium* was published bearing the subtitle "in which all questions of conscience are briefly treated."[95] Azor introduced a fourfold division of moral theology: first, the ten commandments; second, the seven sacraments; third, ecclesiastical censures, penalties, and indulgences; and, fourth, states of life and the last things.[96] Azor also included seven general topics which he claimed were borrowed from Thomas's *Summa*: first, human acts; second, the division of action into good and bad; third, the passions or affections; fourth, *habitus*; fifth, virtues in general; sixth, sins in general (understood as infractions against law and rights); seventh, law in all its senses (human, divine, and natural along with the precepts of the church).[97] Not surprisingly, given the *ratio* of the Jesuit Order, there was no mention of beatitude, grace, or the Holy Spirit.

The influence of Azor's syllabus is evident in most of the manuals that followed him. Even in the nineteenth century, Jean Gury, the eminent Jesuit casuist, said that Azor "is, among authors, the most commendable for his wisdom, learning and the weight of his reasoning."[98] The success of the syllabus was due first to the authority of the Society but also to the fact that Azor systematically organized the pre-

---

93. See Pinckaers, *Sources*, 260.

94. See ibid., 260–62, 265–66.

95. Jonsen and Toulmin, *Abuse of Casuistry*, 149.

96. Pinckaers, *Sources*, 261.

97. The preceding was outlined by Pinckaers in *Sources*, 261–62.

98. Jonsen and Toulmin, *Abuse of Casuistry*, 155, quoting Jean Gury in "Azor," *Dictionnaire de Théologie Catholique* (Paris: Letouzey et Ané, 1930), I, col. 2653.

sentation of moral theology. His logic was clearly in line with what Pinckaers has identified as a morality of obligation. By emphasizing the exteriority of action in its relation to the law, Azor had no concern for the end of man and beatitude or the internal workings of grace and the Holy Spirit. Azor's method was generally accepted without question. We lament with Pinckaers that

many believed, with Azor, that in it the moral teaching of St. Thomas, the Catholic moral teaching of all times lay revealed. A mere glance at the *Summa theologiae* and the Church Fathers, a smattering of critical sense, would have shown the profound differences. But the new system was so cogent, its appeal to contemporary ideas so direct, that the possibility of any other line of thought had become quite unimaginable.[99]

There was a proliferation of manuals of moral theology, all based on this casuistic style, into the seventeenth century. Jonsen and Toulmin report that by the end of the sixteenth century there were approximately six hundred volumes of moral theology manuals, all casuistic and all remarkably similar.[100] Between the seventeenth and twentieth centuries, all moral theology textbooks adopted the same structure outlined by Azor for fundamental theology, providing treatises on human acts, conscience, law, and sin. In his review of the manuals, Pinckaers observes that there were some minor variations and some manualists even included a treatise on virtue and man's final end, but these were included only superficially and had no impact on the structure of the manuals. The primary concern was exterior human action in relation to obligations imposed by law. The only difference one can note among moral theologians of this period is their position with regard to questionable opinions of the authorities in the resolution of cases of conscience: whether they were laxist, rigorist, probabilist, probabiliorist, or equiprobablist.[101] There is no need to explain these movements here, only to say that they all concern the licit course of action in the face of doubts about the obligations of law. Even Alphonsus Ligouri, the doctor of moral theology, was caught in the mindset of his time and so situated his own theol-

---

99. Pinckaers, *Sources*, 266.
100. Jonsen and Toulmin, *Abuse of Casuistry*, 150.
101. For a summary of these different modes of casuistry, see Mahoney, *Making of Moral Theology*, 135–43; Pinckaers, *Sources*, 273–77.

ogy within this framework when he coined the equiprobablist position. This methodology would govern Catholic moral theology well into the twentieth century.

The Birth of Neo-Thomism

In his history of neo-Thomism, Gerald McCool offers a broad definition: "The term Neo-Thomism is generally employed to designate the movement in philosophy and theology which assumed a leading place in Catholic thought in the latter portion of the nineteenth century and retained its dominance until the middle of the twentieth."[102] Neo-Thomism was a part of a third wave of scholasticism. The second scholastic movement of Trent had fallen to the Enlightenment in the eighteenth century. Jesuit Thomism led by Francisco Suarez (d. 1617) virtually disappeared after the suppression of the Jesuits in 1772. But even the Thomism based on the commentatorial tradition, the more speculative theological descendants of Thomas, was disdained in the face of the rationalism and the secularism of the Enlightenment.[103]

While there were several different reactions in the church to Enlightenment rationalism (within the church), the renewal of Thomism in the face of European rationalism can be attributed to a group of scholars in Italy, many of whom joined the Jesuit Order upon its reestablishment in 1814. One of the most significant of these, Serafino Sordi (d. 1865), "came to recognize the value of Thomism for refuting those philosophical positions that, since they exemplified for the most part either a developed Kantianism or an accommodated Hegelianism, proved ill-suited to elucidate Christian theology."[104] Sordi's own manuals were still in use well into the mid-twentieth century. In 1824, Pope Leo XII returned the Gregorian University to the newly re-founded Society of Jesus and its new rector, the young Luigi Taparelli d'Azeglio, and attempted to unify the faculty by encouraging the study of Thomas. But the faculty strongly resisted, following the lead of their champion theologian Giovanni Perone who "felt none of the hostility toward modern German theology."[105] Thus, the initial effort to spark a Thomistic revival in Rome failed.

102. McCool, *Neo-Thomists*, 9.
104. Cessario, *Short History*, 83.
103. See ibid., 26–27.
105. McCool, *Neo-Thomists*, 32.

The interaction between the neo-Thomists and those some came to call the "traditionalists" (who emphasized faith over reason) was nowhere more clear than a half century later, at the First Vatican Council. The neo-Thomist Jesuit Joseph Kleutgen and the traditionalist Jesuit Johannes Franzelin were commissioned to draft the council's document on faith and reason. Franzelin had little concern for scholasticism or Thomism: "He did not wish to make mediaeval theology the norm for all theology. That might upset the balance of Catholic theology, and it might diminish the important role which the Fathers of the Church should play in it."[106] Still, Kleutgen's Thomistic influence can be recognized in the council's constitution on faith and reason.[107]

While a Jesuit revival of Thomism failed in both Rome and later in Naples, D'Azeglio was very influential on a young student, Gioacchino Pecci, who "in 1828 was prompted to send home for a copy of the *Summa theologiae* that he remembered seeing on the shelves of his family library."[108] After the death of Pope Pius IX on February 7, 1878, Cardinal Gioacchino Pecci was elected pope the following April. He took the name Leo XIII. It was this pope who issued the landmark encyclical *Aeterni Patris* in 1879, which initiated the institutional revival of Thomism in the Catholic church. The document bore the subtitle, "On the Restoration of Christian Philosophy according to the Mind of St. Thomas Aquinas, the Angelic Doctor." After offering a history of philosophy and its use by Christian theologians, including the Church Fathers, in responding to the needs of their day, this doc-

---

106. Ibid.

107. The final paragraph of the chapter on faith and reason in the Dogmatic Constitution on the Catholic Faith (*De Fide Catholica*) explains the relationship between faith and reason in much the same way that the first question of the *Summa Theologiae* does. Specifically, the chapter concludes with the observation that the human sciences should be left to operate upon their own principles and methods. Nevertheless, the role of faith is to prevent these sciences from extending beyond their limits or from conflicting with the faith. The principles and conclusions of other science, rightly practiced, can be assumed into the faith by confirming theology's own fundamental principles: those truths revealed by God. See Vatican Council I, *De Fide Catholica*, April 24, 1870, in Tanner, *Decrees*, 1:809 (chap. 4); *ST* I, q. 1, aa. 1, 2, 5, 8; and Lawrence J. Donohoo, OP, "The Nature and Grace of *Sacra Doctrina* in St. Thomas's *Super Boetium de Trinitate*," *The Thomist* 63 (1999): 343–401.

108. Cessario, *Short History*, 85.

ument extols the wisdom of Thomas and highlights his useful contribution for church doctrine even in the present day. The encyclical praises movements that seek to restore the Angelic Doctor's teaching to its former importance. The pope goes on to insist that the philosophy of Thomas would respond most suitably to the needs of the time and, therefore, he instructed all universities to offer his teaching.

McCool reports that the reaction to *Aeterni Patris* was generally favorable by the bishops of the world. They had grown weary of the eclectic and variant forms of philosophy and theology being taught in seminaries and houses of study.[109] Pope Leo XIII made strategic appointments to guarantee the success of his encyclical. He forced the appointments of Thomists to the official Jesuit journal, *Civiltà Cattolica*, and Joseph Kleutgen's appointment as prefect of studies for the Society of Jesus. A form of Thomism was thus established in the Society of Jesus before the turn of the century.

The manuals of the twentieth century, some published even on the eve of the Second Vatican Council, took their cue from this revival of Thomism. The twentieth century manualists seem to have little knowledge or concern for the challenges to this initial revival of Thomism that were offered by Etienne Gilson, Jacques Maritain, or Joseph Marechal. Rather, these later manuals assumed many of the hallmarks of neo-Thomist theology: the distinctions between the natural and supernatural, nature and grace, faith and reason, body and soul, philosophy and theology, on the one hand, and the unifying theological theme which they took to be Thomas's, "the idea of God, considered, in his inner being and his exterior creative and redemptive work."[110]

John Gallagher provides a helpful synopsis of the major manualists published in the twentieth century.[111] He notes six theological themes found in most of the manuals of the twentieth century, all of which were imported from the neo-Thomist theology popular in the

109. See McCool, *Neo-Thomists*, 40.
110. See Gallagher, *Time Past, Time Future*, 40, quoting Gerald McCool, SJ, *Catholic Theology in the Nineteenth Century* (New York: Seabury Press, 1977), 196.
111. The manuals Gallagher surveys include those by John A. McHugh, OP, and Charles J. Callan, OP; Aloysio Sabetti, SJ, and Timotheo Barrett, SJ; Marcellinus Zalba, SJ; F. Hürth, SJ, and P. M. Abellan, SJ; Francis J. O'Connell, CSSR; and Dominic Prümmer, OP.

day.[112] The first theme is that moral theology is its own theological discipline. Here, he notes two distinct ideas running through most of the manuals: first, that moral theology has as its goal the attainment of man's end, even though the manuals spoke very little of the content of that end, and second, that moral theology's primary task was "the determination of sins and duties in order to prepare seminarians for the proper administration of the sacrament of penance."[113] In the post-Vatican I church, the sources of moral theology were not just scripture and tradition but also the teachings of previous moralists and the teachings of the church (for example, the *responsia ad dubia* issued by various offices in the Holy See). In this period, the papacy and the Holy See were clearly in control of theological discussion, as evidenced by the plethora of official responses to theological questions offered in the first half of the twentieth century.[114]

The second theological theme of the manuals that Gallagher identifies concerns the goal of humanity, which "could be adequately known only through revelation and was primarily mediated to the Catholic community through dogmatic theology."[115] Gallagher notes that the end of the human person was defined so as to emphasize "the religious significance of human acts."[116] There is, however, no mention of interiority or the growth in virtue and holiness that was so central to Thomas's moral theology. In fact, the end of human nature is itself defined in terms of obligation. Gallagher says that the for most of the manuals, "the end of human beings is both an *obligation of* and a perfection of their nature, but its achievement is totally a consequence of God's gratuitous grace."[117] Here lies the conundrum of the neo-Thomist manualist tradition: the relationship between nature's obligations and supernatural grace. Hence, the third theme preoccupying the manuals is the question of the relationship between merit and grace, nature and supernature.

112. Gallagher, *Time Past, Time Future*, 50–62.

113. Ibid., 50.

114. See Mahoney, *Making of Moral Theology*, 116–74, for a historical review of the impact that magisterial authority had on theologians from the end of the nineteenth century through the twentieth century.

115. Gallagher, *Time Past, Time Future*, 54.

116. Ibid.

117. Ibid., 55.

The fourth concern, the theological virtues, was also elucidated in terms of obligation and exteriority, even if interior necessity was acknowledged. Here, Gallagher uses the Dominic Prümmer's manual, one of the last manuals before the council, to summarize the point:

The gift of the [theological] virtues imposed upon their recipient the obligation of eliciting acts of faith, hope, and charity, as well as the obligation of performing external acts consistent with each of the virtues. An elicited act is one which remains within the will; in itself it does not require any external act. Thus Prümmer argued that there was an obligation to elicit interior acts of faith when God's revelation had been sufficiently proposed to one, when a dogma of faith was proposed by the church, frequently during life, and probably at the moment of death. The same author proposed that, since human nature was embodied, there were also external acts of faith incumbent upon a Christian: a positive duty to worship and to profess one's faith when questioned by public authority as well as the negative duty to deny one's faith. Similar interior and exterior acts, elicited and commanded, were also entailed by the virtues of hope and charity.[118]

This conception of theological virtues and grace figured prominently in the manualists' view of the new law, the fifth theme identified by Gallagher. The new law of the gospel has both interior and exterior elements. The interior elements are the grace of the Holy Spirit and the theological virtues. The exterior elements are the required and commanded external acts of the Christian life: works of mercy, the sacramental life of the church, etc. Gallagher notes the obvious fact that "as one studies the special moral theology of the manualists one begins to suspect that the primacy of the inner aspect of the new law was being obscured by the requirements of the external law."[119] The new law of the manualists was plagued with duty and obligation.

Finally, as noted earlier, sin was a major preoccupation. In true scholastic form, the manualists were certain to distinguish between actual and habitual sin, personal and original sin, mortal and venial sin, and formal and material sin. For the manualists, sin is evil for two reasons: first, because it is a turning away from God as the person's ultimate end and second, because it frustrates the divine order, which was the eternal law of God (though the manualists seemed to accept the voluntarist conception that law was primarily in the will

118. Ibid., 57.   119. Ibid., 60.

of God).[120] The theological presuppositions that influence the manualist moral theory are in continuity with the tradition of casuistry (traceable more to the nominalist Ockham than to Aquinas); even though the twentieth-century manualists aligned themselves with the neo-Thomist movements of the time, or perhaps because of this fact, they were still steeped in a morality of obligation.

CONCLUSION

As we have seen, Servais Pinckaers, Romanus Cessario, John Mahoney, and John Gallagher all share the same critique of the manualist tradition. In our exploration of Pinckaers's widely-known critique, we gave special focus (as he does) to Juan Azor's syllabus in the sixteenth century. Azor, who was among the first to exclude a treatise on beatitude and the happiness of man from his moral system, has served as one of our primary examples of the shift in outlook, whereby the topic of beatitude was increasingly seen as too speculative for moral theology. Pinckaers sees a deeper reason "unclear perhaps to Azor but nonetheless operating in influencing him and his followers.... [Namely, Azor] could no longer see the importance of the treatise on beatitude within the context of his conception of a morality of obligation."[121] Despite the fact that Azor apparently intended to include beatitude in the final section of his study on the ends of man but died before completing the work, had he done so he would have inverted the order that Thomas himself had followed: "St. Thomas placed the question of happiness at the beginning of moral theology, considering it to be primary and principal.... Finality no longer held a preponderant place in this system. The end, henceforth, was only one element of a moral action— one among others."[122]

The manualists certainly mentioned man's last end, and believed it was God himself, but an action was judged according to its extrinsic relationship to norm and law. Obedience, law, and norm were the primary referents when considering man's end. For example, morality was, according to John McHugh and Charles Callan's manual, "the agreement or disagreement of a human act with the *norms* that regu-

---

120. Ibid., 62.
122. Ibid., 262–63.

121. Pinckaers, *Sources*, 262.

late human conduct with reference to man's last end."[123] Similarly, the Aloysio Sabetti and Timotheo Barrett manual instructs: "The essence of morality consists primarily in the condition of the human act to the eternal law which is the divine plan, the will of God ordering natural order to be preserved and condemning its perturbation.... The secondary essence of morality consists in the relation of human acts to right reason."[124] Even when manualists attempted to introduce a transcendent conception of man's end, it was still under the rubric of norm and obligation. Gallagher writes, "[Francis] O'Connell proposed that morality meant 'a transcendental relation of a human act, either of agreement or disagreement, to a norm or rule of goodness and evil, based on man's nature in its entirety.'"[125] The manualists were more concerned with whether a particular act violated God's divine will expressed primarily in the norms of nature (such as biological processes) or revealed in revelation, than with the question of the reasons why an act would be evil and, therefore, why it would be against nature and God's will.

This view of morality as obligation is the direct result of the freedom of indifference that views the will as the primary locus of morality and freedom as the fundamental ability to choose between contraries. This in turn was precipitated and confirmed by nominalism which, as we have seen, held that natures were convenient labels of the mind, but do not exist in reality. The only means of circumscribing freedom in such a view is the imposition of law. Thomas's idea that natural law was an intrinsic image of the eternal law, the *ratio* of God, in the human person had no place in the manualist tradition. Rather, as Cessario says, "all law represents something extrinsic to the human person and constitutes a limitation on the person's God-given autonomy."[126]

123. Gallagher, *Time Past, Time Future*, 76, quoting John A. McHugh, OP, and Charles J. Callan, OP, *Moral Theology: A Complete Course Based on St. Thomas Aquinas and the Best Modern Authorities* (New York: Joseph F. Wagner, 1929), 1:23 (emphasis added).

124. Gallagher, *Time Past, Time Future*, 76, quoting Aloysio Sabetti, SJ, and Timotheo Barrett, SJ, *Compendium Theologiae Moralis*, ed. Daniel F. Creeden, SJ, 34th ed. (Neo Eboraci: Frederick Pustet, 1939), 27.

125. Gallagher, *Time Past, Time Future*, 77, quoting Francis J. O'Connell, CSSR, *Outlines of Moral Theology* (Milwaukee, Wis.: Bruce Publishing Company, 1953), 18.

126. Romanus Cessario, OP, *Introduction to Moral Theology* (Washington, D.C.: The Catholic University of America Press, 2001), 238.

This bracketing of beatitude in Catholic moral theory and the exaltation of absolute freedom of indifference led to what both Cessario and Pinckaers have referred to as the atomization of moral action. Since this system "does not directly envision man as set between God as the first principle and God as our beatitude, casuistry does not adequately cognize or explain the dynamism of the moral life."[127] Each human act is an absolute choice between contraries and has no bearing on the acts which follow. Morality was simply the evaluation of particular acts in their relationship to the divine law. Thus, the extrinsic aspects of those acts were emphasized to the detriment of the interior life of the human person. Pinckaers observes, astutely:

> The distinction between interior and exterior acts was blurred. The ethicist lost sight of the interior dimension, for he felt that it was necessary to study only the exterior aspects of human acts as found in the legal ordinances. The ethicist focused on the material elements covered by the law; for him, this was objectivity. Whence the danger of objectivism, or the reduction of the moral act to its material object as opposed to all that emanated from the agent.[128]

The concern the manualists had with sin and cases of conscience confirms these criticisms. Identifying sin and human acts in relationship to the law through cases of conscience is a chief identifying characteristic of a system concerned primarily with exteriority.

Finally, the primacy of the freedom of the will in this methodology fostered a dualist anthropology. If the will must be absolutely free and under no constraint, then aside from the virtue of obedience to the law, the primary virtue for the human person is stoicism: the command of all forces that might sway the will. This necessarily includes the passions. Cessario speculates that this explains casuistry's "disproportionate interest in regulating sexual morality. No greater threat to the liberty of indifference could be imaged than the sudden upsurge of lust. So every precaution had to be taken to maintain the serene 'indifference' of the will in the face of some *de facto*, especially unexpected, compelling good."[129] Excessive attempts to keep the will in control of all emotion would contribute, at least in part, to the widespread dismissal of traditional moral theology during the sexual revolution of the 1960s.

127. Ibid., 237.
128. Pinckaers, *Sources*, 271.
129. Cessario, *Introduction*, 238.

We have seen how the manuals departed from the theology of Aquinas. Thomas articulated a moral theory that was grounded on God as man's beatitude and end. This fact, he believed, was written into man's nature and provided the sources for human action in the form of natural inclinations that seek the good and the true, that is, that seek God himself. Aquinas's synthesis was displaced by William of Ockham's nominalism and voluntarism. Ockham's rejection of realism—the idea that there are any universal natures outside of the mind—corroborated his exaltation of the will over the intellect. In his view, the will is unfettered from human nature and natural inclination. It becomes simply the power to choose at any given moment between absolute contraries. The only locus of morality in such a worldview is the divine will to which the human will must be obedient. The divine will issues norms that simply must be obeyed. These norms can be seen in revelation and in the structures of nature, which is itself often understood in purely biological terms.

Thus, morality was reoriented from its former concern with beatitude and growth in virtue through a succession of acts to a concern for the evaluation of particular and isolated actions and the relationship of those actions with the law. This meant that moral theologians and confessors were solely concerned with the exterior aspects of the human act, which could be identified and evaluated. This led to a separation between the interior and exterior aspects of the human person, and ultimately to an emphasis on human nature above the human person, with human nature "dissolved or reduced to sheer biological facticity."[130] The narrative we have developed here and will develop further in the next chapter suggests that this overemphasis on biological facticity would be exposed as insufficient in the debate on the birth control pill in the twentieth century. In the next chapter, we move to that debate itself, principally as it is articulated in the light of a growing school of thought that would be particularly important for the work of Karol Wojtyła—personalism—and in Pope Paul VI's critical 1968 encyclical *Humanae Vitae*.

130. Grabowski, *Sex and Virtue*, 16.

2

Personalism and the Debate on
Marriage and Contraception

In this chapter, we will see how the methodology of moral theology
and ethics, presented in chapter 1, was challenged substantially in the
twentieth century. The manualist tradition emphasized the physical
structure of human action and strict obedience to law (as manifested
in nature and in scripture) in moral evaluation. In the centuries that
followed, the natural *telos* of biological processes began to give way to
scientific progress, which was increasingly efficient in altering those
processes for the perceived good of the human person. Responding
to this development and the perceived insufficiency of the manuals,
some Catholic moral theologians began to favor the notion of the
acting person rather than the purposes of nature as the category of
theological discourse. This trend was particularly evident in the birth
control movement at the turn of the century, which found sympathy
within the church in the 1960s. At this same time, there was a renewal
in the understanding of marriage in the Catholic church, particularly
within the personalist school of thought. These two trends were piv-
otal in the debate among theologians and laity both before and after
the promulgation of Pope Paul VI's 1968 encyclical *Humanae Vitae*.
By considering all of these issues, this chapter will thus conclude the
historical background necessary to appreciate Pope John Paul's con-

tribution to the discussion on marriage and sexuality that culminated in *Theology of the Body* and the notion of a "spousal meaning of the body."

The chapter consists of four sections. The first section outlines the stirrings for change in the church's teaching on sex and marriage before 1953. The second section concentrates on what William Shannon calls the first phase of the birth control debate, beginning with the introduction of the birth control pill in 1953. The third section reviews the second phase of that debate, which begins with John Rock's book *The Time Has Come* (1963), arguing for the permissibility of the birth control pill, and lasts until completion of the work by the papal commission on birth control in 1966. Finally, the fourth section provides a glimpse of the immediate aftermath of *Humanae Vitae's* publication. In a way, the Catholic church is still experiencing the aftermath of the encyclical as a strong majority of Catholic couples reportedly practice contraception. To report the complete reaction to the encyclical from 1968 to the present would be its own study. Rather, the fourth section of this chapter offers the immediate setting for Karol Wojtyła's unique contribution to these debates as a bishop and eventually as Pope John Paul II.

THE STIRRINGS FOR CHANGE BEFORE 1953

The Anglican Communion and *Casti Connubii*

When a papal commission was formed by Pope John XXIII to discuss the issue of birth control, eminent historian John Noonan was invited to give a lecture on the history of the church's teaching on contraception.[1] In his book on contraception, Noonan shows that historically the Christian church has, at least until 1930, always taught that contraception was immoral. He summarizes his findings in the introduction: "The teachers of the Church have taught without hesitation or

---

1. See Robert McClory, *Turning Point: The Inside Story of the Papal Birth Control Commission, and How* Humanae vitae *Changed the Life of Patty Crowley and the Future of the Church* (New York: Crossroad, 1995), 68–69.

variation that certain acts preventing procreation are gravely sinful. No Catholic theologian has ever taught, 'Contraception is a good act.' The teaching on contraception is clear and apparently fixed forever."[2] Noonan, however, closes this same introduction with a suggestion that the doctrine might change given "the circumstances in which the doctrine was composed, the controversies touching it, [and] the doctrinal elements now obsolete."[3] Janet Smith observes that Noonan's prejudice in favor of reversing the prohibition on artificial contraception makes his historical conclusion "particularly forceful," as he is clearly suggesting a departure from the teaching of the historical church.[4] This tradition was ruptured on August 14, 1930, when the Lambeth Conference of the Anglican Communion permitted the use of contraception for its members.

Noonan reports that the birth rate per thousand persons had been steadily falling since 1771, when it was 38.6 in France, to 1860, when it was just 26.3.[5] The birth control movement had gone international as early as 1900 with the First International Birth Control Congress in Liège.[6] By 1935 there were some two hundred mechanical contraceptive devices employed in most Western countries. A vast array of chemical solutions were also used.[7] Standard medical practice began to approve the use of contraception as early as 1905 in France and 1922 in England. This trend was coupled with the overpopulation movement, which took its cue from the now-discredited work of Thomas Malthus (d. 1834) who argued that population was increasing faster than the world's resources for human subsistence (particularly agricultural resources). The competition for basic subsistence, he argued, leads to many of society's ills.[8] The 1925 international con-

2. John T. Noonan, *Contraception: A History of Its Treatment by the Catholic Theologians and Canonists*, rev. ed. (Cambridge, Mass.: Harvard University Press, 1986), 6.

3. Ibid.

4. See Janet E. Smith, *Humanae vitae: A Generation Later* (Washington, D.C.: The Catholic University of America Press, 1991), 3. Noonan would later explicitly argue for a development in the doctrine on contraception. See John T. Noonan, *A Church That Can and Cannot Change: The Development of Catholic Moral Teaching* (South Bend, Ind.: University of Notre Dame Press, 2005).

5. Noonan, *Contraception*, 387.

6. See ibid., 407.

7. See ibid., 408.

8. See Thomas R. Malthus, *An Essay on the Principle of Population* (New York:

gress on birth control held in New York had precisely this theme: "Overpopulation produces war."[9]

These trends definitely had an influence on Christians. The Anglican Communion experienced a rapid shift in its teaching. In 1908 and again in 1920 the Lambeth Conference condemned contraception.[10] But in 1930, with a vote of 193 to 67, the Anglican bishops approved the following resolution:

> Where there is a clearly felt moral obligation to limit or avoid parenthood, the method must be decided on Christian principles. The primary and obvious method is complete abstinence from intercourse (as far as may be necessary) in a life of discipline and self-control lived in the power of the Holy Spirit. Nevertheless in those cases where there is such a clearly-felt moral obligation to limit or avoid parenthood, and where there is a morally sound reason for avoiding complete abstinence, the conference agrees that other methods may be used, provided that this is done in the light of the same Christian principles. The Conference records its strong condemnation of the use of any methods of conception control from motives of selfishness, luxury, or mere convenience.[11]

The statement provided no methodology for determining when contraception is illicit other than to insist that contraception cannot be used for impure motives.

The Catholic response was swift. Less than five months later, Pope Pius XI issued his landmark encyclical *Casti Connubii* on Christian marriage.[12] In his encyclical, Pius XI implicitly refers to the Anglican bishops when he writes: "Openly departing from the unin-

---

Oxford University Press, 1993), originally published in 1798; Samuel Hollander, *The Economics of Thomas Robert Malthus* (Toronto: University of Toronto Press, 1997); William Peterson, *Malthus: Founder of Modern Demography*, 2nd ed. (Piscataway, N.J.: Transaction Publishers, 1998). Malthus had developed the idea of the "Malthusian disaster." He theorized that a series of natural disasters and human troubles eventually equalizes population *vis-à-vis* resource and thus balancing the supply and demand ratio. Since its publication, Malthus's controversial view has been rebutted. For a recent example, see Antony Trewavas, "Malthus Foiled Again and Again," *Nature* 418 (August 8, 2002): 668–70.

9. Noonan, *Contraception*, 408.

10. See Edward M. East, *Mankind at the Crossroads* (New York: Charles Scribner's Sons, 1923), vii, 167, 340; Noonan, *Contraception*, 409.

11. Quoted in Noonan, *Contraception*, 409.

12. See ibid., 410–14.

terrupted Christian tradition some recently have judged it possible solemnly to declare another doctrine regarding this question."[13] In direct contradiction to the Lambeth Conference, Pius XI wrote: "*No reason, however grave, may be put forward by which anything intrinsically against nature* may become conformable to nature and morally good. Since, therefore, the conjugal act is destined primarily by nature for the begetting of children, those who in exercising it deliberately frustrate its natural power and purpose sin against nature and commit a deed which is shameful and intrinsically vicious."[14]

Casti Connubii defends the intrinsic integrity of the conjugal act according to the same principles common to the manualist tradition:

> The Catholic Church, to whom God has entrusted the defense of the integrity and purity of morals, standing erect in the midst of the moral ruin which surrounds her, in order that she may preserve the chastity of the nuptial union from being defiled by this foul stain, raises her voice in token of her divine ambassadorship and through our mouth proclaims anew: any use whatsoever of matrimony exercised in such a way that the act is *deliberately frustrated in its natural power to generate life is an offense against the law of God and of nature, and those who indulge in such are branded with the guilt of a grave sin.*[15]

On the one hand, the tone of this paragraph reveals a *contra mundum* tendency. The church is depicted as "standing erect in the midst of the moral ruin which surrounds her." On the other hand, when read as a whole, I think the encyclical does more than simply rehash manualist principles.

The 1917 Code of Canon Law had declared: "The primary end of marriage is the procreation and education of children; the secondary [end] is mutual support and a remedy for concupiscence."[16] Interest-

---

13. Pope Pius XI, *Casti Connubii*, Encyclical Letter, December 31, 1930, par. 56 [hereafter, *CC*]; the official Latin text is found in *Acta Apostolicae Sedis* (Città del Vaticano: Typis Polyglottis Vaticanis, 1909–), 22 [hereafter, *AAS*]: 539–92; all English translations are drawn from www.vatican.va.

14. *CC*, par. 54 (emphasis added).

15. *CC*, par. 56 (emphasis added).

16. *Codex Iuris Canonici* (Città del Vaticano: Typis Polyglottis Vaticanis, 1917), can. 1013, §1. This passage is on page 352 in the unofficial English translation: Edward N. Peters, *The 1917 Pio-Benedictine Code of Canon Law in English Translation with Extensive Scholarly Apparatus* (San Francisco, Calif.: Ignatius Press, 2001).

ingly, the code mentioned nothing of the mutual love of the spouses as either a primary or a secondary end. Unlike the Code, Pope Pius XI includes a third object among the secondary ends of marriage, "the cultivating of mutual love."[17] He says the love between husband and wife "pervades all duties of married life and holds pride of place in Christian marriage."[18]

[The] mutual molding of husband and wife, this determined effort to perfect each other, can in a very real sense ... be said to be the chief reason and purpose of matrimony, provided matrimony be looked at not in the restricted sense as instituted for the proper conception and education of the child, but more widely as the blending of life as a whole and the mutual interchange and sharing thereof.[19]

John Gallagher has argued that while Pope Pius XI uses physicalist language to condemn contraception, he is not using the language in the same mode as the manualists and older moral theologians. "In the content of the whole encyclical, however, it seems that what is 'according to nature' is to be determined not by considering the physical aspect by itself but by looking at the nature and purpose of matrimony."[20] Indeed, the encyclical speaks more of the nature of marriage as established by God and unalterable by man than it does about the nature of the conjugal act.[21]

This is why Pope Pius XI explicitly accepted that couples could engage in sexual intercourse even when they know they will not conceive. There are other goods to be gained—mutual aid, the cultivation of mutual love, and the quieting of concupiscence—that the couple are permitted to seek "so long as they are subordinated to the primary end [the procreation and education of offspring] and so long as the intrinsic nature of the act is preserved."[22] Gallagher may be right that Pius XI was attempting to express an idea for which the

17. CC, par. 59.   18. CC, par. 23.
19. CC, par. 24.
20. John Gallagher, "Magisterial Teaching from 1918 to the Present," in *Human Sexuality and Personhood, Proceedings of the Workshop for the Hierarchies of the United States and Canada Sponsored by the Pope John Center Through a Grant from the Knights of a Columbus* (Braintree, Mass.: Pope John Center, 1990), 196.
21. See CC, pars. 6, 49, 50, 95.
22. CC, par. 59.

theology of his day did not yet have an adequate vocabulary.[23] In effect, Pius XI's attempt to articulate the importance of the spouses' life of love, even as he was committed to the terminology of primary and secondary ends, was just the beginning of a shift to an emphasis on the personalist value of marriage.

Personalism and Marriage: Dietrich Von Hildebrand and Herbert Doms

The shift to a personalist understanding of marriage began some years before the promulgation of *Casti Connubii*. One of the most notable lay scholars on marriage in the twentieth century was Dietrich von Hildebrand, a professor of philosophy at the University of Munich. While a detailed review of von Hildebrand's theology of marriage is beyond the scope of this study, it should be noted that von Hildebrand stood diametrically opposed to the physicalist methodology which he thought was at work in most of the Catholic theology of his day.[24] He lamented that "our epoch is characterized by a terrible anti-personalism, a progressive blindness toward the nature and dignity of the spiritual person.... Human life is considered exclusively from a biological point of view and biological principles are the measure by which all human activities are judged."[25]

In 1928, he wrote that the marital act is "not only a function, the generation of children; it also possesses a significance for man as a human being—namely to be the expression and fulfillment of wedded love and community of life—and, moreover, it participates after a certain fashion in the sacramental meaning of matrimony."[26] Noonan notes that "for the first time, a Catholic writer taught that love was a requirement of lawful, marital coition. He tied this novel demand

---

23. See Gallagher, "Magisterial Teaching," 195.

24. See Dietrich von Hildebrand, *In Defense of Purity: An Analysis of the Catholic Ideals of Purity and Virginity* (Baltimore: Helicon Press, 1962). For an excellent analysis of von Hildebrand's thought on this matter, see Kevin Schemenauer, *Conjugal Love and Procreation: Dietrich Von Hildebrand's Superabundant Integration* (Lanham, Md.: Lexington Books, 2011).

25. Dietrich von Hildebrand, *Marriage* (New York: Longmans, Green, 1942), v.

26. Von Hildebrand, *Defense*, 20.

to an ancient term—*fides*, fidelity. Fidelity required that person meet person in a giving of self."[27] For von Hildebrand, the conjugal act has not only an objective end (the procreation of children) but also an intrinsic significance for the couple: "The act of wedded communion has indeed the object of procreation, but in addition the *significance* of a unique union of love."[28] He argued that conjugal love is not simply an advancement on the love of friendship that now included sensuality, but rather he suggested that conjugal love is a unique self-gift of one person to another, an "I-thou communion."[29] Marriage establishes the community in which this communion is fully actualized, while the conjugal act expresses the meaning of that communion.[30]

Von Hildebrand's obvious disposition in favor of the implications of the conjugal act for the persons involved did not deter him, however, from condemning contraception, which he viewed as a rupture between the biological objective and the personal significance of the act.[31] Thus, von Hildebrand was one of a new breed of Catholic scholars who, in the words of John Grabowski, "strove to balance the primacy of procreation as the end of marriage by delineating a new category—that of meaning—in which love could be accorded primacy. Each value was seen as having primary importance in its own sphere. Hence the natural value of procreation was balanced by the new focus on personal self-giving love."[32] The interaction between the meaning of personal self-giving love and the natural ends of marriage, traditionally understood, would occupy the thought of many Catholic moral theologians in the twentieth century concerned with marriage and contraception.

This shift in thinking about marriage was not an enterprise restricted to professional theologians and philosophers. William Shannon has pointed out that the laity increasingly viewed marriage as a vocation, their love expressed through sexual intercourse as a means to sanctity,

---

27. Noonan, *Contraception*, 495.

28. Von Hildebrand, *Defense*, 22.   29. See ibid., 5–8.

30. See ibid., 25.

31. Dietrich von Hildebrand, *The Encyclical* Humanae vitae—*A Sign of Contradiction: An Essay on Birth Control and Catholic Conscience* (Chicago: Franciscan Herald Press, 1969).

32. John S. Grabowski, "Person or Nature? Rival Personalisms in 20th Century Catholic Sexual Ethics," *Studia Moralia* 35 (1997): 306.

and were increasingly realizing that marriage was better characterized as self-gift rather than merely a juridical contract. This sentiment was catalyzed by various lay movements of the time.[33] Shannon concludes: "In the context of this growing appreciation of the personal values of married life and married love, it seemed increasingly unrealistic to think that the nature of marriage could be adequately expressed in the impersonal categories of primary and secondary purposes."[34]

Publishing after von Hildebrand, Herbert Doms further advances the personalist view of marriage, but in a way perhaps unforeseen by von Hildebrand. Doms was critical of the emphasis placed on the procreation and education of children as the primary meaning of marriage. While not denying this *end* or *purpose* of marriage, he believed the *meaning* of marriage—the union of the spouses—was primary.[35] "The principal and primary purpose of marriage is not the child, but the mutual forming and perfecting of husband and wife in the metaphysical, natural and, above all supernatural orders."[36] Therefore, he argued that the church should abandon all reference to primary and secondary ends in marriage.[37]

For Herbert Doms, marriage and sexual desire are fundamentally about the completion and fulfillment of persons.[38] The sexual instinct, although natural, is not simply natural; it is personal. Moreover, he suggests, "the sexual act is always a result of the power of the

---

33. The Family Renewal Association was founded in the early 1940s in New York City by Fr. John P. Delaney, SJ. During their meetings, married couples heard conferences on the vocation of marriage, the love of spouses, and the meaning of sexuality in marriage. This initial association was followed upon by the Cana Conference Movement and the Christian Family Movement. All of these movements tended to emphasize the personalist dimensions of marriage instead of juridical notions. See William H. Shannon, *The Lively Debate: Response to* Humanae vitae (New York: Sheed and Ward, 1970), 15–17.

34. Shannon, *Lively Debate*, 16–17.

35. Doms, *Meaning of Marriage*, 87. He says here, for example, "Marriage ... fulfills its primary and secondary *purposes* through the realization of its *meaning*." In *Love and Responsibility*, Karol Wojtyła would argue along similar lines that love should not be confused with the purpose of mutual help of the spouses (*mutuum adiutorium*) lest it be set in competition with the primary purpose of procreation. Rather, he said, love is what "norms" the ends or purposes of marriage (see Wojtyła, *Love and Responsibility*, 68–69). Doms likewise insisted that the union of the spouses not be confused with *mutuum adiutorium* (see Doms, *Meaning of Marriage*, 88).

36. Doms, *Meaning of Marriage*, 87.   37. See ibid., 88.

38. Ibid., 36.

personality to make a free gift of itself."[39] It is able to communicate the total gift of self in an act that creates the "two-in-oneship" of the couple.[40]

John Noonan has identified the benefits of Doms's approach.[41] However, John Grabowski has showed that Doms's view in *The Meaning of Marriage* was not entirely consistent or complete.[42] While in some places Doms suggests personal union is primary only in the subjective sphere, leaving open the possibility that procreation is primary in the biological sphere, ultimately Doms argues that given the time separation between intercourse and conception, procreation cannot be a primary end.[43] By reversing the order of the ends of marriage, and in some way abolishing them, Grabowski believes Doms "anticipates the trajectory of much revisionist personalism over the course of the century."[44]

Regarding family planning and contraception, Doms generally resorts to a voluntarist defense of the integrity of the sexual act. Since the human person cannot control the natural processes of insemination once the act is complete, "we have to recognize that nature itself imposes certain limits on human rights.... If they [the married couple] do interfere with these [natural] movements, they are presuming that state of sovereignty which God has manifestly reserved for Himself."[45] Though Doms attempts to argue that there is a relationship between the biological end of sex and the personalist meaning, Grabowski notes he does not use this argument consistently.[46] In many parts of his book Doms appeals to the voluntarist defense such as the one just mentioned.[47] His voluntarist appeal "is clearly a weak defense of many of the conclusions which he attempts to defend. Such arguments would unravel quickly when subjected to the pressure of later developments."[48] The most significant challenge to

---

39. Ibid., 32.   40. See ibid., 33.

41. See Noonan, *Contraception*, 498.

42. See Grabowski, "Person or Nature," 287.

43. See Doms, *Meaning of Marriage*, 175–76, 183–84.

44. Grabowksi, "Person or Nature," 288.

45. Doms, *Meaning of Marriage*, 72; see also 88, 165–66; Grabowski, "Person or Nature," 288.

46. See Grabowski, "Person or Nature," 288.

47. See also Doms, *Meaning of Marriage*, 88, 165–66.

48. Grabowski, "Person or Nature," 288; see also 307.

this view will be the development of the progesterone pill in 1953, which seemingly does, in fact, work with the biological processes of a woman's body. Doms's argument simply could not respond to such a challenge.

The Roman Rota and Pope Pius XII

On January 22, 1944, the Roman Rota issued a decree on the nature of marriage.[49] The document clarifies the meaning of the word "end" (*finis*) in the church's language about marriage. When the word *finis* is used in canon law, it "is taken in a technical sense and means a benefit which is meant to be obtained both on the part of nature and by the deliberate intention of the agent."[50] Following traditional Thomistic language, the decree goes on to speak of both a *finis operis* and a *finis operantis* in marriage. The *finis operis* in marriage "is that good (*bonum*) which matrimony tends of its very nature to obtain, and which God the Creator gave to the institution of matrimony."[51] The *finis operantis* is that which the person intends in any action. This is the subjective aspect of marriage, why people choose to marry, and can be as varied as the couples themselves: personal fulfillment, a desire for a family, economic advantage, etc.

The secondary ends mentioned in the Code of Canon Law—mutual help and the remedy for concupiscence—are each also a *finis operis*, but they are secondary ends *contingent* upon the primary end of procreation and the education of children. The procreation and education of children cannot properly be carried out without the mutual life of the spouses and a remedy for concupiscence.[52] The decree of the Roman Rota is here primarily concerned with the relationship between the various ends of marriage—the primary and secondary ends (*fines operis*) and the intention of the spouses (*finis operantis*). The *finis operantis* need not always coincide with the *fines operis*. Indeed, the decree recognizes that the two are not often aligned. Some-

---

49. See *AAS* 36 (1944): 179–200. The whole of this document is not pertinent to the discussion on marriage. The relevant texts were extracted and translated by Odile Liebard in *Love and Sexuality* (Wilmington, N.C.: McGrath Publishing Company, 1978), 71–83.

50. Liebard, *Love and Sexuality*, 71–72.   51. Ibid.

52. See ibid., 77.

times the "*finis operantis* is completely *extra* or *praeter* to the *finis operis.*"[53] However, a marriage entered into in which the *finis operantis* is contrary to any of the three *fines operis* is invalid and immoral, as is any conjugal act.[54] A *responsio ad dubium* by the same Roman Rota on April 1, 1944, would confirm that when the ends of marriage are equated, the relationship between them becomes confused.[55] The whole thrust of the Roman Rota's response is that the conjugal act has multiple ends, but also that there is a hierarchy among those ends.

Though Pope Pius XII never wrote an encyclical on marriage, a number of his addresses to various groups concerned marriage and sexuality.[56] The limited scope of this chapter prevents a full summary of each address.[57] Nevertheless, some significant themes are apparent in his allocutions. For example, in one of his central addresses on the topic, an October 1951 address to midwives, he emphasizes the importance of the secondary ends of marriage but insists they have "been placed by the will of nature and the Creator at the service of the offspring."[58] Sometimes he uses biologistic or physicalist language to argue for non-interference in the conjugal act as when he speaks early in his pontificate, in 1944, to the Italian Medico-Biological Union of St. Luke.[59] However, in the 1951 address he argues from the nature of marriage itself.[60]

53. Ibid., 72.   54. See ibid.
55. See *AAS* 36 (1944): 103.

56. English translations of most of these addresses are collected in Liebard, *Love and Sexuality*, 84–134, 160–243.

57. For a summary of Pius XII's teaching on marriage, see Paulette Huber, AdPPS, *The Teachings of Pius XII on Marriage and the Family* (PhD diss., The Catholic University of America, 1950); Noonan, *Contraception*, 451–75; Donald P. Asci, *The Conjugal Act as a Personal Act* (San Francisco, Calif.: Ignatius Press, 2002): 45–61; Gallagher, "Magisterial Teaching," 199–200; Shannon, *Lively Debate*, 24–39.

58. Pope Pius XII, "Address to Midwives," October 29, 1951, in Liebard, *Love and Sexuality*, 117. Original Italian text available in *AAS* 43 (1951): 850. See also Pope Pius XII, "Address to the Second World Congress on Fertility and Sterilitym" May 19, 1956, *AAS* 48 (1956): 469–70; unofficial English translation in Liebard, *Love and Sexuality*, 175–76. During his pontificate, Pope Pius XII gave several audiences to newlywed couples. The collection of these insightful addresses have been collected in Pope Pius XII, *Dear Newlyweds: Pope Pius XII Speaks to Young Couples* (Kansas City, Mo.: Sarto House, 2001).

59. See Pope Pius XII, "Address to the Italian Medical-Biological Union of St. Luke," November 12, 1944, in Liebard, *Love and Sexuality*, 84–95. Official Italian text: *Discorsi e Radiomessaggi di Sua Santita Pio XII* (Rome: Tipografia Poligotta Vaticana, 1944), 6:192.

60. See Pope Pius XII, "Address to Midwives," in Liebard, *Love and Sexuality*, 116.

Pope Pius XII repeats Pope Pius XI's suggestion that it is legitimate for couples to have sexual intercourse during the woman's infertile period for "serious reasons" such as "medical, eugenic, economic and social grounds, [which] can exempt from that obligatory service [of procreation] even for a considerable period of time, even for the entire duration of marriage."[61] He warns, however, that if there are no serious objective reasons "deriving from external circumstances" then "the habitual intention to avoid the fruitfulness of the union, while at the same time continuing fully to satisfy sensual intent, can only arise from a false appreciation of life and from motives that run counter to true standards of moral conduct."[62]

Finally, he mentions to the midwives the development of a theology grounded on "personal values" in which "the bodily union is the expression and actuation of the personal and affective union."[63] He concludes that if the rise of personalism is only a matter of emphasis, then it is a welcome contribution. His concern is apparently not with personalism itself but with the conclusions of some personalists who place the mutual affection of spouses over the procreation of children.[64] The primary end God instituted for marriage is the procreation and education of children. All other ends are subordinate to that primary end. Even sterile couples are ordered to that primary end regardless of the condition which renders them incapable of reproduction.[65] We can presume that couples who struggle with fertility demonstrate, nonetheless, the primacy of children in the marital relationship precisely because they desire children.

---

61. Ibid., 113.   62. Ibid.

63. Ibid., 115.

64. Though Pius XII does not mention Herbert Doms, it was Doms's position that he was criticizing.

65. See Pope Pius XII, "Address to Midwives," in Liebard, *Love and Sexuality*, 115–17.

THE FIRST PHASE OF
THE DEBATE (1953–62)

The Hesperidin Pill and the Principle
of Double Effect

Benjamin Sieve developed the first commercially available oral contraceptive in the form of a pill.[66] This first pill was phosphorylated hesperidin, an enzyme that occurs naturally in many citrus fruits. In Sieve's study, three hundred couples experienced a suspension of fertility if both the men and women took the pill as directed. He hypothesized that the pill worked by making the ovum impenetrable, thus eliminating the possibility of fertilization.[67]

The Jesuit John Lynch was one of the more prominent critics of Sieve's pill. In an August 1953 article, he not only condemned this pill as direct sterilization, but insisted it was a violation of the fifth commandment.[68] A more thorough reading of Lynch's argument reveals a moral viewpoint excessively dependent on the exteriority of human action, the finality of biological mechanisms, and the sovereign will of God. Citing *Casti Connubii*, which says that persons have limited dominion over their bodies, Lynch offers a rebuttal grounded in the purposes (or *telê*) of nature.

Lynch rightly argues that we are stewards of our lives and our bodies as well as our bodies' members.[69] He continues: "As stewards therefore we must respect the exclusive right of God over bodily in-

---

66. Much has been written on the origins of the controversy surrounding the birth control pill and contraception in the Catholic church in the mid-twentieth century. John Noonan's book, *Contraception*, is an invaluable resource. Other books written in the same era include Shannon, *Lively Debate*, and Ambrogio Valsecchi, *Controversy: The Birth Control Debate 1958–1968*, trans. Dorothy White (Washington, D.C.: Corpus Books, 1968). See also Robert Blair Kaiser, *The Politics of Sex and Religion* (Kansas City, Mo.: Leaven Press, 1985). Valsecchi's book is especially helpful for the impressive bibliography he catalogues and analyzes. The next two sections are indebted to these scholars' historical review.

67. Benjamin Sieve, "A New Anti-Fertility Factor," *Science* 116 (October 10, 1952): 373–85.

68. See John Lynch, SJ, "Fertility Control and the Moral Law," *Linacre Quarterly* 20 (1953): 83–89.

69. See ibid., 85.

tegrity, guarding as His, and not as our own, the members and faculties with which we have been entrusted."[70] Only if the body as a whole is threatened may a faculty or member be sacrificed in virtue of the principle of totality. Lynch's definition of mutilation is consistent with this perspective. Inasmuch as mutilation violates God's dominion over life, it violates the fifth commandment. While acknowledging the existence of possible therapeutic uses for the pill, and accepting the possibility of its use according the principle of double effect, Lynch nonetheless equates the oral contraceptive with the much more physical procedures of sterilization and mutilation.[71]

Hesperdin was never widely used as a contraceptive pill. There was no evidence that it worked as reliably as Sieve had hoped. Its fate on the commercial market was sealed by the more successful and more widely promoted progesterone pill, which was developed in 1953 and was legalized in the United States in 1960. Because its primary mechanism was the hormone progesterone, the introduction of this second contraceptive pill would prove to be a catalyst for the debate on birth control and the subsequent interventions of Pope Pius XII and Pope Paul VI.

The Therapeutic Uses of the Progesterone Pill

In its first stage, the debate on progesterone revolved primarily around legitimate therapeutic uses for the pill in virtue of the principle of double effect. The primary concern of this period of the debate was determining the appropriate use of biology in the service of the person. Some moral theologians were more permissive than others, though all agreed that direct sterilization was immoral because of its intentional circumvention of the natural finality of the procreative process. Therefore, they were concerned with identifying those legitimate reasons in which the good of the person might justify the temporary sterilization caused by the pill.

John Lynch had already accepted the possibility of therapeutic uses for contraceptive pills, although he did not identify any use in

---

70. Ibid.
71. See John Lynch, SJ, "Another Moral Aspect of Fertility Control," *Linacre Quarterly* 20 (1953): 120–22.

particular.[72] In 1957, another Jesuit, William Gibbons, further argued that the pill must be distinguished from physical contraception precisely because it does not interfere with copulation as such.[73] While he himself does not support direct contraception, this is the first suggestion that the pill will have to be rebutted using argumentation that does not solely rely on the finality of the sexual act.

Returning to the debate in 1958, John Lynch maintained his earlier distinction of the licit therapeutic uses of the pill from the illicit contraceptive uses.[74] In addition, he identifies several infertility disorders that might legitimize the use of the pill. Lynch argued that these treatments could not be considered the suspension of sterility, in any sense of the word, since the woman would have already been proven to be sterile in the first place.[75]

The correction of menstrual and fertility disorders were not the only licit therapeutic uses of the pill that were identified by the literature of the time. Two other possibilities were mentioned, but without universal agreement. The first, generally more accepted, suggested the use of the pill for the regulation of a woman's ovulatory cycle. Though Gibbons had suggested the validity of such a use, to my knowledge, its first explicit endorsement came from Louvain theologian Louis Janssens in a 1958 article.[76] Mentioning nothing of the contraceptive purposes of the pill, Janssens focuses entirely on its possible therapeutic uses and identifies a principle whereby the pill corrects pathologies to the natural mechanisms of a woman's body. He writes, "*Salvo mediore iudicio*, I am inclined to believe that this saying is realized

---

72. In agreement with Lynch's observation, but likewise not identifying any particular therapeutic uses were: André Snoeck, "Fecundation inibée et morale Catholique," *Nouvelle Revue Theologique* 75 (1953): 690–702, and Francis J. O'Connell, CSSR, provides the same simple moral criteria in "The Contraceptive Pill," *The American Ecclesiastical Review* 137 (1953): 50–51.

73. See William J. Gibbons, SJ, "Antifertility Drugs and Morality," *America* 98 (1957): 346–48.

74. See John Lynch, SJ, "Progestational Steroids: Some Moral Problems," *Linacre Quarterly* 25 (1958): 93–99.

75. See ibid., 98. For a brief summary of the preceding articles, see Valsecchi, *Controversy*, 1–11.

76. See Louis Janssens, "L'inhibition de l'ovulation est-elle moralement licite?" *Ephemerides Theologicae Lovanienses* 34 (1958): 357–60; Gibbons, "Antifertility Drugs and Morality," 348.

when one intervenes to support natural mechanisms which are defective or to correct pathological situations."[77] That being the case, the pill could legitimately be used, he argued, to regularize a women's fertility cycle.

Janssens suggested another, more controversial, therapeutic use. In his article, he noted that typically a woman is sterile during the period of lactation following a pregnancy. This "natural mechanism" is sometimes lacking in women, who then experience fertility while nursing their new infants. Janssens argues, therefore, that the use of the progesterone pill after childbirth and during the period of lactation is therapeutic and morally licit in order to ensure the new mother is, in fact, sterile during those months following the birth of her child.[78] He identified this as an exercise of the principle *licit corrigere defectus naturae*. The position was not universally supported.[79]

Valsecchi summarizes the debate as it existed in September 1958:

Almost all the authors agree in rejecting the deliberately anti-ovulatory use of progestational drugs, which they deem to be direct sterilization: Janssens alone is silent about this. All agree in justifying their therapeutic use (concerning which an interesting discussion is now taking place) on the grounds of the two principles of double effect and total good. The therapeutic use, moreover, is enlarged to include interventions aiming and the regulation of the female cycle, at least when the irregularities in question are of a pathological nature. But the opinion is being put forward that it is licit to administer progestational drugs also *in order to effect what nature herself requires but which for some unknown reason she seems unable to procure* [as in the case of sterility during lactation].[80]

Pope Pius XII's address to the Seventh International Congress of Hematology takes up these issues.[81] Pius XII accepts the legitimacy of reasoning from the principle of double effect and the principle of totality to allow the use of progesterone drugs for therapeutic purposes as long as the sterilization is not within the intention of the person.

77. Ibid., 359 (author's translation).

78. See ibid.

79. For a summary of the responses to Janssens's position, see Valsecchi, *Controversy*, 1–6.

80. Ibid., 6 (emphasis added).

81. See Pope Pius XII, "Address to the Seventh International Hematological Congress" (September 12, 1958), *AAS* 50 (1958): 732–40; unofficial English Translation in Liebard, *Love and Sexuality*, 234–43.

He warns, however, that it is "necessary to reject the view of a number of doctors and moralists who permit these practices when medical indications make conception undesirable .... In these cases the use of medication has as its end the prevention of conception by preventing ovulation. They are instances, therefore, of direct sterilization."[82]

Pope Pius XII furthermore cautions against the use of the principle *licet corrigere defectus naturae* in what seems to be an implicit warning against the use of progesterone to suspend sterility during lactation: "In an attempt to justify such sterilization, a principle of morality, correct in itself but badly interpreted, is often cited: '*licet corrigere defectus naturae.*' And since in practice it suffices, for the application of this principle, to have a reasonable probability ... it is still necessary to examine the means by which natural defects are corrected and to avoid the violation of other principles of morality."[83] The intervention of Pope Pius XII did nothing to quell the debate that had begun in the early 1950s. Since the address was imprecise, many moral theologians proceeded along the same paths upon which they had begun. The late 1950s and early 1960s would see the emergence of the distinction between the good of the person and the finality of human nature in the debate regarding various uses of the birth control pill. This trend would achieve its full import in the years leading to and following upon *Humanae Vitae*.

The Emergence of Personalist Arguments in the Birth Control Debate

The emergence of personalist arguments in the birth control debate was the result of continued discussion of the possible therapeutic uses of the pill. Most moral theologians supported the use of the progesterone pill to increase fertility.[84] A much different case was the possibility of using the pill to regulate a woman's menstrual cycle. In this case, the woman was not already sterile and so the temporary suspension of ovulation would in theory be required to regularize her

---

82. Pius XII, "Address to the Seventh International Hematological Congress," in Liebard, *Love and Sexuality*, 238.

83. Ibid.

84. See Valsecchi, *Controversy*, 16–17. Notably, at that time, it was still unknown whether the progesterone would serve this purpose.

cycle. A number of moral theologians were against such therapeutic use since it required the frustration of the finality of biological processes.[85]

Valsecchi reports that the arguments for or against the imposition of order on a woman's menstrual cycle were fundamentally about "whether this kind of action belongs to a human being's legitimate control over his own body, or whether it exceeds this and constitutes an illicit interference in 'natural' bio-physical processes."[86] This question was especially important in the ongoing debates about progesterone therapy during lactation and the suspension of fertility in the case of cyesophobia, which is the fear of pregnancy. The position particular Catholic scholars would ultimately take on the question of artificial contraception was largely determined by his or her answer to this prior question of what constitutes legitimate control over the biological processes of one's own body.

Using the pill to defer menstruation when convenient would be condemned by those theologians who disagreed with the suspension of sterility except in cases of true pathology. Others, however, saw the intervention as simply the suspension of menstruation (that is, the pill was simply suspending the shedding of the endometrium). Marcelino Zalba was the most forthright in his suggestion that the human person has complete control over the nature of his sexual organs. He wrote that "no intervention is forbidden to man."[87] For Zalba, Valsecchi observes, "the sexual organs, although given to man 'primarily for the sake of the species and not for his own personal and individual use' do in fact exist in the individual as a part to be controlled for the good of his own person."[88]

The physicalist methodology that so dominated Catholic moral theology at the beginning of the twentieth century, which tended toward a moral evaluation based on the physical structure of human action and an identification of the purposes of nature with biophysical processes, had underemphasized the notion of the person. Retrieving

---

85. See ibid., 17–21.

86. See ibid., 19.

87. Marcelino Zalba, SJ, "Casus de usu artificii contraceptive," *Periodica de re morali, canonica et liturgica* 51 (1962): 176 (author's translation).

88. See Valsecchi, *Controversy*, 25, citing Zalba, "Casus de usu artificii contraceptive," 176–77.

the notion of the person as a concrete instance of human nature, Janssens, Zalba, and others were defending what they believed to be legitimate therapies that placed the purposes of nature at the service of the person. In this first period of the debate, those who maintained a traditional stance against contraception, except in the most absolutely pathological necessity, were arguing with an older methodology. Even the American Jesuit Paul Quay, who in a 1961 article attempts to make a solidly personalist defense of the traditional teaching, inevitably resorts to an implicit emphasis upon nature's purposes instead of the person.[89]

Before 1963, the increased interest in the person *vis-à-vis* nature dominated the debate and the conclusions reached by those theologians prepared for the position proclaimed by John Rock in his 1963 book *The Time Has Come* that the progesterone pill and its contraceptive effects were natural.

THE SECOND PHASE
OF THE DEBATE (1963–68)

John Rock and the Widening of the Birth Control Debate

In 1963, John Rock, a Catholic medical doctor, explicitly rejected the exclusive emphasis on the biophysical processes of the human body in favor of an emphasis on the needs of the person and of the couple.[90] He had already expressed support for anti-ovulant use of the progesterone pill, which he helped to develop.[91] His position was criticized by a number of theologians, including John Lynch, yet he was undeterred.[92]

---

89. See Paul Quay, "Contraception and Conjugal Love," *Theological Studies* 22 (1961): 18–40. For a summary and a critique of Quay's argument, see Grabowski, "Person and Nature," 297–300, 308. Grabowski shows that while Quay evokes the language of personalism, he ultimately believes the person is only fulfilled by working in virtue of his nature (see Quay, "Contraception," 26). Grabowski's critique is subtle and penetrating. Nevertheless, given the era in which Quay wrote this article, his idea of sex as language was prescient of similar ideas in Pope John Paul's own thought.

90. See John Rock, *The Time Has Come: A Catholic Doctor's Proposals to End the Battle over Birth Control* (New York: Alfred A. Knopf, 1963).

91. See John Rock, "We Can End the Battle over Birth Control," *Good Housekeeping* (July 1961): 44–45, 107–9.

92. See John Lynch, SJ, "Notes on Moral Theology," *Theological Studies* 23 (1962): 242. See also Shannon, *The Lively Debate*, 44.

In his book, *The Time Has Come*, Rock's argument in favor of the use of the pill to regulate births begins with a redefinition. Rather than a contraceptive or artificial birth control, he said that using the pill was analogous to the rhythm method, which was already approved by Pope Pius XI in 1930. Progesterone is the natural hormone, secreted by the ovaries, which suspends ovulation during the "safe period" of a woman's menstrual cycle. Rock, therefore, concluded there is no moral difference between the natural safe period and the pill-induced safe period.[93] Even though the pill was synthetic, by noting the "naturalness" of the pill, John Rock was responding to a physicalist or biologist view of morality. Effectively Rock used physicalist terminology against the physicalist arguments for the traditional condemnation of contraception. Furthermore, he notes, "the pills, when properly taken, are not all likely to disturb menstruation, nor do they mutilate any organ of the body, nor damage any natural process."[94]

Both Pope Pius XI and Pope Pius XII supported periodic continence—the abstinence from intercourse during the "safe period" of a woman's cycle—in certain circumstances.[95] Since the discernment of the presence of these conditions in a couple's life is the role of the intellect, Rock writes, "it is difficult not to believe that God gave man his intellect to safeguard him whenever his inner biology is inadequate."[96] Thus, John Rock furthered the distinction between person and nature by highlighting the traditional Catholic emphasis on the uniqueness of human reason.

Rock's book was met with immediate criticism in the United States.[97] John Lynch's response was emblematic. He argued that im-

---

93. See Rock, *Time Has Come*, 168.   94. Ibid., 169.

95. See *CC*, par. 59; Pius XII, "Address to Midwives," in Liebard, *Love and Sexuality*, 113. Pope Pius XI does not mention periodic continence specifically as a means of birth regulation, nor does he countenance the idea that a couple may have reason to avoid giving birth. He does, however, make clear that couples are free to make use of their "marital right" to the conjugal act even if they know that procreation is not possible "on account of natural reasons either of time or of certain defects" (*CC*, par. 59).

96. Rock, *Time Has Come*, 169.

97. See Joseph S. Duhamel, "The Time Has Come" (book review), *America* 108 (April 27, 1963): 610; John J. Lynch, "The Time Has Come" (book review), *Marriage* 45 (June 1963): 16–17; John C. Ford and Gerald Kelly, *Contemporary Moral Theology* (Westminster, Md.: The Newman Press, 1964), 2:376–77. See also Shannon, *Lively Debate*, 46–47; Noonan, *Contraception*, 468–69.

itating natural occurrences is not always within our rights, as in the case of the natural circumstances surrounding death. "It is quite obvious, for example, that death from natural causes is a very common occurrence. But that biological fact does not justify one's anticipating nature in this respect by deliberately and directly terminating innocent human life."[98] But if Rock's ideas were initially rejected in the United States, they would receive a more than fair reception in Europe.

On March 21, 1963, just months before the publication of *The Time Has Come*, William Bekkers, the bishop of the diocese of Den Bosch in Holland, gave a televised speech in which he suggested that a marriage must be morally evaluated within the entire "kaleidoscope" of a life lived together in love. From this perspective, the regulation of births can be seen as a responsibility of a couple to each other and to their children. The means used, the bishop said, should be left to the couple.[99]

Louis Janssens also resurfaced in 1963 with a lengthy article arguing that the anti-ovulant use of the pill to regulate child births was already permissible.[100] Following a long exposition of the history of the church's teaching from Augustine to his own time, he argues that the use of the pill is no different than sexual intercourse during a woman's infertile period of her menstrual cycle. The permissibility of the rhythm method reveals, says Janssens, that procreation need not be a positive intention in every act of sexual intercourse provided the act itself maintains its own integrity.

The distinction between periodic continence and the use of chemical or physical contraceptives is the difference they make for the integrity of the sex act. Janssens writes: "It suffices to note that the practice of periodic continence positively excluded procreation:

---

98. Lynch, "*The Time Has Come*" (book review), 17.

99. Excerpts from this televised speech along with excerpts from an article which the bishop published in his diocesan paper the same month can be found in Leo Pyle, ed., *The Pill and Birth Regulation* (Baltimore, Md.: Helicon Press, 1964), 5–8. See also Shannon, *Lively Debate*, 47–49, and Noonan, *Contraception*, 469.

100. See Louis Janssens, "Morale conjugale et progesogènes," *Ephemerides Theologicae Lovanienses* 39 (1963): 787–826. Abstracts translated into English can be found in Pyle, *The Pill*, 14–19. See also Valsecchi, *Controversy*, 38–41; Shannon, *Lively Debate*, 50–51; Noonan, *Contraception*, 470–72.

it creates an obstacle in the *temporal* order through the choice to engage in sexual relations exclusively during the periods of infertility. Similarly, the use of artificial conception constitutes an obstacle in the *spatial* order by erecting a material wall between the organs of the spouses."[101] Precisely because the church has already accepted the possibility of intentionally excluding procreation in a particular conjugal act for specific reasons, Janssens argues, therefore, the nature of the act itself is more than simply procreative. It is rather an "expression and incarnation of conjugal love."[102]

This conjugal love is a mutual self-giving of the spouses, "without reserve and without restriction" (*sans resérve et sans restriction*). The incarnation of this unreserved and unrestricted love is the "intrinsic meaning" (*le sens intrinsèque*) of the conjugal act. To introduce any reservation, any restriction, any barrier is to vitiate the act by abandoning this intrinsic meaning.[103] The pill introduces no barrier nor does it interfere with the self-gift of the spouses. In this way, Janssens argues, it is no different than the rhythm method.[104] Janssens was not alone in his early support of the use of anti-ovulant pill to regulate childbirth.[105]

The initial response to Janssens's position in Europe was favorable, even if some authors expressed reservations about the logical conclusions that might be drawn from it.[106] In the United States, however, the initial response was as critical to Janssen's article as it had been to the work of John Rock.[107] The Americans rejected Jans-

---

101. Janssens, "Morale conjugale et progesogènes," 817 (author's translation).

102. Ibid., 819 (author's translation). 103. Ibid.

104. Ibid., 820–21.

105. See W. van der Marck, OP, "Vruchtbaarheidsregeling. Poging tot antwoord op een nog open vraag," *Tijdschrift voor Theologie* 3 (1963): 379–413; J. M. Reuss, "Eheliche Hingabe und Zeugung: Ein Diskussionsbeitrag zu einem differenzierten Problem," *Tubinger Theologische Quartalschrift* 143 (1963): 454–76. An English translation of abstracts from the latter appears in Pyle, *The Pill*, 8–13. For a concise summary of the arguments of these two articles see Valsecchi, *Controversy*, 41–45, and Noonan, *Contraception*, 470–71. Louis Janssens is the most often cited of the three Belgian theologians supporting an expanded use of the pill.

106. See Valsecchi, *Controversy*, 47–48, for a bibliography and summary of arguments.

107. See Gerald Kelly, SJ, "Confusion: Contraception and 'The Pill,'" *Theology Digest* 12 (1964): 123–30; John Lynch, SJ, "Notes on Moral Theology. The Oral Contraceptives," *Theological Studies* 25 (1964): 237–49; Francis J. Connell, CSSR, "Is Contra-

sen's tenuous link between periodic continence and the pill. An editorial in the April 25, 1964, issue of *America* provided a standard reply. The difference between the rhythm method and the pill was *"non-*performance of the conjugal act during the fertile period.... No amount of word juggling can make abstinence from sexual relations and the suppression of ovulation one and the same thing."[108] Respondents to the editorial likewise all commented that the church's teaching had not changed and, therefore, that Catholics were not free to use the contraceptive pill.

A younger generation of Catholic moral theologians, more favorable to contraception, also began publishing at this time. Many of these would play a significant role in the aftermath of the promulgation of *Humanae Vitae.*[109]

The Second Vatican Council

Three months after the close of the Second Vatican Council's first session, in March 1963, Pope John XXIII established a commission to examine the question of contraception. The Pope died three months later but his successor, Pope Paul VI, decided that the commission should continue its work. It would meet periodically from 1963 to 1966.[110]

In the fall of 1965, during its fourth and final session, the Sec-

---

ception Intrinsically Wrong?" *The American Ecclesiastical Review* 150 (1964): 434–39. See also Shannon, *Lively Debate,* 52–54; Noonan, *Controversy,* 49–53.

108. "Time Bomb" (editorial), *America* (May 25, 1965): 563.

109. The most notable of these was Charles Curran. See Charles Curran, "Christian Marriage and Family Planning," *Jubilee* 12 (August 1964): 8–13.

110. There have been few detailed histories of the commission's work. Shannon devotes a chapter in his book, *The Lively Debate,* to the commission and correlates all the material published up to the time of the book's publication (see 76–104). Janet Smith offers a brief outline of the commission's work and an analysis of the two reports issued by the commission (see Smith, *Humanae Vitae,* 11–35). Finally, Robert McClory offers a popular history of the "inside story of the papal birth control commission." Besides his own research, McClory follows the account offered by Patty Crowley, a founder of the Christian Family Movement and among the lay married persons added to the commission in 1964. According to McClory's own depiction, Crowley makes no secret of her disappointment with *Humanae Vitae* and accepts the legitimacy of dissent to the papal teaching. McClory agrees with her sentiments, which is a prejudice that colors his presentation of the commission (see McClory, *Turning Point,* 38–137).

ond Vatican Council was reviewing *Schema XIII*, the document on the church in the modern world that would eventually be known as *Gaudium et Spes*. The council fathers were divided regarding whether the schema should reference the traditional primary and secondary ends of marriage. In his historical survey of this session of the council, Gilles Routhier notes that "a number of the fathers did regard conjugal love as the reality that ought to be the basis for thinking about marriage."[111] The struggle between those who wanted a more personalist approach to marriage, which emphasized conjugal love as primary, and those who wanted a more traditional approach that would reference primary and secondary ends was central to the debate on marriage.

The council's subcommission on marriage completed its work on the final draft of the schema on November 20 and thus began a tumultuous time of debate in the mixed commission, which was responsible for the agenda of the council.[112] On November 24, as the mixed commission began to consider the final draft of the schema, a letter arrived from the Vatican's Secretary of State, Amleto Cardinal Cicognani. It proposed "in the name of a higher authority" four amendments (*modi*) to the text, one of which included a reference to the hierarchy of ends. It was clear to everyone in the room that the higher authority was Pope Paul VI.[113] When the mixed commission

111. Gilles Routhier, "Finishing the Work Begun: The Trying Experience of the Fourth Period," in *History of Vatican II*, ed. Giuseppe Alberigo and Joseph A. Komonchak, trans. Matthew J. O'Connell (Washington, D.C.: The Catholic University of America Press, 2006), 5:155.

112. See Peter Hünermann, "The Final Weeks of the Council," in *History of Vatican II*, ed. Alberigo and Komonchak, 5:406, 408.

113. See Shannon, *The Lively Debate*, 85. For a summary of the papal *modi*, their history, the debate in the mixed commission, and its resolution, see Hünnerman, "Final Weeks," 408–19; Shannon, *The Lively Debate*, 84–87; Kaiser, *Politics*, 115–21; McClory, *Turning Point*, 83–85. The text of Cicognani's letter and the four papal *modi* are available at *Acta Synodalia Sacrosancti Concilii Oecumenici Vaticani II* (Vatican City: Typis Polyglottis Vaticanis, 1970–92), V/3, 604–6 [hereafter, *AS*]. In article 47 of the schema, practices such as polygamy, divorce, free love, selfishness, and hedonism would be condemned as against the nature of married love. The first papal *modus* asked that contraceptive practices (*artes anticonceptionales*) be included in this list. The second *modus* wanted a phrase on the preeminent place the gift of children has for a marriage. The third *modus* wanted the document to condemn all birth control practices that "are" proscribed or "will be" proscribed, as well as a direct reference to *Casti Connubii* and

descended into argument on the papal *modi*, a second letter from Cicognani arrived only two days later, which indicated that the four amendments were only "counsels" and the commission was free to discern their merit and their incorporation into the text.[114]

Rather than include birth control in the list of dangers against marriage found in the early paragraphs of the schema, as the pope suggested, the commission used instead the words "illicit practices contrary to conception."[115] The mixed commission agreed with the pope that a paragraph of the schema was ambivalent on the ends of marriage, so the mixed commission accepted the pope's advice to insert a reference to children as the preeminent gift of marriage. Without mentioning the ends of marriage, the commission added that sharing lovingly in the work of God as creator and redeemer was the orientation of marriage "without prejudice to the other ends of marriage."[116] The text thus refers to the ends of marriage but does not include a hierarchy of those ends.[117]

In deference to the papal *modi*, a footnote reference to *Casti Connubii* and to Pius XII's address to midwives was added to the schema's discussion of legitimate methods of birth control. Additionally, another footnote (the famous footnote 14) was added that referred directly to the papal commission on birth control. The council deferred to the pope's decision on birth control once the papal commission concluded its work and, therefore, the footnote said "the council is not aiming immediately to propose specific solutions."[118] Finally, "the commission wanted to avoid giving the impression that conjugal chastity was the only possible means of birth control. For this reason the reference to conjugal chastity that the pope had requested in his fourth *modus* was introduced at a different place than the one called for."[119]

Pius XII's address to midwives. The final *modus* wanted chastity discussed in the section of the document that concerns the difficulties married couples face.

114. For the text of this second letter, see *AS* V/3, 610.

115. See Vatican Council II, *Gaudium et Spes*, December 7, 1965, par. 47 [hereafter, *GS*], in *Decrees*, ed. Tanner, 2:1100: "illicitis usibus contra generationem." The official Latin text of *GS* is available in *AAS* 58 (1966): 1025–1115.

116. See *GS*, par. 50, in *Decrees*, ed. Tanner, 2:1103.

117. See Hünermann, "Final Weeks," 415.

118. See *Decrees*, ed. Tanner, 2:1104.

119. Hünermann, "Final Weeks," 415.

Once the mixed commission completed its work, the finalized amended text was presented to the fathers of the council and was promulgated on December 7, 1965. *Gaudium et Spes* was the final document the council issued. The chapter on marriage, while not overturning the traditional teaching on marriage, offers a fresh presentation. The central point of the constitution's treatment of marriage is the notion of conjugal love. John Gallagher notes that "as a matter of human will, this love is much more than physical desire, but it includes physical expression."[120] Conjugal love, the council said, "embraces the good of the entire person and is therefore capable of endowing human expressions with a particular dignity and of ennobling them as special features and manifestations of married friendship."[121]

It is this conjugal love and the institution of marriage that is directed to the procreation of children:

> The institution of marriage and *conjugal* love are, of their nature, directed to the *procreation* and *education* of children and they find their culmination in this. Thus it is that a man and a woman, who "are no longer two but one flesh" (Mt 19:6) in their marital covenant, help and serve each other in their intimate union of persons and activities, and from day to day experience and increase their sense of oneness. Such intimacy, as a mutual giving of two persons, as well as the good of their children require complete faithfulness between the partners, and call for their union being indissoluble.[122]

Here, Gallagher rightly notes, "the council fathers are arguing not from a narrowly biological basis. It is the nature of marriage itself and of conjugal love to be oriented toward procreation."[123] One could go further and say that the council has insisted that while marriage and conjugal love are directed to the procreation of children, the existence of children in the marriage further confirms and strengthens that love. This is why *Gaudium et Spes* reaffirms later that marriage and married love are "directed towards the begetting and bringing up of children" and goes on to say that "children are the supreme gift of marriage and they contribute greatly to the good of their parents."[124]

---

120. Gallagher, "Magisterial Teaching," 201.
121. *GS*, par. 49, in *Decrees*, ed. Tanner, 2:1112.
122. *GS*, par. 48, in *Decrees*, ed. Tanner, 2:1101.
123. Gallagher, "Magisterial Teaching," 201.
124. *GS*, par. 50.

While the primary concern of *Gaudium et Spes* is conjugal love and the institution of marriage, the conjugal act and procreation are certainly not absent from the document. Rather, these are presented in their relationship to conjugal love and marriage.

The document does not present an argument against contraception, though it does speak against "illicit practices against conception" at the request of Pope Paul VI. It simply said that methods of birth regulation should be decided by objective criteria according to "the nature of the person and his acts" with the understanding that the faithful may not choose a means proscribed by the magisterium.[125] More importantly, *Gaudium et Spes* does not mention the distinction between the primary and secondary ends of marriage. Nor does it mention the idea of mutual help of spouses as subordinate to the procreation and education of children. Some have speculated that this omission means that the council intended to overturn the traditional teaching of the church by according equal status to the ends of marriage.[126] Others have said that the document does not overturn the traditional hierarchy of ends, but only reformulates its expression.[127] The promulgation of *Gaudium et Spes* with its dynamic presentation of marriage and the inclusion of footnote 14 increased speculation on the results of the work of the papal commission on birth regulation. The world awaited eagerly the pope's decision on the matter.

---

125. *GS*, par. 51, in *Decrees*, ed. Tanner, 2:1104.

126. See James P. Hanigan, *What Are They Saying about Sexual Morality?* (New York: Paulist Press, 1982), 33; Grabowski, "Person and Nature," 308n107. While the other authors argue generally from silence, Grabowski offers a cogent argument in three points. "First, it is not the reading of most scholars [that *Gaudium et Spes* did not repudiate the hierarchy of the ends marriage utilized in the 1917 Code of Canon Law]. Second, it ignores the theology of covenant present within the Pastoral Constitution which serves as the vehicle for its embrace of personalist ideas. Third, it overlooks the fact that subsequent magisterial documents, including *Humanae Vitae* (esp. par. 12), effectively settle the question by treating the two ends as not only equally important but inseparable."

127. See Janet Smith, *Humanae Vitae*, 47–48; Ramón García de Haro, *Marriage and the Family in the Documents of the Magisterium: A Course in the Theology of Marriage*, trans. William E. May (San Francisco, Calif.: Ignatius Press, 1989): 195–98, 241–45; William E. May, *Marriage: The Rock on Which the Family Is Built* (San Francisco, Calif.: Ignatius Press, 1995): 109–15; and Asci, *Conjugal Act*, 68–71. Pope John Paul II suggested that the hierarchy was reaffirmed by both *Gaudium et Spes* and *Humanae Vitae* but reoriented their relationship by orienting the ends to conjugal love. See *TOB*, no. 127.

The Reports of the Papal Commission

The papal commission on birth control met five times between 1963 and 1966. At each meeting, more members were added to the group.[128] Its final meeting began on April 18, 1966, and concluded three months later on June 25. The structure of the group for this final meeting had been reconstituted. In February, Pope Paul VI appointed sixteen bishop members to form an executive committee to the commission.[129] Only these bishops would have a vote on the deliberations of the commission. In effect, those members of the commission who had labored in the previous four meetings were reconstituted as advisers (*periti*) to this executive committee. The work of the papal commission came to an end on June 25, 1966. On June 28, Cardinal Julius Doepfner and Fr. Henri de Riedmatten presented the commission's work to Pope Paul VI.

Three principal documents emerged from the papal commission. All three were subsequently leaked to the media. First, there was a minority report written by four theologians who were against reversing the church's condemnation of contraception. Second, a schema, which was approved by a majority of the bishops on the executive committee, advocated a change of the teaching. Finally, there was a majority rebuttal of the minority report.[130] Very brief observations

128. For a list of the various members added for each meeting, see McClory, *Turning Point*, 188–90.

129. See Shannon, *Lively Debate*, 88; McClory, *Turning Point*, 96–97. The sixteen members of the executive committee were Archbishop Leo Binz (United States), Bishop Carlo Colombo (Vatican), Archbishop John Dearden (United States), Juilies Cardinal Doepfner (Germany), Archbishop Claude Dupuy (France), Valerian Cardinal Gracias (India), John Cardinal Heenan (England), Joseph Cardinal Lefebvre (France), Archbishop Thomas Morris (Ireland), Alfredo Cardinal Ottaviani (Vatican), Lawrence Cardinal Shehan (United States), Leo Joseph Cardinal Suenens (Belgium), Archbishop José Rafael Pulido-Méndez (Venezuela), Bishop Joseph Reuss (Germany), Archbishop Karol Wojtyła (Poland), and Archbishop Jean Baptiste Zoa (Cameroon). Wojtyła, however, did not attend this final meeting, having been denied an exit visa by the Communist government in Poland (see Weigel, *Witness to Hope*, 207).

130. The shorthand references to these three documents vary depending on the authors consulted. For the sake of clarity, I will be following Janet Smith's nomenclature. In this study, the paper drafted by the minority theologians will be referred to as the "minority report"; the paper intended as a draft of a final document will be referred to as "the schema"; and the rebuttal prepared by the majority theologians will be referred

on each of the reports are in order before we discuss of the encyclical.

The minority report relies fundamentally on the strength of the church's tradition in condemning contraception. After defining the terms of the question, the report goes on to provide a brief survey of the church's teaching on contraception and marriage, focusing especially on the twentieth century. Referencing Noonan's book, the report states: "One can find no period in history, no document of the Church, no theological school, scarcely one Catholic theologian, who ever denied that contraception was always seriously evil. The teaching of the Church in this matter is absolutely constant. Until the present century this teaching was peacefully possessed by all other Christians."[131] Acknowledging that the church's presentation of marriage and sexuality had moved away from an excessively juridical emphasis toward a more personalist view that sees marriage as its own means to holiness, the minority report then responds to the typical arguments advanced in favor of changing the church's teaching on contraception.

When the minority report addresses positive arguments in favor of the church's teaching, it admits: "If we could bring forward arguments which are clear and cogent based on reason alone, it would not be necessary for our commission to exist, nor would the present state of affairs exist in the Church as it is."[132] It is in this section that the minority theologians defend the church's teaching against the charge of physicalism. The inviolability of intercourse has always been taught because it is generative, and "this inviolability is always attributed to the act and to the process, which are biological; not inasmuch as they are biological, but inasmuch as they are human, namely inasmuch as they are the object of *human acts* and are destined by their nature to the good of the human species."[133] The report also argues that the teaching can-

---

to as the "majority rebuttal." All three of these reports were never meant for public consumption, but they were leaked and published in the spring of 1967 in both *The Tablet* and *The National Catholic Reporter*. The translation published in the *National Catholic Reporter* is available in *Pope and Pill: More Documentation on the Birth Regulation Debate*, ed. Leo Pyle (Baltimore, Md.: Helicon Press, 1969): 257–305. All references to these reports in this book will be from Pyle's compilation.

131. See "Minority Report," in *Pope and Pill*, ed. Pyle, 275–76.

132. Ibid., 278–79.

133. "Minority Report," in *Pope and Pill*, ed. Pyle, 279.

not be based on a faulty medieval notion of "nature," because "the teaching of the Church was first fully formulated and handed down constantly for several centuries before scholastic philosophy was refined."[134] Also, theology has never argued for the inviolability of nature generally, but the inviolability of human generative process "precisely because they are generative of new *human life.*"[135] The reason the teaching is irreformable, according to the report, is that the teaching has been stated as true by the church constantly and consistently. If error is admitted, "the authority of the ordinary magisterium in moral matters would be thrown into question."[136] This is why, the minority theologians suggest, that those who seek to change the teaching have redefined the notions of the magisterium and its authority.

The report then summarizes the philosophical foundations for those arguments in favor of changing the church's teaching. Here we find a brief summary of the debate of the twentieth century presented from the perspective of those defending the traditional teaching.[137] The foundations are by now familiar: a reverence for God, an emphasis on the person over nature, and the duty of humanizing nature according to reason. The report is critical of the view that nature is "a complex of physical and psychic powers in the world, granted to the dominion of man, so that he can experience them, foster change, or frustrate them for his own earthly convenience."[138] The minority report concludes by suggesting the consequences of changing the teaching on contraception: an increase in premarital sex, masturbation, illicit acts of copulation within marriage, and sterilization.

The majority rebuttal begins by placing the condemnation of contraception in *Casti Connubii* in its historical context. Specifically, the majority theologians suggest that the tone of that encyclical was appropriate for the context in which it was issued, that is, immediately following the Anglican declaration at the Lambeth Conference and amid fears of the possibility of population decline with the use of contraception. It says: "Today no one holds that the solemn declaration of the encyclical *Casti Connubii* constitutes a true doctrinal definition."[139] Similarly, the rebuttal seeks to contextualize the con-

---

134. Ibid., 278.
136. Ibid., 281.
138. Ibid., 289–90.

135. Ibid.
137. See ibid., 285–89.
139. Ibid., 297.

stant condemnation of contraception in the church's history, insisting those condemnations were made for larger dogmatic concerns that are no longer problematic in the church.[140] The problem with the natural law argument offered against contraception is that "the gifts of nature are considered to be immediately the expression of the will of God, preventing man, also a creature of God, from being understood as called to receive material nature and to perfect its potentiality."[141]

The rebuttal notes that in fact the church's teaching on marriage and the conjugal act had evolved over recent decades with an emphasis on conjugal love as expressed in the act of intercourse. The rebuttal offers many reasons in favor of change: social changes in marriage, the differing roles of women, advances in science, and the growing consensus of the faithful, to name just a few. A change in teaching would be nothing more than an acknowledgement of this evolution.[142]

The rebuttal's rejection of any natural law argument rests upon the authors' emphasis on the person and human freedom over nature. The dignity of man consists in "that God wished man to share in his dominion. God has left man in the hands of his own counsel .... Therefore the dominion of God is exercised through man, who can use nature for his own perfection according to the dictates of right reason."[143] Thus, man recognizes his dignity "when he uses his skill to intervene in the biological processes of nature so that he can achieve the ends of the institution of matrimony in the conditions of actual life, than if he would abandon himself to chance."[144] For all that, though, the rebuttal insists that there are moral criteria that must be respected. Specifically, actions must be in conformity with rational nature and respect the ends to which nature has things ordered. Undoubtedly, the rebuttal is vague as to its meaning on this point.[145]

In a decisive shift in favor of the notion that the human person rather than human nature should be considered normative, the rebuttal argues that persons, not natures, are the sources of life. It is up to married persons to exercise reason in appropriate planning of children. "In virtue of this decision [on the planning of children] they

140. See ibid., 298.   141. Ibid.
142. See ibid., 300.   143. Ibid., 301.
144. Ibid.   145. Ibid.

use the sexual organs to gain the predetermined goal, but the organs themselves are not *per se* the sources of life. The biological process-es in man are not some separated part (animality) but are integrated into the total personality of man."[146] After recounting the now typical emphasis on the conjugal act as an expression of conjugal love, the rebuttal concludes there is no difference between acts that are fertile and acts that are infertile. From this perspective, the rebuttal argues that reasonable intervention in fertility is completely within the lim-its of classical doctrine. A person using the pill is not excluding fertili-ty permanently but only regulating it reasonably in order to direct the whole marriage toward conjugal union and fecundity.[147] The rebuttal concludes by disagreeing with the minority report's grim predictions of a future with contraception. It reaffirms the majority's condemna-tion of both abortion and the unreasonable or selfish use of contra-ception.

With Janet Smith, then, we can identify four major areas of funda-mental disagreement between the two documents.[148] First, the docu-ments disagree on the meaning and purpose of the church's tradition-al condemnation of contraception. Second, they differ on the impact a change in the teaching would have on the moral authority of the church. Third, the understanding of natural law differs in the docu-ments. Finally, they each offer their own outlook on a future in which contraception is universally accepted and practiced.

The schema begins with a striking observation: "In creating the world God gave man the power and the duty to form the world in spirit and freedom and, through his creative capacity, to actuate his own personal nature."[149] Here it is clear: nature is subject to human freedom. In the first part, then, the schema turns to the impact this lofty vocation of man has on marriage. Emphasizing the value of conjugal love as mutual self-giving, the schema nevertheless asserts that married life is not complete merely by self-gift. "Married peo-ple know well," it says, "that they are only able to perfect each other

146. Ibid., 302.
147. See ibid., 302–5.
148. See Smith, *Humanae Vitae*, 14. For a thorough comparison of the minority re-port and the majority rebuttal from the perspective of a scholar supportive of *Humanae Vitae*, see Smith, *Humanae Vitae*, 14–30.
149. "The Majority View," in *Pope and Pill*, ed. Pyle, 257.

and establish a true community if their love does not end in a merely egotistic union but according to the condition of each is made truly fruitful in the creation of new life."[150] In this view, the procreation and education of children is only reasonable when the community of self-gift already exists in the parents, a community which the presence of children confirms and strengthens. Thus, "conjugal love and fecundity are in no way opposed, but complement one another in such a way that they constitute an *almost* indivisible unity."[151]

The schema goes on to suggest the many ways in which parenthood has become a more difficult responsibility. One of the major difficulties presented to conjugal love and parenthood is the "new possibilities for the education of children."[152] Other conditions may be economic, psychological, and physical. Regulation of fertility appears, therefore, to be necessary. Because the good of the children requires the existence of a stable and loving familial community, the schema argues that "the morality of sexual acts between married people takes its meaning first of all and specifically from the ordering of their actions in a fruitful married life, that is one which is practiced with responsible, generous and prudent parenthood. It does not then depend upon the direct fecundity of each and every particular act."[153]

The schema follows this argument with an explanation of the reasons for the development of the doctrine, following the arguments of the majority rebuttal. Then, before concluding the section on the fundamental principles, the schema offers four criteria to discern the various means of contraception.[154] First, following upon *Gaudium et Spes* (par. 51), the "action must correspond to the nature of the person and of his acts so that the whole meaning of the mutual giving and of human procreation is kept in a context of true love."[155] Second, the means chosen "should have an effectiveness proportionate to the degree of right or necessity of averting a new a conception tempo-

---

150. Ibid., 260.

151. Ibid. (emphasis added). The strength of the union between the procreative and unitive aspects of the conjugal act was precisely what was at issue. The Majority believed that the two aspects were only "almost" indivisible. Pope Paul VI will disagree in *Humanae Vitae* (par. 12) by insisting that the two are simply inseparable.

152. "The Majority View," in *Pope and Pill*, ed. Pyle, 261.

153. Ibid., 263.   154. See ibid., 267.

155. Ibid.

rarily or permanently."[156] Third, the means chosen should be the one "which carried with it the least possible negative element, according to the concrete situation of the couple."[157] The schema here refers to a certain amount of "physical evil" which the couple "more or less" seriously feels. The evil can be biological, hygienic, or psychological, among other things. Finally, the choice often "depends on what means may be available in a certain region or at a certain time or for a certain couple; and this may depend on the economic situation."[158] Exactly how this final statement qualifies as a moral criterion and not a mere indicative statement is unclear.

The second part of the schema on pastoral necessities concerns only the need for various reforms and renewals in the church and in society, which while important, does not offer any new insight into the majority's thinking on the morality of contraception itself. The commission's report was presented to Pope Paul VI in June, 1966. It would be two years before he would make a decision on the issue.

HUMANAE VITAE
AND THE AFTERMATH
The Encyclical

Humanae Vitae was signed by Pope Paul VI on July 25, 1968, and released to the public four days later.[159] The document represents the careful and prudent reflection of the pontiff upon the report of the papal commission. The encyclical follows the same structure as the sche-

156. Ibid. It is unclear what exactly this criterion means. What is clear, however, is that it represents a furtherance of the position put forth by many progressive theologians that the permanent prevention of conception would be immoral, a position that was seemingly adopted earlier in the same schema which insisted that married life cannot be entirely complete without the complement of children. Janet Smith's rhetorical suggestion that the second criterion "seems to mean that if the spouses are very determined not to have a child, they should use the most effective means possible" is probably misplaced (Smith, *Humanae Vitae*, 33).

157. "The Majority View," in *Pope and Pill*, ed. Pyle, 267.

158. Ibid.

159. See Pope Paul VI, *Humanae Vitae*, Encyclical Letter, July 25, 1968, in *AAS* 60 (1968): 481–503 [hereafter, *HV*]; all English translations of encyclicals are drawn from www.vatican.va. Another English translation is available in print: Paul VI, "On Human Life (*Humanae Vitae*)" (Boston: Daughters of St. Paul, 1968).

ma submitted by that commission. It is divided into three parts: first, an introduction; second, a presentation of the relevant doctrinal principles; and third, some pastoral directives.

After reaffirming the authority of the church to interpret matters of the natural moral law and alluding to the difficulty of his own discernment of the question which was compounded by the lack of unanimity on the papal commission, the second part of the encyclical on doctrinal principles begins in such a way that Paul VI suggests fundamental agreement with the personalist view of marriage which had begun in the 1920s and which many were using to advocate for the use of contraception.[160] In these opening paragraphs, he writes that marriage is a "provident institution of God the Creator."[161] It is in marriage that "husband and wife, through that mutual gift of themselves, which is specific and exclusive to them alone, develop that union of two persons in which they perfect one another, cooperating with God in the generation and rearing of new lives."[162] Married love, he says, is "fully human" and not merely a question "of natural instinct or emotional drive." It is a total and "very special form of personal friendship."[163] Married love is "faithful and exclusive of all others, and this until death."[164] Finally, married love is fecund. "It is not confined wholly to the loving interchange of husband and wife; it also contrives to go beyond this to bring new life into being."[165] Here, the pope inserts a direct quote of *Gaudium et Spes* (par. 50).

A discussion of responsible parenthood follows.[166] The pope addresses biological processes and says that "responsible parenthood means an awareness of, and respect for, their proper function. In the procreative faculty the human mind discerns biological laws that apply to the human person."[167] The encyclical acknowledges the necessity of rational control over "innate drives and emotions" along with the possibility of not having "additional children for either a certain or an indefinite period of time."[168] It encourages couples to maintain

---

160. See *HV*, pars. 6, 8–9.
162. Ibid.
164. Ibid.
166. See ibid., par. 10.
167. Here the encyclical cites *ST* I-II, q. 94, a. 2.
168. *HV*, par. 10.

161. Ibid., par. 8.
163. Ibid., par. 9.
165. Ibid.

the "right order of priorities, [and] recognize their own duties toward God, themselves, their families and human society."[169]

So similar are the sentiments that are expressed in these early paragraphs of the encyclical to those of the papal commission schema that William Shannon observes "up to this point, i.e., the second last paragraph of Article 10, the encyclical could have moved in either direction—toward a change in the Church's teaching on contraception or toward a reaffirmation of the norms of the past."[170] But the encyclical makes a decisive shift in the final paragraph of article ten:

> From this it follows that they [the married couple] are *not free* to act as they choose in the service of transmitting life, as if it were wholly up to them to decide what is the right course to follow. On the contrary, they are bound to ensure that what they do corresponds to the will of God the Creator. The very nature of marriage and its use makes His will clear, while the constant teaching of the Church spells it out.[171]

The pope shifts to the traditional argument from the ends of nature, both the ends of the conjugal act and the ends of marriage itself.

Then Pope Paul VI offers a brief summary of natural law.[172] There, the pope acknowledges that involuntary infertility does not affect the moral status of the conjugal act because of "its natural adaptation to the expression and strengthening of the union of husband and wife is not thereby suppressed." He also acknowledges the fact that "new life is not the result of each and every act of sexual intercourse." These natural occurrences are the result of God, who "has wisely ordered laws of nature and the incidence of fertility in such a way that successive births are already naturally spaced through the inherent operation of these laws." Nevertheless, the encyclical reaffirms the church's teaching that "each and every marital act must of necessity be intrinsically ordered [*per se destinatus*] to the procreation of human life."[173] Here the pope footnotes both *Casti Connubii* and Pope Pius XII's 1951 address to midwives.

The following article, article 12, has been the subject of much speculation and disagreement. In full, it reads:

169. Ibid.   170. Shannon, *Lively Debate*, 108.

171. *HV*, par. 10 (emphasis added). Here the encyclical refers again to *GS*, pars. 50–51.

172. See *HV*, par. 11.   173. Ibid.

This particular doctrine, often expounded by the magisterium of the Church, is based on the inseparable connection, established by God, which man on his own initiative may not break, between the unitive significance and the procreative significance which are both inherent to the marriage act. The reason is that the fundamental nature of the marriage act, while uniting husband and wife in the closest intimacy, also renders them capable of generating new life—and this is a result of laws written into the actual nature of man and of woman. And if each of these essential qualities, the unitive and the procreative, is preserved, the use of marriage fully retains its sense of true mutual love and its ordination to the supreme responsibility of parenthood to which man is called. We believe that our contemporaries are particularly capable of seeing that this teaching is in harmony with human reason.[174]

This article is significant for a number of reasons, not the least of which is that Paul VI here definitively decides against the majority of bishops and theologians on his own commission. Whereas the schema had indicated the connection between the two aspects of the conjugal act were "almost indivisible," Paul VI's draws a different conclusion. The two ends of the conjugal act are not simply indivisible sides of a personal choice, but rather inseparable ends of an act specified by the nature of man and woman. This is precisely the issue of the debate—the connection between the unitive and procreative aspects of the conjugal act—and the encyclical offers a centrally unique contribution to the discussion.

Article twelve of *Humanae Vitae* is a capstone of the development of the church's presentation of marriage, which began in the 1920s and was implicitly manifest in *Gaudium et Spes*. Donald Asci has noted that the novelty is evident in the lack of any citation in the article to previous magisterial teaching.[175] John Gallagher's observation that Pope Paul VI's rejection of the commission and his affirmation of the ban on contraception is primarily the result of a loyalty to the magisterium is thus misplaced.[176] The encyclical as a whole reveals that Paul VI had taken a turn toward a more personalist presentation of marriage while maintaining the traditional position on one issue: the inseparability of the procreative and unitive ends of the conjugal

---

174. *HV*, par. 12.
175. See Asci, *Conjugal Act*, 111.
176. Gallagher, "Magisterial Teaching," 206–7.

act.[177] He expresses his fundamental disagreement with the majority of the theologians of his commission who held only that conjugal love and fecundity were *almost* an indivisible unity.[178] Paul VI thus espouses a view of the conjugal act that is at once both personalist and faithful to the natural law, even though he does not fully elaborate how the two views coincide.

The pope offers no arguments for why it is the case that the unitive and procreative meanings of the conjugal act are inseparable. He simply states that an honest reflection on the nature of marriage will reveal "that an act of mutual love which impairs the capacity to transmit life which God the Creator, through specific laws, has built into it, frustrates His design which constitutes the norm of marriage, and contradicts the will of the Author of life ... and is consequently in opposition to the plan of God and His holy will."[179]

Paul VI clearly sides with the minority theologians on a number of other points. First, he agrees that reason does not have absolute dominion over nature. Man does not have complete dominion over his body let alone his sexual faculties because "these are concerned by their very nature with the generation of life, of which God is the source."[180] Second, no action can be chosen "which either before, at the moment of, or after sexual intercourse, is specifically intended to prevent procreation—whether as an end or as a means."[181] Third, against the majority's invocation of the principle of totality, the encyclical asserts that a lesser evil cannot be chosen in preference to a greater one. Nor can it be held that contraceptive intercourse could "merge with procreative acts of past and future to form a single entity, and so be qualified by exactly the same moral goodness

---

177. In his general audience on July 31, 1968, the pope stated that when he was writing the encyclical he "willingly adopted the personalist concept which is proper to the Council's doctrine on conjugal society and which gives to the love that generates and nourishes it the preeminent place that befits it in the subjective evaluation of marriage." *AAS* 60 (1968): 529; English translation from "Church in the Word," *The London Tablet* 222 (August 10, 1968): 803.

178. It should be noted here that Paul VI introduces the word "unitive" to describe the conjugal meaning of the sexual act. Donald Asci has provided a thorough investigation of this development as well the difference between the notions of end, purpose, and meaning. See Asci, *Conjugal Act*, 240–69.

179. *HV*, par. 13.   180. Ibid.
181. Ibid., par. 14.

as these."[182] *Humanae Vitae* considers contraceptive intercourse evil and, traditionally, one may never do evil that good may come of it. "Consequently, it is a serious error to think that a whole married life of otherwise normal relations can justify sexual intercourse which is deliberately contraceptive and so intrinsically wrong."[183]

After recognizing the moral permissibility of therapies that result in (but do not intend) infertility, the encyclical promotes recourse to infertile periods as a legitimate means for spacing births. Moreover it identifies the difference between this method and contraception. "In the former the married couple rightly use a faculty provided them by nature. In the latter they obstruct the natural development of the generative process."[184] The encyclical then turns to the consequences of the use of artificial contraception.[185] It restates the consequences written in the minority report: a rise in marital infidelity, a lowering of moral standards, an irreverence toward women, and government-sponsored population control. Limits on man's reason and power "are expressly imposed because of the reverence due to the whole human organism and its natural functions."[186]

Before turning to the pastoral directives, with which this study is not properly concerned, the doctrinal section concludes by anticipating that "not everyone will easily accept this particular teaching."[187] Nevertheless, the church cannot change the moral law. "It could never be right for her to declare lawful what is in fact unlawful, since that, by its very nature, is always opposed to the true good of man."[188] The pope clearly understood the ramifications of the encyclical, but it is difficult to know whether he anticipated the heated reaction it would receive.

Reactions to the Encyclical

Immediately following upon the encyclical's release, episcopal conferences around the world issued supplemental statements.[189] Just

---

182. Ibid.
184. Ibid., par. 16.
186. Ibid.
188. Ibid.

183. Ibid.
185. See ibid., par. 17.
187. Ibid., par. 18.

189. In a popular summary of the debate surrounding birth control, Robert Hoyt reports that *Humanae Vitae* included a cover letter from Cardinal Cicognani in which he

under half of the episcopal conferences that issued statements expressed clear and unmitigated agreement with the encyclical. Other conferences emphasized the priority of conscience and that the content of the encyclical was not infallible. Still other statements seemed uncertain in their approach.[190] Since Monsignor Ferdinando Lam-

---

asked the bishops to give their full report. Hoyt quotes the letter as stating, "And now, he (the Pope) turns to his brothers, the bishops of the Catholic world, asking them to stand beside him more firmly than ever ... and to help present this delicate point of the church's teaching to the Christian people, to explain and justify its reasons." Robert G. Hoyt, ed., *The Birth Control Debate: The Interim History from the Pages of* The National Catholic Reporter (Kansas City, Mo.: National Catholic Reporter Publishing, 1968), 143. Unfortunately, Hoyt does not cite his source for this letter and I have been unable to locate the original text even in the *AAS*.

190. Most of these statements are collected in John Horgan, ed., Humanae Vitae: *The Encyclical and the Statements of the National Hierarchies* (Shannon: Irish University Press, 1972). In his doctoral dissertation, Joseph Selling categorizes the various episcopal conference statements into three categories based on their reaction to *Humanae Vitae*. There were statements which exhibited "clear acceptance" of the encyclical; statements which offered "clear mitigation"; and statements which were "uncertain" and offered elements of both of the previous categories. Though some conferences issued more than one statement with variant positions, ultimately Selling identifies sixteen conferences in the category of "clear acceptance," thirteen in "clear mitigation," and eight that are "uncertain." Joseph Selling, *The Reaction to* Humanae vitae: *A Study in Special and Fundamental Theology* (PhD diss., Catholic University of Louvain, 1973): 26–27, appendix B3. Philip Kaufman disagreed with both Selling's approach and conclusion. He thinks it is too simplistic to assert that forty-two percent of the world's episcopal conferences clearly accepted the encyclical. Rather, he suggests that Selling's study be interpreted as though the conferences were an electoral college. Thus, Poland's clear acceptance would be mitigated in the light of the Latin American Episcopal Conference (CELAM) which is an umbrella organization of over twenty national episcopal conferences. Poland's twenty-six dioceses (and, therefore, twenty-six votes) would pale in comparison to CELAM's 442 dioceses/votes. Additionally, Kaufmann challenges Selling's categorization of the United States as "uncertain" and he places the U.S. (with its 159 dioceses/votes) in the category of "critically mitigating." Furthermore, he subsumes Brazil (192 dioceses/votes), Colombia (45 dioceses/votes), and Mexico (66 dioceses/votes) under the CELAM mitigation vote. Selling had placed none of these three conferences in that category. Using this process, he concludes that only seventeen percent of the world's *bishops* clearly accepted *Humanae Vitae*. Philip S. Kaufmann, *Why You Can Disagree and Remain a Faithful Catholic*, rev. ed. (New York: Crossroad, 1995), 96. However, Kaufmann's conclusion is questionable. He not only shuffles the conferences differently than Selling without explanation, his method is fundamentally flawed. Episcopal conferences do not normally issue statements with unanimous approval. Sometimes a statement requires only a simple majority to be approved. Suggesting that because a conference has issued a statement, therefore all of its bishops were in agreement with that statement is akin to suggesting that every voter in a particular state voted for

bruschini, one of the Vatican spokesmen who introduced the encyclical to the press, specifically noted that the encyclical is not infallible, many argued that for serious reasons a Catholic may dissent from its teaching in good conscience—provided his conscience was properly and honestly formed.[191] This distinction between fallible and infallible teaching, along with the priority of conscience, significantly affected the responses offered by various theologians around the United States.

For theologians around the world who had disagreed with the conclusions of the encyclical, freedom of conscience and the right to dissent from non-infallible magisterial teaching were used to buttress their more fundamental objections to the document. The case of the American theologians led by Charles Curran, then professor of moral theology at the Catholic University of America, is the most well known. Having obtained a copy of the encyclical on the day of its publication, by three o'clock in the morning he had obtained the signatures of eighty-seven theologians from around the country for a statement expressing dissent from the encyclical.[192] Citing the non-infallible nature of the encyclical, the statement goes on to say that "history shows that a number of statements of similar or even greater authoritative weight have subsequently been proven inadequate or even erroneous."[193] It ends with the observation: "It is com-

---

a presidential candidate simply because the candidate received all the state's electoral votes.

191. Ten episcopal conferences of the twenty that Selling studied had made this distinction: Holland, Germany, Belgium, Austria, Canada, Scotland, Scandinavia, the United States, and Switzerland. An English translation of extracts from Lambruschini's speech on the presentation of the encyclical is available in *Pope and Pill*, ed. Pyle, 101–5.

192. For a history of the drafting of this statement and its repercussions for those involved, see Charles E. Curran, Robert E. Hunt, et al., *Dissent In and For the Church: Theologians and* Humanae vitae (New York: Sheed and Ward, 1969), and Larry Witham, *Curran vs. Catholic University: A Study of Authority and Freedom in Conflict* (Riverdale, Md.: Edington-Rand, 1991). The statement was presented to the press on July 30, 1968, and was subsequently published in various media outlets. The full text of the statement is still available in numerous books on the topic of the response to the encyclical. Quotations from the text in this study are taken from Charles Curran et al., "Statement by Catholic Theologians, Washington, D.C., July 30, 1968," in Charles Curran, and Richard A. McCormick, eds., *Readings in Moral Theology*, no. 8, *Dialogue about Catholic Sexual Teaching* (New York: Paulist Press, 1993), 135–37.

193. Curran, "Statement," 135.

mon teaching in the Church that Catholics may dissent from authoritative, non-infallible teachings of the magisterium when sufficient
reasons for so doing exist," and, therefore, that Catholic couples
should feel free to decide according to their own conscience the path
they would take.[194]

The statement offers many reasons for dissent. First, the theologians believe that the ecclesiology of the encyclical is deficient. It
does not take into consideration the experience of Catholic couples
or non-Catholic Christians. Second, by rejecting the findings of the
papal commission and "the conclusions of a large part of the international Catholic theological community," the encyclical betrays a
positivistic view of papal authority. Third, the conclusion on contraception is "based on an inadequate concept of natural law."[195] Additionally, the statement includes a paragraph, which reads more as an
angry diatribe, that includes no less than six faults of the encyclical.
One of those faults is the "overemphasis on the biological aspects of
conjugal relations as ethically normative."[196] In subsequent days, the
statement was sent to theologians and teachers of theology all over
the United States. The list of signatures grew to over six hundred.[197]

In addition to this statement and the debate it generated in the
pages of the *National Catholic Reporter*, a number of theologians initially began publishing articles in theological journals expressing
their dissent.[198] Generally, the articles dissenting from the teaching

194. Ibid., 136.
195. Ibid.
196. Ibid. *The National Catholic Reporter* served as a sounding board for scholars
on both sides of the American theologians' statement. These statements were collected by Robert G. Hoyt in his book, *The Birth Control Debate* (181–97). John T. Noonan,
Albert C. Outler, and Richard A. McCormick each offered the *National Catholic Reporter* analyses in support of the Curran's statement. Austin Vaughn and Charles R. Meyer
published responses to the dissenting theologians. This was an interesting discovery for
me personally; Fr. Meyer was still on faculty at the University of St. Mary of the Lake/
Mundelein Seminary when I was student there in the early 2000s, and was still highly
regarded among the seminarians as a professor with an unmatched Thomistic intellect.
197. See Shannon, *Lively Debate*, 150.
198. For initial articles, see Richard A. McCormick, "Notes on Moral Theology,"
Theological Studies 29 (1968): 732–41; Bernard Häring, "Statement in the *National Catholic Reporter*," *National Catholic Reporter* (August 7, 1968), 8; and Louis Janssens, "Considerations on *Humanae Vitae*," *Louvain Studies* 2 (1969): 231–53. See also the collection
of essays edited by Charles Curran, *Contraception: Authority and Dissent* (New York:

of *Humanae Vitae* focused on two overarching themes. First, many of the theologians argued for the right to conscientious dissent, with good reason, from non-infallible magisterial teaching. Second, some theologians said that the methodology employed in the encyclical was based on a faulty view of natural law that emphasizes the physical structure of the conjugal act to the detriment of personal and familial obligations.

The second of these themes concerns this study more directly. Two principal proponents of this theme in particular were Charles Curran and his teacher Bernard Häring.[199] Häring praises the encyclical for recognizing the "positive value of the marital act as expressive of conjugal love" and thus dismissing the necessity for every conjugal act to include the specific intention to procreate.[200] Nevertheless, Häring questions the internal consistency of the encyclical's conclusion on birth control since it also accepts the positive value of the sexual act for infertile couples. As he sees it, *Humanae Vitae* argues from the presupposition that "biological laws ... [are] absolutely binding on the conscience of men."[201] But this would seem to reduce human action to a mere natural instinct shared with animals. Like most personalists arguing for change, Häring argues that man's reason elevates him above natural instinct. "The absoluteness of biological laws can apply to the human person to the extent that he *knows* them."[202] The basic question is whether man is subject absolutely to biological laws or if he is, rather, their steward.

Medicine, Häring says, is "generally based on the principle that biological functions may be interfered with and even destroyed if it is necessary for the well being of the *person*. It is evident that the final perspective of an anthropologically grounded medicine is not the mere restoration of the *organism* but the wholeness of a *person* in community."[203] The Catholic solution to personal difficulties with-

---

Herder and Herder, 1969). The collection includes essays by Curran himself, Joseph Noonan, Joseph A. Komonchak, Daniel C. Maguire, and Bernard Häring.

199. See Charles E. Curran, "Natural Law and Contemporary Moral Theology," in *Contraception: Authority and Dissent*, 151–75, and Bernard Häring, "The Inseparability of the Unitive-Procreative Functions of the Marital Act," in *Contraception: Authority and Dissent*, 176–92.

200. Häring, "The Inseparability," 177.   201. Ibid., 180.
202. Ibid. (emphasis added).   203. Ibid., 193.

in a marriage through recourse to periodic continence already acknowledges that the human person has some authority over his use
of nature. From this personalist perspective, the prohibition against
the birth control pill is incomprehensible to society. "Today man
thinks much more in terms of the good of the whole person than in
terms of absolutely sacred but often dysfunctional 'natural laws and
rhythms.'"[204]

Finally, Häring argued that had the relationship between the unitive and procreative aspects of the conjugal act received more attention in theology in the decades before 1968, the encyclical may have
been worded differently. In line with the majority of the theologians
on the papal commission, he states: "There is and must be a close
linkage of the two meanings, and great care must be exercised never
to separate them unduly or totally in any aspect of sexual morality."[205]
Again, the pope thought that the two aspects of the conjugal act were
always inseparable.

Charles Curran carries Häring's dispute with the encyclical's natural law methodology further by naming it "physicalism." Curran
writes: "Christian ethics cannot absolutize the realm of the natural as
something completely self-contained and unaffected by any relationships to the evangelical or supernatural."[206] A Christian theory of natural law, he argues, must include reference to creation and sin, on the
one hand, and the incarnation and redemption of Christ, on the other. Natural law is, for the Christian, Christocentric.[207] The encyclical
fails in this regard by not recognizing the corrupting influence of sin
on human reason and nature, both of which are the foundational to
any natural law theory.

Curran claims that *Humanae Vitae* employs a physicalist methodology "which tends to identify the moral action with the physical and biological structure of the act."[208] Curran thus condemns
the methodology of the manualist tradition, especially in the area of
medical ethics, sexuality, reproduction, moral conflicts, killing, abor-

---

204. Ibid., 185.   205. Ibid., 188.
206. Curran, "Natural Law," 154–55.
207. See ibid., 155. Curran no doubt learned this from Häring himself, who was his
professor. See, for example, Bernard Häring, *The Law of Christ: Moral Theology for Priests
and Laity*, 3 vols., trans. Edwin G. Kaiser (Paramus, N.J.: Newman Books, 1961–66).
208. Curran, "Natural Law," 159.

tion, euthanasia, and divorce. The manualists "have tended to define the moral action in terms of the physical structure of the act considered in itself apart from the person place the act and the community of persons within which he lives."[209] Actions which the manualists prohibit definitively because of their intrinsic immorality are usually grounded in the physical structure of the act. Curran suggests that the harsh reaction to *Humanae Vitae* is a result of its physicalist approach. It is in response to physicalism, Curran believes, that theologians have adopted a personalist approach which "always sees the act in terms of the person placing the act."[210] These new approaches are not simply added to the natural law theory but affect the conclusions arising from that theory. These new approaches "logically lead to the conclusion that artificial contraception can be a permissible and even necessary means for the regulation of birth within the context of responsible parenthood."[211]

Thus, Curran effectively set the boundaries for the birth control debate. Those who wanted to preserve the church's traditional prohibition against artificial contraception and to defend the conclusions of the encyclical were thus required to rearticulate their natural law methodology. Otherwise, they would easily be dismissed as "physicalist," a word whose negative connotations were quickly assumed by scholars. Nobody would want to be labeled a physicalist.

CONCLUSION

This was the highly-charged arena in which Karol Wojtyła began to develop his own personalist approach to defending *Humanae Vitae*. As we have seen, prior to the advent of nominalism in the fourteenth century, Catholic moral theologians were primarily concerned with the virtue and beatitude of the person. The influence of nominalism led to a more juridical understanding of the moral life based fundamentally on law, obligation, and conscience. With the spiritual principles of the human person thus reduced, the manualists were left with only the manifest physical structure of the human action and its re-

---

209. Ibid., 161.   210. Ibid., 172.
211. Ibid., 175.

lationship to natural finality to determine the morality of human action.

Although after the council most moral theologians turned almost exclusively to the category of person and saw the good of the person superseding natural finality, Karol Wojtyła articulated a personalist philosophy that respected the natural law. This was part of his larger ambition to reconnect theology with the subjective experience of the human person while exploring the relationship between the categories of human nature and the human person. This was a project he would pursue throughout his pontificate. As we move forward, keep in mind that in this study we are focusing on *Theology of the Body* and, specifically, on Wojtyła's notion of the spousal meaning of the body as a particularly poignant contribution to that project.

3

The Moral Theology of
Karol Wojtyła

Born in 1920 in Wadowice, Poland, Karol Wojtyła lived through some of the worst horrors not only in the history of his native land but in the history of the world. In the course of his youth, Poland fell, first, under Nazi occupation during World War II, and later, under the control of the Soviet Communist regime. Wojtyła's young life was filled with a depth of experience, both rich and tragic. His innate ability to articulate those experiences in the arts—poetry, prose, and theater—proved a saving grace for both him and his friends. While the purpose of this chapter is not to provide a historical narrative of Wojtyła's life, these early experiences profoundly affected the man who would be Pope John Paul II.[1] He became a man dedicated to the dignity of

1. This work has already been done. George Weigel has written what many consider to be the definitive biography of Pope John Paul II. See Weigel, *Witness to Hope*. Weigel's follow-up effort should not be missed: *The End and the Beginning: Pope John Paul II—The Victory of Freedom, the Last Years, the Legacy* (New York: Image, 2011). Another important biography of note was written by Wojtyła's childhood friend and seminary classmate. It provides several personal accounts known to the biographer alone. Its only weakness is that it was written shortly after Wojtyła's election to the papacy. See Mieczyslaw Malinksi, *Pope John Paul II: The Life of Karol Wojtyła*, trans. P. S. Falla (New York: Seabury Press, 1979). Several books have been written which are less biographical and more concerned with the development of Wojtyła's thought. This chapter is indebted, in part, to the work of these scholars. See Rocco Buttiglione, *Karol: The*

the human person, having personally witnessed atrocities committed against that dignity. Consequently, Wojtyła's interest in love and marriage, his defense of *Humanae Vitae*, and his explication of the spousal meaning of the body in the *Theology of the Body* catecheses, while concrete matters, are not isolated elements of his thought. They are practical applications of his general moral theory. Moreover, his moral theory bears the influence of the thought of Thomas Aquinas. Karol Wojtyła was just as concerned as other theologians, philosophers, and pastors with the experience of human persons in the context of love and marriage, but he was not willing to abandon magisterial teaching or metaphysical ontology in favor of those experiences. He was unwilling to disconnect the philosophical category of the human person from the category of human nature. On the contrary, though he spent much of his life before his pontifical election focusing on the philosophical categories of experience and the human person, he never abandoned ontology—specifically, Thomistic ontology. He cannot be accused of subjectivism however much he focuses on subjective experience.

This chapter outlines the development of Wojtyła's thought from his first studies of Thomism to his encounter with phenomenology of Max Scheler and his final works on philosophy and ethics before his election to the papacy. What this survey will show is that Wojtyła consistently attempts to connect ontology and phenomenology. Though his emphasis shifts to one or the other at various moments in his career, he abandons neither.

Thought of the Man Who Became Pope John Paul II, trans. Paolo Guietti and Francesca Murphy (Grand Rapids, Mich.: Eerdmans, 1997); Kenneth L. Schmitz, *At the Center of the Human Drama: The Philosophical Anthropology of Karol Wojtyła/Pope John Paul II* (Washington, D.C.: The Catholic University of America Press, 1993); Jarosław Kupczak, OP, *Destined for Liberty: The Human Person in the Philosophy of Karol Wojtyła/John Paul II* (Washington, D.C.: The Catholic University of America Press, 2000); and, George Hunston Williams, *The Mind of John Paul II: Origins of His Thought and Action* (New York: Seabury Press, 1981).

KAROL WOJTYŁA'S EARLY STUDIES

Experience and Theology: Wojtyła Studies
St. John of the Cross

The first chapter of this study recounted briefly the trends in twenti-eth-century Thomism, which, in different ways, attempted to respond to the Enlightenment and modernity. Wojtyła's first encounter with Thomism occurred during his years in the underground seminary in Cracow led by Cardinal Adam Sapieha. In September 1942, he was as-signed to read Kazimierz Wais's book on metaphysics, *Ontologia czy-li metafizyka* (*Ontology and Metaphysics*).[2] Wais's text was influenced by the transcendental Thomism of Louvain's Désiré Mercier, which attempted to place Thomas's thought in relation to that of Immanuel Kant.[3] It was unlike anything Wojtyła had read before and it initial-ly presented a significant challenge.[4] Wojtyła's background in the hu-manities had not prepared him to handle the difficult scholastic the-ses he was expected to learn. Nevertheless, he would later admit that the metaphysics he learned in that text gave confirmation to what he had previously only known intuitively by experience.[5]

The young Wojtyła was ordained a priest on November 1, 1946, and was immediately sent to the Angelicum in Rome for doctoral stud-ies. While there, he continued to develop his conviction that Thomis-tic philosophical and theological categories can aid in both confirming and articulating experience. The topic for his doctoral dissertation was the question of faith according to John of the Cross.[6] His director was

2. Kazimierz Wais, *Ontologia czyli metafizyka ogólna* (Lwów: Biblioteka Religijna, 1926).

3. See Williams, *The Mind of John Paul II*, 87; Buttiglione, *Karol Wojtyła*, 31; Weigel, *Witness to Hope*, 69–71.

4. Malinski, *Pope John Paul II*, 47.

5. John Paul II and André Frossard, *Be Not Afraid! Pope John Paul II Speaks Out on His Life, His Beliefs, and His Inspiring Vision for Humanity*, trans. J. R. Foster (New York: St. Martin's Press, 1984), 17.

6. Karol Wojtyła, *Doctrina de fide apud S. Joannem a Cruce* (STD diss., Pontifical University of St. Thomas Aquinas, 1948); English translation: Karol Wojtyła, *Faith Ac-cording to Saint John of the Cross*, trans. Jordan Aumann, OP (San Francisco, Calif.: Igna-tius Press, 1981). Wojtyła had been introduced to the Carmelite mystics long before en-tering the seminary by Jan Tyranowski, a layman who eventually led the youth group of young Wojtyła's parish (see Weigel, *Witness to Hope*, 58–62). But it was Fr. Ignacy Róży-cki, a professor of Sapieha's underground seminary, who first suggested to Wojtyła not

Reginald Garrigou-Lagrange, OP, who was himself an expert on John.[7] Wojtyła's dissertation follows closely not only upon Garrigou-Lagrange's work but also upon that of two other authors who were concerned with the differences between John of the Cross and the scholastics on the nature of faith: Jane Baruzi and Michel Labourdette, OP. Whereas scholasticism viewed faith as a virtue residing in the intellect, John's emphasis on the dark night of faith, in which the intellect can say nothing about God, placed more emphasis on the experience of God. The difference here is that between dogmatic faith (or intellectual propositions about God) and mystical faith (the experience of God).

In his dissertation, Wojtyła had hoped to show that mystical faith and dogmatic or intellectual faith were not opposing concepts but different aspects of a single virtue. In the introduction to the dissertation, he writes:

The doctrine we shall study is a testimony of experience. It is expressed in scholastico-mystical language, using words and concepts well known in Scholastic theology, but its primary value and significance is a witness of personal experience. It is there, in fact, that we can discover the living and dynamic reality of the virtue of faith, its activity in the human intellect, its corollaries and the effects on the movement of the soul toward union with God. For that reason we take the experiential witness of St. John of the Cross as the material for our investigation. It will be our task to discover the concept of faith that can be gleaned from that witness and the theological precisions that are latent in it.[8]

Later in the same introduction, he writes: "We should emphasize that the texts not only expound a theology based on experience, but to a great extent they do so in a descriptive manner. The description is often couched in Scholastic terminology, but the experience that is described will often give a different nuance or a new meaning to that technical terminology."[9]

Faith according to St. John of the Cross is divided into two parts. The first and more substantial part analyzes the passages concerning

---

only that he was competent to write a doctoral dissertation but that it should be on the subject of faith according to John of the Cross (see Malinski, *Pope John Paul II*, 88–89).

7. Garrigou-Lagrange had published several books and articles on the relationship between faith and experience, and one book, in particular, on John of the Cross's understanding of the relationship between faith and experience. For a brief summary of these works and a bibliography, see Williams, *The Mind of John Paul II*, 103–4.

8. Wojtyła, *Faith according to St. John of the Cross*, 23.

9. Ibid., 25.

faith and love in John's four major works (*The Ascent of Mount Carmel*, *The Dark Night of the Soul*, *The Spiritual Canticle*, and *The Living Flame of Love*), while the second offers a synthesis of his conclusions on the nature of faith in these works. The dissertation also includes a very brief appendix, which attempts to correlate John of the Cross's understanding of faith with that of Thomas Aquinas.

According to Wojtyła, faith for John of the Cross is itself an "essential likeness" to God, which by the power of an "excessive light" is able to create a proportion between man's intellect and God so that man can be united to God.[10] Our union with God exists both ontologically and psychologically, he says. Ontologically, the virtue of faith alters the natural operation of the intellect. Following the thought of Aquinas, Wojtyła notes that the intellect naturally attains knowledge through the senses and the formation of intentional species. There is, he says, an "incapacity of the intellect to attain such knowledge of the divine object by means of an intentional species."[11] God cannot be known through sense impressions, and the intellect cannot contain the divine as an object of knowledge.

Faith therefore provides an ontological transcendence in which the intellect is proportioned so as to be capable of uniting with God.[12] Faith, however, is not union with God, not even intellectually. Faith involves "no clear apprehension of the divine essence in the intentional order, no 'substance as understood.'"[13] Does John of the Cross believe that the intellect is therefore frustrated by the virtue of faith? No, Wojtyła responds:

The senses fail to form a species because that which is given in revelation is totally inaccessible to the senses. As a result, the agent intellect lacks material or sense species on which it can focus, so that the revealed truths seem doomed to remain only words or meaningless names of an unknown object. But the virtue of faith is infused into the intellect, and with faith the intellect receives the excessive light by which it is attracted to the revealed truths and united with them. This was explained in chapter 3, book II of *The Ascent*.[14]

This ascent to revealed truths, however, cannot provide a clear and distinct object to the intellect principally because the intellect re-

---

10. See ibid., 238–39, 265.   11. See ibid., 242.
12. See ibid., 245.   13. Ibid., 241.
14. Ibid., 245.

mains limited, even with the virtue of faith, by its natural tendency toward conceptual knowledge. So this adherence is always somewhat obscure and dependent on a more general knowledge since "adherence to particular and clear truths introduces a natural element of knowledge that is psychologically satisfying, but precisely because of that, it lacks the required proportion to the substance of revealed truths [which is the divine essence]."[15]

In the brief appendix, Wojtyła collects references from Aquinas's works to illustrate his theory that both John of the Cross and Thomas had a similar understanding of faith. Faith is a means of union for Aquinas, not directly, but through adhering to revealed truths.[16] Wojtyła also observes that faith, for Aquinas, likewise involves an element of purgation.[17] However, where John of the Cross places the complete intellectual purification from intentional species in the realm of the faith as commanded by charity, Aquinas "with greater theological precision" identifies this task with the gift of understanding.[18]

Wojtyła's engagement with John's texts shows his belief that union with God is more than an intellectual enterprise of theological expertise; it is a dynamic process. He writes, "all the elements that contribute to union will be discovered, not through an abstract and theoretical consideration, but as actuated in the unifying process itself."[19] Wojtyła elucidates, and seems to agree with, John's preference for love over faith which draws the person into a real ontological and psychological union with God.[20] We may also note Wojtyła's observation that for John of the Cross, God is objective but not objectivizable to the intellect, which naturally lends itself to the personalistic norm that will eventually hold pride of place in Wojtyła's thought. Like the person of God, no human person can ever be a mere object of our actions but must be understood in relationship.[21]

---

15. Ibid., 253.
16. See ibid., 269–71. See also *ST* II-II, q. 1, a. 2 and ad 2; *De Veritate*, q. 14, a, 8, ad 5; q. 14, a. 12; *In III Librum Sententiarum*, dist. 24, a. 1, q. 2, ads. 1 and 2; *In VI Metaphysica*, 8 and ad 3.
17. See Wojtyła, *Faith according to St. John of the Cross*, 271. See also *ST* II-II, q. 7, a. 2 and ad 2.
18. See Wojtyła, *Faith according to St. John of the Cross*, 272. See also *ST* II-II, q. 8, a. 7.
19. Wojtyła, *Faith according to St. John of the Cross*, 110.
20. For example, see ibid., 99.
21. This is the insight of Rocco Buttiglione (*Karol Wojtyła*, 52).

Experience and Philosophy: Wojtyła
Studies Max Scheler

Wojtyła furthered his interest in experience and the person in his habilitation thesis, *An Evaluation of the Possibility of Constructing a Christian Ethics on the Basis of the System of Max Scheler*, which addresses Scheler's work *Der Formalismus in der Ethik und die material Wertethik*.[22] Scheler was primarily responding to Immanuel Kant's ethical system, which was founded upon a pure rationalism and the notion of duty. With his assertion that the person cannot perceive the foundation behind reality (the *noumena*) but only phenomena passing through *a priori* categories in the mind, Kant effectively disallowed for any experience of reality apart from these rational categories. To put it simply, the philosophical school of phenomenology sought to reconnect experience with access to the world beyond the mind.[23] The fact that he opposed Kant and emphasized the mind's access to reality made Scheler a natural candidate for Catholic moral theologians struggling to respond to Kant's system.[24]

In the opening section of the thesis, Wojtyła is emphatic that Scheler's system is not Christian even though he at times employs

22. Karol Wojtyła, *Ocena możliwości zbudowania etyki chrześcijańskiej przy założeniach systemu Maksa Schelera* (Lublin: Towarzystwo Naukowe KUL, 1959). There is no English translation of this work available. In this study, I will be using the Spanish translation: Karol Wojtyła, *Max Scheler y la etica cristiana* (Madrid: Biblioteca de Autores Cristianos, 1982). It is not entirely clear why Wojtyła chose Scheler as the subject of his habilitation thesis. It was most likely Fr. Ignacy Różycki, the same professor who had recommended John of the Cross to Wojtyła, who suggested Scheler. Różycki was himself influenced by Roman Ingarden, who like Scheler, was a student of Edmund Husserl. Through Ingarden, Rozycki would have been aware of the attractiveness of Scheler's philosophy for Catholic moral theologians (see Williams, *The Mind of John Paul II*, 115, 124). Wojtyła was not entirely unfamiliar with Scheler, however. He had heard at least one lecture by Max Scheler in 1938, his first year at the Jagiellonian University; see Tad Szulc, *Pope John Paul II: The Biography* (New York: Scribner, 1995), 88. The principal work of Scheler is *Der Formalismus in der Ethik und die materiale Wertethik* (Bern: Franke Verlag, 1966); English translation: Max Scheler, *Formalism in Ethics and Non-Formal Ethics of Values*, trans. Manfred S. Frings and Roger L. Funk (Evanston, Ill.: Northwestern University Press, 1973).

23. See Williams, *The Mind of John Paul II*, 116, for a brief description of the agenda of phenomenology.

24. See Buttiglione, *Karol Wojtyła*, 55–57; William, *The Mind of John Paul II*, 124.

New Testament texts. Interestingly, he says the role of the Catholic moralist is to present revealed truths using philosophy. Wojtyła writes that Scheler's is "a philosophical system, constructed according to the premises of phenomenology and axiology, in order to describe and explain all moral facts and ethical problems."[25] Scheler is not interested in defending the norms of Christian morality. Wojtyła, on the other hand, wanted to know whether Scheler's system could be used by a Christian philosopher for that purpose. This is the goal of his habilitation thesis.[26]

As Wojtyła sees it, the New Testament presumes that the person is the cause of his actions.[27] Moreover, actions have a direct effect on the person's character. Good actions make man good, bad actions make him bad.[28] In Wojtyła's reading, Scheler does not and cannot acknowledge this fact—an assertion in which we see a hint of Aquinas's moral theory at work in Wojtyła.

Nevertheless Wojtyła thinks that Scheler, by grounding his ethical system upon experience, which he thinks is accessible to the faculties of the human person, was attempting to situate ethics within an objective realm without the rigor of Kant's formalism. "For Scheler, the subject recognizes value in the experience of objects. What we have here is a materialist ethics of values."[29] In the *Formalismus*, Scheler identifies two types of values: material values and ethical values. Jarosław Kupczak summarizes the difference: "Values that stand as goals for intentional acts of a person are material values. Right and wrong are ethical values."[30]

Interestingly, as Kupczak understands him, it seems Scheler did not believe that ethical values should be chosen for their own sake. Scheler insisted that only material values could be actively chosen. Ethical values can only be experienced and even then, only accidentally.[31] Ethical values are always experienced under the rubric of love or hate, with varying intensity.[32] For Wojtyła, this understanding of ethical value is the direct result of Scheler's emotionalist reaction

25. Wojtyła, *Max Scheler*, 40 (author's translation).
26. See ibid.   27. See ibid., 109.
28. See ibid.   29. Buttiglione, *Karol Wojtyła*, 55.
30. Kupczak, Destined for Liberty, 11.   31. Ibid.
32. See ibid.; Williams, *The Mind of John Paul II*, 126.

to Kant's ethics of duty.[33] Since value is only experienced emotive-
ly, the desire for an ethical value is, for Scheler, the desire "to experience one's own ethical righteousness."[34] Scheler refers to this as moral
"pharisaism" and he rejects it.[35] This presented somewhat of a paradox since Scheler set out to present an ethical system for the moral
perfection of the person.

Wojtyła isolates the problem of the paradox in Scheler's inability to explain human causality. In the Thomistic system, the intellect
presents goods to the will for selection.[36] But Scheler's system reduces the role of the intellect by strongly emphasizing the role of the
emotions and the will, which together discern value. Thus, intellectual representation has no role to play in human action for Scheler.[37]

As Wojtyła reads him, since Scheler identifies love as an ethical
value, it cannot be part of any causal tendency in the person, and,
therefore, there is no way left to inform the will in human choice.
Wojtyła writes: "An intentional emotional feeling of value is a sort
of knowledge that originates in the depth of the person's emotional
life. The source of this knowledge is love, in which the subject experiences values in a purely emotional way. Precisely for this reason, according to Scheler's teaching, love has absolutely nothing in common
with any element of tendency."[38] This has several ramifications in Wojtyła's view. "As a result of this understanding, any element of choice
or decision disappears from Scheler's account of human action. Since
the will's participation in the acts of willing is totally passive, the human person cannot be a cause of his own actions.... One does not
know how the person can become morally right or wrong."[39]

Furthermore, since emotion alone discerns value, Scheler allows the conscience no role in ethical action. Indeed, the role of con-

---

33. See Wojtyła, Max Scheler, 117–19.   34. Kupczak, Destined for Liberty, 11.
35. See Wojtyła, Max Scheler, 117–19.

36. While there are disagreements between Thomists on the interpretation of minor points in Aquinas's theory of action, all are agreed on this point. For a detailed analysis on action according to Aquinas, see Lawrence Dewan, OP, "St. Thomas and Moral
Taxonomy," in Wisdom, Law, and Virtue: Essays in Thomistic Ethics (New York: Fordham
University Press, 2008), 444–77; Joseph Pilsner, The Specification of Human Actions in
St. Thomas Aquinas (New York: Oxford University Press, 2006); Westberg, Right Practical Reason.

37. See Wojtyła, Max Scheler, 121–22.   38. See ibid., 123–24.
39. Kupczak, Destined for Liberty, 13.

science is nothing more than the guardian of a person's ethical ideal.[40] The point is summarized by Kupczak: "The individual will choose his own moral goods from the moral values he encounters, making them part of his own ethical ideal and moral ethos. The moral values that the person chooses as his own are summarized in the conscience. Therefore, the conscience guards and preserves the moral identity of the person and ethical ideal."[41] This is in stark contrast to the New Testament understanding of conscience which is presented as an "inner conviction about the moral goodness or badness of a specific deed."[42] For Christians, the judgment of conscience is a subjective norm for the morality of human action.[43] It is this subjective conviction concerning the goodness or badness of an action that obliges the person to perform or to avoid the action, as the case may be. Thus "the conscience as a conviction shows us the practical character of moral values; the conscience as an obligation shows directly the causal relation of the person in respect to the good and the bad."[44]

Such is the legacy that Wojtyła sees in Scheler's reaction to Kant's theory of moral obligation. As Wojtyła writes: "Scheler attempts to suppress obligation from his ethical system because he wants to suppress any source of negativism from ethics."[45] Since Scheler reduced causality to a passive willing of material value, he was unable to ascribe a positive role to obligation. For Scheler, the human person is nothing more than one who experiences values, and since values indicate no tendency toward human fulfillment, the Christian notion of obligation as a pedagogical means toward human perfection is simply absent. Wojtyła notes that "an obligation always manifests itself when we experience the nonexistence of a specific positive value that 'should be,' or the existence of a negative value that 'should not be' in our experience."[46] But this description of positive values that "should be" or negative values that "should not be" is simply not possible without a robust conception of the human person dependent on something more than emotion and feeling.

40. See Wojtyła, *Max Scheler*, 132–33.
41. Kupczak, Destined for Liberty, 14.
42. Wojtyła, *Max Scheler*, 136 (author's translation).
43. See ibid., 136–37.   44. Ibid., 138 (author's translation).
45. Ibid., 139 (author's translation).   46. Ibid., 144 (author's translation).

Wojtyła offers two theses in the conclusion of his study of Scheler. The first is: "The ethical system of Max Scheler is fundamentally inadequate for the scientific formulation of the Christian ethic."[47] Revealed Christian ethics identify the human person as the source of his own actions, and, moreover, Wojtyła insists that persons actually experience themselves as the agents of their actions, both the good and the bad.[48]

Nevertheless, while Scheler's phenomenology may be inadequate to justify and defend Christian ethics, it may still serve as "an aid in a scientific study of the Christian ethic. Concretely, it facilitates for us the analysis of the ethical facts in the phenomenological and experiential plane."[49] Phenomenology, Wojtyła argues, allows us to explore the dynamism of experiencing values and how they mold the human person. Mary Shivanandan has isolated Wojtyła's point: "Through the phenomenological experience we are able to discover how moral good and bad shape the experience of the person but we cannot define through the phenomenological method what makes an act of the person morally good or bad."[50]

In the closing pages of his thesis, Wojtyła asserts that it is the task of ontology and metaphysics to identify objectively what makes an act good or bad "in the light of an objective principle."[51] Though phenomenology has a vital role in identifying the values present in a given experience, it is secondary to ontology's role, which is to discover the objective moral value of human actions.[52] Thus, at the end of his first major study of phenomenology, Wojtyła shows himself favorable to its method but keenly aware of its limitations. He is fully aware of the need for ontology and metaphysics and he will reaffirm this at the very end of his life in his last published work.[53] As with his doctoral

47. Ibid., 206 (author's translation).

48. See ibid., 206–8. Wojtyła would explain the human person's experience of his own action further in *The Acting Person*.

49. Wojtyła, *Max Scheler*, 214 (author's translation).

50. Mary Shivanandan, *Crossing the Threshold of Love: A New Vision of Marriage in the Light of John Paul II's Anthropology* (Washington, D.C.: The Catholic University of America Press, 1999), 27.

51. Wojtyła, *Max Scheler*, 217 (author's translation).

52. See ibid., 218.

53. John Paul II, *Memory and Identity: Conversation at the Dawn of a Millenium* (New York: Rizzoli, 2005), 12.

dissertation on John of the Cross, he reveals an interest in the theological and philosophical system of Thomas Aquinas and in supplementing it with a system more concerned with experience.

WOJTYŁA'S EARLY TEACHINGS

The Lublin Lectures: The Relationship of Phenomenology and Ontology

By the fall of 1953, Wojtyła had completed the thesis and all requirements for receiving the university degree of docent. The Communist regime, however, began to forbid the granting of degrees by the Jagiellonian University in Cracow in early 1954, and months later it disbanded the faculty.[54] This formality notwithstanding, Wojtyła went on to teach at the Catholic University of Lublin. As we will see, in the early lectures and articles of this time, Wojtyła further clarifies his concerns about phenomenology, the use of its method, and the need for ontology in ethics.

Karol Wojtyła began teaching at the Catholic University of Lublin in the fall semester of 1954. That academic year he delivered the first of his Lublin lectures, "Ethical Act and Ethical Experience." The following year, he delivered another lecture entitled "Good and Value." Finally, in the 1956–57 academic year, he turned his attention to "The Problem of Norm and Happiness."[55] At the time, the university's department of philosophy was developing a new school of Thomism under the Dominican Mieczysław Albert Krapiec. Jarosław Kupczak nicely summarizes the principles of this new school of "Lublin Thomism": "First, all [the contributors to Lublin Thomism] were convinced that metaphysics had primacy of place in the realm of philosophy. Second, they emphasized the importance of anthropological reflection. Third, they strongly opposed irrational trends in con-

---

54. See Kupczak, *Destined for Liberty*, 23.

55. Though they bear the name "lectures," these lectures were more akin to courses. Thus the first lecture is fifty-three pages of published text. These three lectures, or courses, by Wojtyła were later published. See Karol Wojtyła, *Wykłady lubelskie* (Lublin: Wydawnictwo Towarzystwa Naukowego Katolickiego Uniwersytetu Lubelskiego, 1986). A German translation is available: *Erizehung zur Liebe* (Munchen: Wilhelm Heyne Verlag, 1981).

temporary philosophy. And fourth, they all felt a need for historical analysis of philosophical problems."[56] Wojtyła would find a sounding board in this school in which he could continue the development of his own vision of the human person, action, and morality.[57] It should be noted that as early as 1949, Wojtyła was already publishing articles in two Catholic journals: *Tygodnik Pwoszechny* and *Znak.*[58] He was not entirely unknown when he arrived at the university.

The first year's lecture, "Ethical Act and Experience," developed many of the same themes that Wojtyła had already established in his dissertation thesis. In the first part of the lecture, he summarizes Scheler's philosophy of ethics and then offers a critique similar to that found in his habilitation thesis. He goes further in the lecture, however, by incorporating modern psychology's empirical observation that human persons experience their own volition (hence we use words, "I want," "I should," or "I must").[59] Wojtyła believed that Scheler's system denies even the possibility of experiencing efficacy of causing one's actions, and he was somewhat stunned by that conclusion. Wojtyła argues, every person experiences himself or herself to be engaging the will in human action. This experience seems to be ignored by Scheler in what, according to Wojtyła, is an overly emotionalistic view of the human person.[60] This failure to recognize human causality is precisely why Scheler does not and is not able to explain what makes an act good or bad. Wojtyła is opposed to any ethic that is based on experience, subjectivity, or value.

In the conclusion of his first lecture at Lublin, Wojtyła notes the similarities between Aquinas's approach to the will and the approach found in contemporary psychology. Granted, there are differences in

---

56. Kupczak, *Destined for Liberty,* 28.

57. Kenneth Schmitz has suggested that Wojtyła's habilitation thesis and his Lublin lectures are important hermeneutical keys to understanding Wojtyła's later work. He expresses disappointment at their dismissal by most scholars of John Paul's work, especially in the English speaking world. Yet, this dismissal by English-speaking scholars is likely due to the fact that neither has been published in English. See Schmitz, *At the Center,* 41.

58. Most of these articles have been collected and translated into French. See Karol Wojtyła, *En esprit et en vérité: Recueilde texts 1949–1978,* trans. Gwendoline Jarczyk (Paris: Le Centurion, 1978).

59. See Karol Wojtyła, *Wykłady,* 35.

60. Ibid., 32.

suppositions between the two. Contemporary psychology studies the act of the will phenomenologically and empirically as an experiential living experience.[61] Thomas, on the other hand, is much more metaphysical when he discusses the will and human action.[62] He continues by outlining Aquinas's understanding of the interplay between reason and will in human action.[63] Specifically, while the will is attracted to the good as to its exercise (*quod exercitium*), it still requires the representations of specific goods by the intellect so as to be specified by those goods (*quod specificationem*).[64]

Wojtyła is quick to assert that Aquinas is not giving reason power over the will, as Kant had done. For Thomas, the command of reason alone would not be enough since the will is what rouses the reason to act (*quod exercitium*). The reason presents various goods to the will (as reason apprehends those goods). This, according to Wojtyła, is what permits the will to realize its own natural inclination to the good.[65] It is this relationship between reason and will that Wojtyła identifies as the proof that the human person always seeks ethical values, that is to say ethical fulfillment, in each human action, contrary to what Scheler thought.

Development from the Lublin Lectures to *Love and Responsibility*

From the time he began delivering his lectures in Lublin until he published *Love and Responsibility* in 1960, Wojtyła produced several articles that advance the project begun in the habilitation thesis and the Lublin lectures.[66] In all but one of these articles, Wojtyła summariz-

61. Ibid., 36.
62. Ibid.
63. See ibid., 64–65.
64. Wojtyła cites *ST* I-II, q. 1 and q. 10; q. 9, a. 3, ad 3 and a. 5.
65. Wojtyła, *Wykłady*, 66 (trans. McDonald).
66. These articles have been translated into English in Karol Wojtyła, *Person and Community: Selected Essays*, trans. Teresa Sandok (New York: Peter Lang, 1993). The following are the articles that I am concerned with here (all page numbers within this footnote refer to *Person and Community*). "The Problem of the Will in the Analysis of the Ethical Act," 3–22; "The Problem of the Separation of Experience from Act in Ethics in the Philosophy of Immanuel Kant and Max Scheler," 23–44; "In Search of the Basis of Perfectionism in Ethics," 45–56; "On the Directive or Subservient Role of Reason in

es his view of Scheler's philosophical system of an ethics based on value.[67] In each of these articles, Scheler's thought is presented in contradiction to Immanuel Kant's. Generally, he contrasts Immanuel Kant with Scheler, but at least once Scheler is presented on his own terms.[68] Only once does Wojtyła use the language of contemporary psychology to criticize Kant and Scheler, and that was in the first article published after he began his professorship at Lublin.[69] It reads as a summary of Wojtyła's first Lublin lecture, "Ethical Act and Experience." But in every one of these early articles following his habilitation thesis, Wojtyła judges Scheler's, Kant's, and, in one place, David Hume's various philosophies of ethics to be inadequate in the face of Aristotle's, and especially Aquinas's, philosophy of being.[70]

In these articles, Wojtyła identifies in Kant's system a separation between experience and reality in his famous phenomena-noumena distinction. Wojtyła writes: "Kant believes that empirical knowledge provides us with only a chaos of impressions, whereas it gives us no basis for such concepts as substance or cause. These are, in Kant's opinion, categories that derive solely from reason, and so they are completely *a priori*."[71] Anything we experience in human action is subject to this distinction for Kant, and thus in our empirical experience "we find no trace of ... free will in the human being."[72] For Kant, the *a priori* cate-

---

Ethics in the Philosophy of Thomas Aquinas, David Hume, and Immanuel Kant," 57–72; "On the Metaphysical and Phenomenological Basis of the Moral Norm in the Philosophy of Thomas Aquinas and Max Scheler," 73–94; "Human Nature as the Basis of Ethical Formation," 95–99.

67. See Wojtyła, "The Problem of the Will," 8–11; "The Problem of the Separation," 32–39; "In Search of the Basis," 51–54; "On the Metaphysical and Phenomenological Basis," 81–87.

68. See Wojtyła, "The Problem of the Will," 7–8; "The Problem of the Separation," 25–32; "In Search of the Basis," 49–51; "On the Directive or Subservient Role of Reason," 67–69.

69. See Wojtyła, "The Problem of the Will," 4–7, 12.

70. See Wojtyła, "The Problem of the Will," 14–21; "The Problem of the Separation," 24, 40–43; "In Search of the Basis," 46–49, 53–55; "On the Directive or Subservient Role of Reason," 58–61, 69–70; "On the Metaphysical and Phenomenological Basis," 74–81, 88–93. The sixth article, "Human Nature as the Basis of Ethical Formation" (94–99), is a short summation of a lecture Wojtyła delivered in February 1959 and is concerned mostly with Aquinas. It does not mention Scheler or Kant.

71. Wojtyła, "The Problem of the Separation," 26.

72. Ibid.

gories of theoretical reason are simply given and through them reason organizes all empirical data. Practical reason, too, has an *a priori* category—duty to law.[73]

Wojtyła isolates two problems in Kant's system. The first is that he "removed the very essence of ethical life from the realm of personal experience and transferred it to the noumenal, trans-empirical sphere."[74] Second, "he crystallized the whole ethical experience of the personal subject into a single psychological element: the feeling of respect for the law."[75]

Wojtyła's criticism of Scheler is now familiar. Scheler thought he was rejecting only Kant's exaltation of moral duty and denigration of experience. In fact, by emphasizing value as emotion, Wojtyła thinks "he did not manage effectively to extricate himself from Kant's assumptions, which entails the divorce of experience from the norm and the reduction of the whole of ethics to logic and psychology."[76] For Scheler, "ethical value manifests itself in the background, and the very act, the very realization, in which (if we go by experience) this value actually arises remains outside this experience of ethical value."[77] Wojtyła wonders outright whether there are, in fact, "remnants of Kantian noumenalism in his [Scheler's] ethics."[78]

Wojtyła employs the ethics of Aristotle, and moreover of Thomas, to refute the fallacies of Kant and Scheler. He claims numerous times that Aristotle's and Aquinas's view of human action is both dynamic and correct. He even says that "their view of the ethical act is the *only* proper and adequate description of ethical experience."[79] Just as in his lectures in Lublin, Wojtyła explains again the will's dual motion (*quod exercitium* and *quod specificationem*) in relationship to reason and the emotions in Thomas's work.[80]

The importance of the Aristotelian-Thomistic ontological distinction between act and potency cannot be underestimated in Wojtyła's reading of the Angelic Doctor. Wojtyła observes: "A conscious hu-

---

73. See ibid., 27.   74. Ibid., 31.
75. Ibid.   76. Ibid., 42.
77. Ibid.   78. Ibid.
79. Wojtyła, "The Problem of the Separation," 43 (emphasis added). Cf. ibid., 24; "The Problem of the Will," 16.
80. See Wojtyła, "The Problem of the Will," 14; "In Search of the Basis," 47.

man act is for St. Thomas not merely a stage upon which ethical experience is enacted. It is itself an ethical experience because it is an act of the will. An act of the will is for St. Thomas a passage from potency, since the will is a faculty (*potentia*) of the soul."[81] It is this dynamism in the human person—the movement from potency to act—that Wojtyła identifies as the purpose of human action.[82] This is why Wojtyła also insists, contrary to Scheler, that "human fulfillment is brought about by moral perfection."[83]

A series of short articles on "Elementary Ethics" published in the weekly Catholic journal, *Tygodnik Powszechny*, represent another step in Karol Wojtyła's intellectual project, which sought to reconcile ontology and phenomenology.[84] For example, in the second article of the series, "The Problem of Scientific Ethics," Wojtyła notes that it is only by "an honest reflection on the human being and on his finality" that a true scientific ethic, based on an authentic knowledge of good and evil, can be achieved.[85] Wojtyła goes on to say that revealed Christian principles do not contradict reason but must, nonetheless, be given a "character of science" by incorporating within them "all that human thought has gained or is gaining in the domain of ethics."[86] Wojtyła singles out Aquinas's incorporation of Aristotle as a particularly fine example of such a project.[87]

Wojtyła maintains the observation from his habilitation thesis that ethics is fundamentally a system of norms.[88] Still, this system of norms must be grounded in reality. In fact, the whole system must stem from the basic principle, "in all your activity be in accord with objective reality."[89]

This reality is made up, on the one hand, of the acting subject endowed with a rational nature, and on the other hand, it is made up of the whole series of objective beings which this subject encounters in his activity, each one of

---

81. Wojtyła, "The Problem of the Will," 20.
82. Wojtyła will clarify this point in *The Acting Person*.
83. Wojtyła, "In Search of the Basis," 47.
84. These articles were collected and published in 1979. See Karol Wojtyła, *Aby Chrystus się nami posługiwał* (Cracow: Znak, 1979). French translation: Wojtyła, *En esprit et en vérité*, 103–59.
85. Wojtyła, *En esprit et en vérité*, 108 (author's translation).
86. Ibid., 110 (author's translation).   87. Ibid.
88. See ibid., 111.   89. Ibid., 114 (author's translation).

which has its own nature. This fundamental principle, the principle of being in accord with reality, both objective and subjective reality, is the guarantee of realism in the whole of practical philosophy, and in particular ethics. Ethical norms are based in reality.[90]

Wojtyła reveals here a fundamental trust, contrary to many of his contemporaries, in the ability of reason to grasp reality. As a Thomist, he is a realist moral theologian, that is, a theologian who believes that the human mind can know objective reality.

Wojtyła's understanding of natural law (in his short essay "The Law of Nature") is understandably similar to that of Aquinas.[91] Natural law has for its purpose the perfection of man. Here we see Wojtyła beginning to incorporate in his published works the notion of human perfection. The essay, "Nature and Perfection," proves an excellent summary of the *prima secundae* of Thomas's *Summa Theologiae*, namely the treatise on happiness and human action.[92] Here Wojtyła provides a lucid and succinct analysis of the role of reason and activity in the perfection of being. He writes: "The being acts and becomes to a greater degree itself. In this process of the being's becoming more itself there is contained the fundamental good of every being."[93] The same process occurs in man through his activity. "Various kinds of goods become the end of his desires and activities in the measure that they contribute to man's perfection in one or another respect.... Among all these goods only the moral good perfects human nature itself: through the moral good a man becomes simply a better man."[94]

Wojtyła also clarifies the distinction between perfectionism and normitivism in ethics in a scholarly article written contemporaneously with his "Elementary Ethics" texts.[95] The perfectionist aspect of ethics "consists in emphasizing that the person who acts well is perfected morally.... [It] is not identical in ethics with the normative aspect, which concerns only the definition of what is morally good and

---

90. Ibid. (author's translation).

91. See ibid., 123–26.

92. See ibid., 116–19. I am grateful to Schmitz, *At the Center*, 55, for suggesting the similarities between these two articles and Thomas's thought.

93. Wojtyła, *En esprit et en vérité*, 117 (author's translation).

94. Ibid., 117–18 (author's translation).

95. See Wojtyła, "In Search of the Basis," 45–56.

evil."[96] All ethical norms should always concern perfection. "Ethics is always in some way about the human being.... Norms, therefore, do not have full meaning apart from the human being, who, by living according to them, simply lives in a good way and is perfected as a human being, or, in the opposite case, deteriorates and loses value."[97] In this essay, Wojtyła goes on to argue that the connection between norm and perfection is adequately understood *only* when the assumptions of ontology are accepted in ethics.

Wojtyła's ontological assumptions mean that, for him, any action in and of itself is not necessarily perfective and fulfilling. In the Thomistic philosophy of being "the good is that which constitutes the object of an aim, i.e., an end—the good is that which perfects a being."[98] Thus for Aquinas, ethics "is a science about human beings, who, in striving for various goods, must seek above all the good most suited to their rational nature."[99] Aquinas reinforces the strict connection between goodness and being. As Wojtyła reads Aquinas, the emphasis on moving from act to potency results from Aquinas's perspective that "the actualization of potency consists in the real coming-into-existence of something previously only existed in potency."[100] Therefore, "every perfection or good consists in existence."[101] Thus, a being is only truly good (*bonum simpliciter*) when it not only exists (*ens simpliciter*) but when it is brought to perfection with all the qualities necessary for fulfillment (*entia secundum quid*).[102]

Love and Responsibility

Even though in this early period Karol Wojtyła had clearly concluded that ontology (and the ontology of Aristotle and Thomas specifically) is necessary for ethics, he had certainly not given up his project of developing an understanding of the human person and human experience. His 1960 book, *Miłość i Odpowiedzialność* (*Love and Responsibility*), brings these moral categories—the person and experience—back to the fore of Wojtyła's thought as he further attempts to do that which he vowed to do when he was studying in Rome: to move be-

96. Ibid., 46.
97. Ibid.
98. Ibid., 47.
99. Ibid.
100. Ibid., 48.
101. Ibid.
102. See ibid.

yond Thomas to his own philosophy.[103] Rocco Buttiglione notes that in *Love and Responsibility* we find "Wojtyła's first positive attempt to build an ethic which would create an organic synthesis of ontology and phenomenology."[104]

Unlike the previous published works of Wojtyła considered thus far in this section, *Love and Responsibility* is concerned with the particular issues surrounding love and marriage rather than general moral theory. But this aspect of the book will be considered more thoroughly in chapter 4. Presently I want to follow Buttiglione's lead and show that *Love and Responsibility* marks the first positive step on the part of Wojtyła to synthesize ontology with an experience-based methodology (that is, phenomenology).

Wojtyła's opening chapter, an analysis on the verb "to use," begins with an important observation on the world. After noting that the world we live in is a world of many objects and the word "object" is the same as "entity," Wojtyła writes:

> This is not the proper meaning of the word, since an "object," strictly speaking, is something related to a "subject." A "subject" is also an "entity"—an entity which exists and acts in a certain way. It is then possible to say that the world in which we live is composed of many subjects. It would indeed be proper to speak of "subjects" before "objects." If the order has been reversed here, the intention was to put the emphasis right at the beginning of the book on its objectivism, its realism. For if we begin with a "subject," especially when that subject is man, it is easy to treat everything which is outside the subject, i.e., the whole world of objects, in a purely subjective way, to deal with it only as it enters into the consciousness of a subject, establishes itself and dwells in that consciousness. We must also, then, be clear right from the start that every subject also exists as an object, an objective "something" or "somebody."[105]

103. Wojtyła, *Love and Responsibility*. While studying at the Angelicum in 1947, Wojtyła wrote to a friend regarding Aquinas: "His entire philosophy is so marvelously beautiful, so delightful, and, at the same time, so uncomplicated. It seems that depth of thought does not require a profusion of words. It is even possible that the fewer words there are the deeper the meaning.... But I still have far to travel before I hit on my own philosophy." George Blazynski, *John Paul II: A Man from Krakow* (London: Weidenfeld and Nicolson, 1979), 57.

104. Buttiglione, *Karol Wojtyła*, 83.

105. Wojtyła, *Love and Responsibility*, 21.

In this opening paragraph, Wojtyła immediately sets himself against all modern philosophies that draw a hard distinction between subject and object.[106] Here, Wojtyła's appropriation of Thomas's philosophy of being serves him well as he seeks a delicate balance between a personalist ethic and a moral theory grounded in objective norms.

In his closing sentence, Wojtyła clarifies that some objects (which are also subjects) that occupy the world are not only "somethings" (as a philosophy of being tends to imagine them) but are occasionally "somebodies." This is the beginning of a philosophical method that is deeply personalist. While all things in the world of being can be categorized as members of genus and species, for man such a taxonomy is not entirely satisfactory. This is the case since

there is something more to him, a particular richness and perfection in the manner of his being, which can only be brought out by the use of the word "person." The most obvious and simplest reason for this is that man has the ability to reason, he is a rational being, which cannot be said of any other entity of the visible world, for in none of them do we find any trace of conceptual thinking.[107]

Therefore, Wojtyła believes that Boethius's definition of the person as an "individual substance of a rational nature" (*individua substantia rationalis naturae*) captures the distinctive character of the human person and differentiates him from "the whole world of objective entities."[108]

Wojtyła then turns to the experience of the human person by noting that the presence of reason means "the person as a subject is distinguished from even the most advanced animals by a specific inner self, an inner life, characteristic only of persons."[109] Cognition and desire come together in the human person in a spiritual manner, Wojtyła says, assisting in the formation of a "genuine interior life."[110] For him, the interior life is the spiritual life, and it is centered upon truth and goodness. The two central questions for man's the interior life are (1) the ultimate cause of everything and (2) the way to be good. The first of these concerns cognition. The second concerns desire.[111]

---

106. Buttiglione summarizes just a few of the positions to which Wojtyła's opening comment responds. See Buttiglione, *Karol Wojtyła*, 84–86.

107. Wojtyła, *Love and Responsibility*, 22.   108. Ibid.

109. Ibid.   110. Ibid.

111. Ibid., 23.

The interior life of the human person is primary for Wojtyła. He does not ignore the world of objects, but the person's contact with the world must go beyond the natural or physical contact he has through his body:

It is true that a human person's contact with the world begins on the "natural" and sensual plane, but it is given the form proper to man only in the sphere of his interior life. Here, too, a trait characteristic of the person becomes apparent: a man does not only intercept messages which reach him from the outside world and react to them in a spontaneous or even purely mechanical way, but in his whole relationship with his world, with reality, he strives to assert himself, his "I," and he must act thus, since the nature of his being demands it.[112]

Wojtyła goes on to say that the nature of man's being fundamentally differs from animals because of free will. Free will entails a self-determination flowing from choice.[113]

This insight provides Wojtyła with the foundation for the maxim that the person is *alteri incommunicabilis*. He is expanding on Aquinas on this point. The reason the person is incommunicable, Wojtyła says, "is not that a person is a unique and unrepeatable entity, for this can be said just as well of any other entity.... The incommunicable, the inalienable, in a person is intrinsic to that person's inner self, to the power of self-determination, free will. No one else can want for me."[114] This observation flows directly to Wojtyła's articulation of the personalistic norm: "Nobody can use a person as a means toward an end—no human being, not even God the Creator. On the part of God, indeed, it is totally out of the question, since, by giving man an intelligent and free nature, He has thereby ordained that each man alone will decide for himself the ends of his activity."[115]

Integrating the Kantian categorical imperative, now understood through the lens of a realist ontology and the biblical commandment of love of neighbor, Wojtyła offers a basic axiom that will guide his moral thought: "Whenever a person is the object of your activity, remember that you may not treat that person as only a means to an end, as an instrument, but must allow for the fact that he or she, too, has, or at least should have, distinct personal ends. This principle, thus formulated, lies at the basis of all the human freedoms, properly understood, and especially the freedom of conscience."[116] This is an important insight that provides a key to much of Wojtyła's moral writings, both before his election to the pontificate and after. He does not make forceful exhortations that seek to impose but rather to convert. Buttiglione observes:

Whereas the objectivist view, holding as it does to the idea of the primacy of objective truth, can go so far as wanting to impose it on those who do not recognize it, the personalistic view, which is rooted in a genuine philosophy of being, maintains that while the person indeed has the moral duty to adhere to the truth, he cannot be made to do so by overriding the choice of his freedom and his conscience.[117]

As we will see in chapter 4, for Wojtyła the ethical substance of love consists of the union of two wills, two freedoms, in the pursuit of a common good.

A PHILOSOPHY MATURES

The Shift after *Love and Responsibility*

Following the publication of *Love and Responsibility*, Wojtyła's articles bear a different tone concerning the ontology of Thomas than before. While maintaining a reverence for the Angelic Doctor, Wojtyła is more likely to point to what he perceives to be Aquinas's deficiencies in confronting the modern world.[118] For example, in an article published the year following *Love and Responsibility*, Wojtyła suggests what a "Thomistic personalism" might look like.[119] Wojtyła explains succinctly that Thomas's understanding of the person, developed in a different historical era, depends more on theology than phi-

---

116. Ibid., 28.

117. Buttiglione, *Karol Wojtyła*, 90–91.

118. This shift already began in *Love and Responsibility*. For example, while Wojtyła's analysis of sexual desire follows Aquinas's treatises on the concupiscible appetite and the passions (see *Love and Responsibility*, 147–54), he nonetheless believes Aquinas is mistaken to place chastity under the virtue of temperance rather than under charity (see *Love and Responsibility*, 166–74).

119. See Wojtyła, "Personalizm tomistyczny," *Znak* 13 (1961): 664–75; English translation: "Thomistic Personalism," 165–75.

losophy. Indeed, Thomas uses the word "person" only in treatises on the Trinity and the incarnation in the *Summa Theologiae*. Nevertheless, Wojtyła says, Aquinas's understanding of the person as an individual substance of a rational nature along with his understanding of the *compositum humanum* allows later Thomists to identify the concrete human individual as a person.[120]

Still, in what appears to be his first explicit critique of Aquinas, Wojtyła says that a Thomistic view of the human person is often too objectivistic and it allows no room for consciousness and self-consciousness. Wojtyła writes: "According to St. Thomas, consciousness and self-consciousness are something derivative, a kind of fruit of the rational nature that subsists in the person, a nature crystallized in a unitary rational and free being, and not something subsistent in themselves. If consciousness and self-consciousness characterize the person, then they do so only in the accidental order, as derived from the rational nature on the basis of which the person acts."[121] While Aquinas presents a full view of the objective activity of the human person, accomplished in the faculties of the soul, Wojtyła believes that in Aquinas's "objectivistic view of reality" there is no place to examine the subject.[122]

Four years later in "The Problem of Catholic Sexual Ethics," Wojtyła will openly declare that because modernity has withdrawn from teleology, an ethical theory based on the notion of final ends, such as the theories found in Aristotle and Thomas, is no longer tenable.[123] The contemporary shift was caused "on the one hand, by a new, more critical attitude toward metaphysics, and, on the other—and this, in my opinion, is the more important cause—by a more basic grasp of the moral facts themselves, by a reestablished contact with moral experience."[124] The dialogue with modernity requires moral theology likewise to move to the normative approach of ethics that characterizes this shift away from metaphysics and toward moral experience.

120. See Wojtyła, "Thomistic Personalism," 167–69.
121. Ibid., 170.
122. Ibid.
123. See Wojtyła, "The Problem of Catholic Sexual Ethics: Reflections and Postulates," 279–80. This is Theresa Sandok's English translation of Karol Wojtyła, "Zagadnienie katolickiej etyki seksualnej: Refleksje i postulaty," *Roczniki Filozoficzne* 13, no. 2 (1965): 5–25.
124. Ibid., 280.

Wojtyła does not argue for the abandonment of teleology in ethics. Yet, during this period of his life, Wojtyła is going to argue that ethics needs a more normative approach.[125] When moral theology assumes the methodology of normative science, it concerns properly the "norms of morality contained in divine revelation and proclaimed by the magisterium of the Church in solemn and ordinary teachings."[126] The task of the moral theologian, Wojtyła continues strikingly, "is to scientifically interpret these norms and, above all, to justify them in the light of reason and revelation. A justification of the norms of morality is more than interpretation of them.... To justify the norms of morality means to give reasons for their rightness."[127] Wojtyła calls this process a "justifying interpretation."[128] He goes on to say that the justification requires a complete vision of the reality of revelation in which the norms are situated.

Two years later, Wojtyła will argue that teleology is not enough to justify revealed norms.[129] Though scripture testifies to the possibility of knowing some revealed norms by reason alone, Wojtyła will by then argue that "such a purely rational interpretation of revealed norms involves a certain 'compression' and 'abbreviation' of them."[130] Only a full view of revelation can provide a substantial justification of Christian moral norms. Wojtyła writes: "Without theology, there is no way to give a fully adequate interpretation of moral norms or of the so-called theological virtues."[131] Here we see Wojtyła explicitly turning away from any sort of purely naturalistic or ontological morality to one dependent primarily, if not exclusively, on revealed principles. However, it was still necessary for him to present his understanding of the human person. He did this with the publication in 1969 of *Osoba i Czyn* (*Person and Act*), published in English in 1979 under the title *The Acting Person*.[132]

---

125. Ibid.   126. Ibid.
127. Ibid.   128. Ibid.
129. See Karol Wojtyła, "Etyka a teologia moralna," *Znak* 19 (1967): 1077–82; English translation: "Ethics and Moral Theology," 101–6.
130. Wojtyła, "Ethics and Moral Theology," 105.
131. Ibid.
132. Wojtyła, *The Acting Person*.

The Acting Person

In *The Acting Person* we see the full fruition of Karol Wojtyła's many years of labor of studying the phenomenology of Max Scheler and contrasting it with ontology. There is no doubt that Wojtyła intended this work to be a synthetic presentation of phenomenology and ontology. He writes in one of the two prefaces to the English edition: "The first question which was born in the mind of the present student of St. Thomas (certainly a very poor student) was the question: What is the relationship between action as interpreted by the traditional ethic *actus humanus*, and the action as an experience. This and other similar questions led me gradually to a more synthetic formulation in the present study *The Acting Person*."[133] Unlike his previous work, which seemed to portray phenomenology and ontology in opposition, *The Acting Person* is an explicit attempt to synthesize the two philosophies into a coherent whole that will compensate for the limitations of each.

Thus, we find our author less critical of Scheler in this work. In the preface, he writes: "Granted the author's acquaintance with traditional Aristotelian thought, it is however the work of Max Scheler that has been a major influence upon his reflection."[134] But this is not a reversal of his previous position on Scheler, for Wojtyła's appropriation of Scheler is a critical one. Though there is less explicit reference to Aquinas in *The Acting Person*, Wojtyła's criticisms of Scheler remain. The prime issue of the post-Cartesian era, according to Wojtyła, is the fracturing of the human person from reality, even the reality of what it means to be a person.[135]

He believes, therefore, that it is imperative for every philosopher to seek the unity of the human person. Modernity had been unsuccessful in that project thus far. "In fact, in spite of the fundamental Schelerian, and for that matter generally phenomenological, efforts conducive to the cognition of the complete man, this unity, its basis, as well as its primordial manifestation, are still missing in the present-day philosophical conception of man."[136] Wojtyła goes on to say that for Ar-

133. Ibid., xiii–xiv.   134. Ibid., viii.
135. See ibid., vii.   136. Ibid., viii.

istotle, "it was the very conception of the 'human act' which was seen as the manifestation of man's unity as well as its source."[137] Essentially, he reverses the traditional analysis of Aristotelian-Thomistic philosophy (or any philosophy of being, for that matter), which begins with metaphysical presuppositions about the agent before moving to action. Wojtyła begins with analyzing action in order to reveal the person who acts. But in doing so, he also reacts to the Cartesian subjectivism, which held that only in thinking does man know his existence. Wojtyła wants to say that it is in all sorts of actions that the person is revealed, both to the world and to himself.

Wojtyła maintains a Thomistic realist perspective by insisting, in opposition to Kant, that experience has a direct connection with objective reality. It need not pass through Kantian *a priori* categories.[138] Moreover, experience includes a basic understanding without first having to pass through consciousness.[139] Here we see Wojtyła purposefully separating himself from a facet of Edmund Husserl's phenomenology, which runs strikingly close to viewing consciousness as constitutive of both experience and reality.

For Wojtyła, cognition is distinct from consciousness. Experience and cognition stem from an "intrinsic cognitive dynamism."[140] Wojtyła's presentation of cognition appropriates the Aristotelian-Thomistic theory of apprehension. This cognitive dynamism consists in the "comprehension and knowledge [which] contribute in an intentional way to the formation of the object."[141] Whereas for the phenomenologists consciousness is always intentional—which is to say constituting the object to be experienced—for Wojtyła this process is left to cognition itself, which identifies and grasps the object experienced.[142] Consciousness, therefore, is not intentional for Wojtyła. On the contrary, consciousness is "the understanding of what has been constituted and comprehended" by cognition.[143] Wojtyła thus brings the role of consciousness, exalted by the phenomenologists and largely ignored by the scholastics, into alignment with the other faculties of the soul.

---

137. Ibid.
139. See ibid., 3–5.
141. Ibid.
142. Wojtyła explains this nicely in ibid., 303n16.
143. Ibid.

138. See ibid., 6–7.
140. Ibid., 32.

In this system, consciousness has two primary functions: mirroring and reflectivity. Consciousness "mirrors" objects that are apprehended through cognition. This mirroring is more than simple duplication. The consciousness "interiorizes in its own specific manner what it mirrors, thus encapsulating or capturing it in the person's ego."[144] In my view, this mirroring in Wojtyła's phenomenology does much of the same work that phantasms and abstraction do in the Aristotelian-Thomistic epistemology. The reflective aspects of consciousness concern our action. The reflexive function of consciousness allows one "to *experience* one's self as the subject of one's own acts and experiences."[145] This experience, Wojtyła says, is quite different from being the subject of action, on the one hand, and cognizing one's self as the subject of one's action, on the other. In some ways, being the subject of action is the result of our natural dynamisms.[146] To cognize one's self as a subject of action is to reflect upon one's self as an object of knowledge. Reflection, therefore, bears upon the *experience* of being a subject.

The reflective function of consciousness reveals two types of experiences. The experience of action (*agere*) and the experience of being acted upon (*pati*). "When acting I have the experience of myself as the agent responsible for this particular form of the dynamization of myself as the subject. When there is something happening to me, then the dynamism is imparted without the efficacious participation of my ego."[147] The possibility of experiencing these dynamisms, both acting and being acted upon, flows from our very being.[148] It is the potentialities of our nature, in the Aristotelian-Thomistic sense, that give rise to the various dynamisms we experience.[149]

It is our human nature that yields the cognitive dynamism that allows us to apprehend the world. Consciousness and its reflective function depends on objective reality: an objective world and an objective nature. Left to itself, Wojtyła argues, phenomenology would not be able to hold the two fundamental dynamisms (*agere* and *pati*) together.[150] Edmund Husserl's thinking evolved from understanding

144. Ibid., 35. Wojtyła also notes that emotions and passions can affect the consciousness, interfering with this mirroring function. See ibid., 50–56.

145. Ibid., 44.   146. Ibid., 44–45.

147. Ibid., 66.   148. See ibid., 72–73.

149. See ibid., 88–87.   150. See ibid., 80.

the self as stream of consciousness to understanding the self as a transcendental ego as experiencing that consciousness.[151] Still, Wojtyła was not satisfied with the notion of the transcendental ego as it still seemed to him to reify too absolutely the separation of self from experience. For Wojtyła, when the person acts, the ego "has the experience of its own efficacy in action." When it is acted upon, the ego "does not experience its own efficacy ... but it does have the experience of the inner identity of itself."[152] This experience of unity and identity is the experience of being, and it is more basic than a mere collection of experiences, as Husserl seemed to suggest.[153] The fact that nature grounds this experience eliminates, for Wojtyła, any hard separation between nature and person, even if both concepts must be suitably distinguished.[154]

In the middle section of *The Acting Person*, Wojtyła outlines his vision of human action and self-determination in an analysis of the transcendence of the human person.[155] The very act of willing some good means that the agent is himself also somehow determined. Self-determination is not willed but is the "return" from what is willed back on to the agent.[156] This is to say that action somehow determines and molds us. This idea classically belongs to Aristotelian-Thomistic virtue theory. This understanding of self-determination is protected from falling into relativism by Wojtyła's constant insistence that volition is guided by self-knowledge and a knowledge of reality, which is provided by cognition.[157] The role cognition plays also guarantees that both consciousness (which provides a subjective experience of action) and reality (objectivized by cognition) are always in relation.[158] By calling attention to the transcendence of the person, Wojtyła means only to assert that the person is more than volition, since no one action perfects the human person.[159]

---

151. For an analysis of this development, see David Woodruff Smith, "Mind and Body," in *The Cambridge Companion to Husserl*, ed. Barry Smith and David Woodruff Smith (Cambridge: Cambridge University Press, 1995), 323–93.

152. Ibid.   153. See ibid., 81, 91.

154. See ibid., 80–83.   155. See ibid., 105–16.

156. See ibid., 109.   157. See ibid., 113–14.

158. See ibid., 114. Truth is always the criterion for moral choice according to Wojtyła (See ibid., 135–43). The function of conscience is to provide the truth of the value of the goods presented by the cognition to the will (see ibid., 151–61).

159. See ibid., 111.

In Wojtyła's anthropology, integration complements transcendence. Since the human person experiences more than agency, transcendence "does not ... exhaust all the contents of the dynamic reality of the person."[160] The person is also acted upon. The person must integrate the experiences of being acted upon, especially when the person is acted upon by the natural dynamisms of the body or of the psyche.[161] As we will see in the next chapter, integration will play a significant role in Wojtyła's sexual ethics.

The Acting Person closes with a brief chapter on the idea of intersubjectivity and participation in community.[162] As Wojtyła sees it, participation in community avoids both individualism and collectivism, neither of which respect the value of the person upon which society and community must be based.[163] Kenneth Schmitz identifies Wojtyła's point: "Human relationships are possible only insofar as personal reality is present and operative in the relationships."[164]

Wojtyła is interested to show in this final chapter that action is always within a community of persons and so there is a "genuinely personalistic structure of human existence in a community."[165] The personalist value of action must always, therefore, be respected. For Wojtyła, this personalist value is the self-fulfilling aspect of action that he has spent the whole of the book developing.[166] In concluding, Wojtyła turns to the commandment of love and to the idea of neighbor, insisting that the interaction between persons is more than the interaction of a group of individuals within in community but rather an interaction of individuals identified in terms of love and neighborliness.[167]

---

160. Ibid., 189.

161. See ibid., 191–92, for an understanding of this integration; see 196–202 for psychosomatic unity and 220–31 on the *psyche* and the *soma*. Wojtyła also has something to say in this section of *The Acting Person* (203–6) on the relation of the body to action and as an expression of the person, but this will be more properly dealt with in the next chapter.

162. See ibid., 261. The English edition of *The Acting Person* provides two versions of this last chapter since Wojtyła was unable to review modifications made by the edition's editor, Anna-Teresa Tymieniecka. The literal translation of the final chapter as in the 1969 *Osoba i Czyn* can be found on 317–57.

163. See Wojtyła, *The Acting Person*, 271–76.

164. Schmitz, *At the Center*, 87.   165. Wojtyła, *The Acting Person*, 282.

166. See ibid., 270.   167. See ibid., 292–99.

In the short postscript to the book, the author acknowledges that the final chapter is a mere sketch of an ongoing project. Wojtyła admits to some limitations given the limited scope of his project which was "to extract from the experience of action everything that would shed some light on man as a person, that would help, so speak, to visualize the person."[168] His aim, he says, "was never to build a theory of the person as a being, to develop a metaphysical conception of man. Even so, the vision of man who manifests himself as the person in the way which we have tried to disclose in our analyses seems to confirm sufficiently that his ontic status does not exceed the limits of his contingency—that he is always a being."[169]

After The Acting Person

In December 1970, the Catholic University of Lublin held a conference to discuss *Osoba i Czyn*. The conference included nineteen commentators who were given permission by the author himself to discuss the issues freely and frankly. The basic critiques of the commentators were as follows:

That the book was neither a rounded anthropology nor a developed ethics of action; that it mingled without due care to discrimination the intersecting vocabularies of two philosophical languages, Thomist and phenomenological; that the author too readily equated Aristotle and Thomas on man in the phrase Aristotelian-Thomist, not giving full recognition to the differences between the historic Aristotle and the historic Thomas free from glosses; that the author was, despite the two sets of terminology, Aristotelian-Thomist and phenomenological, often more involved in "the etymological hermeneutics of words than in the hermeneutics of the realities signified" ... and, indeed, that the author was not himself clear or consistent in his efforts to integrate the two main philosophical terminologies of the book.[170]

The difficulties with *Osoba i Czyn* would become more pronounced with the problematic English translation. The connection with Thomism is no longer readily apparent, since traditional Aristotelian-Thomistic language is paraphrased or transliterated rather than translated.[171]

---

168. Ibid., 300.   169. Ibid.
170. Williams, *The Mind of John Paul II*, 196.
171. Oceans of ink have been poured on the English translation of *Osoba i Czyn*. Most often *The Acting Person* was criticized for not rendering faithfully Wojtyła's Polish (and when he uses it, Latin) into English. Wojtyła's English collaborator, Anna-Teresa

Given Wojtyła's phenomenological style, it is difficult to follow his line of argument. Perhaps most frustrating of all is that he never actually explains what good and evil are, and how properly to evaluate particular human actions as good and evil.[172] At the conclusion of his introductory remarks, Wojtyła surprisingly renounced "any attempt at combining these two philosophies [Thomism and phenomenology].... Such a melding is completely out of the question."[173] He may, however, be offered some latitude in this final criticism because his scope was more anthropological and epistemological rather than ethical and moral.

Much of Wojtyła's writing after *The Acting Person* sought to further the project of the final chapter of that book: a phenomenological description of the human person within community and as the subject of his own self-determination.[174] For our present purposes, three articles merit special mention. Wojtyła published two articles in 1969 following upon the publication of *Osoba i Czyn*: "The Problem of Experience in Ethics" and "The Problem of the Theory of Morality."[175]

Tymieniecka, often bears much of the brunt of this criticism, and is charged with overly paraphrasing key concepts in Wojtyła's original. As a result, the intellectual ancestry of Wojtyła's terms is not readily apparent to the English reader. For more details on this dispute, as well as a bibliography of articles and sources on the translation, see Kupzcak, *Destined*, 67n55; Schmitz, *At the Center*, 58–60; Williams, *The Mind of John Paul II*, 197–218, 378–81.

172. See Williams, *The Mind of John Paul II*, 203.

173. Williams, *The Mind of John Paul II*, 196. This is a surprising comment, as Wojtyła seemingly claims otherwise in prefaces to the English edition, as I reported above. See ibid., 378n23: "*Analecta Cracoviensia*, Vols. 5 and 6 (1973–74), pp. 49–272, with resumés in French, pp. 256–77; the quoted renunciation of a melding is on p. 249." Williams's summary appears on 196–97.

174. See the following articles by Karol Wojtyła: "Uczestnictwo czy alienacja," *Summarium* 7, no. 27 (1978): 7–16 (this paper was written in 1975); English translation: "Participation or Alienation?," in *Person and Community*, 197–207. "Podmiotowość i to, co nieredukowalne' w człowieku," *Ethos* 1, nos. 2–3 (1988): 21–28 (this paper was written in 1975); English translation: "Subjectivity and the Irreducible in the Human Being," in *Person and Community*, 209–17. "Osoba: Podmiot i wspólnota," *Roczniki Filozoficzne* 24, no. 2 (1976): 5–39; English translation: "The Person: Subject and Community," in *Person and Community*, 219–61. "The Intentional Act and the Human Act, that is, Act and Experience," *Analecta Husserliana* 5 (1976): 269–80. "Problem konstytuowania się kultury poprzez ludzką "praxis," *Ethos* 2, no. 8 (1989): 38–49 (this paper was written in 1977); English translation: "The Problem of the Constitution of Culture Through Human Praxis," in *Person and Community*, 263–75.

175. See Karol Wojtyła, "Problem doświadczenia w etyce," *Roczniki Filozoficzne* 17, no. 2 (1969): 5–24; English translation: Karol Wojtyła, "The Problem of Experience in

In the first of these articles, he recounts much of the argument from *Osoba i Czyn* on the nature of experience in the life of the human person. He goes on to argue that morality is grounded in the experience of self-determination, that is, the subjective experience of our action and its effects on our person.

In the second article, however, Wojtyła moves beyond experience itself in an attempt to identify the source of moral norms for good and bad actions. He locates the validity of these norms in the experience of happiness and guilt.[176] We experience happiness when our actions are good and make us good. We experience guilt or shame when they are evil, and make us evil. The articulation of moral norms are beyond experience and result from teleology, but without considering the experience of the human person, Wojtyła fears that teleology becomes too objectivist.[177]

Finally, in the 1974 article, "The Personal Structure of Self-Determination," Wojtyła makes direct reference to the December 1970 colloquium on *Osoba i Czyn* discussed above.[178] He notes that the commentators at the Catholic University of Lublin were most concerned with his appropriation of Thomism in the book. In this short article, Wojtyła asserts that his phenomenology remains connected to Aquinas's ontology.[179] He suggests that Aquinas would agree with the concept of action affecting not only the object but also the subject.[180] As will be shown in my discussion in chapter 4 of Aquinas's notion of virtue, I would have to agree.

Ethics," in *Person and Community*, 107–27. Karol Wojtyła, "Problem teorii moralnosci," in *W nurcie zagadnień posoborowych*, ed. Bohdan Bejze (Warszawa: Sióstr Loretanek, 1969), 3:217–49; English translation: Karol Wojtyła, "The Problem of the Theory of Morality," in *Person and Community*, 129–61.

176. See Wojtyła, "The Problem of the Theory of Morality," 137–39.

177. See ibid., 147–50.

178. See Karol Wojtyła, "The Personal Structure of Self-Determination," 187. This is the Theresa Sandok's English translation of Karol Wojtyła, "Osobowa struktura samostanowienia," *Roczniki Filozoficzne* 29, no. 2 (1981): 5–12 (this article was written in 1957).

179. See Wojtyła, "The Personal Structure," 190.

180. See ibid., 191.

CONCLUSION

As we have seen, Karol Wojtyła cannot be understood properly if he is seen as a philosopher concerned only with the philosophical categories of the human person and human experience. Indeed, he understands the modern situation and the alienation of persons from their selves. For that reason, he argues repeatedly that Christian ethics must restore a sense of personal experience in its justification of moral norms.

However, to assume that for this reason Wojtyła abandons ontology would be to misinterpret grossly his published writings. Though he had clearly begun to emphasize the phenomenological method and the human person in his writings immediately before his election to the pontificate, he always felt the need to refer to the basic necessity of Thomas's philosophical system. He knew that without a realist ethic grounded in a philosophy of being, we cannot properly evaluate good and evil.

He would hold this position throughout his life. In his last published work, *Memory and Identity: Conversations at the Dawn of a Millennium,* Pope John Paul II wrote:

> If we wish to speak rationally about good and evil, we have to return to Saint Thomas Aquinas, that is, to the philosophy of being. With the phenomenological method, for example, we can study experiences of morality, religion, or simply what it is to be human, and draw from them a significant enrichment of our knowledge. Yet we must not forget that all these analyses implicitly presuppose the reality of the Absolute Being and also the reality of being human, that is, being a creature. If we do not set out from such "realist" presuppositions, we end up in a vacuum.[181]

It is a different question, beyond the scope of this study, whether Wojtyła was ultimately successful in incorporating Thomism into phenomenology, or whether the two schools can, in fact, be reconciled. However, what this final quote reveals is Wojtyła's conviction that the realist philosophical presuppositions include not only a philosophy of being but also an acknowledgement of a divine creator.

It is this conclusion that propels Wojtyła's moral work. For Wo-

---

181. John Paul II, *Memory and Identity,* 12.

jtyła, the task of the moral theologian is to justify moral norms revealed in scripture and taught by the magisterium. The theologian is to use whatever philosophical and theological tools are at his disposal to present a "justifying interpretation" of these norms. The church's teaching on sexual morality provided an apt opportunity for Wojtyła to put his theory into practice. In the next two chapters, we will survey Wojtyła's grand defense of the church's norms on love and marriage, culminating in his notion of the spousal meaning of the body.

4

Karol Wojtyła's Ethics of Sexuality

Now that we have discussed the context in which Karol Wojtyła began his scholarly and pastoral work, this chapter advances the line of argument by introducing Wojtyła's ethics of sexuality. Over the course of this chapter, it will become clear that Wojtyła's sexual ethics are a practical application of his general moral theory. He clearly believed that the church's difficulty in defending Christian sexuality was due not only to cultural trends but also to what might be described as the rigid objectivistic method of the manualist tradition.

This chapter is intended to show the intellectual lineage in Karol Wojtyła's pre-pontificate publications for the concept of spousal meaning of the body in his papal *Theology of the Body* catecheses. *Love and Responsibility*, *The Acting Person*, and articles written from 1953 to 1978 all demonstrate, as we will see, that the relevant themes present in *Theology of the Body* more or less occupied the mind of Wojtyła from his earliest published writings on love, sexuality, and marriage.

To that end, we will explore the following particular themes: the personalistic norm, the sexual instinct, the gift of man and woman to each other (and the related impact on parenthood), the role of the conjugal act in this gift, and the body as a means of self-communication. What we will see is that in his ethics of sexuality, Wojtyła continues his larger project of balancing personalism with its attendant focus on the human person with a realist Thomistic ontology and its focus on human nature.

We will first survey Wojtyła's thought on sexuality and marriage. We will then consider his thought on the human body in these early works of his career. Finally, we will explore Wojtyła's vigorous defense and exegesis of Pope Paul VI's encyclical on birth control, *Humanae Vitae*. This final section will bring this study to the year of Wojtyła's election to the papacy, the tenth anniversary of *Humanae Vitae*.

SEXUALITY AND MARRIAGE

The Personalistic Norm and Sexual Instinct

In chapter 3, I mentioned Wojtyła's use of the personalistic norm only briefly. This norm can be found in the opening pages of his 1960 book, *Love and Responsibility*. The human person's rich inner life, which stems from the gift of reason and free will, distinguishes him from all other animals.[1] This is the foundation for Wojtyła's insistence that each person is incommunicable (*alteri incommunicabilis*). It is not that the person is simply ontologically unrepeatable; this is true of every being. Rather, he is referring to "the incommunicable, the inalienable, in a person [that] is intrinsic to that person's inner self, to the power of self-determination, free will. No one else can want for me."[2] In one place, Wojtyła formulates the personalistic norm in a way that is reminiscent of Kant: "Whenever a person is the object of your activity, remember that you may not treat that person as only the means to an end, as an instrument, but must allow for the fact that he or she, too, has, or at least should have, distinct personal ends."[3] He explains further:

The personalist norm rests on the unique interior life of the human person: A person must not be *merely* the means to an end for another person. This

1. See Wojtyła, *Love and Responsibility*, 22, 24. George Williams argues that this reveals an Aristotelian-Thomistic connotation in Wojtyła's notion of person (see Williams, *The Mind of John Paul II*, 152).

2. Wojtyła, *Love and Responsibility*, 24.

3. Ibid., 27. Wojtyła also asserts that not even God can use a person as a means to an end. He writes, "On the part of God, indeed, it is totally out of the question, since, by giving man an intelligent and free nature, he has thereby ordained that each man alone

is precluded by the very nature of personhood, by what any person is. For a person is a thinking subject, and capable of making decisions: these, most notably, are the attributes we find in the inner self of a person. This being so, every person is by nature capable of determining his or her aims. Anyone who treats a person as the means to an end does violence to the very essence of the other, to what constitutes its natural right.[4]

In his excellent summary of Pope John Paul's vision of love and marriage, Walter Schu provides a necessary conclusion for this norm in the context of love. "A young man may come to fall deeply in love with a young woman and reach the conclusion that he can never be happy without her. But if he truly loves her, he realizes that he must respect who she is as a person, what she desires in life. He cannot treat her simply as a means to his own happiness. He cannot compel her to love him or to marry him."[5] Between persons, love must replace use. Love is the positive reformulation of the personalistic norm: "the person is a good towards which the only proper and adequate attitude is love."[6]

According to Wojtyła, love begins between persons when both accept a common end. "If this happens," he writes, "a special bond is established between me and this other person: the bond of a *common good* and of a common aim. This special bond does not mean

---

will decide for himself the ends of his activity, and not be a blind tool of someone else's ends. Therefore, if God intends to direct man towards certain goals, he allows him to begin to know these goals, so that he may make them his own and strive towards them independently. In this amongst other things resides the most profound logic of revelation: God allows man to learn His supernatural ends, but the decision to strive towards an end, the choice of course, is left to man's free will. God does not redeem man against his will" (ibid.). This understanding of the verb *to use* (as a means to an end) is only the first sense that Wojtyła describes. He goes on to describe as second sense of the verb in which something is used (i.e., enjoyed) for the purposes of pleasure (ibid., 31). In this sense, too, if a person of the opposite sex is used only to obtain pleasure and avoid pain, "then that person will become only the means to an end," which reverts to *use* in the first sense (ibid., 33).

4. Ibid., 26–27.

5. Walter J. Schu, *The Splendor of Love: John Paul II's Vision of Marriage and Family* (New Hope, Ky.: New Hope Publications, 2002), 57.

6. Wojtyła, *Love and Responsibility*, 41. Wojtyła also compares Christ's commandment to love with the personalistic norm, in which he states that only the personalistic norm can justify such a commandment (ibid., 31). He will return to this theme five years later in an article on Catholic sexual ethics. See Wojtyła, "The Problem of Catholic Sexual Ethics," 279–99.

merely that we both seek the common good, it also unites the persons involved internally, and so constitutes the essential core round which any love must grow."[7] For Wojtyła, the pursuit of a common good puts two people on the equal footing necessary to build a relationship. This, of course, is identical with the Aristotelian-Thomistic view of friendship which will be explored in chapter 7.

The pursuit of a good, however, does not guarantee that a particular person is capable of love or that a relationship is grounded in love. This instinct to the good is present even in animals.[8] "Man's capacity for love depends on his willingness consciously to seek a good together with others, and to subordinate himself to that good for the sake of others, or to others for the sake of that good. *Love is exclusively the portion of human persons.*"[9] This is an important element in Wojtyła's sexual anthropology. For Wojtyła, marriage is the realm in which the principle of seeking the common good is applied to the relationship of a man and a woman. But not every common pursuit can be the foundation for an authentic and lasting love.

Pursuing certain ends prevents a man and a woman from using each other, even in the relationship of marriage. There are certain common pursuits, certain common ends, that guarantee authentic love. The ends that a couple pursue should exclude the possibility of selfishness. "Such an end, where marriage is concerned, is procreation, the future generation, a family, and, at the same time, the continual ripening of the relationship between two people, in all the areas of activity which conjugal life includes. These objective purposes of marriage create in principle the possibility of love and exclude the possibility of treating a person as a means to an end and as an object for use."[10] Though Wojtyła articulates these conclusions in personalist terms, in chapter 8 we will see that they are essentially the same conclusions reached by Aquinas—one of many correlations between the thought of John Paul and the Angelic Doctor.

The drive of man toward woman and woman toward man in the pursuit of a common good and the relationship of love manifests itself in what Wojtyła refers to as the "sexual urge."[11] The sexual urge

---

7. Wojtyła, *Love and Responsibility*, 28.   8. See ibid., 29.
9. Ibid.   10. Ibid., 30.
11. See ibid., 45.

in man is more than instinct. Since man has reason and free will, he is capable of self-determination. Therefore *"man is by nature capable of rising above instinct in his actions."*[12] When he speaks of the sexual urge, Wojtyła is speaking less of an innate instinct than "a certain orientation in man's life implicit in his very nature."[13] This is a key conclusion for what Wojtyła will later refer to as the "spousal meaning of the body."

The sexual urge and the directionality which it entails is rooted in the division of humanity into two sexes: male and female. The person recognizes specific values in a person of the opposite sex. Wojtyła says that "we may therefore speak of sexual values which are connected with the psychological and physiological structure of man and woman."[14] The sexual urge, therefore, compels the person not to the other sex abstractly but to a particular human being. "It is because it is directed towards a particular human being that the sexual urge can provide the framework within which, and the basis on which, the possibility of love arises."[15] Since a person cannot be used, even for self-completion, love of the other must transcend this urge.[16]

The sexual urge is not properly satisfied in the absence of another person (as in the case of the solitary sin of masturbation) or in violence to another person (as in the case of sexual assault).[17] For Wojtyła, the sexual urge is only rightly understood in the light of the existential significance of the complementarity of two sexes and the orientation of the two to each other. Indeed, the reason sexual relations are often difficult "is certainly the fact that in his mind, in his reason, man often accords the sexual urge a merely biological significance and does not fully realize its true, existential significance."[18]

---

12. Ibid., 46.

13. Ibid. 14. Ibid., 48.

15. Ibid., 49.

16. See ibid., 50.

17. See ibid., 52.

18. Ibid., 53. The theme of the existential significance of sexuality reappears during Wojtyła's pontificate. It is explicitly mentioned in his 1981 apostolic exhortation on the family in the modern world: "Sexuality, by means of which man and woman give themselves to one another through the acts which are proper and exclusive to spouses, is not something simply biological, but concerns the innermost being of the human person as such. It is realized in a truly human way only if it is an integral part of the love by which a man and woman commit themselves totally to one another until death." John Paul II, *Familiaris Consortio*, Apostolic Exhortation of November 22, 1981, par. 11 [hereafter, *FC*]; the official Latin text is available in *AAS* 74 (1982): 81–191.

Unless man and woman consciously recognize the importance of love as the goal (*telos*) of both the sexual urge and that urge's natural disposition to procreation, their love will not grow according to the natural and metaphysical order.[19] It will rather denigrate into selfishness which uses the other as a means to personal satisfaction.

Love and the Gift of Self

Wojtyła begins his metaphysical analysis of love with the observation that "*love is always a mutual relationship between persons.*"[20] Since this relationship is directed toward the good, Wojtyła suggests that some metaphysical distinctions on the nature of love are necessary before exploring the psycho-physiological or bio-psychological aspects of love. He writes of love in three aspects: love as attraction, love as desire, and love as goodwill. Although these elements are accessible in love between various persons, our author limits himself to the love between man and woman.

As the name implies, love as attraction is the recognition of another person as a good. The sexual urge catalyzes attraction as a natural force which is raised to the consciousness of one person for another person.[21] Attraction entails seeing the other person not only as a good, but as a certain good to be possessed.[22] This attraction need not be merely erotic or sexual. Alluding to the Aristotelian-Thomistic theory of cognition and discernment of goods, Wojtyła notes that attraction is more than mere cognition; it involves the emotions and the will.[23]

The richness of a person's emotional life lies precisely in the dynamic at work in attraction. Specifically, a person finds himself, more or less, attracted to various goods of the other person and not just one aspect of this person. Hence, "*Attraction is of the essence of love and in some sense is indeed love, although love is not merely attraction.*"[24] In fact, attraction can be entangled by emotive reactions such that values may be projected on to the person who is the object of our attraction. These projected values may not in fact actually exist in this

---

19. See Wojtyła, *Love and Responsibility*, 53.
20. Ibid., 73.   21. See ibid., 74.
22. See ibid., 75.   23. See ibid.
24. Ibid., 76.

person.[25] This is why Wojtyła will insist that attraction be measured by the truth of the other person's reality, not merely by the genuineness of emotion for the other.[26]

Love as desire differs from the love of attraction. Love of attraction identifies goods as such. Love as desire includes love as attraction but is directed toward the lover's own completion. This distinction is especially manifest in the relationship between the sexes:

> The human person is a limited being, not self sufficient and therefore—putting it in the most objective way—needs other beings. Realization of the limitation and insufficiency of the human being is the starting point for an understanding of man's relation to God.... A human being, a human person, is either man or woman. Sex is also a limitation, an imbalance. A man therefore needs a woman, so to say, to complete his own being, and woman needs man in the same way. This objective ontological need makes itself felt through the sexual urge.[27]

Unlike love as attraction, love as desire "originates in a need and aims at finding a good which it lacks."[28] Wojtyła goes on to note that love as desire is different from sensual desire itself. Sensual desire recognizes deficiency and seeks to remedy that lack. In the case of persons, this can devolve into the use of another for one's own satisfaction (which is contrary to the personalistic norm). Love as desire, on the other hand, moves beyond mere sensuality to the whole person, to whom the lover says "I want you because you are good for me."[29]

Wojtyła continues his analysis, finally, with the love of goodwill. He writes: "Love between man and woman would be evil, or at least incomplete, if it went no farther than love as desire. For love as desire is not the whole essence of love between persons. It is not enough to long for a person as a good for oneself, one must also, and above all, long for that person's good."[30] Wojtyła says that the love of goodwill is completely selfless. It has no ulterior motive, and as a complete act of selflessness, perfects both the lover and the beloved.[31] The love between man and woman necessarily includes the love of desire, but for Wojtyła this love must eventually move to a love of goodwill. Ev-

---

25. See ibid., 78.
27. Ibid., 80–81.
29. Ibid.
31. See ibid.

26. See ibid.
28. Ibid., 81.
30. Ibid., 83.

ery personal love should develop into a love of goodwill and this, he says, is especially true in marriage. It is important to note that love of goodwill does not compete with desire but purifies it.[32]

Authentic love demands reciprocity for its durability and security. It is only when love is returned that two persons become an acting "we." Love exists not only in a subject but also between two subjects. Wojtyła writes: "The fact is that a person who desires another as a good desires above all that person's love in return for his or her own love, desires that is to say another person above all as co-creator of love, and not merely as the object of appetite."[33] The very interpersonal character of love means for Wojtyła that to seek reciprocity is not, in fact, an act of selfishness since reciprocity is in the very nature of love.

This reciprocity must be tied to an enduring good. Reciprocity may not be self-interested or pragmatic; it cannot tend simply toward mutual sensual pleasure. Wojtyła astutely notes:

A woman and a man can afford each other pleasure of a sexual nature, can be for each other the source of various enjoyment. However, mere pleasure, mere sensual enjoyment is not a good which binds and unites people for long.... A woman and a man, if their "mutual love" depends merely on pleasure or self-interest, will be tied to each other just as long as they remain a source of pleasure or profit for each other. The moment this comes to an end, the real reason for their "love" will also end, the illusion of reciprocity will burst like a bubble.[34]

For Wojtyła, love must be understood not only according to its psychological aspects but also according to its ethical import. Ignoring the importance and dignity of the human person results in a less than stable form of reciprocity.[35] Ultimately, couples need to move from an emotive love of one another (what Wojtyła calls "sympathy") to true friendship in which each can say to the other, "I desire your good as if it were my own good."[36] To this point, Wojtyła has followed the Aristotelian-Thomistic understanding of love exclusively.

But he will move beyond the obvious Thomistic view when he begins to connect love to the incommunicability of the person. When

---

32. See ibid., 84.   33. Ibid., 85.
34. Ibid., 87.   35. See ibid., 88.
36. Ibid., 90.

a couple has moved into the "love of goodwill," charged by a love of desire and friendship, they find themselves at the threshold of betrothed love which is distinct from all other forms of love. Betrothed love exists when a man and a woman become gift to one another. This does not necessarily contradict Wojtyła's earlier claim that the person is incommunicable. He confirms that "the very nature of the person is incompatible with such a surrender."[37] However, he goes on to say, "what is impossible and illegitimate in the natural order and in a physical sense, can come about in the order of love and in a moral sense. In this sense, one person can give himself or herself, can surrender entirely to another, whether to a human person or to God."[38]

The gospels, in fact, call for such a self-gift—see, for example, Matthew 10:39. For Wojtyła, it is an uncompromising gift of love in which the inalienable "I," incommunicable and non-transferable, is surrendered to the other.[39] This self-gift is more than sexual. A sexual offering without the gift of self is vacuous and utilitarian, whereas an authentic sexual offering, as we will see, becomes a means of expression of the true gift of self.[40]

The Nature of Marriage

In Wojtyła's sexual ethics, the mutual self-gift of a man and woman, along with the sexual relationship it entails, is only properly ordered within the institution of marriage.[41] Marriage is not only an intrapersonal reality but a social institution. As an institution, marriage protects not only the persons involved from becoming objects one to the other, but it also justifies the consequence of their relationship: their progeny.[42] Society is itself dependent upon marriage for its existence and, therefore, it is interested (or at least should be interested) in protecting the family.[43] The institution of marriage legitimizes and protects the unique love between a man and a woman. As their

---

37. Ibid., 96.
38. Ibid.
39. See ibid., 96. He argues on this same page that such an act cannot be taken. It is, rather, an act of the whole person, determined to dispose himself in love in a particular way to another.

40. See ibid., 99.   41. See ibid., 211.
42. See ibid., 216.   43. See ibid., 217.

love matures through courtship, it "must also gain acceptance by other people."[44] This is why marriage is necessary, "to signify the maturing of the union between a man and a woman, to testify that there is a love on which a lasting union and community can be based."[45]

Wojtyła recalls the order of nature and its relationship to reason. Reason allows each person to understand his dependence on the creator for his existence. The justification of marriage is that "it creates an objective framework for a lasting union of persons."[46] This justification is not only for the union itself, but also for each sexual act between the spouses. "Every such act must have its own internal justification, for unless justice is done there can be no question of a union of persons."[47] Each sexual act between the spouses cannot violate his or her personal dignity; it cannot violate the personalistic norm.

Wojtyła insists that in the sexual act the order of nature and the personal order meet. By the order of nature, Wojtyła means more than simply a biological order. For him, "the order of nature is above all that of existence and procreation."[48] In the order of nature, the primary purpose of the sexual act is procreation. "Looked at objectively the marital relationship is therefore not just a union of persons, a reciprocal relationship between a man and a woman, but is essentially a union of persons affected by the possibility of procreation."[49] The two orders cannot be separated since they depend on each other.[50] This conclusion is reminiscent of Wojtyła's earlier analysis of the sexual urge and the difference between animals and human persons.

The correct attitude to procreation is a condition of the realization of love. In the animal world there is only reproduction, which is achieved by way of instinct. In that world there are no persons, hence there is no personalistic norm to proclaim the principle of love. In the world of persons on the other hand instinct alone decides nothing, and the sexual urge passes, so to speak, through the gates of the consciousness and the will, thus furnishing not merely the conditions of fertility but also the raw material of love.[51]

Following this passage, Wojtyła goes on to say that consciousness and free choice are the foundation of love and procreation between per-

44. Ibid., 219.
46. Ibid., 225.
48. Ibid., 226.
50. See ibid.

45. Ibid., 220.
47. Ibid.
49. Ibid.
51. Ibid.

sons. Spurred on by the sexual urge, when a couple chooses to marry they are also choosing the possibility of procreation.

Parenthood, therefore, is intricately bound to the unique love that exists between a man and woman. Becoming a parent, Wojtyła says, is "not merely a biological fact but also a personal significance.... It has profound effects upon the 'interior' of a person.... For human parenthood implies the whole process of conscious and voluntary choice connected with marriage and with marital intercourse in particular."[52] The full value of sexual relations between the two persons is not fully guaranteed, Wojtyła argues, unless there is conscious acceptance of the possibility of procreation. The two orders, the personal order and the order of nature, thus reaffirm each other.[53] In fact, when the possibility of procreation is excluded from the marital relationship, the "danger arises that objectively speaking there will be nothing left except 'utilization for pleasure,' of which the object will be the person."[54]

Wojtyła further clarifies the relationship between the order of nature and the order of the person in his 1965 article, "The Problem of Catholic Sexual Ethics: Reflections and Postulates."[55] In chapter 3, I noted that this article was among those written after *Love and Responsibility* that called for a more normative approach to Catholic sexual ethics without abandoning a teleological view.[56] Admittedly, the task of incorporating the personalistic norm is more difficult in the realm of sexual ethics as it is very easy only to consider the biological or physiological aspects of sex itself.[57] The fact that the sexual urge is rooted in human nature is itself not remarkable for Wojtyła. What he does find significant, however, is the fact that "human nature actually

---

52. Ibid., 227.   53. See ibid.
54. Ibid., 228.
55. See Wojtyła, "The Problem of Catholic Sexual Ethics," 279–99.
56. Recall that for Wojtyła, "*Moral theology is a science that, in the light of revelation, makes justified statements concerning the moral value, or goodness or badness, of human actions*" ("The Problem of Catholic Sexual Ethics," 279). His project is to justify revealed norms using whatever philosophical system (or combination of different systems) serves that end. As the previous chapter showed, over the course of his early career, he became increasingly interested in presenting a phenomenological and personalist justification combined with an ontological realism.
57. See ibid., 284.

exists always in a concrete *suppositum* that is a person. Consequently, the sexual properties and the sexual urge in humans are always and in every instance attributes of a person."[58] It is the person who acts sexually, not the human nature that acts. Wojtyła reaffirms here that marriage is the consequence of this fact.[59]

Revelation reveals that marriage "is not just a sexual union of a man and a woman in which these persons use the urge to realize the ends of marriage, particularly its primary end—procreation. Marriage is also a genuine union of persons, a union that, according to revelation, bears the mark of indissolubility. This union arises from a mutual choice, and, according to Catholic teaching, the interpersonal relationship expressed and realized in this choice ought to be true love."[60] Again, in this article, Wojtyła affirms the need for free and conscious acceptance of both the natural purpose of the sexual urge (procreation) and the personal purpose of the sexual urge (love). This acceptance must be "ongoing, systematic, [and] habitual."[61] Accepting one without the other renders the sexual relationship loveless, as it thereby denigrates into mutual use of one person by the other.[62]

In chapter 3, I noted that for Wojtyła norms are vacuous if they are not grounded in an ontological view of reality. This remains true for sexual norms as well. Without a view of the human person as a substance (as is the case in the Kantian or Schelerian anthropology), Wojtyła says, the person becomes merely a "'source' of experiences, and not really even a source, but just a background."[63] Ontologically speaking, "every being—or, more precisely, the essence, or nature, of every being—can serve as the basis of an ethical norm and of the positing of norms. A being's essence, or nature, determines how free we are to behave with respect to that being, how we should or ought to behave when that being is an object of our activity."[64]

Recalling that the human person is a highly organized being with reason, Wojtyła understands "all norms, including the personalistic norm, as based on the essences, or natures, of beings, are expressions of the order that governs the world. This order is intelligi-

58. Ibid.
60. Ibid.
62. See ibid., 290.
64. Ibid., 287.

59. See ibid., 285.
61. Ibid.
63. Ibid., 286

ble to reason, to the person."[65] Wojtyła makes appropriate use here of the scholastic adage that the person participates in the eternal law and is conscious of a natural law (*particeps legis aeternae et conscia legis naturae*).[66] The person is able to perceive the normative force of his human nature, and therefore the natural purpose of the sexual urge: procreation.

But this natural purpose is necessarily supplemented by the personalistic norm as the sexual urge requires a person of the opposite sex for its fulfillment. Wojtyła writes:

> The necessity of combining these two norms into one—which involves, of course, the necessity of properly situating the norm that emerges from an understanding of the purpose of the sexual urge within the objective content of the personalistic norm—is indispensible for preserving the order of nature.... In integral theological (as well as philosophical) reasoning in Catholic sexual ethics, the aims of nature must always come together with the value of the person.[67]

Thus, it is easy to understand why in *Love and Responsibility* Wojtyła insisted that "the proper way for a person to deal with the sexual urge is, on the one hand, consciously to make use of it for its natural purposes, and on the other to resist it, when it threatens to degrade the relationship between two persons to a level lower than that of love, lower than the level on which the value of the person is affirmed in a union with a truly personal character."[68] Far from subordinating the person to nature, Wojtyła argues that instead this challenge assists the person in adapting himself to the dynamic of nature. Nature, he insists, is not conquered by violating its laws.[69]

Any Catholic presentation that fails to incorporate the personalistic norm runs the risk of slipping into a physicalism, or what Wojtyła calls "naturalism" which would reduce ethical discourse to mere biological and physiological requirements.[70] Finally, incorporating the personalistic norm in our understanding of the sexual urge requires that the person be considered in any explanation of the traditional ends of marriage. The primary end of marriage, procreation,

---

65. Ibid.
66. See ibid. Cf. *ST* I-II, q. 91, a. 2.
67. Wojtyła, *Love and Responsibility*, 288.
68. Ibid., 229.
69. See ibid.
70. Wojtyła, "The Problem of Catholic Sexual Ethics," 290.

is the natural purpose of the sexual urge. Likewise, the two second-ary ends—the mutual aid of the spouses and the remedy of concupis-cence—cannot be understood by a wholly naturalistic or excessively juridical interpretation.[71] Rather, the gospel's command of love must "shape the realization of all the ends of marriage—and it must do so according to that objective hierarchy over which the Church keeps watch."[72]

Before turning to the particular difficulty of contraception in the early thought of Karol Wojtyła, and particularly to his early exegesis

71. In this article, Wojtyła notes that the hierarchy of these ends has not changed and that the church has resoundly rejected any attempt to do so. Attempting to place the mutual aid of the spouses above procreation, he writes, "would not be in keeping with the plan of the Creator either in the order of nature and in the light of reason or in the order of grace and in the light of revelation" (see ibid., 291). This article, howev-er, was published the same year that *Gaudium et Spes* was promulgated by the Second Vatican Council. I noted in chapter 2 of this study that some have argued that the coun-cil intended to overturn the church's traditional language of the hierarchy of the ends of marriage. Wojtyła's statement here cannot in any way be read as a response to such arguments. Indeed, in this article Wojtyła gives no evidence of having read *Gaudium et Spes*. However, as pope, he suggested that the hierarchy was reaffirmed by both *Gaudi-um et Spes* and *Humanae Vitae*, but that it was deepened by referring it to conjugal love. See *TOB*, no. 127. In 1979, the Congregation for the Doctrine of the Faith issued a noti-fication against the book, *Human Sexuality: A Study Commissioned by the Catholic Theo-logical Society of America*, edited by Anthony Kosnik for, among other things, claiming that Vatican II had relativized the ends of marriage. See Congregation for the Docrine of the Faith, "Observations about '*Human Sexuality: A Study Commissioned by the Catholic Theological Society of America*,'" *Origins* (December 7, 1979): 1–2.

72. Wojtyła, "The Problem of Catholic Sexual Ethics," 291. Wojtyła goes on to dis-pute any theologian who would translate *mutuum adiutorium* as "love" and thereby es-tablish a competition between procreation, love, and a remedy of concupiscence (see ibid.). One wonders if he has in mind here the attempt made by Herbert Doms in the 1930s, which was discussed in the first chapter of this study. Interestingly, in his 1969 article, "The Teaching of *Humanae Vitae* on Love," he seems to reverse this position by referring to *mutuum adiutorium* explicitly as "conjugal love," while maintaining his insistence that the ends of marriage cannot be placed in opposition to each other: "I should also point out at the very outset that neither the conciliar constitution nor the encyclical anywhere explicitly mentions the traditional view concerning the hierarchy of the ends of marriage. In that view, the primacy of *procreatio* (procreation) over *mu-tuum adiutorium* (which today we would call conjugal love) was always emphatically stressed. Neither the conciliar constitution nor the encyclical appeals to such a hierar-chy of the ends of marriage, *much less places these ends in opposition to one another*." Wo-jtyła, "The Teaching of *Humanae Vitae* on Love," in *Person and Community*, 302; origi-nally published as Karol Wojtyła, "Nauka encykliki 'Humanae vitae' o miłości," *Analecta Cracoviensia* 1 (1969): 341–56.

of *Humanae Vitae*, it will be necessary to explore the role the human body plays in Wojtyła's early works on sexual ethics.

THE BODY IN WOJTYŁA'S EARLY WORKS

The Religious Experience of Purity

One of the earliest published articles by Karol Wojtyła discussing the importance of the body appeared in 1953: "The Religious Experience of Purity."[73] It has been suggested recently that this article "contains the nucleus of *The Theology of the Body*, which our author would develop thirty years later."[74] It also shares many themes in common with *Love and Responsibility*. The article begins by noting that Christianity is fundamentally a personal religion in which a personal God reveals his interior life to man and engages man in a personal relationship with himself.[75] According to Wojtyła, only the personalistic view of religion can clarify the virtue of purity.[76]

Just as God is a person who is inviolable and incommunicable, so also is the human person. The locus of the connection between religion and purity is this notion of the person:

Anybody can easily confirm the fact that man experiences in a profound way the fundamental inviolability of his person. He is conscious of belonging to himself, of possessing his own interior world of things, of plans, of decisions and of feelings, a whole interior life of which he is the owner and to which nobody else has access. He experiences his own personal individuality, autonomy, and unique character, and all come together in the profound consciousness of the inviolability of the person. For this reason, we can speak of

73. See Karol Wojtyła, "Religijne przeżywanie czystości," *Tygodnik Poweszechny* 6 (1953): 1–12; French translation: "L'expérience religieuse de la pureté," in Wojtyła, *En Esprit et en Vérité: Recueil de texts 1949–1978*, trans. Gwendoline Jarczyk (Paris: La Centurion, 1980), 46–55; Spanish translation: "La experiencia religiosa de la pureza," in Wojtyła, *El don del amor: escritos sobre la familia*, 2nd ed., trans. Antonio Esquivias and Rafael Mora (Madrid: Ediciones Palabra, 2001), 69–81. I am grateful to a recent doctoral dissertation by Ailbe Michael O'Reilly for suggesting this article's importance in understanding the importance of the body in Wojtyła's later works. See "Conjugal Chastity in Pope Wojtyła" (PhD diss., Pontifical University of St. Thomas, 2007).

74. O'Reilly, "Conjugal Chastity," 195.

75. See Wojtyła, "La experiencia religiosa de la pureza," 69–70.

76. See ibid., 70.

the *virginity* of the human person. Man is a *virgin* by nature, in the sense that he possesses his own interior world, his own interior life which he himself shapes and which he alone is responsible.[77]

In this passage, there is an initial but expanded formulation of what Wojtyła eventually refers to as the personalistic norm. Each person has his own rich interior world which is unique and unrepeatable. No other person has a right to access that world or is even able to access it.[78]

In his doctoral study, Ailbe Michael O'Reilly notes that for Wojtyła man's interior life is inviolable not because he is man but because he is a person.[79] According to Wojtyła, the uniqueness of the human person's inviolability (*vis-à-vis* that of God and of the angels) is located, at least in part, in the body: "The totality of the human person also includes the body, where, on the one hand, the acts of the interior life have their origin and, on the other hand, find expression and resonance. Because of this strict union between the human body and the person, the natural virginity of man, his claim to this natural inviolability that he experiences interiorly, finds a particular mode of expression."[80] It is clear that for Wojtyła the interior life of the person begins with the body and is expressed by the body, but he does not here explain exactly how the interior life originates in the body.

The import of this observation for Wojtyła's later work in sexual ethics is clear. This union between the body and the soul means "that physical relations between man and woman acquire an interior motivation. The unity that exists between the human person and his body implies that physical (sexual) relations should always be an expression of that which is truly interior, of that which is personal."[81] The relationship between the person and the body in sex must be one of gift.[82] When the two, person and body, are not aligned in self-gift, that is to say, when the offering of one's person is not the interior motivation of sex, the other person experiences the worst violence done

77. Ibid., 76 (author's translation).
78. Wojtyła goes on to say, however, that God, as the "Infinite Person," has the right to possess the content of a lesser person's inviolable world (ibid., 77).
79. See O'Reilly, "Conjugal Chastity," 197.
80. Wojtyła, "La experiencia religiosa de la pureza," 76 (author's translation).
81. O'Reilly, "Conjugal Chastity," 197.
82. See Wojtyła, "La experiencia religiosa de la pureza," 77.

to "the entire human person, and not only on his body."[83] This, Wojtyła says, suggests that "man experiences in his body the fundamental right to virginity and to personal inviolability."[84]

The remainder of the article is devoted, then, to the conclusion that the self-gift of man and woman to each other in marriage necessarily includes the gift of their bodies to each other. He goes on to contrast this with the gift of physical virginity that the religious person makes to God as personal gift of self. It is precisely the gift of the body in conjugal consummation that is not accessible to the person giving himself over to God in vowed celibacy or consecrated virginity.[85] The point here is that though a human person is inviolable in his interior life and in his body, he is able to communicate his interior life through the body to another. In that unique betrothed relationship between a man and a woman, a person "can allow another person to enter into his or her most physically intimate sphere. Through personal consent, there can exist total personal self-giving in the sphere of human sexuality."[86] In *Theology of the Body*, Wojtyła will expand on the corporal aspects of the self-gift between husband and wife, especially those aspects that can illegitimate or obscure the meaning communicated by the body.

The Body in *Love and Responsibility*

Wojtyła's understanding of the body is a key theme in *Love and Responsibility*. The sexual urge discussed above, which provides the initial foundation upon which love is based, finds its origin in the body as a certain natural instinct.[87] The instinct is directed toward particular persons of the opposite sex; it is a primal recognition of the complementarity of the sexes.[88] This orientation toward the other is the foundation for what Wojtyła calls "love as attraction."[89] However, for love to be authentic, it has to move beyond simple attraction to the body and find its true *terminus* in love of the person.[90] For love of at-

83. Ibid. (author's translation). 84. Ibid. (author's translation).
85. See ibid., 77–81. 86. O'Reilly, "Conjugal Chastity," 199.
87. See Wojtyła, *Love and Responsibilty*, 45–51.
88. Wojtyła notes that attraction to persons of the same sex is the homosexual deviation (see ibid., 49). Further, see ibid., 106–7.
89. Ibid., 74. 90. See ibid., 123.

traction to grow into that betrothed love in which the gift of self in sexual relations is authentically manifest, it has to be integrated by the virtue of chastity. Wojtyła notes that man is blessed above all of material creation with the faculties of reason and free will. The integration of attraction into reason and freedom is the work of chastity, and this is a difficult work.

Wotyla's reliance on Aristotelian-Thomistic anthropology is evident in his explanation of sensuality as sensory experience and impression. He writes: "Any immediate contact between a woman and a man is always the occasion of a sensory experience for both of them. Each of them is a 'body,' [and] is therefore exposed to the senses of the other and creates some impression."[91] Wojtyła further states that sensuality is directed to the enjoyment of the other as body. It is a "'consumer orientation'—it is directed primarily and immediately towards a 'body': it touches the person only indirectly, and tends to avoid direct contact."[92] When sensuality and love as attraction are allowed to progress unchecked and in a disintegrated fashion, a person is not loved but only objectified. True beauty is, for Wojtyła, an object of "contemplative cognition" which, although apprehended sensually, is integrated by the virtue of chastity.[93]

Love will not mature if it "is dominated by an ambition to possess, or more specifically by concupiscence born of sensual reactions, even if these are accompanied by intense emotion."[94] Love "*develops on the basis of the totally committed and fully responsible attitude of a person to a person, erotic experiences are born spontaneously from sensual and emotional reactions.*"[95] Chastity is the ability to transcend the spontaneity of erotic reactions that develops in the attraction of man and woman to each other. The virtue of chastity takes hold of these spontaneous reactions so that the other person may not be used merely for the enjoyment of his or her body but actually loved for who he or she is. Far from suppressing the value of the body, Wojtyła writes, the "essence of chastity consists in quickness to affirm the value of the person in every situation, and in raising to the personal level all reactions to the value of 'the body and sex.'"[96]

91. Ibid., 104.
92. Ibid., 105.
93. See ibid., 105–6.
94. Ibid., 145.
95. Ibid.
96. Ibid., 171.

All of this means that for Wojtyła the gift of self has deeper origins than sexual differentiation and the sexual urge. The innate desire of each person to offer himself is first of all found in the spiritual and metaphysical nature of the person created in the image of a God who is love.[97] Only in betrothed love, the love between husband and wife, is the innate desire for the other fulfilled in this world. In betrothed love, neither the man nor the woman wishes to possess the other. Rather, in betrothed love "the lover 'goes outside' the self to find a fuller existence in another."[98]

This mutual self-surrender is an interior movement of the will. In this 1960 book, then, Wojtyła continues the theme from his 1953 article, "The Religious Experience of Purity." What is happening in the body, sensually and emotionally, should correspond to the interior movements of the person. "The sensual and emotional experiences which are so vividly present in the consciousness form only the outward expression and also the outward gauge of what is happening, or most certainly should be happening, deep inside the persons involved."[99] Sexual intercourse finds its proper place within marriage, the institution that guarantees the mutual self-surrender of spouses, because it serves as an expression of betrothed love.[100]

In 1960, Wojtyła reaffirmed his conclusions from 1953: that love involves the body but must transcend its mere sensual urges, integrate it, and grow into self-gift; and that sexual intercourse is morally legitimate only when it serves as an expression in marriage of the betrothed love of the spouses. He also reaffirmed the incommunicability of the person and the possibility of radical self-communication in sexual intercourse. Still, he had yet to concern himself with the possibilities of miscommunication, so to speak, with the sexual act and the elements that might hamper or alter exactly what is communicated in the conjugal act.

The Body in *The Acting Person*

In chapter 3, I briefly described Wojtyła's understanding of human action and dynamism in *The Acting Person*.[101] For Wojtyła, the human

---

97. See ibid., 249–55.
98. Ibid., 126.
99. Ibid.
100. See ibid., 126–27.
101. See pages 117–22.

person has two basic experiences: action (*agere*) and passion or being acted upon (*pati*).[102] When the person is acting, he acts intentionally and his act moves outward, but when he is acted upon he is the subjective ego receiving the action.[103] When a person is acted upon, various potentialities (which Wojtyła refers to as "dynamisms") are actualized and the person finds himself in one way or another in a state of becoming.[104]

Chapter 3 also showed that for Wojtyła personal agency also invokes a certain dynamism in the subject. Wojtyła writes, "When acting I have the experience of myself as the agent responsible for this particular form of the dynamization of myself as the subject."[105] What is willed by the agent is reflected back on the agent so that what is willed affects not only an object exterior to the person but also affects the person himself.[106] In this second half of the book, we will see that this is precisely Aquinas's theory regarding action, *habitus*, and virtue. For Wojtyła, self-determination is the unique hallmark of the transcendence of the human person. The human person is determined not only by the purposes of nature but also by his own free actions.[107]

Nevertheless, in the latter chapters of *The Acting Person*, Wojtyła goes on to write: "The notion of the 'transcendence of the person in action' does not, however, exhaust all the contents of the dynamic reality of the person."[108] The self-determination that characterizes transcendence requires, according to Wojtyła, that the person have both self-possession and self-governance. This is the case since "only the things that are man's actual possessions can be determined by him; they can be determined only by the one who actually possesses them."[109]

When Wojtyła speaks of the *pati* of the human person, of things happening to him, he is referring not only to action upon the person from the outside but also things that happen within man. These dynamisms are intrinsically bound up with the body. Jaroslaw Kupczak explains:

102. See Wojtyła, *The Acting Person*, 66, 71.
103. See ibid., 71.
104. For Wojtyła's understanding of dynamism as potentiality, see ibid., 86–87. For the actualization of dynamism as "becoming" see ibid., 96.
105. Ibid., 66.   106. See ibid., 105, 109.
107. See ibid., 105–16.   108. Ibid., 189.
109. Ibid., 106.

Wojtyła's theory of transcendence led him into a dialogue with the nine-teenth- and twentieth-century German philosophy of human freedom. He was aware, however, that a large part of this philosophy treats the human person from a dualistic and idealistic perspective. What is required, there-fore, for a complete and successful explication of his theory of the acting per-son is an account of the human body and an explanation of the role that hu-man biology and physiology play in *actus humanus*.[110]

In *Love and Responsibility*, Wojtyła introduced the notion of integra-tion of the body with human action and love, in *The Acting Person* he further explains the dynamisms present in the body and their neces-sary integration in action.

Wojtyła identifies two dynamisms that are beyond the control of the human person: the somato-vegetative dynamism and the psy-cho-emotive dynamism.[111] The somatic refers directly to the human body. The dynamisms of the *soma*, Wojtyła writes, are primarily reac-tive to stimuli.[112] The somatic dynamisms have two aspects because the body has two aspects: an interiority and an exteriority. When he writes of the exteriority of the body, Wojtyła means that "the body is material, it is a visible reality, which is accessible to sense; the access to it is first of all from the 'outside.'"[113] This exteriority serves a two-fold purpose. On the one hand, the image of the body contributes to the self-image of the person, but the body is also the means of the person's expression and communication. Wojtyła writes: "It is gener-ally recognized that the human body is in its visible dynamism the territory where, or in a way even the medium whereby, the person ex-presses himself."[114] This will become the overriding theme of *Theolo-gy of the Body*.

Any description of the body, or of the somatic dynamisms, is not exhausted by the material appearance of the body. The body also has its own interior dynamisms which constitute what we call the "hu-man organism" according to Wojtyła.[115] He chooses this specifical-ly biological language because the interiority of the body refers to "the system and the joint functioning of all the bodily organs."[116] The

---

110. Kupczak, *Destined for Liberty*, 132.
111. See Wojtyła, *The Acting Person*, 88–90.
112. See ibid., 200.   113. Ibid.
114. Ibid., 204.   115. See ibid., 201.
116. Ibid., 201; see 207.

functioning of this interior somatic dynamism is largely beyond the person's consciousness unless the organism of the body breaks down in some way or another.[117]

Wojtyła incorporates an understanding of nature in his treatise on the acting person:

> Because of his body, the man-person genuinely belongs to nature. This implies, on the one hand, his similarity to the rest of nature and, on the other, his partaking in the whole of the external conditions of existence that we also refer to as "nature".... The close connection existing between the human organism and nature, so far as nature constitutes the set of conditions of existence and life, helps us to define the somatic dynamism of man. It seems that this dynamism may be contained and expressed in the concept of reactivity and also by the attribute *reactive*.... The human body has the ability to react like other bodies in nature.[118]

The body is reactive both to other bodies and to the transcendent volition of the person (that is, in the willed movements and expressions of the body). It is also, in a certain sense, reactive to natural instincts, which concern more than just the *soma* but also the *psyche*.[119]

The words *psyche* or *psychical*, according to Wojtyła, "apply to the whole range of manifestations of the integral human life that are not in themselves bodily or material, but at the same time show some dependence on the body, some somatic conditioning."[120] The *psyche* for Wojtyła is not the equivalent of the soul. The *psyche*, although immaterial, is dependent on the *soma*. For Wojtyła, *psyche* is the conscious awareness of emotion in the human person.[121]

Wojtyła is very concerned to explain the *soma*'s (and by necessary connection, the *psyche*'s) reaction to the natural instincts of self-preservation and reproduction. He writes that these "instinctive reactions are indicative of a dynamization that is appropriate to nature itself, while instinct with its inherent drive tells of nature's dynamic orientation in a definite direction."[122] Self-preservation and reproduction have a specific "emotive urge" in the *psyche*.[123] They are of particular import because they concern the human being as a whole. The

117. See ibid., 89–90.
118. Ibid., 208.
119. See ibid., 15.
120. Ibid., 201.
121. See ibid., 222–23.
122. Ibid., 215.
123. See ibid., 216.

instinct for self-preservation, for example, governs and motivates all aspects of the somatic-psychical life of the human person—feelings of hunger, urges to eat, to defend oneself, as well as somatic functions that enable these, such as eating, digestion, and bodily movement.[124]

Wojtyła claims that the instinct for reproduction lies deeper than the *soma*, as even a brief analysis of sexuality reveals.[125] Recalling his conclusions from *Love and Responsibility*, our author reaffirms that "the drive of sex, which relies on the momentous division of mankind into male and female individuals, stems from the somatic ground and also penetrates deeply into the psyche and its emotivity, thereby affecting even man's spiritual life."[126] He goes on to say that while the instinct for self-preservation arises from a basic desire to maintain personal preservation, the sexual instinct develops from "the desire for sharing with another human being."[127] Simultaneously, the sexual instinct is the source of reproduction and a drive to the other.[128] The sexual urge is powerful. However, it is not beyond our control. Wojtyła writes:

> The reproductive, procreative trait is most clearly manifested at the somatic level of the instinctual dynamism, the dynamism manifesting itself in strictly defined reactions of the body that to some extent automatically or spontaneously *happen* in man. In spite of all their specificity and automatism, however, these reactions remain sufficiently conscious to be controllable by man. Essentially, this control consists in the adaptation of the body's instinctual dynamism of sex to its proper end.[129]

Here, Wojtyła claims that like other dynamisms, the sexual instinct must be directed by the person to its proper end. The sexual dynamism presents itself to the consciousness by passing through the *psyche* so that the person is aware of the sexual instincts within. Controlling this sexual instinct is implicit in the larger process of the integration of the human person.

The integration of the person is, according to Wojtyła, necessary for the transcendence of the human person. In fact, without integration, the self-determination that characterizes transcendence is

---

124. See ibid., 217–18.
126. Ibid.
128. See ibid.

125. See ibid., 218.
127. Ibid.
129. Ibid.

not possible.[130] In Wojtyła's system, integration is synonymous with self-possession and self-governance.[131] Integration's *sine qua non* relationship to transcendence is clear: one cannot determine that which one neither possesses nor governs. Integration is the "subordination of the subjective ego to the transcendent ego—that is to say, the synthesis of efficacy and subjectiveness."[132] The self-governance and self-possession that characterizes integration primarily regards the dynamisms of the *psyche* and the *soma*, and brings those dynamisms into line with human action.[133] The importance of integration in Wojtyła's thought cannot be overstated.[134]

Finally, failure to achieve self-governance and self-possession generally leads to the disintegration of the person. Although personal disintegration may manifest itself in varying degrees of intensity, a disintegrated person "appears to be completely destitute of the specifically 'personal' structures manifested in and with the action."[135] The action of the disintegrated person is vacuous. Disintegration is the "'insubordinativeness' or 'unpossessibility' of the subjective ego."[136] This insubordination of the psychosomatic element of the person impinges upon his cognitive function, making him unable to make the correct associations and this, in turn, leads to an inability to make correct choices.[137]

130. See ibid., 106, 189–90, 220.   131. See ibid., 189–99.
132. Ibid., 196.   133. See ibid., 198–99.
134. Kenneth Schmitz notes that in Wojtyła's thought, "The structure of the human person … is such that the individual human being is called to integrate his or her complex dynamisms and to redeem the promise of what is both a received human nature and a unique personal project. The realization of the value of one's person comes through actions that are responsible, that are self-determined and yet responsive to the enlarged sense of reality in which both the subjective and objective sides of human existence are in play" (Schmitz, *At the Center of the Human Drama*, 89).
135. Wojtyła, *The Acting Person*, 193–94.
136. Ibid., 195.
137. Ibid. Here we see another indication of Wojtyła's attempt to bring Thomas Aquinas and Max Scheler into dialogue: "Regarding Aquinas, Wojtyła shares with him the conviction that emotions should be subjected to the will guided by the intellect and that this subjection is the function primarily of proficiencies and virtues. Scheler, on the other hand, helped Wojtyła to appreciate the richness of human emotions and their role in the process of value cognition. Balancing the Thomistic emphasis on human rationality and Scheler's emphasis on human affectivity, Wojtyła, in *The Acting Person*, presents a convincing understanding of soma and psyche" (Kupczak, *Destined for Liberty*, 140).

The understanding of self-possession, self-governance, and self-determination is important for the purposes of this study. It is now apparent that according to Wojtyła persons can act without first integrating their nature. This is to say that persons can, and do, act in contradiction to the purposes of nature, but such action is disintegrated. Moreover, in an article following upon the publication of the original Polish edition of *The Acting Person*, Wojtyła notes that "both self-possession and self-governance imply a special disposition to make a 'gift of oneself,' this is a 'disinterested' gift. And only if one governs oneself can one make a gift of oneself."[138] In my exegesis (below) of the spousal meaning of the body in the *Theology of the Body* catecheses, this theme will be repeated and amplified: the authentic spousal meaning of the body can be subverted by a disintegrated use of sexuality.

KAROL WOJTYŁA'S ANALYSIS OF *HUMANAE VITAE*

With his publication of *Love and Responsibility* in 1960, Karol Wojtyła inserted himself into the debate on love and sexuality. Pope Paul VI was aware of the book and had appointed Wojtyła to the papal commission on birth control before its final meeting in 1966, but he could not attend the meeting because he was denied a passport by the Polish Communist government.[139] Throughout the 1960s, he was aware of the difficulties in the church's understanding of sexual ethics.[140] In 1966, he established his own diocesan commission in Cracow to study the question of birth control and conjugal love. When that commission completed its work, a memorandum entitled "The Foundations of the Church's Doctrine on the Principles of Conjugal Love" was sent to Paul VI by Wojtyła in February 1968.[141]

138. Karol Wojtyła, "The Personal Structure of Self-Determination," 194; in the original Polish: "Osobowa struktura samostanowienia," *Roczniki Filozoficzne* 29, no. 2 (1981): 5–12.

139. See Weigel, *Witness to Hope*, 207. Weigel reports this based on a personal conversation with John Paul II. This account contradicts Tad Szulc's claim that Wojtyła had purposely missed the meeting. See Szulc, *Pope John Paul II*, 254.

140. One example of this is his 1965 article, "The Problem of Catholic Sexual Ethics."

141. Karol Wojtyła et al., "Les fondements de la doctrine de l'Eglise concernant les principles de la vie conjugale," *Analecta Cracoviensia* I (1969): 194–230; English transla-

As early as January 1969, almost six months after the publication of *Humanae Vitae*, Wojtyła began publishing a series of articles that both defended and explained the document's teaching.[142] On the occasion of the tenth anniversary of *Humanae Vitae*, the same year he would be elected to the papacy, Wojtyła published two important articles on the document.[143] These were his last published works on the issue of conjugal love before beginning the *Theology of the Body* catecheses.[144]

In his exegesis of *Humanae Vitae*, we see two basic elements of Wojtyła's anthropology and ethics come together in practical conclusions on love and marriage. First, conjugal love and responsible

---

tion: "The Foundations of the Church's Doctrine Concerning the Principles of Conjugal Life: A Memorandum Composed by a Group of Moral Theologians from Krakow," trans. Thérèse Scarpelli Cory, *Nova et Vetera* 10 (2012): 321–59.

142. See Karol Wojtyła, "La verità dell'Enciclica «*Humanae Vitae*»," *L'Osservatore Romano* (January 5, 1969): 1–2; Spanish translation: "La verdad de la Encíclica *Humanae Vitae*," in Wojtyła, *El don del amor*, 185–99; French translation: "*Réflexions sur la vérité de l'encyclique «Humanae Vitae»*," in *Pour relire «Humanae Vitae»: Déclarationes épiscopales du monde entire*, ed. Philippe Delhaye, Jan Grootaers, and Gustave Thils (Gembloux: Éditions Duculot, 1970), 185–93. See Wojtyła, "Wprowadzenie do Encykliki «*Humanae Vitae*»," *Notificationes e curia Metropolitana Cracoviensi* 1–4 (1969): 1–3; Spanish translation: "Introducción a la Encíclica *Humanae Vitae*," in *El don del amor*, 201–4. See also Wojtyła, "The Teaching of the Encyclical *Humanae Vitae* on Love," in *Person and Community*, 301–14; Spanish Translation: Karol Wojtyła, "La enseñanza sobre el amor de la encíclica *Humanae Vitae*," in Wojtyła, *El don del amor*, 163–83. Finally, see Wojtyła, "Crisis in Morality," in *Crisis in Morality: The Vatican Speaks Out* (Washington, D.C.: United States Catholic Conference, 1969), 1–7. I have been unable to ascertain whether this final article is a translation of an original. The edition does not mention whether this is a translation. However, I have not found this article in any of the collected works of John Paul in English, French, Spanish, or German to which I have access.

143. The first article was an address given to an international congress in Milan. See Karol Wojtyła, "Amore fecondo responsabile, a dieci anni della *Humanae Vitae*, in *Atti del Congresso Internazionale a Milano, 21–25 Guigno 1978* (Milan: Centro Internazionale Studia Famiglia, 1979), 9–18; English translation: "Fruitful and Responsible Love," in Wojtyła, *Fruitful and Responsible Love* (New York: Seabury Press, 1979), 12–34. See also Wojtyła, "La vision anthopologica della *Humanae Vitae*," *Lateranum* 44 (1978): 125–45; English translation: "The Anthropological Vision of Humanae Vitae," trans. William E. May, *Nova et Vetera* 7 (2009): 731–50.

144. If Michael Waldstein's research is accurate, Wojtyła may indeed have had the manuscript of *Man and Woman He Created Them* finished by the time these articles were published. This manuscript was left unpublished after Wojtyła's election to the pontificate and became the basis for the *Theology of the Body* catecheses. See Michael Waldstein's introduction to *Man and Woman He Created Them*, 6–11.

parenthood are ontologically connected. Second, a man and woman must be fully integrated to understand the significance and meaning of the conjugal act.

Conjugal Love and Responsible Parenthood

Reading *Humanae Vitae*, Wojtyła notes that Paul VI acknowledged the difficulties of the family by placing conjugal morality squarely within an ontologically integral vision of man in order to resolve the question of artificial contraception and parenthood (see *HV*, par. 8).[145] It is not that this ontology is purely philosophical; in fact, it begins with the love of God. Wojtyła notes that Paul VI begins the document with the fundamental premise that God is love and that conjugal love enables spouses to participate in that love.[146]

In his analysis, Wojtyła focuses on *Humanae Vitae's* emphasis on the connection between conjugal love and responsibility (see *HV*, pars. 7 and 14), since he treated a similar theme in *Love and Responsibility*. The connection between conjugal love and responsible parenthood is found in the notion of the gift of self that comprises love (see *HV*, par. 8).[147] The responsibility that is inherent in conjugal love, Wojtyła writes, "finds its expression in an abiding consciousness of having received that gift of love and at the same time in discerning and appreciating the tasks which accompany the gift."[148] Love comes to us as both a gift and a task in response to the gift. Marriage is a communion of persons (*HV*, pars. 8 and 9). Moreover, this conjugal love "requires in husband and wife an awareness of their mission of 'responsible parenthood'" (*HV*, par. 10). Here, Wojtyła notes, "*The proper parenthood of the love between persons is a responsible parenthood*. We can say that in the encyclical *Humanae Vitae* responsible parenthood becomes the proper name of human procreation."[149]

---

145. See, for example, Wojtyła, "The Teaching of the Encyclical *Humanae Vitae*," 313; Wojtyła, "The Anthropological Vision," 733.

146. See "The Teaching of the Encyclical *Humanae Vitae*," 303; Wojtyła, "La verdad de la Encíclica *Humanae Vitae*," 194; Wojtyła, *Fruitful and Responsible Love*, 16.

147. See also *GS*, par. 51.

148. See Wojtyła, *Fruitful and Responsible Love*, 19.

149. Wojtyła, "La verdad de la Encíclica *Humanae Vitae*," 188–89 (author's translation).

Responsible parenthood is not simply about procreation. Ac
cording to *Humanae Vitae*, responsible parenthood is "either … the
thoughtful and generous determination either to have a large family, or … the decision to avoid a new birth provisionally or even for an
indeterminate time" (*HV*, par. 10). From this Wojtyła draws the conclusion that

> if conjugal love is a fecund love, that is to say orientated to parenthood, it is
> difficult to think that the meaning of responsible parenthood … can become
> identified only with the limitation of births. Responsible parenthood can be
> achieved by the couple who, by their thoughtful and generous decision, de-
> cide to bring up numerous offspring, but equally so by those who determine
> to restrict this parenthood "for serious motives and respecting moral law"
> (HV, 10).[150]

Given the communion of persons that comprises conjugal love and
orients it to responsible parenthood, one of the central tasks of conjugal love according to Wojtyła is to "resolve itself into an incessant effort which tries to personalize sexual values, and not the opposite."[151]

Responsible parenthood and the values from which it stems, values grounded in the person and in the communion between persons,
cannot be exchanged for a scientific technique.[152] In fact, the conjugal
act loses its character as a personal act between persons with the intervention of artificial methods of contraception. The conjugal act as
such is deeply personal but also deeply interpersonal. Man cannot renounced the attitude of self-control in this act. Wojtyła insists, "If he
[man] thinks that he can be replaced by artificial methods and means,
he ought to know at the same time that he is ridding himself of his
basic values, namely, those values which determine his dignity as a
person and the authenticity of his love for the other person and their
mutual communion."[153]

The importance of this assertion is fully apparent when we recall
what Wojtyła had already written on the values of the human person,
that is, self-determination and self-possession *vis-à-vis* the gift of self as

---

150. Ibid., 189 (author's translation).
151. See Wojtyła, "Crisis in Morality," 5.
152. See Wojtyła, "La verdad de la Encíclica *Humanae Vitae*," 189–90; Wojtyła, *Fruitful and Responsible Love*, 26; Wojtyła, "Crisis in Morality," 6.
153. See Wojtyła, "Crisis in Morality," 6.

articulated in *The Acting Person*. Wojtyła argues that an "integral view" of the person is necessary to understand responsible parenthood.[154] More than that, however, a person himself must be integrated in order to experience conjugal love and responsible parenthood fully.

Integration and the Conjugal Act: Its Signification and Meaning

Karol Wojtyła's analysis is particularly focused on Pope Paul VI's reliance on the meanings of the conjugal act and their inseparable unity. Recall that Paul VI asserts there is an "inseparable connection, willed by God and unable to be broken by man on his own initiative, between the two meanings of the conjugal act: the unitive meaning and the procreative meaning" (*HV*, par. 12). The encyclical's reference to the will of God certainly represents for Wojtyła a nod to the purposes of nature.[155]

However, it is important to note that in this paragraph, Pope Paul VI does not emphasize the purposes of nature in the conjugal act. Wojtyła notes:

By appealing to the meaning of the conjugal act, the Pope places the whole discussion not only and not so much in the context of the nature of this act, but also and even more in the context of human awareness, in the context of the awareness that should correspond to this act on the part of both the man and the woman—the persons performing the act. One can detect in this part of the encyclical *a very significant passage from what some might call a "theology of nature" to a "theology of the person."*[156]

As Wojtyła reads it, *Humanae Vitae*, while not dismissing the nature of the act, brings, rather, the subjectivity of the acting persons into the discussion. The meanings of the conjugal act must be present in the consciousness of the couple.

For Wojtyła, *Humanae Vitae*, par. 12, finds its intellectual lineage in *Gaudium et Spes*, par. 51, which speaks of the "nature of the human person and his acts" in reference to conjugal morality, insisting upon the preservation of "the integral sense of mutual donation and of hu-

---

154. See ibid.
155. See Wojtyła, "The Teaching of the Encyclical *Humanae Vitae*," 308.
156. Ibid.

man procreation in the context of true love."[157] Both the Second Vatican Council and *Humanae Vitae* encourage an analysis not only of the nature of action but also of the acting human person. He writes: "If we wish to analyze this action, we cannot do this without detaching it from the person as the subject who is conscious of the meaning of his own acting."[158]

Wojtyła thinks that Pope Paul VI is "not only writing about the meaning of the conjugal act, which results from its nature, *he is also writing on the intended meaning and the sign* [of the conjugal act]."[159] In fact, Wojtyła believes that "a man or a woman is not only conscious of this meaning [of the conjugal act], but that in realizing this act, can and must give it this precise meaning and no other, can and must intend this sign and no other."[160] While the authentic meaning of the conjugal act follows from its nature, and it is this meaning that should be in the couple's intention, they can, nonetheless, give the act some other purely subjective meaning.

In his 1978 article, "The Anthropological Vision of *Humanae Vitae*," Wojtyła further explains the difference between the objective meaning and the intended meaning. For Wojtyła, par. 12 of *Humanae*

157. *GS*, par. 51. See Tanner, *Decrees*, 2:1104.
158. Wojtyła, "The Anthropological Vision," 742.
159. Wojtyła, "La enseñanza sobre el amor de la encíclica *Humanae Vitae*," 174. I have chosen to provide my own translation of the Spanish version of this article because I believe the phraseology of this English translation is confusing. Throughout his writing, Wojtyła speaks of the nature of the conjugal act and the objective meaning that stems from that nature, on the one hand, and here he introduces the possibility of other meanings intended by the couple. There is nothing to suggest in his writing, or in the Spanish, that when he speaks of the nature of the act and its objective meaning (rather than the subjective meaning intended by the couple) that this meaning results from the couple's "understanding of its nature" as the English phraseology implies, but which is not present in the Spanish.
160. Wojtyła, "La enseñanza sobre el amor de la encíclica *Humanae Vitae*," 174. Again, I revert to a translation of the Spanish, but here even the English translation confirms my observations of the English phraseology in the previous note: "The personal subject of this act—a man or a woman—is not only aware of its meaning, but in performing this act can and should give it precisely this and not some other meaning, can and should signify only this and not something else by it" (Wojtyła, "The Teaching of the Encyclical *Humanae Vitae*," 308). The English here suggests that the objective meaning of nature does exist apart from the couple's understanding and, therefore, that they should align their subjective meaning with this objective meaning. This is, in fact, what Wojtyła argues as the article proceeds.

Vitae advances the anthropological vision of *Gaudium et Spes*. He writes: "Indeed, it seems that by engaging in an analysis of the act, or rather the cooperation of the spouses in the act we call the 'conjugal act,' *Humanae Vitae* 12 emphasizes even more the subjectivity of the cooperating persons [than *Gaudium et Spes*, par. 51, does]."[161] *Humanae Vitae*, in Wojtyła's reading, presupposes the objective dimension of the "action-cooperation" of the spouses while stressing the "subjective moment proper to this action-cooperation."[162]

The objective dimension of the action-cooperation is the unitive and procreative meaning of love and the conjugal act is naturally a sign signifying both these meanings.[163] But Wojtyła insists that *Humanae Vitae* is concerned just as much, if not more, with the conjugal act "realized subjectively by concrete persons—a man and a woman—as an act effected and experienced together."[164] In his very lucid analysis, Wojtyła writes:

The author of *Humanae Vitae* does not limit himself to ascertain, therefore, what that act, that singular act-cooperation of man and woman, objectively, "signifies" (*significa*) but broadens his analysis to the "meaning" (*significato*) that the man and the woman can and must attribute to themselves as acting and cooperating subjects. The author of the encyclical *Humanae Vitae* therefore affirms that, in this subjective dimension of the act-cooperation, "man may not break on his initiative [the bond] between these two meanings (*significati*) of the act." There must be actualized a harmony between what the act objectively "signifies" (*significata*) and the "meaning" (*significato*) that the spouses ... confer on it in the subjective dimension of their action-cooperation.[165]

This harmony is achieved when the couple intends the authentic (or objective) meaning (the union of procreative and unitive) of the conjugal act. In 1969, Wojtyła wrote the same thing: "They can and should intend by it precisely what it means essentially. It means both a special union of persons and, at the same time, the possibility (not the necessity!) of fecundity, of procreation. *If, in acting jointly, this is precisely what they intend to signify by their activity, then the activity is intrinsically true and free of falsification.*"[166]

161. Wojtyła, "The Anthropological Vision," 742.
162. Ibid.   163. Ibid.
164. Ibid., 743.   165. Ibid.
166. Wojtyła, "The Teaching of the Encyclical *Humanae Vitae*," 309. This idea reap-

Periodic continence as a means of ethical regulation of birth differs from contraception in precisely this way. "The former does not undermine the order of meanings contained in the conjugal act, whereas the latter does.... *In the ethical regulation of birth, spouses can signify by their activity in the conjugal act what this activity essentially means, whereas contraception makes this impossible.*"[167] Since the meaning of union cannot be separated from the meaning of procreation, when procreation is intentionally limited from the act, the meaning of union is not properly expressed. An "active undermining of the 'meaning and purpose' that corresponds to the plan of the Creator *must work against the 'intimate union' of the spouses.* One could say ... the conjugal act *then lacks the value of a true union of persons.*"[168] Undermining the objective significance or meaning of the conjugal act necessarily undermines whatever subjective meaning the spouses intend. They are acting at cross purposes with nature.

This subjective element in the conjugal act, as with all of the conjugal life and responsible parenthood, "above all implies a more profound relationship to the objective moral order established by God, of which a right conscience is the faithful interpreter" (*HV*, par. 10). Recalling themes from *The Acting Person*, Wojtyła insists that a right conscience "makes its decisions from the maturity and fullness of human subjectivity; it determines (judges) because it is the 'faithful interpreter' (one would rather say, 'the *truthful* interpreter') 'of the objective moral order established by God.'"[169] He believes that this mature subjectivity entails "equitable objectivity" in keeping the hierarchy of values in conjugal life.[170]

---

pears in *FC*: "The innate language that expresses the total reciprocal self-giving of husband and wife is overlaid, through contraception, by an objectively contradictory language, namely, that of not giving oneself totally to the other. This leads not only to a positive refusal to be open to life but also to a falsification of the inner truth of conjugal love, which is called upon to give itself in personal totality.... The difference, both anthropological and moral, between contraception and recourse to the rhythm of the cycle ... involves in the final analysis two irreconcilable concepts of the human person and of human sexuality" (par. 32).

167. Wojtyła, "The Teaching of the Encyclical *Humanae Vitae*," 309–10.

168. Ibid., 311. Wojtyła is here commenting on *HV*, par. 13. See also Wojtyła, "La Verdad," 194–95.

169. Wojtyła, "The Anthropological Vision," 743.

170. See ibid.

More importantly, Wojtyła concludes that it is the true objectivity of a right conscience that "allows the spouses to establish an authentic harmony between what the conjugal act objectively 'signifies' (*significa*) and the 'meaning' (*significato*) that the spouses themselves attribute to it in their own inner attitude, in their subjective action and in their intimate experience."[171] The two aspects, the objective and the subjective (otherwise referred to by Wojtyła as the ethical aspect and the psychological aspect, respectively) must be integrated.[172] In fact, for a love to be a truly honest and human love, "its psychological value must be integrated with its ethical value."[173]

When he speaks of integration, Wojtyła is referring once again to the composite of the human person—body and soul—and insisting that the somatic processes must be included in such integration. The body cannot be regarded simply as biological organism that may be manipulated by technique.[174] *Humanae Vitae*, he argues, understands the body not as an autonomous being but "as a component of the whole man in his personal constitution.... The respect due to the body, particularly in its procreative functions—functions rooted in the whole specific somatic quality of sex—is respect for the human being, that is, for the dignity of the man and the woman."[175] Only with this integrated view of the human person, in which the *soma*, the *psyche*, and the soul are understood as united in one person, can the scientific interventions of bio-physiological techniques be evaluated, "those techniques that interfere efficiently in the bio-physiological processes themselves."[176] This imposes a limit on man's dominion over his own body which is rooted "in the profound structure of personal being."[177]

Here, finally, Wojtyła has recourse to the theme of self-mastery (self-governance and self-possession). He writes: "Man cannot exercise power over his own body by means of interventions or techniques that, at the same time, compromise his authentic personal dominion over

---

171. Ibid.
172. See Wojtyła, "The Teaching of the Encyclical *Humanae Vitae*," 311; Wojtyła, "The Anthropological Vision," 743.
173. Wojtyła, "The Teaching of the Encyclical *Humanae Vitae* on Love," 312.
174. See Wojtyła, "The Anthropological Vision," 746.
175. Ibid.   176. Ibid.
177. Ibid.

himself and that even, in a certain way, annihilate this dominion."[178] Artificial contraception subverts that self-mastery. And self-mastery is necessary for the authentic gift of self to another person.[179]

CONCLUSION

In this chapter, I have sought to provide a glimpse of the intellectual pedigree of John Paul's notion of the spousal meaning of the body as articulated in the *Theology of the Body* catecheses. The salient themes that have emerged here are: (1) his understanding of the relationship of conjugal love as a self-gift and responsible parenthood in the institution of marriage; (2) the possibility of the body serving in the self-communication of that self-gift in the conjugal act; (3) the idea that there is both an objective meaning or significance and a subjective meaning or significance in the conjugal act; and (4) his view that integration of the *psyche* and *soma* is necessary for an authentic self-gift and the proper alignment of meanings in the conjugal act.

Wojtyła knew the difficulties the church's teaching on contraception presented to the world. He knew the anxieties married couples faced.[180] In his view, *Humanae Vitae* was an exercise of the magisterium's vocation to serve the faithful in distinguishing between opinion and truth.[181] In 1965, three years before the publication of *Humanae Vitae*, Wojtyła argued that four circumstances militated against the church's presentation of the issue: "1) The habit of thinking and judging in a utilitarian way; 2) the inclination to judge the value of an act solely on the basis of its effects; 3) the enormous pressure exerted by the subjective, emotional element; and 4) the whole set of difficulties, real or illusory, connected with the use of natural methods of birth control."[182]

After reading *Humanae Vitae*, he saw that "a comprehensive ontology of marriage, an integral vision of the human being, a vision

---

178. Ibid.
179. See ibid., 748; Wojtyła, "La verdad de la encíclica *Humanae Vitae*," 195.
180. See, for example, Wojtyła, "La verdad de la encíclica *Humanae Vitae*," 197–99; Wojtyła, "Crisis in Morality," 3–4; Wojtyła, *Fruitful and Responsible Love*, 32–34.
181. See Wojtyła, "Introducción a la Encíclica *Humanae Vitae*," 202–3.
182. Wojtyła, "Problem of Catholic Sexual Ethics," 294.

of man and woman as persons" was absolutely necessary.[183] He believed that *Humanae Vitae* was a first step to this presentation inasmuch as "it points to the possibility and even necessity, of in some way transforming the optics of the issue, while at the same time preserving—*and even for the sake of preserving*—a more precise identity of doctrine."[184] One way of reading *Theology of the Body* is to read it as Karol Wojtyła's attempt to transform "the optics of the issue" at work in *Humanae Vitae* and in the twentieth century ecclesial debate on marriage and sexuality in general. And, indeed, in the very last catechesis of the *Theology of the Body* series, John Paul suggests this interpretation.[185] The next chapter will offer an exegesis of one of the central themes of those catecheses, one of the principal subjects of this study, namely, the spousal meaning of the body.

183. Wojtyła, "The Teaching of the Encyclical *Humanae Vitae*," 314.
184. Ibid.
185. See *TOB*, no. 133.

5

The Spousal Meaning of the Body
in *Theology of the Body*

As I mentioned in the introduction to this book, Pope John Paul II's Wednesday catecheses, which eventually became known as *Theology of the Body*, were largely based on an unpublished manuscript entitled *Man and Woman He Created Them*. In a new critical translation of the catechetical lectures, Michael Waldstein has incorporated the original headings from that unpublished manuscript. These headings reveal the systematic nature of Wojtyła's project by offering an outline of the work as a whole. For the first time, readers can approach *Theology of the Body* not as a work of disjointed talks but as a unified whole.[1]

The headers of the manuscript divide the work into two parts. The first part concerns the words of Christ. Here, the pope focuses on

1. Charles Curran can be excused for his criticism to the contrary since it was made before the publication of Waldstein's translation. See Charles Curran, *The Moral Theology of Pope John Paul II* (Washington, D.C.: Georgetown University Press, 2005), 167: "The talks occasionally cite philosophers and other secular thinkers; the talks also come complete with footnotes. But the theology of the body is not developed in a systematic way. The very nature of short talks presented every week to a different audience militates against a totally systematic approach. Because the talks are not a complete and systematic presentation of the pope's teaching on marriage, many aspects remain somewhat unclear and certainly less developed than they would be in a truly systematic presentation."

three "words": the beginning, the human heart, and the resurrection. In the first chapter, John Paul offers a catechesis on creation, particularly addressing Christ's assertions that divorce was not present in the beginning (Mt 19:3–8) and that adultery may be committed in the heart and not only in the flesh (Mt 5:27–28). Building upon his analysis of Genesis, the pope then lays out his moral teaching on concupiscence and love. The third chapter of this first part concerns Christ's words about the body and the resurrection (Mt 22:24–30), and addresses the role of the body in the resurrection and continence for the kingdom of God.

The second part of *Theology of the Body* is about the sacrament of marriage itself. It also is divided into three chapters. The first chapter is an exegesis on the words of scripture, primarily of the prophets, the gospels, and Paul on the dimension of the covenant and grace at work in the sacrament. The second chapter concerns the dimension of sign, specifically the sign of consent in marriage and the sign or language of the body. The final chapter is a direct commentary on *Humanae Vitae* in light of the language of the body that John Paul develops throughout the work. This final chapter is central to the whole work.[2] Indeed, *Humanae Vitae* was central to the pope's thought when writing the catecheses.[3] As the pope himself put it, the whole of *Theology of the Body* is intended to "face the questions raised by *Humanae vitae* above all in theology, to formulate these questions, and to look for an answer to them."[4]

The previous two chapters of this book have surveyed Wojtyła's thought on a number of relevant issues: nature, the person, the body, and the conjugal act. Given the trajectory of his thought and the turmoil after the promulgation of *Humanae Vitae*, it is not surprising that Wojtyła was prepared to publish a book not only defending the 1968 encyclical but, in a sense, rereading it in the light of a biblical and theological anthropology. In this work, John Paul clarifies several

2. It should be noted that in his final Wednesday audience, Pope John Paul II identified three main parts to his catechetical lecture. The first two mentioned above, and the part concerning *Humanae Vitae* (see *TOB*, no. 133:1–2, 4). This differs from the headings of the unpublished manuscript upon which the audiences were based. For an analysis of this difference, see Waldstein, "Introduction," 105–28.

3. See *TOB*, no. 133:4.

4. Ibid.

aspects of his moral theology which are central to an understanding of his view of the spousal meaning of the body. Further, many of the themes found in *Theology of the Body* recur throughout the pontificate of John Paul II in his writings on marriage and the family.[5]

The purpose of this chapter is not to provide a complete survey of *Theology of the Body*. As I mentioned in the general introduction of this book, that task has largely been accomplished. Rather, this chapter will elucidate John Paul's understanding of several key features important to this study, not the least of which is his articulation of the spousal meaning of the body. Since the pope nowhere provides a precise definition of the spousal meaning of the body, it will be necessary for this chapter to provide an exegesis of the key concepts underpinning John Paul's use of the term, including man's unique position in creation, the role and language of the body in this position, the impact of sin on the human person and the body, the redemption of the body by Christ, and, finally, the import of all this for understanding *Humanae Vitae* and the spousal union of a married couple.

Therefore, this chapter is composed of a four-part exegetical reading of *Theology of the Body*. First, we discuss John Paul's analysis of creation and man's place in it. In the second section, we turn to the fall and redemption: the effects of sin, shame, and concupiscence on the body along with the impact that the redemption of Christ has on the body. In the third section, we explore John Paul's understanding of the language of the body as it is lived in marriage and articulated in *Humanae Vitae*. In the conclusion of this chapter, then, we offer a summary view of what Pope John Paul means by the spousal meaning of the body so that it will be evident exactly which elements of his understanding stem from Thomas Aquinas.

---

5. The second part of *FC* (written in 1981) follows the same outline as *TOB*. See *FC*, pars. 11–17. Similar themes can also be found in his apostolic letter on the dignity and vocation of women: John Paul II, *Mulieris Dignitatem*, Apostolic Letter of August 15, 1988 [hereafter, *MD*], in *AAS* 80 (1988): 1653–1729. The following two texts also contain themes culled from these Wednesday catecheses: John Paul II, *Gratissimam Sane*, Apostolic Letter of February 2, 1994, in *AAS* 86 (1994): 868–925; and John Paul II, "Mulieribus ex Omnibus Nationibus Missus," June 29, 1995; official Italian text: *AAS* 87 (1995): 803–12.

THE ANALYSIS OF CREATION

Creation and Original Solitude

At the very beginning of his catechetical talks, John Paul continues a trend that he began with his doctoral dissertation on John of the Cross. Namely, he continues to emphasize the subjective element of human experience while respecting the objective and ontological categories of the Christian theological tradition. For example, he writes that the first scriptural account of creation (Gn 1:1–2:4) "is concise, free from any trace of subjectivism: it contains only the objective fact and defines the objective reality."[6] And again, "The first account of the creation of man ... contains hidden within itself a powerful metaphysical content."[7] After explaining the traditional metaphysical distinction between being (*ens*) and existence (*esse*), the pope concludes "that the first chapter of Genesis has formed an incontrovertible point of reference and solid basis of a metaphysics and also for an anthropology and an ethics according to which '*ens et bonum convertuntur*' [being and good are convertible]. Of course, all of this has its own significance for theology as well, and above all for the theology of the body."[8] As God brings creatures into existence, he declares them good. Metaphysics and ontology are consistently implicit in *Theology of the Body*, even if they are not always fully explained. Created from nothingness, declared good, man is directed to communion with God.

Regarding the second account of creation (Gn 2:4–25) and the story of the fall (Gn 3:1–24), however, John Paul is clear. The accounts differ from the first account in more ways than their authorship. He writes, "We must observe that the whole text, *in formulating the truth about man, strikes us with its typical depth*, different from that of the first chapter of Genesis. One can say this depth is above all subjective in nature and thus in some way psychological. Chapter 2 of Genesis constitutes in some way the oldest description and record of man's self-understanding and, together with chapter 3, it is the first witness of human consciousness."[9]

---

6. *TOB*, no. 2:4.   7. Ibid., no. 2:5.
8. Ibid.   9. Ibid., no. 3:1.

It is this subjective and psychological aspect, the biblical record of human consciousness, with which John Paul is concerned in *Theology of the Body*. The pope declares that "theology has built *the overall image of man's original innocence and justice before original sin* by applying the method of objectivization specific to metaphysics and metaphysical anthropology. In the present analysis, we are trying rather to take into account the aspect of human subjectivity."[10] Here John Paul states explicitly that he is purposely not employing a metaphysical and teleological method in *Theology of the Body*. This is not surprising since, as I noted in chapter 3, in the 1970s he began to turn to phenomenology as a means of discourse on moral norms, even though he continued to assert the value of natural teleology and metaphysics for any moral theory.

If the previous two chapters of this study have shown anything, it is that John Paul does not deny the importance of objective and metaphysical categories. One of the motivating aspects of this chapter is to highlight the places in *Theology of the Body* where that which is objective, metaphysical, and ontological is necessary for the account of the spousal meaning of the body even though John Paul is more concerned to incorporate human experience into theology. John Crosby has astutely noted that Wojtyła spent much time explaining and defending the norms of *Humanae Vitae* from an experiential perspective because the encyclical represents a vast truth about man and because the faithful more easily follow the truth when they understand the truth.[11] From this perspective, it is true, John Paul presents modest critiques of theologians who rely primarily on a metaphysical account, including Aquinas.[12] In the *Theology of the Body* catecheses, he is more concerned with the "*biblical, theological sphere.*"[13]

The primal experience of man revealed in the second Genesis narrative is solitude, or "original solitude" as John Paul calls it. In Genesis 2:18, God speaks the words that identify this solitude: "It is not good

10. Ibid., no. 18:1.

11. See John F. Crosby, "The Personalism of John Paul II as the Basis of His Approach to the Teaching of '*Humanae vitae*,'" *Anthropotes* 5 (1989): 48–49.

12. In *TOB*, no. 54, for example, John Paul disagrees with Aquinas's conception that purity "consists above all in holding back the impulses of sense-desire." See also ibid., no. 130.

13. Ibid., no. 133:4.

that the man should be alone; I will make him a helper fit for him."[14] And God brings all the animals to the man. The pope draws two conclusions from this. First, "*created man* finds himself from the first moment of his existence *before God* in search of his own being, as it were; one could say, in search of his own definition; today one would say, in search of his own 'identity.'"[15] Here, John Paul brings together both the objective and the subjective elements of his study by introducing the *subjective* search for the identity of one's *objective* being. His "anthropology calls man to *become* what or who he is by accepting and living out the identity and vocation that God has inscribed in his very being."[16]

The second conclusion is this:

Self-knowledge goes hand in hand with knowledge of the world, of all visible creatures, of all living beings to which man has given their names to affirm his own dissimilarity before them. Thus, consciousness reveals man as the one who *possesses the power of knowing* with respect to *the visible world*. With this knowledge, which makes him go in some way outside his own being, *man* at the same *reveals himself to himself in all the distinctiveness of his being* .... Man is alone because he is "different" from the visible world, from the world of living beings.[17]

This idea that man is unique in all of creation and that he is in search of his own identity will play a significant role in John Paul's understanding of the conjugal act and the spousal meaning of the body. It also relies on the blending of the two categories: the objective and the subjective. As John Paul sees it, this experience of original solitude in creation is the effect of man's ontological uniqueness. But that uniqueness is itself the direct result of man being created in the im-

---

14. Unless otherwise stated, all English passages of scripture are taken from the *Holy Bible*, Revised Standard Version, Second Catholic Edition (San Francisco, Calif.: Ignatius Press, 2005).

15. *TOB*, no. 5:5. This theme of man finding himself appears throughout Pope John Paul's theological writings. A leitmotif of his pontificate was the theological idea that in man's search for his identity, Christ reveals not only God but also man to himself. This idea was explicitly stated in *GS*, par. 22. This is one of the principal themes of the Pope's first encyclical, published in 1979, *Redemptor Hominis*, in *AAS* 71 (1979): 257–324. See also John Paul II, *Gratissimam Sane*, par. 9.

16. Asci, *The Conjugal Act*, 124.

17. *TOB*, no. 5:6.

age of God and brings with it a subjective urge for self-definition and self-identity.

The pope argues that being created in the image of God is the equivalent of being called to a community of persons (*communio personarum*).[18] Mary Shivanandan has effectively shown the uniqueness of John Paul's thought on this point. Man's solitude in creation reveals a directionality to the other, to a *communio*, and to a capacity for union with others. This directionality, as we will see, is part and parcel of man's fundamental existence. Here the pope does not disparage the tradition of seeing the *imago Dei* only in the intellectual faculties of intellect and will. Rather, he supplements the tradition by incorporating a biblical anthropology which he has drawn from a reading of the Genesis narrative.[19] The *communio personarum* to which man is called is ultimately the Trinitarian communion of Father, Son, and Holy Spirit. John Paul is clear that though man has self-consciousness and even self-determination, these exist as parameters within his relationship with God.

The nature of the relationship is expressed in the primordial command not to eat of the tree of knowledge (Gn 2:16–17). According to the pope, because man is made in the image of God, he is "a subject constituted as a person, constituted according to the measure of 'partner of the Absolute,' inasmuch as he must consciously discern and choose between good and evil, between life and death.... *Man is 'alone': this is to say that through his own humanity, through what he is, he is at the same time set into a unique, exclusive, and unrepeatable relationship with God himself.*"[20] Self-determination exists within a covenantal relationship with God. Freedom is not absolute or autonomous. This is a foundational point in John Paul's anthropology and moral theology.

18. See ibid., no. 9:2–3.

19. See Mary Shivanandan, *Crossing the Threshold of Love: A New Vision of Marriage in the Light of John Paul II's Anthropology* (Washington, D.C.: The Catholic University of America Press, 1999), 72–80.

20. *TOB*, no. 6:2. The final sentence here hints at *GS*, par. 24, in which the council declares, "Man is the only creature on earth whom God has willed for his own sake, he is unable to find himself except through a sincere gift of himself" (Tanner [ed.], *Decrees of the Ecumenical Councils*, 2:1083–84). This paragraph of the council's Pastoral Constitution is another theme of the Pope's pontificate. See Pascal Ide, "Une théologie du don: Les occurrences de *Gaudium et spes*, n. 24, §3 chez Jean-Paul II," *Anthropotes* 17 (2001): 149–78, 313–44.

The body plays a significant role in man's awareness of solitude, of being alone in the world. The pope writes: "The body, by which man shares in the visible created world, makes him at the same time aware of being 'alone.' Otherwise he would not have been able to arrive at this conviction, which in fact he reached (as we read in Gen 2:20), if his body had not helped him to understand it, making the matter evident to him."[21] Man learns his own solitude by recognizing the structure of his body, through which he recognizes that his being differs from other creatures.

The Body in Creation

At the beginning of creation, John Paul says, the body was a visible sign of man's transcendence, of being different from the animal kingdom.[22] But the body's structure also reveals man's subjectivity just as much as self-consciousness and self-determination do. He writes: "Man is a subject not only by his self-consciousness and by self-determination, but also based on his own body. *The structure of the body is such that it permits him to be the author of genuinely human activity.* In this activity, the body expresses the person."[23] This is the leitmotif of John Paul's catecheses: the body expresses the person.[24] It reappears in different ways throughout the Wednesday audiences. For example, he says later that "the body, as the expression of the person, was the first sign of the presence of man in the visible world. In that world, from the very beginning, man was able to distinguish himself, to identify himself, as it were—that is, to confirm himself as a person—also through his body."[25]

---

21. *TOB*, no. 6:3; cf. no. 27:3.   22. See ibid., no. 27:3.
23. Ibid., no. 7:2.

24. This is repeated several times throughout the catechetical lectures, in some way or another. The body "expresses" the person, it "manifests" man. See, for example, *TOB*, nos. 12:4, 12:5, 14:5, 27:3, and 123:4. It also appears throughout John Paul's other magisterial writings. See, for example, *FC*, par. 11; *Gratissimam Sane*, par. 19; *Veritatis Splendor*, Encyclical Letter of August 6, 1993, pars. 46 and 48, in *AAS* 85 (1993): 1133–1228; *Evangelium Vitae*, Encyclical Letter of March 25, 1995, par. 23. See also Richard A. Spinello, *The Genius of John Paul II: The Great Pope's Moral Vision* (New York: Sheed and Ward, 2007), 57–88, for an illuminating study of the pope's attempt to reconnect the human person with human nature and the body.

25. *TOB*, no. 27:3.

In the previous chapter, I surveyed the importance of the body in Wojtyła's moral theory, especially his account of sexual ethics. That the body expresses the person was already present in his writings before *Theology of the Body*. This is not surprising given his own Thomistic background. Throughout these catecheses, the pope routinely affirms the importance of the body and obedience to nature as morally normative. Yet part of the delicate balance of John Paul's method in *Theology of the Body* is not to subordinate the freedom of the human person to the dynamics of nature so that he becomes guilty of the same pure naturalism or physicalism that he had criticized in the past. He wants to insist upon man's uniqueness but at the same time the pope articulates man's indebtedness to the creator of nature who has given him the gift of existence. This indebtedness to nature is key not only to a proper understanding of the spousal meaning of the body but also to its effective communication between persons.

The recognition of the first man's uniqueness, of his solitude, leads to the creation of the woman (Gn 2:21–22).[26] The man's immediate reaction—"this at last is bone of my bone and flesh of my flesh" (Gn 2:23)—is instructive. The man recognizes not the somatic differences between him and the woman, but that she is a person. This means that "bodiliness and sexuality are not simply identical. Although in its normal constitution, the human body carries within itself the signs of sex and is by its nature male or female, *the fact that man is a 'body' belongs more deeply to the structure of the personal subject than the fact that in his somatic constitution he is also male or female.*"[27]

The solitude experienced by man is experienced by both males and females. They are "two 'incarnations' of the same metaphysical solitude before God and the world—*two reciprocally completing ways*

26. In ibid., no. 5:2, and in 8:3, John Paul notes that until the creation of the woman, the biblical word for "man" is *'adam,* which denotes the whole human race. The words for "male" and "female," *'is* and *'issah,* are not employed until after the creation of the woman. On the creation of the woman, the pope observes that the "sleep" into which Adam is cast is less "sleep" as it is torpor—an almost going out of existence—so that the creation of the woman is, in fact, a reemergence of man in his "double unity as male and female" (*TOB,* no. 8:3). In Genesis, *'Adam* is recreated as *'is* and *'issah.*

27. *TOB,* no. 8:2; cf. *FC,* par. 11. This passage is somewhat problematic, it seems to contradict the point of the *Theology of the Body* catecheses, which is to emphasize the complementarity of man and woman in the spousal meaning of the body. This is an isolated statement in the catecheses and should be considered in that context.

of *'being a body'* *and at the same time of being human*—as two complementary dimensions of self-knowledge and self-determination and, at the same time, *two complementary ways of being conscious of the meaning of the body."*[28] Here, John Paul introduces the concept of reciprocal complementarity between the sexes, which he articulated in his earlier writings.[29]

When the two sexes unite in the conjugal act, the union *"carries within itself a particular awareness of the meaning of that body in the reciprocal self-gift of the persons."*[30] The catalyst of self-gift is deeper than sexual difference. Self-gift lies in the metaphysical fact that creation itself is a gift: *"Creation is a gift, because man appears in it, who, as an 'image of God,' is able to understand the very meaning of the gift in the call from nothing to existence."*[31] One of the ways the pope speaks about the body is as *"a witness* to creation as a fundamental gift, and therefore a witness *to Love as the source from which this same giving springs.* Masculinity-femininity—namely, sex—is the original sign of a creative donation and at the same time <the sign of a gift that> man, male-female, becomes aware of as a gift lived so to speak in an original way. This is the meaning with which sex enters into the theology of the body."[32] This gift has a directionality to it. It is the gift manifest in a creature sprung from nothingness into existence and directed toward the other, and, ultimately, toward God himself. The somatic (that is, bodily) differences between men and women are not unimportant in *Theology of the Body.* He writes that "sex is not only decisive for man's somatic individuality, but at the same time it defines his personal identity and concreteness."[33] Later, he writes: "Woman's constitution differs from that of man; in fact, we know today that it is different even in the deepest bio-physiological determinants."[34]

---

28. *TOB*, no. 10:1.

29. This concept is also present in *FC*, par. 19, and "Letter to Women," Apostolic Letter of June 29, 1995, par. 7, in

AAS 87 (1995): 803–12. Vatican translation found in Boston: Pauline Books and Media, 1995.

30. *TOB*, no. 10:4. See also *FC*, par. 18; *MD*, par. 7; *Gratissimam Sane*, par. 11.

31. *TOB*, no. 13:4.

32. Ibid., no. 14:4 (text in angled brackets supplied by Waldstein from the Polish manuscript).

33. Ibid., no. 20:5.

34. Ibid., no. 21:4.

The somatic difference of the sexes concerns procreation, it is true. But for John Paul the body's meaning and value goes beyond biological procreation to the expression of love, of communion: "The human body, oriented from within by the 'sincere gift' of the person [*Gaudium et Spes*, par. 24:3], reveals not only its masculinity or femininity on the physical level, but reveals also such a *value* and such a *beauty that it goes beyond the simply physical level of 'sexuality.'*"[35] The value that the pope speaks of here is the spousal meaning of the body, which is itself connected to the procreative aspect of the body.[36] Marriage is intended not only for biological procreation, but to propagate the gift of creation from nothingness through the gift of self from one generation to the next.[37]

This is why the pope insists that from the beginning the union of husband and wife was intended to be subordinate to procreation and fruitfulness of life. He writes: "This communion had been intended to make man and woman mutually happy through the search of a simple and pure union in humanity, through a reciprocal offering of themselves, that is, through the experience of the gift of the person expressed with soul and body, with masculinity and femininity—'flesh of my flesh' (Gen 2:23)—and finally through the subordination of such a union to the blessing of fruitfulness with 'procreation.'"[38] I note the pope's use of quotation marks around the word "procreation" to distinguish his meaning from a mere biologism. How does it differ? For John Paul, procreation continues the divine donation, the generation of new persons from nothingness and granting them the urge to seek others and to seek God himself.

It is instructive how John Paul describes the "spousal meaning of the body" the first time the word appears in his catechetical lectures. Referring to the original condition in which man and woman felt no

---

35. Ibid., no. 15:4. See also *FC*, par. 11; "Letter to Women," par. 8.

36. See *TOB*, nos. 14:6, 15:1.

37. See ibid., no. 96:7: "As for marriage, one can deduce that—instituted in the context of the sacrament of creation in its totality, or in the state of original innocence—it was to serve not only to extend the work of creation, or procreation, but also to spread the same sacrament of creation to further generations of human beings, that is, to spread the supernatural fruits of man's eternal election by the Father in the eternal Son, the fruits man was endowed with by God in the very act of creation."

38. *TOB*, no. 30:3.

shame in their nakedness, which John Paul calls "original innocence," he writes:

Seeing and knowing each other in all the peace and tranquility of the interior gaze, they "communicate" in the fullness of humanity, which shows itself in them as reciprocal complementarity precisely because they are "male" and "female." At the same time, they "communicate" based on the communion of persons in which they become a mutual gift for each other, through femininity and masculinity. In reciprocity, they reach in this way a particular understanding of the meaning of their own bodies. The original meaning of nakedness corresponds to the simplicity and fullness of vision in which their understanding of the meaning of the body is born from the very heart, as it were, of their community-communion. We call this meaning "spousal."[39]

From this passage, two points are evident. First, for John Paul, there must be an awareness of the meaning of the body in the understanding of the acting person. Crosby clarifies the importance of this: "Spousal self-donation [self-gift] is by its very nature something consciously lived through; spouses could not possibly perform this self-donation without being aware of it; they are necessarily present to themselves as donating themselves to each other."[40] Indeed, immediately after the passage above, John Paul notes that "the man and the woman in Genesis 2:23–25 emerge, precisely at the very 'beginning,' with this consciousness of the meaning of their own bodies."[41] Later in this chapter, I consider the pope's insistence that this original consciousness of the spousal meaning of the body is lost with sin and must be reacquired through a "rereading" of the body in the truth.[42]

The fact that meaning must be in the consciousness of the acting person does not mean that nature and the body have no objective qualities that contribute to the meaning (whether the spousal meaning of the body or any other meaning). The body itself, accord-

39. Ibid., no. 13:1.
40. Crosby, "The Personalism of John Paul II," 52.
41. *TOB*, no. 13:1. See also ibid., no. 19:1: "If 'they did not feel shame,' this means that they were united by the consciousness of the gift, that they had reciprocal *awareness of the spousal meaning of their bodies*, in which the freedom of the gift is expressed and *the whole inner richness of the person as subject is shown*."
42. See, for example, ibid., no. 19:2: "After original sin, man and woman were to lose the grace of original innocence. The discovery of the spousal meaning of the body was to cease being for them a simple reality of revelation and of grace."

ing to Wojtyła, contains "the 'spousal' attribute, that is, *the power to express love: precisely that love in which the human person becomes a gift and—through this gift—fulfills the very meaning of his being and existence.*"[43]

This brings me to a second conclusion of John Paul's understanding of the spousal meaning of the body. Because man is free, he is not entirely dominated by nature. Somatic sexual difference is only the beginning in understanding the uniqueness of each human person: "One must keep in mind that each of them, the man and the woman, is not only a passive object, defined by his own body and his own sex, and in this way determined 'by nature.' On the contrary, precisely through being man and woman, each of them is 'given' to the other as a unique and unrepeatable subject, as 'I,' as person."[44] Precisely because the "body *manifests* man" and allows for the communication of a communion between man and woman, "any 'naturalistic' criterion is bound to fail, while the 'personalistic' criterion can be of great help."[45] From this standpoint, he notes that Genesis tells us "relatively little about the human body in the naturalistic and contemporary sense of the word."[46] Nevertheless, the third section of this chapter argues that John Paul still insists, as he did in *Love and Responsibility*, that the person must be obedient to nature in order to communicate love.[47]

The shape of the pope's project in these catecheses now begins to be clear. The human person, man and woman, is created in the image of God through a gratuitous divine gift. This gift, imprinted within the *imago Dei* in which they are made, gives men and women a uniqueness in all of creation as free persons since they are called to communion with each other and with God (who is himself a *communio Personarum*). Human existence, while characterized by an original solitude separating man from all other creatures, is nonetheless marked by this drive from nothingness to the other. This drive

---

43. *TOB*, no. 15:1.   44. Ibid., no. 20:5; cf. no. 21:1.
45. Ibid., no. 12:5; cf. 55:2.   46. Ibid., no. 23:4.
47. This insight is argued forcefully in the work of Mary Shivanandan and Michael Waldstein. See Shivanandn, *Crossing the Threshold of Love*, 107, and Waldstein, "John Paul II: A Thomist Rooted in St. John of the Cross," *Faith & Reason* 30 (2005): 199. Cf. Wojtyła, *Love and Responsibility*, 30.

is manifest in the human body just as much as it is written in man's very existence. This drive for the other, the capacity for love and self-giving, is this spousal meaning of the body which is the fulfillment of man's existence. But this capacity for self-giving, in John Paul's view, is threatened by sin and concupiscence. The spousal meaning of the body, the capacity for self-giving, was redeemed by Jesus Christ.

THE MEANING OF
THE BODY AFTER THE FALL

Sin, Shame, and Concupiscence

One of the fundamental tenets of *Theology of the Body*, detailed above, is that the body expresses the person, bearing a meaning both in itself and in the consciousness of the person. The conjugal union is more than sexuality; it is an expression of love. In John Paul's own words, the body is a sort of "primordial *sacrament*" of the image of God at work in the human person.[48] He goes on to say: "The body, in fact, and only the body, is capable of making visible what is invisible: the spiritual and the divine. It has been created to transfer into the visible reality of the world the mystery hidden from eternity in God, and thus be a sign of it."[49]

After the Fall, the relationship between male and female changes with the introduction of concupiscence. The body ceases to express the person simply. John Paul notes that in the lapsarian state

the body is not subject to the spirit as in the state of original innocence, but carries within itself a constant hotbed of resistance against the spirit and threatens in some way man's unity as a person, that is, the unity of the moral nature that plunges its roots firmly into the very constitution of the person. The concupiscence of the body is a specific threat to the structure of self-possession and self-dominion, through which the human person forms

48. See *TOB*, no. 19:4.

49. Ibid. To my mind, the Pope in no way intends to denigrate the sacraments of Christ and his church. Rather, he is suggesting that "in man, created in the image of God, the very sacramentality of creation, the sacramentality of the world, was thus in some way revealed" (ibid., no. 19:5). The sacraments "work" as they do because the body-soul composite of men and women. The Catholic principle of sacramentality is that invisible grace is communicated through material signs. For John Paul, man is the primal example of this.

itself.... In any case, *the man of concupiscence does not rule his own body in the same way, with the same simplicity and "naturalness" as the man of original innocence.*[50]

The threat to self-possession and self-dominion means also that concupiscence threatens the self-mastery which, as Wojtyła had written previously and as he reaffirms in these catecheses, is necessary for the self-gift that characterizes spousal union.[51] Concupiscence brings about "the loss of the interior freedom of the gift."[52] Concupiscence "limits and restricts self-mastery from within, and thereby *in some sense makes the interior freedom of the gift impossible.*"[53]

Analyzing the effects of original sin from the scriptural perspective, John Paul takes special note of Genesis 3:16 ("Your desire shall be for your husband, and he shall rule over [dominate] you"). The pope writes: "On the one hand, the 'body,' which is constituted in the unity of the personal subject, does not cease to arouse the desires for personal union, precisely due to masculinity and femininity ('Your desire shall be for your husband'); on the other hand, concupiscence itself simultaneously directs these desires in its own way; this is confirmed by the expression, 'he will dominate you.'"[54] Whereas in original innocence the man and woman existed in a state of communion, with concupiscence this relation "is replaced by a different mutual relationship, namely, by a relationship of possession of the other as an object of one's own desire."[55]

The relationship of domination carries with it the further consequence that the conjugal union becomes unsatisfying. The man and the woman "are no longer only called to union and unity, but are also *threatened by the insatiability of that union and unity,* which does not cease to attract man and woman precisely because they are persons."[56] Since the union is both insatiable and redefined as domination, the body becomes a "'terrain' of appropriation of the other person."[57]

In the union of their bodies, and in their relationship with each

---

50. Ibid., no. 28:3.
51. See ibid., no. 15:2, on the relationship of self-mastery to self-gift.
52. Ibid., no. 32:6.   53. Ibid.
54. *TOB*, no. 31:3.   55. Ibid. See also *MD*, par. 10.
56. *TOB*, no. 30:5.   57. Ibid., no. 33:3.

other, the man and the woman now experience a fundamental disorder in their humanity. This disorder, caused by concupiscence, is marked by shame. "That shame," the pope writes, "which shows itself without any doubt in the 'sexual' order, reveals *a specific difficulty in sensing the human essentiality of one's own body*, a difficulty man had not experienced in the state of original innocence."[58] The inability to recognize the humanity of one's own body, or the essential relationship between soul and body (that both together constitute the "I" of the person), results in an alienation of the person from his body.[59] Later, John Paul will argue that this separation between person and the body is the fundamental reason that secular culture does not understand the church's teaching on marriage and contraception.[60]

In his opening catecheses on the theology of the body, Pope John Paul II insists that there is continuity between the original order of innocence and the fallen order of sin and concupiscence. He draws this conclusion based on our Lord's words in Matthew 19:1–12, in which Jesus references the "beginning" to answer the Pharisees' question about divorce.[61] More importantly, in his answer to the Pharisees' question, Jesus notes that Moses had allowed divorce only because of the hardness of the human heart (Mt 19:8). John Paul asserts that Jesus's movement to go behind the Mosaic law "means that this order [the original order of innocence] has not lost its force, although man has lost his primeval innocence. *Christ's answer* is decisive and clear. For this reason, *we must draw the normative conclusions from it*."[62]

In original innocence, the body communicates the person and the spousal meaning of the body simply. But after original sin "the discovery of the spousal meaning of the body was to cease being for

---

58. Ibid., no. 28:2.

59. See ibid., no. 29:4: "'That which is in the world,' *namely, concupiscence*, brings with it an almost constitutive *difficulty in identifying oneself with one's own body*, not only in the sphere of one's own subjectivity, but even more so *in regard to the subjectivity of the other human being*, of woman for man and man for woman."

60. See FC, par. 32: "In the context of a culture which seriously distorts or entirely misinterprets the true meaning of human sexuality, because it separates it from its essential reference to the person, the Church more urgently feels how irreplaceable is her mission of presenting sexuality as a value and task of the whole person, created male and female in the image of God."

61. See *TOB*, no. 3:2–3.

62. Ibid., no. 3:4.

them a simple reality of revelation and grace."[63] The spousal meaning of the body, however, is not entirely lost. It is only distorted. "In fact, in the whole perspective of his own 'history,' man will not fail to confer a spousal meaning on his own body. Even if this meaning does undergo and will undergo many distortions, it will always remain [on] the deepest level, which demands that it be revealed in all its simplicity and purity and manifested in its whole truth as a sign of the 'image of God.'"[64] An individual person's experience and assimilation of this truth will affect the meaning he expresses with his body even as the body maintains a definite structure in itself.

The communion of man and woman "had been intended to make man and woman mutually happy through the search of a simple and pure union in humanity, through a reciprocal offering of themselves ... and finally through the subordination of such a union to the blessing of fruitfulness with 'procreation.'"[65] After the Fall, man no longer intuits or experiences the simple meaning of his own body, and so it becomes difficult to communicate its spousal meaning to the other. "What disappears is the simplicity and 'purity' of their original experience, which helped to bring about a singular fullness of mutual self-communication. Obviously, the first parents did not stop *communicating with each other* through the body and its movements, gestures, and expressions; but what disappeared was the simple and direct self-communion connected with the original experience of reciprocal nakedness."[66] Similarly, the procreative attribute of the union was darkened by original sin.[67] Thus, after sin, "man and woman must reconstruct the meaning of the reciprocal disinterested gift with great effort."[68] This is both the gift and the task of redemption.

The Redemption of the Body

In Matthew 19, the foundational passage for John Paul's reflections, Christ appeals to the beginning of creation to emphasize the force of the order of original innocence even though historical man lives with the effects of original sin. But the Lord Jesus, the pope insists, brings hope because historical man "participates not only *in the history of hu-*

---

63. Ibid., no. 19:2.
65. Ibid., no. 30:3.
67. See ibid., no. 97:1.

64. Ibid., no. 15:5.
66. Ibid., no. 29:2.
68. Ibid., no. 22:4.

man sinfulness, as a hereditary, and at the same time personal and un-repeatable, subject of this history, but he also participates *in the history of salvation,* here too as its subject and co-creator. He is thus not merely shut out from original innocence due to his sinfulness, but also at the same time open to the mystery of the redemption realized in Christ and through Christ."[69] In fact, John Paul goes on to say here that had Christ only spoken of the beginning, of original innocence, without opening up the possibility for redemption, his answer would have been incomprehensible. Historical man would have been left with no resources to recapture the order of original innocence. But Christ reveals in his own person, and especially in his suffering and resurrection, the possibility of redemption for man and a redemption for the body. In fact, it is "precisely this *perspective of the redemption of the body* [that] *guarantees the continuity and the unity* between man's hereditary state of sin and his original innocence, although within history this innocence has been irremediably lost by him."[70]

Pope John Paul clarifies that the Christian idea of the "redemption of the body" in no way legitimizes the Manichean notion that the body is evil.[71] Rather, the redemption "points only to *man's sinfulness, by which he lost,* among other things, *the clear sense of the spousal meaning of the body,* in which the interior dominion and freedom of the spirit expresses itself."[72] This follows logically from John Paul's anthropology in which there is not only "the objective reality of the body" but also a "subjective consciousness as well as the subjective 'experience' of the body."[73]

The scriptural warrant for John Paul's understanding of the redemption of the body is the well known passage from Paul's letter to the Ephesians (5:21–33) where we read that the relationship of Christ to his church is analogous to the relationship of husband and wife. Simply put, Christ's gift of himself on the cross for his bride, the church, reveals the true nature of the self-gift of marriage. The pope writes: "That gift of self to the Father through obedience to the point of death (see Phil 2:8) is at the same time, according to Ephesians,

---

69. Ibid., no. 4:3.
70. Ibid. This conclusion also finds its way into *FC,* par. 13.
71. See *TOB,* nos. 44:5–45:5.   72. Ibid., no. 45:2.
73. Ibid., no. 60:1.

an act of 'giving himself for the Church.' In this expression, *redeeming love* transforms itself, I would say, *into spousal love.*"[74]

What this means, according to Wojtyła, is that the resurrection of Christ and the redemption of the body concerns more than mere bodiliness:

The resurrection, according to Christ's words reported by the synoptics, means not only the recovery of bodiliness and the reestablishment of human life in its integrity, through the union of body and soul, but also a wholly new state of human life itself.... There is no doubt that already in the answer given to the Sadducees [concerning marriage in the Kingdom of God; cf. Mt 22:30], Christ reveals the new condition of the human body in the resurrection, and he does so precisely by proposing a reference to and a comparison with the condition in which man shared from the "beginning."[75]

Later, the pope says that in this new human reality the spousal and redemptive dimensions of love "penetrate together with the grace of the sacrament [of matrimony] into the life of the spouses."[76] He goes on to say: "The spousal meaning of the body in its masculinity and femininity, which manifested itself for the first time in the mystery of creation on the background of man's original innocence, is united in the image of Ephesians with the redemptive meaning, and in this way it is confirmed and in some sense 'created anew.'"[77] This understanding of the redemption of the body is one of the aspects of John Paul's vision of marriage and family that appeals to scholars like Mary Shivanandan. *Theology of the Body* is less concerned with concupiscence than it is with the restoration of the spousal meaning of the body through redemption.[78]

This presents a unique challenge to mankind, both male and female. Man today is not exempt from the quest of discovering his own existence. The fallen condition necessitates that quest all the more. John Paul insists that man "must seek the meaning of his existence and the meaning of his humanity by reaching all the way to the mystery of creation through the reality of redemption. There he finds also the essential answer to the question about the meaning of the human

---

74. Ibid., no. 90:6. See *MD*, pars. 23–25, for a similar exegesis of Ephesians.
75. *TOB*, no. 66:3.   76. Ibid., no. 102:4.
77. Ibid. Cf. *FC*, par. 15.
78. See Shivanandan, *Crossing the Threshold of Love*, 138.

body, about the meaning of the masculinity and femininity of the human person."[79]

As I have already noted above, John Paul wants to emphasize man's freedom in relation to nature but without suggesting that nature is unimportant. On the contrary, man's freedom means he is all the more responsible for his actions. For this very reason, John Paul identifies the challenge of Christ's words. The Lord teaches that adultery is more subtle than bodily action and that, in fact, one can commit adultery in the heart simply by a lustful look. Lustful desire objectifies the body of the other. As the result of concupiscence, lust eliminates both the spousal meaning and the procreative meaning of the body, which for the pope are organically linked.[80] John Paul draws the conclusion: *"Christ's words are severe.* They demand that in the sphere in which relationships with persons of the other sex are formed, man has full and deep consciousness of his own acts, and above all of his interior acts, and that he is conscious of the inner impulses of his own 'heart' so that he can identify and evaluate them in a mature way."[81] Man must be "the authentic master of his own innermost impulses" which contributes to the freedom for gift.[82] This whole section of *Theology of the Body*, with its focus on interior impulses and interior as well as exterior action recalls the pope's earlier Thomistic training.

In order for man to live the challenge of the redemption of the body, to live in purity and freedom, John Paul insists that "he must *learn* with perseverance and consistency *what* the meaning of the body *is*, the meaning of femininity and masculinity. He must learn it … in the sphere of the interior reactions of his own 'heart.'"[83] By mastering his interior instincts, man "rediscovers the spiritual beauty of the sign constituted by the human body in its masculinity and femininity."[84]

The spiritual beauty of the body spoken of here by John Paul is fulfilled ultimately in the spiritualization of the body in the kingdom of God. The Lord tells the Sadducees that in the kingdom to come, men will be like angels (Lk 20:26). This does not mean that the hu-

---

79. *TOB*, no. 102:8.
81. Ibid., no. 48:3.
83. Ibid., no. 48:4.

80. See ibid., no. 39:5.
82. Ibid.
84. Ibid., no. 48:5.

man body will be transformed to an ethereal constitution. This would render the resurrection pointless. Rather, it will consist of a "spiritualization of his somatic nature, that is, by another 'system of powers' within man. The resurrection signifies a new submission of the body to the spirit."[85] Unlike "historical" man, "eschatological" man will be free of the various oppositions at work in his faculties.[86]

At the end of time, the redemption of Christ will culminate in "participation in the divine nature, participation in the inner life of God himself, penetration and permeation of what is essentially human by what is essentially divine.... This new spiritualization will be a *fruit of grace*, that is, *of God's self-communication in his very divinity,* not only to the soul, but *to the whole of man's psychosomatic subjectivity.*"[87] This is why the Lord teaches that there is no marriage in the world to come (Lk 20:35). It seems, according to Wojtyła, that biblical eschatology leads to *"the discovery of the 'spousal' meaning of the body above all as the 'virginal' meaning of being male and female in the body."*[88] This is true because God will give himself completely to "eschatological" man, and man will make of himself a complete gift to God. In one of the most beautiful passages of the catecheses, John Paul writes:

In this reciprocal gift of self by man, a gift that will become completely and definitively beatifying as the response worthy of a personal subject to God's gift of himself, the "virginity" or rather the virginal state of the body will manifest itself completely as the eschatological fulfillment of the "spousal" meaning of the body, as the specific sign and authentic expression of personal subjectivity as a whole. In this way, then, the eschatological situation in which "they will take neither wife nor husband" has its solid foundation in the future state of the personal subject when, as a consequence of the vision of God "face to face," *a love of such depth and power of concentration on God himself* will be born in the person that *completely absorbs the person's whole psychosomatic subjectivity.*[89]

The spousal meaning of the body is fulfilled in the virginal meaning of a pure and complete mutual gift between the person and God.

Though *Theology of the Body* is preeminently concerned with the

85. Ibid., no. 66:5.   86. See ibid., no. 67:1.
87. Ibid., no. 67:3.   88. Ibid., no. 67:4.
89. Ibid., no. 68:3.

spousal meaning of the body as it is lived in the marital union, it is apparent now that Pope John Paul does not ignore vocations of continence (that is, celibacy) and virginity. Indeed, continence "for the kingdom of God" is a "sign that the body, whose end is not death, tends toward glorification.... *This* charismatic *sign* of the 'other world' *expresses the most authentic power and dynamics* of the mystery of the 'redemption of the body.'"[90] This is why, he says, those who embrace charismatic continence as a way of life should understand not only the nature of sexual instinct but, more importantly, they must have "*the awareness of the freedom of the gift, which is* organically connected with the deep and mature *consciousness of the spousal meaning of the body.*"[91] Only in this awareness can voluntary continence "*find a full guarantee and motivation.*"[92]

Precisely because the spousal meaning of the body entails freedom for a self-gift in love, it is not entirely surprising that the pope holds that vocations other than marriage are capable of living out that spousal meaning in a non-conjugal way. The spousal meaning of the body can be lived in these various ways of life because Christ's redemptive love is a spousal love. His redemptive love embraces all these vocations, and each mirrors that love in its own way.[93] Though virginity and celibacy are eschatological signs of the authentic and complete spousal meaning of the body, this does not diminish the fact that this spousal meaning of the body is normally expressed in marriage in this life. Thus, when the pope turns to the question of the language of the body, he focuses intently on marriage, consent, and procreation.[94]

90. Ibid., no. 75:1.   91. Ibid., no. 80:5.

92. Ibid.

93. See *TOB*, no. 102:8. See also *FC*, par. 16, on virginity and celibacy. While John Paul does not go to great lengths to treat every possible vocation in the church (he does not mention widows, for example), Charles Curran's contention that *Theology of the Body* has nothing to teach single (presumably non-consecrated, non-celibate) persons and widows seems excessive. See Curran, *Moral Theology of Pope John Paul II*, 168.

94. William Mattison has offered a salient critique of popular presentations of *Theology of the Body* which focus entirely on marriage and sexuality as the normative expression of the spousal meaning of the body. His concern is that such emphasis redirects the pope's thought away from Christian tradition, which has more heavily focused on eschatological virginity and the resurrection of the body. Marriage may be the normative way that men and women live out the spousal meaning of the body in this life,

THE LANGUAGE OF
THE BODY IN MARRIAGE

Consent, the Body, and Truth

When John Paul reads scripture, especially the prophets (for example, Mal 2:14; Is 54:5–6, 10; Hos 1:2; Ezek 16 and 23), he is able to reaffirm his fundamental conviction that "the human body speaks a *'language'* of which it is not the author. *Its author is man,* as male or female, as bridegroom or bride: man with his perennial vocation to the communion of persons. Yet, man is *in some sense unable to express* this singular language of his personal existence and vocation *without the body.*"[95] Here, the pope introduces a new concept in his writing on meaning and the body.

Man, he says, must "reread" the language of the body to communicate the spousal meaning:

He [man] thus rereads that spousal meaning of the body as integrally inscribed in the structure of the masculinity or femininity of the personal subject. A correct rereading "in the truth" is an indispensable condition for proclaiming this truth or instituting the visible sign of marriage as a sacrament. The spouses proclaim exactly this "language of the body," reread in the truth, as the content and principle of their new life in Christ and in the Church.[96]

---

but it is not the definitive or only way for doing so. Mattison disagrees with the "ultimacy" of marriage some promoters of *Theology of the Body* espouse but he argues that the catecheses lend themselves to this misinterpretation. See William Mattison, "'When they rise from the dead, they neither marry nor are given to marriage': Marriage and Sexuality, Eschatology, and the Nuptial Meaning of the Body in Pope John Paul II's Theology of the Body," in *Sexuality and the U.S. Catholic Church: Crisis and Renewal,* ed. Lisa Sowle Cahill et al. (New York: Crossroad, 2006), 32–51. I agree with his concerns that popular writers are over-romanticizing marriage and sexuality. However, I would suggest that if there are elements in *Theology of the Body* that contribute to this confusion, it is because the focus of *Theology of the Body,* as I see it, is to articulate an experiential, biblically centered, defense of the notion of marriage and conjugal life found in *Humanae Vitae.*

95. *TOB,* no. 104:7.

96. Ibid., no. 105:2. Following the line of John Paul's thought, Walter J. Schu suggests that "re-reading" the body means reading the intrinsic meaning the body possesses in itself. Schu offers two helpful analogies to explain: "We are called to reread the language of the body in truth—the truth of the intrinsic meaning it possesses in itself and its acts. In a similar way Shakespeare made use of the English language already constituted. If our intentions correspond to the inner meaning of the language of the body,

Man remains the author of the meanings he communicates through the language of the body, but in the pope's anthropology, only "after having reread the 'language of the body' in truth."[97] It will become increasingly clear below that for John Paul the body communicates with a language that is inherent to nature and the structure of the human person. Normally, this language should communicate the spousal meaning of the body (which is the gift of self in love), but because of the effects of sin, this language is often corrupted by individuals and by spouses acting together.

If this is true, it is not surprising that John Paul again says that the body does not act on its own behalf but on behalf of the person. It will speak *"in the name and with the authority of the person."*[98] Through their bodies, the couple engages in "the conjugal dialogue, which is proper to their vocation and based on the language of the body, continually reread on the right occasion and at the proper time: and it is necessary that it is reread in the truth!"[99] This dialogue of bodies includes more than the conjugal act. The pope writes, "Given that a *complex of meanings corresponds to the language,* the couple—through their conduct and behavior, actions and gestures ('gestures of tenderness,' see *Gaudium et Spes,* [par.] 49)—are called to become the authors of these meanings of the 'language of the body,' from which they then build and continually deepen love, faithfulness, conjugal integrity, and the union that remains indissoluble until death."[100] Later in his catecheses, John Paul will reference these gestures of tenderness in his defense of periodic continence within marriage.

Simply put, *"man is the causal origin of actions that have through themselves (per se) clear-cut meanings. He is thus the causal origin of actions and at the same time the author of their meanings."*[101] The man and the woman appropriate the meanings of the language of the body

---

we are living in the truth. If, on the other hand, we attempt to confer on our actions a meaning that contradicts the significance they possess in themselves, we are falsifying the language of the body. We are telling a lie with our bodies. In the Garden of Gethsemane, Judas greeted Christ with a kiss of friendship. But he meant that kiss to betray his Master. Everyone recognizes immediately the terrible nature of violating in this way the language of the body" (*Splendor of Love,* 144).

97. *TOB,* no. 107:4.
98. Ibid., no. 106:2.
99. Ibid.
100. Ibid.
101. Ibid., no. 105:6.

(reread in the truth) in their communion with each other when they consciously ascribe those meanings to their behavior and action. According to Wojtyła, "*There is an organic link between rereading the integral meaning of the 'language of the body' in the truth and the consequent use of that language in conjugal life.*"[102] Thus "if the human being—male and female—in marriage (and indirectly also in all spheres of mutual life together) *gives to* his *behavior a meaning in conformity with the fundamental truth of the language of the body*, then he too 'is in the truth.' In the opposite case, he commits lies and falsifies the language of the body."[103]

The fundamental truth that the language of the body is supposed to communicate within marriage for Wojtyła is contained in the words of consent exchanged by the couple on their wedding day.

The structure of the sacramental sign [of marriage] remains, in fact, in its essence the same as "in the beginning." What determines it is *in some sense "the language of the body,"* inasmuch as the man and woman, who are to become one flesh by marriage, express in this sign the reciprocal gift of masculinity and femininity as the foundation of the conjugal union of persons. The sign of the sacrament of Marriage is constituted by the fact that the words spoken by the new spouses take up again the same "language of the body" as at the "beginning" and, at any rate, give it a concrete and unrepeatable expression.[104]

He goes on to say that the language of the body is, therefore, "*not only the 'substratum,'* but *in some sense also the constitutive content of the communion of persons.*"[105] The man and the woman give themselves to each other precisely in their masculinity and their femininity. The couple is called to use the language of the body to express both the unitive meaning and the procreative meaning of love.[106]

---

102. Ibid., no. 106:3.

103. Ibid.

104. Ibid., no. 103:4–5. All of these ideas are included in the "Letter to Families," pars. 7, 8, and 10. With these reflections, John Paul resituates the discussion of the *ratio et consumatum* of marriage within the context of language and self-gift. The question of what constitutes a marriage was heavily debated in the medieval church. For a brief history of this discussion see Theodore Mackin, SJ, *The Marital Sacrament* (New York: Paulist Press, 1989), 285–93.

105. *TOB*, no. 103:5.

106. See ibid., no. 106:4.

The words of consent "*confirm* the essential '*truth*' of the language of the body and (at least indirectly, *implicitly*) they also *exclude* the essential '*untruth*,' the falseness of the language of the body."[107] The body speaks the truth of consent through "conjugal love, faithfulness, and integrity," while "untruth or falsity is expressed through all that negates conjugal love, faithfulness, and integrity."[108] When John Paul here speaks of untruth in the language of the body, he first of all means the untruth that is adultery.[109] Below, it will become apparent that he believes contraception is also a lie, a falsification of the language of the body. Falsification in the language of the body is the result of concupiscence: "*The one who rereads this 'language' and then expresses it* not according to the needs proper to marriage as a covenant and sacrament, is naturally and morally the man of concupiscence."[110]

However, when a man and woman reread the language of the body in the truth and use that language rightly, they are once again invoking the spousal meaning of the body as it was in the beginning and as it has been redeemed in Christ.[111] In the penultimate audience before turning, finally, to the moral norm of *Humanae Vitae*, Pope John Paul insightfully notes: "The 'language of the body' reread in the truth goes hand in hand *with the discovery of the inner inviolability of the person*. At the same time, precisely this discovery expresses the authentic depth of the reciprocal belonging of the spouses, the beginning and growing *consciousness of belonging to each other*, of being destined for each other: 'My beloved is mine and I am his' (Song 2:16)."[112] This brings redemption of the body back in a full circle to the beginning. The spousal meaning of the body surpasses concupiscence by recognizing the inviolability of the other. Through their consent and the language of the body, the couple, Wojtyła will insist, is called to bear witness both to a spousal love and a procreative love.[113]

---

107. Ibid., no. 105:1.
108. Ibid.
109. See, for example, ibid., no. 104:8: "*The body tells the truth* through faithfulness and conjugal love, and, when it commits 'adultery' it tells a lie, *it commits falsehood.*"
110. Ibid., no. 107:1.   111. See ibid., no. 105:5.
112. Ibid., no. 110:8.   113. See, for example, ibid., no. 106:4.

The Moral Norm of *Humanae Vitae*

Almost five years after he began his catecheses on the theology of the body, Pope John Paul admits: "The reflections about human love in the divine plan carried out so far would remain in some way incomplete if we did not try to see their concrete application in the area of conjugal and familial morality."[114] The theology of the body is not only speculative. It is also practical. And now the pope turns to *Humanae Vitae*, especially to pars. 11 and 12 of that encyclical. Yet, and this should be clear, in writing the final part of these catecheses on *Humanae Vitae*, the pope does not wish these to be considered a mere appendix: "If I draw particular attention precisely to these final catecheses, I do so not only because the topic discussed by them is more closely connected with our present age, but first of all because *it is from this topic that the questions spring* that run in some way through the whole of our reflections. It follows that this final part is not added to the whole, but is organically and homogenously united with it."[115] These were among the last words of John Paul's five-year catechetical project. The norms of *Humanae Vitae* are the formal cause of the *Theology of the Body* catecheses.[116]

John Paul follows upon his earlier observation that the sacrament of marriage is based on the language of the body "reread" in the truth, and the truth is the self-gift first expressed in the words of consent that are exchanged in the liturgy. Now he goes on to say that this truth is constantly reaffirmed: "We are also dealing with a truth that is, so to speak, always affirmed anew. In fact, as man and woman live in marriage 'until death,' in some sense they continuously re-propose the sign they themselves gave—through the liturgy of the sacrament—on the day of their wedding."[117] The conjugal act is the moment *"so rich in meaning"* that it is "particularly important that the 'language of the body' be reread in the truth. This reading becomes an indispensable condition for *acting in the truth* or for behaving *in conformity with the value and the moral norm*."[118] The moral norm he

---

114. Ibid., no. 118:1.
115. Ibid., no. 133:4. See also *FC*, pars. 29 and 31.
116. See *TOB*, no. 133:4   117. Ibid., no. 118:4.
118. Ibid..

defends here is the norm that the conjugal act must remain open to procreation.

The pope notes that the moral norm, expressed in *Humanae Vitae* (par. 12), that the two meanings of the conjugal act (the procreative and the unitive) are inseparable is immediately defended by Paul VI with the following sentence: "By its immediate structure, the conjugal act, while most closely uniting husband and wife, capacitates them for the generation of new lives, according to laws inscribed in the very being of man and woman" (*HV*, par. 12). Wojtyła is fascinated with Pope Paul VI's twin notions of the "innermost structure" of the conjugal act (which he takes to be synonymous with the nature of the act), on the one hand, and the "laws inscribed in the very being of man and woman," on the other. He writes: "The encyclical leads one to look for the foundation of the norm determining the morality of the actions of man and woman in the conjugal act, in the nature of this act itself and more deeply still in the nature of the acting *subjects themselves*."[119]

Thus, John Paul is certain that the nature of the conjugal act must be understood by the couple.

The "*innermost structure*" (or *nature*) of the conjugal act constitutes *the necessary basis for an adequate reading and discovery of the meanings* that must be carried over into the conscience and the decisions of the acting persons. It also constitutes the necessary basis for grasping the adequate relationship of these meanings, namely, their inseparability. Since "the conjugal act"—at one and the same time—"deeply unites husband and wife" and together "makes them able to generate new lives," and since the one as well as the other thing comes about "by its innermost structure," it follows (with the necessity proper to reason, logical necessity) that the human person "should" read, *at one and the same time*, the "*two meanings* of the conjugal act" and also the "*inseparable connection* between the two meanings of the conjugal act."[120]

Here, finally, we see John Paul's concern for the nature of the conjugal act on full display. He argues that meaning is not arbitrary but is dependent on ontology. He even says that "what is at stake here is the *truth*, first *in the ontological dimension* ('innermost structure') and then—as a consequence—in the *subjective and psychological dimen-*

119. Ibid., no. 118:5.
120. Ibid., no. 118:6, quoting *HV*, par. 12.

sions ('meaning')."[121] Meaning "is born in consciousness *with the re-reading of the* (ontological) *truth of the object.* Through this rereading, the (ontological) truth, enters so to speak, into the cognitive, that is, subjective and psychological dimension."[122] The ontological precedes the psychological and the subjective.

When Paul VI referred to the "reasonableness" of the moral norm (cf. *HV*, par. 12), John Paul thought he was referring not only to the ontological dimension of the conjugal act but also to the psychological and subjective dimension. Nevertheless, the reasonableness of the subjective dimension is dependent on *"the right understanding* of the innermost structure of the conjugal act, that is, the adequate rereading of the meanings that correspond to this structure and their inseparable connection in view of morally right behavior.... In this sense, we say that the norm is identical with rereading the 'language of the body' in the truth."[123] The subjective dimension can be neither properly understood nor communicated without reference to the ontological.

John Paul is clear that the conjugal act has its own moral qualification. Thus even if a couple is morally right in deciding not to procreate, "the *moral problem* of the way of acting in such a case remains, and this mode expresses itself in an act that—according to the Church's teaching transmitted in the encyclical—possesses *its own intrinsic moral qualification,* positive or negative. The first, positive, corresponds to the 'natural' regulation of fertility; the second, negative, corresponds to 'artificial contraception.'"[124] Later, he says that natural regulation of fertility is in conformity with the natural law. Conformity with natural law is not legalistic but personal and virtuous for Wojtyła:

By "natural law" we understand here the "order of nature" in the field of procreation inasmuch as it is understood by right reason: this order is the expression of the Creator's plan for the human person. And it is exactly this that the encyclical [that is, *Humanae Vitae*], together with the whole tradition of Christian teaching and practice, particularly underlines: the virtuous character of the attitude expressing itself in the "natural" regulation of fertility is determined, *not so much* by the faithfulness to an impersonal *"natural law,"* but to the personal Creator, the source and Lord of the order that is shown in this law.[125]

---

121. *TOB*, no. 118:6.
122. Ibid., no. 119:1.
123. Ibid., no. 119:2.
124. Ibid., no. 122:3.
125. Ibid., no. 124:6.

The language of the body includes not only masculinity and femininity but also "the inner structures of the organism, of somatic and psychosomatic reactivity. All this should find its fitting place in the language with which the spouses dialogue as persons called to communion in the 'union of the body.'"[126] Since the person is inseparable from his body, self-gift includes the true communion of the body in relationship to the laws inscribed by the Creator of the body.

In *Familiaris Consortio*, John Paul is clear that the body has its own "innate language."[127] When the couple act at cross purposes from the body's innate language they introduce an "objectively contradictory language" into their self-donation.[128] John Paul's reference to an "innate language" recalls his commitment to the idea that man's activity should be obedient to nature. John Crosby sees this as a decisive rebuttal of dualism:

> Their bodies have a nuptial [that is, spousal] meaning, and their bodily union has the meaning of self-donation, *independently of any subjective act of conferring which they might perform.* This is why the bodily union of man and woman in the absence of spousal self-donation and of spousal belonging to one another (that is, the bodily union of fornication or adultery) has something untruthful, it "says" as it were too much, more than is really meant.... We find, then, that the nuptial meaning of the body does not exist merely as conferred by the spouses, it is rather pre-formed in the nature of man and woman, and is so strong a reality that it constitutes a norm for their subjective intentions; and it cannot be ignored without persons misusing each other.[129]

This is exactly what John Paul makes explicit in *Familiaris Consortio*. The couple that uses artificial contraception set themselves as "'arbiters' of the divine plane" and they "'manipulate' and degrade human sexuality—as well as themselves."[130] Whereas those who respect the language of the body "are acting as 'ministers' of God's plan and they 'benefit from' their sexuality according to the original dynamism of 'total' self-giving, without manipulation or alteration."[131]

As in *The Acting Person, Love and Responsibility*, and *Humanae Vitae*, self-mastery is here still presented as necessary for the proper

---

126. Ibid., no. 125:1.   127. FC, par. 32.
128. Ibid.
129. Crosby, "The Personalism of John Paul II," 66.
130. FC, par. 32.
131. Ibid.

rereading of the language of the body.[132] John Paul repeats his earlier observation that self-mastery is not always the same as the domination of the forces of nature. In fact, he is concerned that the extension of the means which dominate nature "threatens the human person for whom the method of 'self-mastery' is and remains specific.... The transposition of 'artificial means' ... *breaks* the constitutive dimension of the person, deprives man of the subjectivity proper to him, and turns him into *an object of manipulation*."[133] The language of the body is "more than mere sexual reactivity."[134] It is "an authentic language of persons, [which] is subject to the demand for truth, that is, to objective moral norms."[135]

By now, it should be clear that the criterion of truth for conjugal life is the total self-gift. This is the truth that is expressed in consent, and it is the truth reaffirmed in the language of the body. The pope writes: "*According to this criterion of truth* ... the conjugal act 'means' not only love, but also potential fruitfulness, and thus it cannot be deprived of its full and adequate meaning by means of artificial interventions."[136] It is not licit to separate these two meanings "because the one as well as the other belong to the innermost truth of the conjugal act. The one is realized together with the other and, in a certain way, the one through the other."[137] John Paul is not clear here whether he is referring to the ontological dimension of the conjugal act or the psychological dimension. The strength of his tone would suggest the former: "When the conjugal act is *deprived of its inner truth* because it is deprived artificially of its procreative capacity, it also *ceases to be an act of love*."[138] A real bodily union is brought about, but it "does not correspond to the inner truth and dignity of personal communion."[139]

Since natural regulation of fertility requires self-mastery, it requires

---

132. See *TOB*, no. 123:5.
133. Ibid., no. 123:1.
134. Ibid., no. 123:4.
135. Ibid.
136. Ibid., no. 123:6.
137. Ibid.
138. Ibid.

139. Ibid., no. 123:7. John Paul provides a strong defense of the inseparability of the unitive and procreative meanings of the conjugal act. He never identifies the unitive meaning of the conjugal act with the spousal meaning of the body. In fact, though he says that the procreative meaning and the spousal meaning are organically united, he routinely speaks of spousal meaning of the body expressed in the conjugal act as only "potentially procreative" (see, for example, *TOB*, no. 132:2). Protecting the dignity of the

also continence. And continence is not simply a technique but a "definite and permanent moral attitude, *it is a virtue*, and thus the whole mode of behavior guided by it becomes virtuous."[140] For the pope, continence is the virtue that opposes concupiscence of the flesh. Continence is "the *ability to master, control, and orient the sexual drives* (concupiscence of the flesh) and their consequences in the psychosomatic subjectivity of human beings."[141] Elsewhere, continence is said to be "the spiritual effort aimed at expressing the 'language of the body' not only in the truth, but also in the authentic richness of the 'manifestations of affection.'"[142] Here he seems to refer back to the gestures of tenderness.

With *Humanae Vitae* (par. 20), Pope John Paul affirms that this effort is possible, that it requires that man be viewed as person with his or her own subjectivity, with his or her own choices. Another person should not be viewed as simply a means to an end.[143] The personalistic norm, articulated in his earlier writings, is fully articulated in John Paul's *Theology of the Body*.

CONCLUSION

The development of Karol Wojtyła's thought on love, sex, and marriage began with his published articles in the 1950s and reached its culmination in these *Theology of the Body* catecheses. Here he brought the insights he had developed in his previous work, which were discussed in chapters 3 and 4 of this book, to bear on an extended explanation and defense of Paul VI's 1968 encyclical *Humanae Vitae*. In *Familiaris Consortio*, John Paul invited theologians to develop an organic presentation of the teaching established in *Humanae Vitae*.[144] He led by example with his *Theology of the Body*.

---

two inseparable meanings of the conjugal act protects the potential of the procreative expression of the spousal meaning (see *TOB*, no. 132:2). I believe he makes this distinction to separate the modes of the spousal meaning's expression. The spousal meaning of the body is expressed in the conjugal act, but it is also expressed in other gestures of affection which are not potentially procreative (see ibid., no. 129:6).

140. Ibid., no. 124:4. This was developed in more detail in *Love and Responsibility*, as I noted in the previous chapter.

141. Ibid., no. 128:1.   142. Ibid., no. 129:1.

143. See ibid., no. 129:2.   144. See *FC*, par. 31.

His presentation in these catecheses is based upon a scriptural exegesis, most notably of Genesis, the gospels, and Paul's letter to the
Ephesians. In doing so, John Paul provides a systematic explanation
of creation as gift and of man called to find himself by giving himself
to another in self-gift.[145] The body, all the while, is manifesting the
person who is created in the image of God, and contains within itself
a spousal attribute directing the person to the other. When the person "rereads" the language built into his body and his actions, he is
able to ascribe meaning to those actions that are congruent with his
nature. Such is the proper expression of spousal love as self-gift: the
body truly speaks the offering of one person to another. When the
body is prevented from communicating this meaning, as in the case
of contraception, or when the person intends to communicate something different from the body, as in the case of adultery, then the person's actions are a lie.

John Paul's emphasis on subjective consciousness, of living the
truth in love, provided a breath of fresh air in what otherwise had
become a rather stale debate in the twentieth century regarding
the theological and philosophical categories of nature and person.
Richard Spinello is right that Wojtyła's moral vision moves beyond
a Thomistic anthropology in his emphasis on consciousness and
self-determination along with his focus on the communitarian nature
of the human person.[146] There is a cottage industry of popular com-

---

145. I disagree with Charles Curran, who, while he notes that *Theology of the Body*
has a generally positive understanding of marriage and sexuality, nonetheless believes
the catecheses do not provide a systematic treatment of love. This is clearly not the case.
Love, for Pope John Paul, is the gift of self. Curran wrote this criticism before the publication of Michael Waldstein's translation of the catechetical talks and the introduction
of the headers found in the original manuscript. Curran's larger criticism is that *Theology
of the Body* in general is not a systematic treatment, since it was delivered piecemeal in
the form of general audiences. As I mentioned in the general introduction of this study,
Waldstein's research has shown this is not the case. Perhaps Curran would view the issue more favorably in light of this new development. See Curran, *The Moral Theology of
Pope John Paul II*, 167, 170.

146. Spinello, *Genius of John Paul II*, 75. Mary Shivanandan lists a series of unique
contributions made by John Paul to the understanding of the human person: the incommunicability of the person yet with a call to communion; the application of Trinitarian
theology of *communio personarum* to anthropology; male and female complementarity; and the relationship of gift and love, to name a few (see Shivanandan, *Crossing the
Threshold of Love*, 141–70). The constraints of this study have prevented me from ad-

mentaries, study guides, and explanations of this vision of marriage and love.[147] It has been argued that the pope's emphasis on the communion of persons effectively responded to a culture dominated by the "'relationship marketplace' ... in which we instrumentalize others, rather than loving them."[148] I think this is true.

There are some Catholic theologians, however, who have been critical of the pope's theology of sex, marriage, and the family, especially as it is articulated in *Theology of the Body*. Some have argued, for example, that the idea of a self-gift manifest in each sexual act is simply too romantic. Interestingly, this criticism is articulated not only by the feminist theologian, Lisa Sowle Cahill, but it is also held by David Matzko McCarthy, each for different reasons. Cahill thinks that John Paul's theology is too romantic and does not take into consideration what she perceives to be the harsh social circumstances of women.[149] McCarthy, on the other hand, is concerned that the overly romantic personalist view of marriage espoused by John Paul lifts sexuality out of the normal routine of married life.[150] Unlike Cahill, who is more interested with the role of women in society, McCarthy believes that John Paul's thought runs the danger of isolating the family from its larger social vocation.[151] I tend to agree with McCarthy's critique here, but only if *Theology of the Body* is read as a work that stands sufficiently on its own as some of its interpreters are unfortu-

---

dressing all of these aspects John Paul's thought. It would be an interesting study to ascertain the true uniqueness of some of these components of pope's thought *vis-à-vis* the Christian tradition.

147. The most popular of these is Christopher West, *Theology of the Body Explained: A Commentary on John Paul II's Man and Woman He Created Them*, rev. ed. (Boston: Pauline Books and Media, 2007).

148. David Cloutier, "Heaven Is a Place on Earth? Analyzing the Popularity of Pope John Paul II's Theology of the Body," in *Sexuality and the U.S. Catholic Church*, ed. Cahill et al., 19. Also arguing from a self-described feminist perspective, Charles Curran criticizes John Paul for overemphasizing women's maternal role while showing no concern for their role in the world and in the social sphere. Given the social condition of women throughout history, he thinks it is a danger to overemphasize women's self-gift and service (see Curran, *Moral Theology of Pope John Paul II*, 193).

149. See Lisa Sowle Cahill, *Sex, Gender, and Christian Ethics* (Cambridge: Cambridge University Press, 1996), 201

150. David Matzko McCarthy, *Sex and Love in the Home*, rev. ed. (London: SCM Press, 2004), 43.

151. See ibid., 8, 118.

nately prone to do. I have argued in this chapter that the pope's task with the catecheses was much more narrow than it seems: to defend *Humanae Vitae* with a biblical and experiential perspective.

Moreover, both Cahill and Charles Curran argue that John Paul's interpretation of scripture is too much indebted to the hierarchical teaching of the church, and particularly to *Humanae Vitae*.[152] They both contend that this has hindered his interpretation of scripture on its own terms. Curran also complains that the pope does not appeal adequately to the experience of the lay faithful; he does not consult the wisdom of the *sensus fidelium*. A more popular and somewhat more visceral version of this criticism is one offered by Notre Dame law professor, Cathleen Kaveny.[153]

Despite the criticisms it has received, *Theology of the Body* has taken hold in the Catholic church. Through the work of Christopher West and others, more and more of the lay faithful, especially engaged and married couples, are exposed to its principal tenets. This study, too, will hopefully serve as a small contribution to the massive secondary material now available on Pope John Paul's wonderful catechetical lectures.

For the present purposes of this study, then, it is important to summarize John Paul's view of the spousal meaning of the body in order to identify which components and characteristics can be supported by Aquinas's mature thought. First, human existence is itself a gift from God out of nothingness. The gift of existence is constitutive of human nature and personhood. Secondly, precisely because they are created in the image of a God who is himself a communion of divine persons, John Paul argues that human existence is inherently directed to the other. Namely, the life of man is characterized by a drive to self-gift—a drive from nothingness to the other.

Third, since man is an embodied person, the human body participates in this spousal character of human existence. The spousal

152. See Lisa Sowle Cahill, "Catholic Sexual Ethics and the Dignity of the Person: A Double Message," *Theological Studies* 50 (1989): 148; Curran, *Moral Theology of Pope John Paul II*, 177.

153. See Cathleen Kaveny, "What Women Want: 'Buffy,' the Pope, and the New Feminists," *Commonweal* 130, no. 19 (November 7, 2003): 18–24; Cathleen Kaveny, "The 'New' Feminism? John Paul II and the 1912 Encyclopedia," *Commonweal* 135, no. 6 (March 28, 2008): 8.

meaning of the body is the capacity to express the person's gift of self to another human person and, ultimately, to God. Since human persons are male or female, this spousal meaning is complementarily and equally expressed in both a masculine and feminine manner. This expression most often occurs in the relationship of marriage, in which there is complete conjugal self-giving, but the spousal meaning of the body is more fundamental than the marital relationship. The spousal meaning of the body is manifest even in (and perhaps especially in) celibate vocations as expressions of the virginal and redemptive aspects of that spousal meaning.

Fourth, because man is a free rational animal, he is not entirely subservient to nature but nonetheless must be obedient to it in order to properly express the meaning of his existence, which is the gift of self to another. This is to say that men and women are not arbitrary authors of the language of the body. However much they may be free to misuse the body (and distort its accompanying communicative value), ultimately they are only truly fulfilled when they communicate love, life, and fidelity in accordance with the body's innermost truth: the spousal meaning.

We will now turn our attention to the anthropology of Thomas Aquinas—and, as will soon be apparent, we will not be turning far from our consideration of *Theology of the Body*. In fact, our investigation of Thomas will prove particularly illuminative of the spousal meaning of the body as expressed above.

6

The Anthropology of
Thomas Aquinas

Long before the events of the fourteenth century precipitated the
downward spiral in moral theology, Aquinas discovered the thought
of Aristotle. His incorporation of Aristotle's hylomorphic view of the
human person as a composite being of soul (form) and body (matter)
has important consequences for his anthropology. Since the human
being is a composite of soul and body, both are involved in man's call
to fulfillment, to beatitude. According to both Thomas Aquinas and
Pope John Paul II, both are involved in human thought and action.
Both shared in the original innocence of our first parents and both
suffered the consequences of original sin. For Aquinas, both are redeemed but continue to suffer from the wounds of sin.

This chapter offers a survey of Thomas's anthropology and how
it relates to sexual difference and sexuality. The first section consists
of an exegesis of Aquinas's conception of man as a composite person.
The second section explores the importance of sexual difference and
the relationship of sexuality to human flourishing. Finally, the third
section reviews Aquinas's understanding of original innocence and
original sin.

The purpose of this chapter is to identify the salient characteristics of Thomas's anthropology, which is contingent upon a robust
union between body and soul. Far from being concerned with "bi-

ological facticity," Aquinas's hylomorphism was evident in every aspect of his description of man: from the interaction of body and soul, to sexual difference, to human flourishing and original sin. Aquinas holds that the body is neither unimportant nor a mere instrument of the human person.

MAN: A COMPOSITE PERSON

A Body and Soul Composite

Aquinas introduces his treatise on man with the following note: "Having treated of the spiritual and of the corporeal creature, we now proceed to treat of man, who is composed of a spiritual and corporeal substance [*qui ex spirituali et corporali substantia componitur*]."[1] In the first several questions of this treatise, he lays out his vision of man as a composite being, a substantial unity between body and soul. He understood himself to be taking a different philosophical approach to human nature than his predecessors and perhaps even his contemporaries.[2] This is clear from the interlocutors he employs in various arti-

1. *ST* I, prologue to q. 75. Gilles Emery, OP, notes that in recent decades "the notion of man as a composite of soul and body often raised a concern over the possibility of dualism" ("The Unity of Man, Body and Soul, in St. Thomas Aquinas," in *Trinity, Church, and the Human Person: Thomistic Essays* [Naples, Fla.: Sapientia Press, 2007], 209). This is undoubtedly true. The mere mention of "two principles" comprising human nature (body and soul) strikes many as dualist. As a result, Emery notes, we are left with two options: either to embrace a Greek anthropology which separates soul from body or to embrace a biblical anthropology that sees man as "a bodily person existing in indissoluble unity" (ibid.). Joseph Ratzinger has offered an insightful critique of recent movements in theology which casts aside any understanding of an immortal soul in favor of an indissoluble unity in which man, body, and soul perish at death. He even notes that the new *Roman Missal* has largely suppressed the word "soul [*anima*]" from its prayers, even from the funeral rites. See Joseph Ratzinger, *Eschatology: Death and Eternal Life*, 2nd ed., trans. Michael Waldstein (Washington, D.C.: The Catholic University of America Press, 2007), 105–61. This is interesting because Aquinas himself was concerned to defend a real unity of the body and soul in which neither could be understood without the other and both were part and parcel of the definition of man, both as a species and as an individual. Nevertheless, the connection is not indissoluble. The soul separates from the body at death and returns to it at general resurrection.

2. For an excellent survey of conception of the body and soul in Thomas *vis-à-vis* his contemporaries, see Anton Pegis, *St. Thomas and the Problem of the Soul in the Thirteenth Century* (Toronto: St. Michael's College, 1934); Richard C. Dale, *The Problem of the Rational Soul in the Thirteenth Century* (Leiden: Brill, 1995); Edouard-Henri Wéber,

cles throughout the treatise.[3] The *antiqui philosophi* to whom Thomas often refers in these articles are the pre-Socratics, who each held some material body or another (wind, fire, air, and water) as the principle of life.[4] Aquinas makes two moves in response.

First, he writes that "it is manifest that not every principle of vital action is a soul, for then the eye would be a soul, as it is a principle of vision and the same might be applied to the other instruments of the soul: but it is the *first* principle of life, which we call the soul."[5] For Aquinas, by definition that not every vital action is a soul, for we do not call an eye or any other instrument of vital action a soul. The soul by definition is the first principle of life that gives rise to all these vital actions.

In his second move, Aquinas appeals to our experience of the world.[6] The Angelic Doctor notes that if a soul were a body, then all bodies would be alive. In effect, the fact that some bodies are living and other bodies are not means that there must be some principle to distinguish a living body from a non-living body aside from corporeality as such. This principle, Aquinas says, is act. A body is alive when

---

OP, *La person humaine au XIIIe siècle: L'avènement chez les Maîtres parisiens de l'acception moderne de l'homme* (Paris: J. Vrin, 1991).

3. Cf. *ST* I, q. 75, a. 1, co.

4. Robert Pasnau, *Thomas Aquinas on Human Nature: A Philosophical Study of* Summa theologiae Ia 75–89 (New York: Cambridge University Press, 2002), 30–34. Pasnau's exegesis of Aquinas's treatise on human nature is generally well done from an analytical standpoint. However, following Aquinas's theory of delayed hominization, he concludes that a "vast majority of abortions, though they may be unfortunate and immoral, are not tantamount to murder" (ibid., 120). There are many Thomists who argue in favor of delayed hominization. See, for example, Joseph Donceel, "Abortion: Mediate v. Immediate Animation," *Continuum* 5 (1967): 167–71, and Donceel, "Immediate Animation and Delayed Hominization," *Theological Studies* 31 (1970): 76–105; William Wallace, "Nature and Human Nature as the Norm of Medical Ethics," in *Catholic Perspectives on Medical Morals,* ed. Edmund D. Pellegrino, John P. Langan, and John C. Harvey (Dordrecht: Kluwer, 1989), 23–52. Some Thomists have been successful in updating Aquinas's scientific viewpoint. See Stephen J. Heaney, "Aquinas and the Presence of the Human Rational Soul in the Early Embryo," *The Thomist* 56 (1992): 19–48, and Nicanor Austriaco, OP, "Immediate Hominization from the Systems Perspectives," *National Catholic Bioethics Quarterly* 4 (2004): 719–38. For a brief introduction to the anthropology of the pre-Socratics, see Joseph Torchia, OP, *Exploring Personhood: An Introduction to the Philosophy of Human Nature* (New York: Rowman and Littlefield, 2008), 17–38.

5. *ST* I, q. 75, a. 1, co.

6. Ibid.

it is a certain type of body that is brought to act, and the actuality of this body which gives it life is called the soul.

In the first article of the first question in his treatise on man, Aquinas concludes that the soul is not a thing. It is a principle of act and the principle of life. But the soul is also much more than a principle. For Thomas, the soul is also subsistent. At first glance, this may be surprising. Since, as an objector points out: "That which subsists is said to be *this particular thing*. Now *this particular thing* is said not of the soul, but of that which is composed of soul and body."[7] If the soul is not a thing *per se*, how can it be subsistent?

Aquinas bases his answer in the human experience of knowledge: "It is clear that by means of the intellect man can have knowledge of all corporeal things."[8] Aquinas concludes, therefore, that the intellectual principle (the soul) has an operation (understanding) which is *per se* apart from the body.[9] Corporeal things cannot coexist in the same place at the same time. Knowledge, which assimilates the thing known to the knower, requires that there is a faculty of knowledge that is not corporeal. It is important to note that Aquinas also tele-

---

7. *ST* I, q. 75, a. 2, obj 1.

8. *ST* I, q. 75, a. 2, co. Aquinas, it should be noted, is writing well before the episte-mological breakdown introduced by the methodical doubt of Rene Descartes in which human understanding was separated from reality. In the *Summa Theologiae*, the Angelic Doctor is not concerned with the epistemological problem of whether our intellect adequately perceives reality or not. Indeed, he presumes it does. This is one of the many ways in which his intellectual milieu differs from Karol Wojtyła, whose work on Max Scheler was an attempt to reconnect knowledge with reality in an age of epistemological doubt. For a concise overview of Thomas's relationship with modern theories of knowledge, see Paul T. Durbin, "St. Thomas and the History of Theories of Knowledge," appendix 6, in Thomas Gilby, ed. *Summa Theologiae* (New York: McGraw-Hill, 1968), 12:181–84; Paul T. Durbin, "Naïve Realism," appendix 7, in Aquinas, *Summa Theologiae*, ed. Gilby, 12:185–87; John F. Peifer, *The Concept in Thomism* (New York: Bookman Associates, 1952). For a historical survey of epistemological trends from Descartes, Immanuel Kant, and Karl Marx, see Benedict Ashley, OP, *Theologies of the Body: Humanist and Christian* (Braintree, Mass.: The Pope John Center, 1985), 51–100. Charles Taylor has also provided an important and thorough history of secularism. See Charles Taylor, *A Secular Age* (Cambridge, Mass.: Belknap Press of Harvard University Press, 2007). Another recent work has outlined the encounter of Thomas's moral theory with the modern separation of practical reason and speculative reason represented in the thought of Immanuel Kant and John Locke. See Luis Cortest, *The Disfigured Face: Traditional Natural Law and Its Encounter with Modernity* (New York: Fordham University Press, 2008).

9. *ST* I, q. 75, a. 2, co.

graphs his full anthropology in this question, namely, that although the intellect understands apart from the body, the body is necessary for the action of the intellect because the body provides the object of the intellectual action, which is the phantasm.[10] It is because the souls of brute animals have no operations apart from the body, because a sensitive soul's operation corresponds to some change in the body, that their souls are not subsistent.[11]

Even though the human soul is subsistent, Thomas is clear: the soul itself is not man. Man is more than his soul. Here, Aquinas emphasizes the importance he ascribes to matter (the body) in the definition of a species. "To the nature of the species belongs what the definition signifies; and in natural things the matter is part of the species; not, indeed, signate [that is, designated or particular] matter, which is the principle of individuality; but the common matter. For as it belongs to the notion of this particular man to be composed of soul, flesh, and bones; so it belongs to the notion of man to be composed of soul, flesh, and bones."[12] The definition of man, whether as a species or as an individual, always includes the body.

Aquinas acknowledges that there are operations in man that belong not only to the soul but also to the body. Sensation, for example, belongs to the soul and to the body.[13] For Aristotle, the principle of potency is matter (ultimately prime matter), which is brought into act by an agent who brings form to that matter (ultimately this process is grounded in the first act of the Prime Mover). How then, if the soul is not a body, if it has no matter, can it move from potency to act? Aquinas circumvents a cosmic antithesis between primordial matter and the first act by noting that there cannot be only one potentiality but must be many potentialities. For if there were only one potentiality to receive the infinite act of the first act then that one potentiality would be brought to infinite act itself and by definition there cannot be two infinite acts. Rather, the processions of the infinite act bring-

---

10. See *ST* I, q. 75, a. 2, ad 3.   11. See *ST* I, q. 75, a. 3.
12. *ST* I, q. 75, a. 4.

13. See *ST* I, q. 75, a. 4, co., and q. 75, a. 3. For a brief overview of Plato's contrasting anthropology, see Torchia, *Exploring Personhood*, 39–69. It would be difficult to find a better summation of how bodily sense perception requires the activity of the soul working on raw sense data than Nicholas Lombardo, *The Logic of Desire: Aquinas on Emotion* (Washington, D.C.: The Catholic University of America Press, 2011), 20–74.

ing other potentialities to act are multiple and, one might say, polyvalent. Primary matter (and matter in general) receives individual forms. The intellect, however, receives absolute forms. For Aquinas, there are different modes of moving from potentiality to actuality.

When Aquinas speaks about the union of the soul and body, he begins by insisting that the soul (the intellectual principle) is the form of the body, which follows upon his earlier statement that the soul is the first principle act of the body.[14] As Gilles Emery states: "For St. Thomas, the principle of intellectual activity is the first principle of all other activities: biological, sensitive, motive, and so on."[15] It will be clear below that Aquinas is not reducing all the activity of the human person to intellectual activity—far from it.

For Aquinas, "the intellectual soul is united by its very being to the body as a form."[16] In fact, he also insists that "although it [the soul] may exist in a separate state, yet since it ever retains its unibility [with the body], it cannot be called an individual substance ... as neither can the hand nor any other part of man."[17] And so, Aquinas says, those who say the soul is united to the body in any way other than as its form must explain the experience each person has of understanding himself.[18] Since the soul is the form of the body there are no intermediaries between the soul and the body. It is a direct union.[19] His insistence that the soul is *the* substantial form of the body is what put Thomas in

14. *ST* I, q. 76, a. 1, co.

15. Emery, "The Unity of Man," in Emery, *Trinity, Church, and the Human Person*, 215.

16. *ST* I, q. 76, a. 6, ad 3.

17. *ST* I, q. 29, a. 1, ad 5.

18. See *ST* I, q. 76, a. 1, co.: "But if anyone says that the intellectual soul is not the form of the body he must first explain how it is that this action of understanding is the action of this particular man; for each one is conscious that it is himself who understands." In this article, Aquinas goes on to argue against both Averroes and Plato, who had both separated the principle of understanding from the body (albeit in different ways).

19. See *ST* I, q. 76, aa. 4–7. In each of these four articles, Aquinas defends his anthropology based on a substantial union between the soul and body against a different objection. In article 4, he argues against the idea that the body requires another form (apart from the intellectual form), since this would suggest that the intellectual soul is not the first principle of life. In the fifth article, he argues that this is a proper union, that the body is not corrupt matter united to a pure spirit. In the sixth article, Aquinas argues that this union is not the result of accidental dispositions. Finally, in article seven, he concludes that the soul is not united to the body through other intermediary bodies.

contradiction with university and ecclesial authorities of his day, all of whom were committed Platonists.[20] He also stands against the modern tendency to see the body as nothing but a tool for the soul.

Anticipating what he will eventually say about the intellectual power of understanding, Aquinas writes that it was necessary for the soul to be united to such a body.[21] While the body "needs" the soul for life, the soul "needs" the body because its nature requires the sense impressions only the body can provide. The human body is particularly apt for the needs of the human soul. Thus it is clear that Aquinas's strict hylomorphism inherently asserts that the body is vitally important for the life of the soul and the soul for the body. He goes on to define in greater specificity the role the body plays in the functions of the soul, as we will see below.

The Powers of a Soul United to a Body

Having stated that the soul is the form of the body, Aquinas's explanation of the various powers of the soul reaffirms the importance of the body. At least in this life, while the body and soul are united in the human composite, the soul needs the body for all of its operations. In this life, the body is implicated in even the intellect's highest operation of understanding since these operations are completed *through* the assistance of the body even if not in virtue of the body. Lawrence Dewan writes: "As beings at home in the world of material, corporeal things, we humans have a mind that finds its nourishment in the consideration of such corporeal things."[22]

Following Aristotle, Thomas says that there are several powers

---

20. Aquinas argues that there could be no multiplicity of forms in man. As the body's substantial form, the intellectual soul subsumes the powers of the vegetative and sensitive souls (see *ST* I, q. 75, a. 5; q. 76, a. 3). For a summary of the debate on the plurality of forms, see Pasnau, *Thomas Aquinas on Human Nature*, 126–30. The debate is related to the development of Aquinas's position on delayed hominization. For a history of the controversies surrounding Aquinas's work especially following upon his death, see Jean-Pierre Torrell, OP, *Saint Thomas Aquinas*, vol 1., *The Person and His Work*, trans. Robert Royal (Washington, D.C.: The Catholic University of America Press, 2005), 296–316; Emery, "The Unity of Man," 216–17; Tugwell, "Aquinas: Introduction," 224–43.

21. *ST* I, q. 76, a. 5, co.

22. Lawrence Dewan, "St. Thomas, Metaphysics, and Human Dignity," in his *Wisdom, Law, and Virtue*, 63.

in the soul.[23] Each of these powers is directed to a particular act. For Aquinas and Aristotle, acts are distinguished according to their objects.[24] However, because he is committed to the composite view of human nature, the Angelic Doctor insists that not all the powers of human nature exist in the soul as their subject. This is to say, the soul is not the exclusive agent of all the powers of human nature.[25]

Aquinas (again, following Aristotle) identifies five genera of powers "in the soul."[26] These are: the vegetative, the sensitive, the appetitive, the locomotive, and the intellectual.[27] The vegetative power "is a power the object of which is only the body that is united to that soul ... [it] acts only on the body to which the soul is united."[28] Beyond the vegetative powers, "there is another genus in the powers of the soul, which genus regards a more universal object—namely, every sensible body and not only the body to which the soul is united."[29] These are the sensitive powers of the soul. Beyond this genus, "there is yet another genus in the powers of the soul, which regards a still more universal object—namely, not only the sensible body, but all being universally."[30] These are the intellectual powers.

Both the sensitive and the intellectual powers are directed toward some body extrinsic to the soul and extrinsic to the body to which the soul is united. Accordingly, Thomas writes that these extrinsic bodies must be related to the soul in two ways. First, "inasmuch as this something extrinsic has a natural aptitude to be united to the soul, and to be by its likeness in the soul";[31] secondly, inasmuch as the soul has an "inclination and tendency to something extrinsic" there are two more powers in the soul.[32] The first is the appetitive in which the soul "is

23. See *ST* I, q. 77, a. 2. Cf. Aristotle, *De Anima*, II.3.414a31.
24. See *ST* I, q. 77, a. 3. Cf. Aristotle, *De Anima*, II.4.415a18.
25. *ST* I, q. 77, a. 5, co.
26. Aquinas's inconsistent use of language should be noted. He says powers are in the soul and not in the human composite. But he also says that some powers need the body to function and hence later he will say that after the soul separates from the body, these powers are in the soul virtually but not actually (see *ST* I, q. 77, a. 8, co.).
27. See *ST* I, q. 78, a. 1.   28. *ST* I, q. 78, a. 1, co.
29. Ibid.   30. Ibid.
31. Ibid. Here, Aquinas is recalling his earlier observation that the likeness or species of forms are in the soul, not the forms in their natural mode of existence, that is, as the forms exist in objects.
32. Ibid.

referred to something extrinsic as to an end."[33] The second is the locomotive in which the soul "is referred to something extrinsic as to the term of its operation or movement."[34]

Aquinas, in fact, divides all created living things into three classifications based upon how each living thing's soul relates to extrinsic bodies. The vegetative souls (plants and the like) have no such relation to extrinsic bodies; they are related only to their own bodies. Sensitive souls (brute animals) are related not only to their own souls (and so have the vegetative powers) but are related to other sensible bodies. Intellectual souls have these two powers but also can consider universal being.[35]

Human beings share the sensitive power's mode of apprehension with brute animals, and for Aquinas the sensitive powers are the beginning of the action of the intellectual power: understanding. For this reason, it is important to analyze precisely how Thomas understands the sensitive powers. The first thing to note is that the sensitive powers are divided between the exterior senses and the interior senses, all of which involve the body (or some "corporeal organ" of the body in some way).

The exterior senses that Thomas identifies are those we all learn in grammar school: sight, hearing, smell, touch, and taste.[36] These are all considered powers by Aquinas, who says that "sense is a passive power, and is naturally altered by the exterior sensible. Wherefore the exterior cause of such alteration is what is per se perceived by the sense, and according to the diversity of that exterior cause are the sensitive powers diversified."[37] The diversity of powers corresponds to the modes in which exteriorly sensible causes affect bodies. These exteriorly sensible causes are any mixture of visibility, aurality, scent,

---

33. Ibid. I refer the reader to the first chapter of this book, in which I offered an analysis of Thomas's understanding of appetite and the good. See also *ST* I, q. 78, a. 1, ad 3, in which Aquinas distinguishes natural appetite and animal appetite. The natural appetite is "that inclination which each thing has, of its own nature for something; wherefore by its natural appetite each power desires something suitable to itself." Animal appetite, on the other hand, "results from the form apprehended." This is the difference between the natural appetite and the animal appetite. The natural appetite of the eye, for instance, is to see. The eye desires to see the visible object. But the animal appetite desires the visible object "not merely for the purpose of seeing it, but also for other purposes."

34. *ST* I, q. 78, a. 1, co.   35. See ibid.

36. See *ST* I, q. 78, a. 3.   37. *ST* I, q. 78, a. 3, co.

tactility, and delectability. The sensitive powers are affected by the exterior sensible causes in five different ways, and therefore there are five different exterior senses.[38]

Corporeal organs are needed to experience and perceive sensible bodies. The body is necessary to see, to smell, to hear, to taste, and to touch. Four interior senses supplement the five exterior senses. Aquinas says there must be interior senses because "nature does not fail in necessary things" and "we must observe that for the life of a perfect animal, the animal should apprehend a thing not only at the actual time of sensation, but also when it is absent. Otherwise, since animal motion and action follow apprehension, an animal would not be moved to seek something absent."[39] Again, Thomas's argument is based on experience. In this same article, he writes that we observe animals seeking goods they do not presently possess. Therefore, he argues, there must be interior senses: the common sense, imagination, the estimative power, and the memorative powers.

The common sense is that interior sense that is "the common root and principle of the exterior senses."[40] Each exterior sense has a proper sense which "judges of the proper sensible by discerning it from other things which come under the same sense; for instance, by discerning white from black or green."[41] But Aquinas goes on to say that the five proper senses are useless in comparing exterior sensible bodies since each proper sense only knows its own proper object. Thus, "neither sight nor taste can discern white from sweet."[42] The task of interpreting the alterations across all the proper senses is left to the common sense.[43]

The sensible forms are received in the exterior senses when an actual agent is directly impinging upon one or more of those five sens-

---

38. Ibid. Thomas goes on to explain that while all sense operations involve some spiritual change in the sense organ, some senses involve natural alteration in the causing object itself, and still other senses involve a concomitant alteration in a particular sense organ. For example, in sight, there is no natural alteration in the object seen that is necessary for it be seen. But for an object to be heard, some natural alteration is necessary to produce sound. Aquinas says the same is true for smell. For tasting and touching, on the other hand, there is both a spiritual alteration and a natural alteration in the sense organs "for the hand that touches something hot becomes hot."

39. *ST* I, q. 78, a. 4, co.   40. *ST* I, q. 78, a. 4, ad 1.

41. *ST* I, q. 78, a. 4, ad 2.   42. Ibid.

43. In the *sed contra* of *ST* I, q. 78, a. 4, Aquinas cites Avicenna as the authority for his list of interior senses.

es. We hear a thing when it is actually making noise. We cease to hear it when it no longer produces noise. Yet in Aquinas's anthropology animals have an imagination which is for "the retention and preservation of these forms … as it were a storehouse of forms received through the senses."[44] Human beings and brute animals can recall the sounds of particular things which they have already heard, even if they do not currently hear them. The same is true for the other four senses. Man's imagination, however, goes beyond animals because he is able not only to recall sensible forms but to combine them. He can recall the form of gold and the form of a mountain to imagine a gold mountain though he has never seen one.[45]

Brute animals have another interior power, not directly connected to the exterior senses, "for the apprehension of intentions which are not received through the senses."[46] Sheep have an natural estimative instinct that the wolf means them harm. In human beings, however, intentions are not perceived through a purely natural instinct but "by means of coalition of ideas. Therefore the power which in other animals is called natural estimative, in man is called the cogitative, which by some sort of collation discovers these intentions. Wherefore it is also called the particular reason."[47]

Finally, animals and human beings have an interior memorative sense which stores the intentions received by the natural estimative (or the cogitative, in the case of man) sense. Aquinas says that we can notice that animals are able to routinely avoid that which they know to be harmful. According to Thomas, however, memory works differently in human beings than it does in animals. Animals only have what he calls a "sudden recollection of the past."[48] Man also has as part of his memory the power of reminiscence in which he syllogistically recalls the past "by the application of individual intentions."[49] The human cogitative and memorative powers, Aquinas writes, "owe their excellence not to that which is proper to the sensitive part; but to a certain affinity and proximity to the universal reason, which, so to speak, overflows into them."[50]

44. *ST* I, q. 78, a. 4, ad 2.
46. Ibid.
48. Ibid.
50. *ST* I, q. 78, a. 4, ad 5.

45. See ibid.
47. Ibid.
49. Ibid.

This is the first hint of the importance of the relationship of the sensitive part of the human soul with the rational part. This relationship elevates the sensitive (that which man shares with all the animals) in dignity. But as I have already said, the relationship is also important for the intellectual powers of the soul, yet for Aquinas the intellect can also work beyond the corporeal sensitive: "The operation of the intellect *has its origin in the senses*: yet, in the thing apprehended through the senses, the intellect knows many things which the senses cannot perceive."[51] This is most especially true in ratiocination, the process of syllogistic argument from premise to conclusion. Aquinas appeals to this process in explaining exactly how natural reason can know of God's existence even though our senses cannot perceive him.[52]

When he begins to discuss the intellect of man specifically, Aquinas immediately notes that the intellect is a passive power in man.[53] This is not surprising given what he has already said about the powers of the soul being moved from potency to act even though there is no matter within the soul. In Thomistic metaphysics, only God is pure act.[54] Every created being, whether an intellect or an atom, is moved from potency to act by some agent other than itself.

The importance of the body for human knowledge in Aquinas's thinking cannot be underestimated. Indeed, it will soon be evident that the body has a lasting legacy on virtually all intellectual activity. The pursuit of knowledge is not the sole purview of a disembodied Cartesian soul inhabiting the material instrument of the body. On the contrary, below I will show that Aquinas thinks the body is so involved in human knowledge that he necessarily admits that the soul's disembodied state in the hereafter is, in a certain sense, unnatural until the soul reunites with the body at the general resurrection of the dead.

The Body and Knowledge

"According to the opinion of Plato," Aquinas writes, "there is no need for an active intellect in order to make things actually intelligible.... For Plato supposed that the forms of natural things subsisted apart

51. *ST* I, q. 78, a. 4, ad 4 (emphasis added).
52. See *ST* I, q. 12, a. 12; q. 1, a. 8.   53. See *ST* I, q. 79, a. 2.
54. See *ST* I, q. 3, a. 1.

from matter, and consequently that they are intelligible: since a thing is actually intelligible from the very fact that it is immaterial."[55] Aristotle, on the other hand, held that the forms of natural things do not exist apart from matter, and as forms in matter they are not intelligible. Therefore, Aquinas says:

It follows that the natures or forms of the sensible things which we understand are not actually intelligible. Now nothing is reduced from potentiality to act except by something in act; as the senses are made actual by what is actually sensible. We must therefore assign on the part of the intellect some power to make things actually intelligible, by abstraction of the species from material conditions. And such is the necessity for an active intellect.[56]

The Angelic Doctor goes on to say that this agent intellect is in the soul itself.[57] He says that "we know this by experience, since we perceive that we abstract universal forms from their particular conditions, which is to make them actually intelligible."[58] He does admit, however, that there must be a separate higher intellect which brings our own agent intellect from potency to act. "The separate intellect, according to the teaching of our faith, is God Himself, who is the soul's Creator, and only beatitude.... Wherefore the human soul derives its intellectual light from Him."[59] The light of reason participates in God's own reason.

Aquinas definitively rejects any sort of body-soul dualism in his account of knowledge. He is especially critical of Plato's theory that "man's intellect is filled with all intelligible species, but that, by being united to the body, it is hindered from the realization of its act."[60] This is unreasonable, Thomas says, because it seems impossible for a soul to forget all of its knowledge. Secondly, "if a sense be wanting, the knowledge of what is apprehended through that sense is wanting also: for instance, a man who is born blind can have no knowledge of colors."[61] The analogy is clear. Just as a blind man would not know the very concept of color, had the soul forgotten all knowledge of immaterial forms, no man (not even Plato) would even know the concept of knowledge and hence would not be able to explain it to another.

---

55. *ST* I, q. 79, a. 3, co.
56. Ibid.
57. See Aristotle, *De Anima*, III.5.430a10.
58. *ST* I, q. 79, a. 4, co.
59. Ibid.
60. *ST* I, q. 84, a. 3, co.
61. Ibid.

The principal reason that Aquinas cannot accept Plato's position is that he rejects Plato's position that the soul merely uses the body. For Aquinas, the soul is the form of the body and is naturally united to the body. Thus "it is unreasonable that the natural operation of a thing be totally hindered by that which belongs to it naturally."[62] Aquinas is fully committed to the concept of a body-soul unity in the acquisition of knowledge. He places the power of human knowledge midway between the sensitive power of animals and the intellect of angels. All three, he says, are cognitive powers.[63] The sensitive power is "the act of a corporeal organ. And therefore the object of every sensitive power is a form as existing in corporeal matter. And since such matter is the principle of individuality, therefore every power of the sensitive part can only have knowledge of the individual."[64] The angelic intellect is a "cognitive power which is neither the act of a corporeal organ, nor in any way connected with corporeal matter.... The object of [this] cognitive power is therefore a form existing apart from matter: for though angels know material things, yet they do not know them save in something immaterial, namely, either in themselves or in God."[65]

The human intellect holds the middle place, "for it is not the act of an organ; yet it is a power of the soul which is the form of the body."[66] This has consequences for knowledge. Plato held that immaterial knowledge had nothing to do with sensible objects. Aristotle, on the other hand, chose another way.[67] Aristotle and Aquinas agree with Plato that the corporeal cannot make an impression on the incorporeal. The corporeal cannot bring the incorporeal to act. Therefore, Aristotle postulated the active intellect which "causes the phantasms received from the senses to be actually intelligible, by a process of abstraction."[68] Following this logic, Aquinas concludes: "On the part of the phantasms, intellectual knowledge is caused by the senses. But since the phantasms cannot of themselves affect the passive intellect but it necessary that they become actually intelligible through the agent intellect, it cannot be said that sensible knowledge is the to-

62. Ibid.
64. Ibid.
66. Ibid.
68. Ibid.

63. See ST I, q. 85, a. 1, co.
65. Ibid.
67. ST I, q. 84, a. 6 (emphasis added).

tal and perfect cause of intellectual knowledge, but rather that it is in a way the material cause."[69]

So important is the union of the intellectual soul with the body for Aquinas that he insists that the intellect can actually understand nothing in this life without making use of the sensitive powers of the soul, which depend on the body. The intellectual soul depends on the interior senses of the imagination and memory even to consider knowledge already acquired and to render judgments. This is because "the proper object of the human intellect, which is united to a body, is a quiddity or nature existing in corporeal matter; and through such natures of visible things it rises to a certain knowledge of things invisible."[70] Aquinas again appeals to experience to explain this. He writes that when we attempt to understand something, we generate phantasms to serve us by way of examples in helping us to understand. In order for the intellect actually to understand its proper object (a nature existing in corporeal matter), it must always turn to sense images (phantasms).[71]

Certainly in this life the body and its dispositions are important for our pursuit of truth and for our contemplation. Aquinas writes that some people understand things better simply because their bodies have a better disposition.[72] Perhaps they are more imaginative in the phantasms they create to lead them syllogistically from one conclusion to another, or maybe they have a better memory. The reverse is also true when the imagination is faulty (as in the case of mental disorder) or the memory is lacking (as in the case of amnesia or laziness), where our understanding is hindered and perhaps even suspended.[73]

The Angelic Doctor acknowledges that his insistence on a strong unity of body and soul in his anthropology creates a tension in holding that the soul continues to live after it is separated from the body, and that it can continue to operate even after death.[74] He writes: "If we admit that the nature of the soul requires it to understand by turning to the phantasms, it will seem, since death does not change its nature, that it can then naturally understand nothing; as the phantasms

69. Ibid.
71. See also *ST* I, q. 85, aa. 1–2.
73. See *ST* I, q. 84, aa. 7–8.
70. *ST* I, q. 84, a. 7, co.
72. See *ST* I, q. 85, a. 7.
74. See *ST* I, q. 89, a. 1, co.

are wanting to which it may turn."[75] His resolution is simple: "The soul, therefore, when united to the body, consistently with that mode of existence, has a mode of understanding, by turning to corporeal phantasms, which are in corporeal organs; but when it is separated from the body, it has a mode of understanding by turning to simply intelligible objects, as is proper to other separate substances."[76] This other mode of understanding that does not make use of corporeal phantasms is, however, "not in accordance with its [the soul's] nature, and likewise to understand without turning to the phantasms is not natural to it."[77]

The separated soul understands by means of "a participated species arising from the influence of the Divine light, shared by the soul as by other separate substances [that is, the angels]; though in a lesser degree."[78] This participation in the divine light is an act of grace, for Aquinas, not an act of nature. However, while it is not natural for the soul to understand in this way, this is not an unnatural mode of knowledge since "God is the author of the influx both of the light of grace and of the light of nature."[79]

---

75. Ibid.

76. Ibid.

77. Ibid. In this same article, Aquinas also explains that while it may be more noble to understand by turning directly to intelligible objects without the use of phantasms, the perfection of the universe requires a gradation of being and intellectual power. The human soul holds the lowest place among intellectual substances.

78. ST I, q. 89, a. 1, ad 3.

79. Ibid. Aquinas goes on to say that the divine light will allow the separated soul to know singulars (ST I, q. 89, a. 4) and to know intelligible species learned in this life without having to resort to phantasms (ST I, q. 89, aa. 5–6). However, he does say that in this state the soul will have knowledge only in a confused and general manner because the soul is not united to its body (see ST I, q. 89, aa. 2–3). Aquinas's solution to the existence the separated soul is not completely satisfying to many of his readers, especially to strict Aristotelians. See, for example, Pasnau, Thomas Aquinas on Human Nature, 366–93. Eleanor Stump offers a more favorable reading in Aquinas (New York: Routledge, 2005), 200–216. For a more detailed treatment on this question, see Anton C. Pegis, "The Separated Soul and Its Nature in St. Thomas," in St. Thomas Aquinas 1274–1974: Commemorative Studies, ed. Armand Maurer (Toronto: Pontifical Institute of Medieval Studies, 1974), 1:131–58; Montague Brown, "Aquinas on the Resurrection of the Body," The Thomist 56 (1992): 165–207.

Person in Aquinas

Our consideration of the Angelic Doctor's anthropology must next consider his notion of personhood. We immediately face a challenge: Aquinas does not use the word "person" in his treatise on man. Aquinas writes of personhood exclusively in his treatise on the Trinity and his treatise on the incarnation of Christ.[80] However, what he says in these two treatises is instructive for his notion of the human person. Commenting on Aquinas's notion of personhood, Joseph Torchia writes: "Thomistic personhood … comprises the spiritual dimension of the rational soul, the corporeal dimension of the human body, and the metaphysical dimension of being or *esse*. By virtue of this multi-dimensionality, the person is the ontological center of a whole range of operations."[81] A brief survey of Thomas's understanding of person will show this to be true.

When Aquinas begins his discussion of the definition of personhood, he notes that substances, by definition, are individualized.[82] We speak of *this* substance. Thomas gives the name *hypostasis* or "first substance" to individual substances. The desk upon which the student writes is, according to Aquinas, a *hypostasis* or first substance. It is individualized and distinguishable from other first substances, and even from every other desk with which it would share a certain commonality and nature. But there is something more particular than first substances. Aquinas continues: "Further still, in a more special and perfect way, the particular and the individual are found in the rational substances which have dominion over their own actions; and which are not only made to act, like others; but which can act themselves; for actions belong to singulars. Therefore also the individuals of the rational nature have a special name even among other substances; and this name is person."[83] A person, therefore, is an individual substance of a rational nature, which is Boethius's classic definition.

In this definition, Aquinas is using the word "substance" in a sec-

---

80. See *ST* I, qq. 27–43, on the Trinity and *ST* III, q. 22, on the personhood of Jesus Christ.

81. Torchia, *Exploring Personhood*, 143.

82. See *ST* I, q. 29, a. 1.

83. *ST* I, q. 29, a. 1, co.

ondary way—as a concrete thing (a first substance).[84] Just as "a thing of nature," "subsistence," and "hypostasis" signify all subjects (particular substances, that is, first substances), "person" signifies the same thing for all rational substances.[85] It is important to understand Thomas's explanation of the relationship of first substances, that is, concrete substance (whether rational or irrational) with the concept of nature or essence (the term "substance" in its primary sense). Essence, nature, or substance refer to the "quiddity of a thing, signified by its definition, and thus we say that the definition means the substance of a thing."[86] In his small but influential work, *De ente et essentia*, Aquinas highlights the importance of matter in the multiplication of individuals within a species or nature.[87] Matter is the principal of individuation among substances composed of matter and form (rational or otherwise). Accidental qualities are inherent in the individuation of substances. Aquinas says that an accident is an essence which is apt to exist in a subject.[88] Whiteness does not exist in the abstract but exists in white things; whiteness is an accidental quality.

Thomas goes on to distinguish between accidents that are proper to matter and accidents that are proper to form. Accidents that characterize matter distinguish individuals of one species from another, while accidents attributed to form characterize the species as a whole. The former he calls the "individual's accidents," while he refers to the latter as "proper attributes [accidents]."[89] Proper accidents are found

84. See *ST* I, q. 29, a. 2, co. In the pages below, we will see that Aquinas will slightly modify this definition when he speaks of the personhood of God and of Jesus Christ.

85. See ibid. Aquinas acknowledges the Latin and Greek differences in the term "*hypostasis.*" See also *ST* I, q. 29, a. 2, ad 2.

86. *ST* I, q. 29, a. 2, co.

87. This small work on being and essence is usually dated to the 1250s, roughly fifteen years before Aquinas began writing the *Summa Theologiae*. On this particular point, however, there is no evidence that he ever changed his thought on the nature of accidents and essence, as it is borrowed from Aristotle, to whom Aquinas was indebted for much of his life. See Torrell, *St. Thomas Aquinas*, 47–50.

88. See *ST* III, q. 77, a. 1, ad 2.

89. See Aquinas, *De ente et essentia*, chap. 6: "As everything is individuated by matter and placed in a genus or species by its form, accidents following upon matter are the individual's accidents, and it is by these that individuals of the same species differ one from another. But accidents which are consequent upon form are proper attributes of the genus or species. Hence, they are found in everything sharing the nature of the genus or species. The capacity for laughter, for instance, comes from man's form, since

in every individual of a species or nature, while individual accidents the individualizing attributes of material difference. All accidents distinguish primary matter from designated (signate or particular) matter. Aquinas says that maleness and femaleness are individual accidents consequent upon matter.[90] In contrast, risibility or laughter is a proper accident of the human species because it is attributed to the form, the human soul—and risibility occurs as an act of knowledge.[91] This important distinction between individual accidents and proper accidents cannot be forgotten in any discussion of Aquinas's view of the body, and, I argue, his view of sexual difference, which I will present below.

Hypostasis and "person" refer to these individual substances (substances individualized by matter designated by individual accidents). In the visible world, according to Aristotelian-Thomistic metaphysics, matter is the distinguishing principle of substance. Thus, in the material world, matter and form are part of the definition (or essence) of things: "In things composed of matter and form, the essence signifies not only the form, nor only the matter, but what is composed of matter and the common form, as the principles of the species."[92] But in the invisible world, in the angelic realm, angels are differentiated from each other not by matter but by differences in their powers and missions.[93] They too fit the definition of an individual hypostasis of a rational nature, and so can rightly be called persons.[94]

The human person is an embodied person. This is why the soul separated from its body after death cannot be called a person. Aqui-

---

laughter occurs because of an act of knowledge on the part of man's soul." English translation from Thomas Aquinas, *On Being and Essence*, trans. Armand Maurer (Toronto: Pontifical Institute of Medieval Studies, 1949).

90. Ibid.: "Among those accidents deriving from matter we find a certain diversity. Some are consequent upon matter in accordance with the relation it has to a special form; for example, among animals, male and female, whose diversity comes from matter." Cf. Aristotle, *Metaphysics*, X.9.1058b21.

91. I am grateful to Paul Gondreau for highlighting the importance of this passage for Thomistic sexual anthropology. See Paul Gondreau, "The 'Inseparable Connection' between Procreation and Unitive Love (*Humanae Vitae*, §12) and Thomistic Hylomorphic Anthropology," *Nova et Vetera* (*English Edition*) 6 (2008): 738–39.

92. *ST* I, q. 29, a. 2, ad 3.

93. See *ST* I, q. 50, aa. 2, 4.

94. See Aquinas, *De ente*, chap. 5, for more of his thoughts on the principle of individuation both for God and for the angelic creatures.

nas writes: "The soul is part of the human species; and so, although it may exist in a separate state, yet since it ever retains its nature of unibility [with the body], it cannot be called an individual substance, which is the hypostasis or first substance, as neither can the hand nor any other part of man; thus neither the definition nor the name of person belongs to it."[95] For Aquinas, the human person is not a part, but the composite of soul and body. The soul is a part of the composite; it is part of human personhood. Aquinas's commitment to hylomorphic unity between soul and body is resolute.[96] In Thomas's anthropology, the category of personhood is not in contradistinction to the category of nature. Rather, the person is the perfection and manifestation of nature. Strictly speaking, we do not know human nature; we know persons. We make abstractions about human nature as a principle of action, but it is a human person who acts. Yet God is a person despite having no principle of limitation. "*Person* signifies what is most perfect in all nature—that is, a subsistent individual of a rational nature. Hence, since everything that is perfect must be attributed to God, forasmuch as His essence contains every perfection, this name *person* is fittingly applied to God; not, however, as it is applied to creatures, but in a more excellent way."[97]

Thomas agrees with an objector that God is not individualized by matter. He writes: "God cannot be called an *individual* in the sense that His individuality comes from matter; but only in the sense which implies incommunicability."[98] He writes approvingly of Richard of St. Victor's addendum to Boethius's definition: "*Person* in God is *the incommunicable existence of the divine nature.*"[99] God is a person not only because

95. *ST* I, q. 29, a. 1, ad 5.
96. See Emery, "The Unity of Man," 230: "The existence of the separated soul must be conceived of in terms of a twofold relation: first, a relation to the earthly existence in which the soul was united to the body in the dignity of a person (the soul did not exist before its union with the body); and second, a relation to the resurrection, which is held by faith, since the general resurrection will restore to the dead the human completeness of the person. The separated soul subsists in this twofold 'tension.'" See also Dewan, "St. Thomas, Metaphysics, and Human Dignity," 60–62.
97. *ST* I, q. 29, a. 3, co. (emphasis added).
98. *ST* I, q. 29, a. 3, ad 4.
99. Ibid. (emphasis added). Cf. Richard of St. Victor, *De Trinitate*, in *Patrologiae cursus completus. Series Latina*, ed. J.-P. Migne (Paris, 1844–64), 196:945 [hereafter, PL]. See also *ST* I, q. 29, a. 4, ad 3.

he is supremely incommunicable, but also because the Father, Son, and Holy Spirit are persons within the Godhead. This is the case for Aquinas because there are real relations in God that are coincident with the divine essence.[100] These relations are really distinguished from each other.[101] For Aquinas, some sort of distinction is the *sine qua non* of personhood.[102]

Unfortunately, Aquinas nowhere speaks in more detail about the incommunicability of the person. In the above-cited passage, Aquinas states that God is an individual (and thus a person) "only in the sense which implies incommunicability."[103] Here Aquinas suggests that individuality is defined not only by being a particular substance but also by being incommunicable. This raises two questions that Aquinas does not answer explicitly.

The first question is whether incommunicability is a property of individuality or a property of personhood. When Thomas speaks about incommunicability and individuality in this reply to his objector, does he mean to suggest that all individual substances are incommunicable? Is it because God is incommunicable that he is therefore an individual even though he is not comprised of matter and form? Certainly, Aquinas would agree that when nonrational substances are seen, they are, in some sense, communicating their existence to those who see. It would seem then that Thomas is using the word "individual" in a more strict sense: an individual rational substance. If this is the case, then what does it mean to be incommunicable?

And this is the second question: what does it mean for Aquinas to say that God is incommunicable? What is incommunicable in persons, whether human or divine, is not a matter of verbal communication or the exchange of information in any way. What is incommunicable, for Aquinas, is one's own distinctive being, one's particular concrete instantiation of one's nature. What is incommunicable (and, I might add, non-transferable) is one's own subsistent reality. And

---

100. See *ST* I, q. 28, aa. 1–2.

101. See *ST* I, q. 28, a. 3.

102. Cf. Gilles Emery, *The Trinity in Aquinas* (Washington, D.C.: The Catholic University of America Press, 2008); Emery, *The Trinitarian Theology of St Thomas Aquinas*, trans. Francesca Murphy (Oxford: Oxford University Press, 2010).

103. *ST* I, q. 29, a. 3, co.

this, in turn, means that one's own operations and actions in nature are just that: one's own.[104]

We have thus progressed through our account of Aquinas's hylomorphism, on the one hand, and his understanding of personhood, on the other. Because Aquinas never fully articulated the incommunicability of the person, the thought of Karol Wojtyła (and later of Pope John Paul II) will be seen to move beyond the limitations established by Aquinas's method and concern. Still, Thomas's strong account of the human person as a body-soul composite is situated within the rich metaphysical categories of matter and form, act and potency. However, precisely because Aquinas is so committed to the material aspect of the body-soul composite that is the human person, it is necessary for him both to offer an account of the purpose of bodily sexual difference and the impact this difference makes on the flourishing of the human person.

SEXUALITY AND HUMAN FLOURISHING

Sexual Difference in the *Summa Theologiae*

For Thomas, bodily sexual difference is natural and serves a purpose. The primary purpose in his view is the generation of offspring.[105] However, he does not believe that sexual difference is solely for the purposes of procreation. In a number of places, he distinguishes the manner in which human beings beget and raise their children from the manner in which brute animals do.[106] The command to "be fertile

104. In ST III, q. 19, a. 1, ad 4, Aquinas writes, "Being and operation belong to the person by reason of the nature; yet in a different manner. For being belongs to the very constitution of the person, and in this respect it has the nature of a term; consequently, unity of person requires unity of the complete and personal being. But operation is an effect of the person by reason of a form or nature."

105. See ST I, q. 92, a. 1.

106. See, e.g., ST I, q. 92, a. 2; II-II, q. 154, a. 2; Supp., q. 41, a. 1; *Summa contra Gentiles* [hereafter, SCG] III.122. On December 6, 1273, while celebrating Mass on the feast of St. Nicholas, Thomas had some sort of mystical experience after which he told his friend and associate, Reginald, these famous words: "I cannot do any more. Everything I have written seems to me as straw in comparison with what I have seen." After that, the Angelic Doctor never wrote or dictated anything again. He died three months later on March 7, 1274 (see Torrell, *Saint Thomas Aquinas*, 289–95). Until the day of the vision,

and multiply" (Gn 1:28), while given to both man and animals, is simply not fulfilled by man in the same way as it is by animals.[107] Indeed, Aquinas remarks that "the human male and female are united, not only for generation, as with other animals, but also for the purpose of domestic life, in which each has his or her duty, and in which the man is the head of the woman."[108] The nature of married domestic life, its relationship to the love of the couple, and the raising of their children will be more fully explored in chapter 7. In addition, I will there address some of the aspects of the complex position of Thomas regarding the nature of biological difference (for example, with regard to Aristotle's assertion that "the female is, as it were, a mutilated [misbegotten] male").[109] What will be clear is that Aquinas's faith in God's act of creation and in human dignity will force him to temper Aristotle's position.

For Aquinas, the image of God in each human person resides in the soul, not in the body. The human body, like all other created realities, bears a trace of God's presence (inasmuch as it is created and sustained by God) but it is not in the image and likeness of God.[110] God himself does not have sexual parts.[111] The soul is the seat of the powers that make us like God: knowledge (reason) and choice (will).

Thomas had been working on the *tertia pars* of the *Summa Theologiae*, which had included treatises on the incarnation, the sacraments, the resurrection, and the last things. Because he did not finish, his students culled responses from his early commentary on Peter Lombard's *Sentences* (begun in 1252) to complete the *Summa* (see Torrell, *Saint Thomas Aquinas*, 332–34). This became known as the *supplementum* to the *Summa Theologiae*. This supplement includes the questions on marriage. Though I will cite the *supplementum* in this study because it is treated by most Thomists as a canonical extension of the *Summa*, I will corroborate Thomas's arguments found in the *supplementum* with arguments from his other *summa*, the *Summa contra Gentiles*, which was completed only a few years before he began working on the *Summa Theologiae*. To assist the reader, when the *supplementum* is cited in this study, if a corresponding passage exists in the *Summa contra Gentiles*, it will be listed in parentheses after the *ST* reference.

107. See *ST*, Supp., q. 42, a. 2, ad 4 (*SCG* III.136).

108. *ST* I, q. 92, a. 2. It is beyond the purview of this study to engage in an exegesis of Aquinas's use of the traditional Christian household code in which the husband was understood to be the head of the woman. Here he is following a long line of Christian thinkers who, until modern times, held for such a code following the practice of early Christianity witnessed by the apostle Paul's writings in the New Testament.

109. Aristotle, *On the Generation of Animals*, II.3.737a27.

110. See *ST* I, q. 93, a. 6.

111. See *ST* I, q. 3.

He understands Genesis 1:28 "not to imply that the image of God came through the distinction of sex, but that the image of God belongs to both sexes, since it is in the mind, wherein there is no sexual distinction."[112] The female sex along with the male sex belongs to the "*perfection* of human nature."[113]

God's will is that the human species reproduce through the union of the two sexes. There would have been reproduction even in original innocence, not for the preservation of the species (since death had not yet entered in human history), but, Aquinas says, for the multiplication of the species, which is a good. If this were not the case, we would have to say that original sin would have been necessary for access to this natural good.[114] Even in original innocence, procreation would have been through sexual intercourse.[115]

This does not mean, however, that sexual difference is meaningless for Aquinas or that it is relegated only to procreation. It is part of our integrity. After the general resurrection, there will no longer be procreation since "the human race will already have the number of individuals preordained by God."[116] Nonetheless, there will be sexual difference after the resurrection.[117] The body will rise in its integrity and with all its members.[118]

This means that sexual difference is inherent in nature itself because it is an accidental quality within signate matter. John Grabowski's caution against overstating that sexual difference is located in nature is well taken.[119] It should not be suggested that sexual difference

112. *ST* I, q. 93, a. 6, ad 2. Recall that when Aquinas uses the word "mind," he means the soul (see *ST* I, q. 75, a. 2). When Aquinas comments on Augustine's position that man is in the image of God but woman is in the image of man, he agrees, but only in a secondary sense: "The image of God, in its principal signification, namely the intellectual nature, is found both in man and in woman.... But in a secondary sense the image of God is found in man, and not in woman: for man is the beginning and end of woman; as God is the beginning and end of every creature" (*ST* I, q. 93, a. 4, ad 1).

113. Ibid. (emphasis indicates author's altered translation): "Sicut autem ad perfectionem universi pertinent diversi gradus rerum, ita etiam diversitas sexus est ad perfectionem humanae naturae."

114. Ibid.

115. See *ST* I, q. 99, a. 2.

116. *ST*, Supp., q. 81, a. 4, co. (*SCG* IV.83).

117. See *ST*, Supp., q. 81, a. 3 (*SCG* IV.88).

118. See *ST*, Supp., q. 80, a. 1 (*SCG* IV.84).

119. See Grabowski, *Sex and Virtue*, 109.

in men and women is so profound so as to delineate two separate species or natures, each with its own inclinations (and, Grabowski warns,
its own moral code). Surely, this is not Aquinas's intention as he indicates that the soul (the seat of the image of God) is without sexual difference and that the proper accidents which flow from the soul determine the species, whereas the accidents of matter (such as maleness
and femaleness) determine only the individuals of the species.[120]

When he first introduces the concept of sexual difference for procreation, Aquinas goes on to say that "man is yet further ordered to a
still nobler vital action, and that is intellectual operation."[121] The nobility of intellectual operation is central to Aquinas's understanding
of the relationship of sexuality to human happiness (beatitude), yet
this intellectual operation, as I have already shown, is in some way
contingent upon the body. Sexuality and the passions that it entails
must be incorporated into an account of human flourishing.

Sexuality and Human Flourishing

For all of his emphasis on sexual difference, Thomas writes virtually
nothing about the conjugal act. He writes in the *Summa* that the generation of offspring is "a great blessing" (*bonum consectum*).[122] In the
Summa contra Gentiles, he writes that carnal union produces a "sweet
association" (*suavem societatem*) between the sexes.[123] Aquinas res-
olutely disagrees with the Gregory of Nyssa and John Chrysostom,

---

120. Grabowski's solution is to draw a solid distinction between person and nature,
locating maleness and femaleness in the human person analogous to the relationality
which distinguishes the divine persons of the Trinity (see Grabowski, *Sex and Virtue*,
109–11). Recently, Paul Gondreau has criticized Grabowski's approach as effectively reducing maleness and femaleness to one relation among many. He argues that the distinction between the divine persons can only analogously be compared to the relationship between men and women. See Paul Gondreau, "The 'Inseparable Connection,'"
739n23. I am grateful to Paul Gondreau for allowing me to preview the manuscript of
his forthcoming book, *Sex and the Human Good: Principles of a Realist (Thomist) Sexual
Anthropology*. It provides more detail than the article cited. Gondreau's salient criticism
deserves a response that lies beyond the constraints of this book. Many of his points are
valid, but I do not think John Grabowski intends in his work to make maleness and femaleness pure accidental properties equivalent to all other relationships. Quite the contrary, if anything, it seems to me that he defines these as essential relationships of the
human person.

121. *ST* I, 92, a. 1, co.   122. See *ST* I, q. 98, a. 1.
123. See *SCG* III.123.

both of whom said that there would have been no sexual activity in original innocence.[124] In fact, Thomas goes so far as to say that sexual delight would have been greater in Eden: "Indeed would sensible delight have been greater in proportion to the greater purity of nature and the greater sensibility of the body."[125]

The above reflection on Aquinas's anthropology reveals that he would place the pleasure that comes from sexual intercourse in the sensitive appetite since it includes bodily affectation, but it also includes delight in the mind. Every created being tends toward its own perfection, the fulfillment of its nature.[126] The good is that which is perfective. Particular objects manifest particular goods which are perfective of other objects.[127] That this is true both of the sensitive souls of brute animals, who are guided by their nature to their own perfection, and of the intellectual soul is vital for any discussion of human sexuality in the *Summa Theologiae* because, for Aquinas, the delight of sex is fundamentally a passion in the sensitive appetite that should be guided by reason.

For Thomas, the appetitive drives in man and in brute animals are principally directed *ad extra*, to things in themselves. In fact, he speaks of passion (the drive of the sensitive appetite) as "being drawn to the agent."[128] Aquinas writes: "Now the soul is drawn to a thing by the appetitive power rather than by the apprehensive power: because the soul has, through its appetitive power, an order to things as they are in themselves: hence the Philosopher says that good and evil, i.e., the objects of the appetitive power, are in things themselves."[129] It should be recalled how this differs from the apprehensive power as described earlier in this chapter, which is directed to the likeness or species of things as they exist in the one who perceives.

The will (the intellectual appetite) differs from the sensitive appetite in this respect. The will is not directed to things as they exist in themselves. Rather, the will is directed to the good of things in them-

124. See Gregory of Nyssa, *De hominis opificio*, in *Patrologiae cursus completus. Series graeca*, ed. J.-P. Migne (Paris, 1857–66), 44:189 [hereafter, PG]. See also John Chrysostom, *Homilae in Genesis* (PG 53:126).

125. *ST* I, q. 98, a. 2, ad 3.   126. See *ST* I, q. 19, a. 1.

127. See *ST* I, q. 16, a. 1.   128. *ST* I-II, q. 22, a. 1, co.

129. *ST* I-II, q. 22, a. 2, co. Cf. Aristotle, *Metaphysics* VI.4.1027b25.

selves as those things are apprehended by the intellect.[130] The sensitive soul, on the other hand, is affected by things in themselves. In sensitive apprehension, as I noted earlier, extrinsic objects cause a corporeal transmutation which allows the sensitive soul to apprehend the presence of the thing (and to remember the thing). The same is true for the sensitive appetite. The sensitive appetite is moved by an agent by way of bodily transmutation.[131] This is why passion is not properly intellectual.[132] This does not mean that man, because he is an intellectual creature, is without passion. Indeed, while passion may not be essentially in the human soul, it is a part of the soul accidentally because the soul is the form of the body, and, therefore, has sensitive functions (both apprehensive and appetitive). Passion is in the human composite, according to Aquinas.[133]

However, because of man's higher status as an intellectual creature, he experiences his passions differently, or rather, passions affect him differently. Men and women differ from animals in exactly how they respond to their passions. For Aquinas, all passions must be governed by reason. In irrational animals this does not happen by following intellectual reason but rather they "are led by a kind of estimative power, which is subject to a higher reason, i.e., the Divine reason."[134] Earlier in the *Summa Theologiae*, Thomas explains that "in other animals the sensitive appetite is naturally moved by the estimative power; for instance, the sheep, esteeming the wolf as an enemy, is afraid."[135] But in man, the estimative power is replaced with practical reason.[136]

Aquinas holds that passions in themselves are not moral. They are neither good nor evil when considered only as corporeal transmutations affected by extrinsic agents. The sensitive appetite, like sensitive apprehension, is, on its own terms, irrational.[137] Nevertheless, the sensitive appetite is related to reason. Thus, Thomas writes: "If, however, they [the passions] be considered as subject to the command of reason and will, then moral good and evil are in them."[138]

---

130. See *ST* I, q. 82, a. 3.
132. *ST* I-II, q. 23, a. 1, co.
134. *ST* I-II, q. 24, a. 4, ad 3.
136. See ibid.
138. *ST* I-II, q. 24, a. 1, co.

131. See *ST* I-II, q. 22, a. 1.
133. See *ST* I-II, q. 22, a. 1, co. and ad 3.
135. *ST* I, q. 81, a. 3, co.
137. See *ST* I-II, q. 24, a. 1.

The Angelic Doctor disagrees with the Stoics, who viewed all passions as evil.[139] The problem with the Stoics was not that they identified passion as evil because it exceeded the limits of reason, but rather that they did not understand that the will moves apart from the sensitive and irrational appetite. Aquinas himself says that "the passions of the soul, in so far as they are contrary to the order of reason, incline us to sin: but in so far as they are controlled by reason, they pertain to virtue."[140] Men and women must govern their passions rationally.

Elsewhere, Aquinas writes that the lower appetite, while sufficient to move irrational animals immediately, is not sufficient to move man unless the higher appetite (the will) concedes.[141] This is why in the treatise on the passions, Aquinas will insist that "the passions, in so far as they are voluntary [consented to by the will], [may] be called morally good or evil."[142] Daniel Westberg notes: "Though it is often convenient for people to excuse their eating habits or sexual behavior on the basis of the strength and irresistibility of sensation and the natural sequence of desire and action, Thomas will have none of this."[143] The will must consent to the direction of the passions.

Here, again, we see the importance of reason in Aquinas's work, especially in his moral theory. Reason is important in the determination of good and evil in human action because the human soul's specific difference from other souls is that it is a rational soul, which is man's natural form.[144] Proper human actions are those actions of which man is the master through reason and free will. This is to distinguish free actions from other general acts of man that do not involve freedom (for example, the beating of the heart or the inadvertent scratching of a beard).[145]

It is God's own reason that governs the universe. To act in accord with his reason is to be good; Aquinas calls this the eternal law.[146] Animals participate in the divine reason inasmuch as their natural form and even their estimative power are created by divine reason to operate in a certain manner. Human beings, on the other hand, participate

---

139. *ST* I-II, q. 24, a. 2, co.
140. *ST* I-II, q. 24, a. 2, ad 3.
141. *ST* I, q. 81, a. 3, co.
142. *ST* I-II, q. 24, a. 1, co.
143. Westberg, *Right Practical Reason*, 80.
144. *ST* I-II, q. 18, a. 5, co.
145. See *ST* I-II, q. 1, a. 1.
146. See *ST* I-II, q. 91, a. 1.

in divine reason through their own God-given power to reason. This is the basis of the natural law.[147] By following the dictates of right reason (which Aquinas calls the natural law), we find the fulfillment of our nature, of our created being, as designed by divine reason.[148]

The sensitive appetite and its passions are only properly ordered when they are governed by reason.[149] In fact, inasmuch as the passions are subject to reason, they are subject to the natural law.[150] While it is true that passions have an "inborn aptitude" to obey reason, they do not always obey due to the effects of original sin.[151] This topic is discussed in depth in chapter 7; for now, I will explore briefly Aquinas's understanding of Adam and Eve's unique original state in order to contrast that with love, marriage, and concupiscence in our fallen state in chapters 7 and 8. That men and women live with the wounds of original sin cannot but affect their mastery of their passions and their relationship with each other. Aquinas is not a Kantian. Sin affects reason's ability to function and to perceive morally upright paths of action.

ORIGINAL INNOCENCE AND ORIGINAL SIN

Thomas writes that original justice, the state in which Adam and Eve were created, "consisted in [man's] reason being subject to God, the lower powers to reason, and the body to the soul."[152] He adds that "the first subjection was the cause of both the second and the third; since while reason was subject to God, the lower powers remained subject to reason."[153] It is only when man is in right relationship with God that he is in right relationship with himself.

It is important to note that this threefold submission is not a natural endowment. In fact, the Catholic tradition has long held that

---

147. *ST* I-II, q. 91, a. 2, co.
148. *ST* I-II, q. 94, a. 3, co.
149. See *ST* I-II, q. 17, a. 7.
150. See *ST* I-II, q. 94, a. 2, ad 2.
151. See *ST* I-II, q. 50, a. 3, ad 1; I-II, q. 17, a. 7. For a brief analysis of our how actions and habits can ingrain in us unnatural behaviors that are contrary to our natural inclinations, see J. Budziszewski, "The Natural, the Connatural, and the Unnatural," in *The Line Through the Heart: Natural Law as Fact, Theory, and Sign of Contradiction* (Wilmington, Del.: ISI Books, 2009), 61–77.
152. *ST* I, q. 95, a. 1, co.
153. Ibid.

Adam and Eve were endowed "with grace and other gifts surpassing what is due to human nature by itself."[154] For Aquinas, original justice is a grace. He writes that "such a subjection of the body to the soul and of the lower powers to reason, was not from nature; otherwise it would have remained after sin.... The primitive subjection by virtue of which reason was subject to God was not a merely natural gift, but a supernatural endowment of grace; for it is not possible that the effect should be of greater efficiency than the cause."[155] The first man and woman were created in grace and this grace is the cause of original righteousness, the state of original justice.[156]

The subjection of the lower powers to the higher powers is necessary for happiness in Aquinas's anthropology. He explains why in the *Quaestiones disputatae de malo*, written contemporaneously with the *Summa Theologiae*.[157] In *De malo*, Thomas provides a key insight:

Every rational creature without exception needs a particular divine help, namely, the help of sanctifying grace, in order to attain perfect happiness.... But in addition to this necessary help, human beings needed another supernatural help because of their composite nature. For human beings are composed of soul and body, and of an intellectual and sensory nature. And if the body and the senses be left to their nature, as it were, they burden and hinder the intellect from being able to freely attain the highest reaches of contemplation. And this help was original justice, by which the mind of human beings would be so subject to God that their powers and their very bodies would be completely subject to them, nor would their reason impede them from being able to tend toward God.... And original sin takes away this help of original justice.[158]

The situation of original justice was wholly unique. Our first parents were uniquely blessed with unmerited grace, which perfected human

---

154. O'Brien, "Original Justice," in Aquinas, *Summa Theologiae*, ed. Gilby, 26:144.

155. *ST* I, q. 95, a. 1. See also *ST* I, q. 100, a. 1, co. and ad 2; I-II, q. 81, a. 2.

156. It should be noted that another grace of the original state was immortality. As Thomas understands it, death entered the world through sin not inasmuch as humanity was naturally immortal before sin, but rather human nature has always been mortal. But in the state of original justice, grace preserved the body from corruption (see *ST* I, q. 97, a. 1).

157. For the historical context of these two works, see Torrell, *Saint Thomas Aquinas*, 1:142–59, 197–223, 327–29.

158. Thomas Aquinas, *De malo*, q. 5, a. 1, co. Unless otherwise noted, all English translations from *De malo* are from Thomas Aquinas, *On Evil*, trans. Richard Regan (Oxford: Oxford University Press, 2003).

nature on a natural level and eliminated deficiencies connatural to that nature (such as suffering and death).[159] In Thomas's view, this was God's plan for us from the beginning. The sensitive appetites pull the creature in various directions toward various goods. This can distract man from his higher pursuits unless the lower appetites are channeled by reason.

In the state of innocence, concupiscence (a desire for sensible pleasure) would have been moderated by reason. This is why Aquinas can say that sexual delight would have been greater in Eden than after the Fall. Reason's role "is not to lessen sensual pleasure, but to prevent the force of concupiscence from cleaving to it immoderately. By immoderately I mean going beyond the bounds of reason, as a sober person does not take less pleasure in food taken in moderation than the glutton, but his concupiscence lingers less in such pleasures."[160] Indeed, the Angelic Doctor does not intend to remove passion from the moral life. He insists "just as it is better than man should both will good and do it in his external act; so also does it belong to the perfection of moral good, that man should be moved unto good, not only in respect of his will, but also in respect of his sensitive appetite."[161] The fact he that devotes his longest treatise in the *Summa Theologiae* (27 questions and 132 articles) to the passions, longer than even his treatise on beatitude, and places it in the heart of the *prima secundae* indicates the seriousness with which he considers human emotion.[162]

159. See *ST* I, q. 97, aa. 1–3, for Aquinas's understanding of the various remedies of grace provided human nature in paradise. See also O'Brien, "Original Justice," in Aquinas, *Summa Theologiae*, ed. Thomas Gilby, 26:146: "Original justice does perfect human nature on a natural level. While a gift and exceeding the claims of human nature, original justice met its wants. Freedom from suffering and death was in keeping with the natural immortality of the soul. The tranquility in the lower appetites was in accord with the control the reason is meant to achieve; man was given that habitual conformity of passion to reason expected after the acquisition of moral virtues. The will itself received a perfection that matched its bent towards God the author of nature and the fulfillment of natural law. By a supernaturally bestowed gift, then, the defects connatural to human nature as composed of body and spirit were overcome; original justice perfected man in his natural and moral well-being."

160. *ST* I, q. 98, a. 2, ad 3.

161. *ST* I-II, q. 24, a. 3, co.

162. The work of the passions in the moral life is often undervalued by Thomists. Some have attempted to retrieve this important aspect of Aquinas's work. For example, see G. Simon Harak, SJ, *Virtuous Passions: The Formation of Christian Character* (New

According to Thomas, original sin "is an inordinate disposition, arising from the destruction of the harmony which was essential to original justice."[163] Rather than living in the harmony of nature-perfecting grace that was original justice, in the fallen state we live disintegrated lives: "As bodily sickness is partly a privation, in so far as it denotes the destruction of the equilibrium of health, and partly something positive, viz. the very humors that are inordinately disposed, so too original sin denotes the privation of original justice, and besides this, the inordinate disposition of the parts of the soul. Consequently, it is not a pure privation but a corrupt habit."[164]

Original sin is not a pure privation because the grace of original justice was not naturally due to man. Since it was grace that gave harmony to human nature in original innocence, original sin is less a privation and more a simple continuation of human existence without the nature-perfecting endowments of grace—a privation that inevitably leads to disorder. Thomas O'Brien puts it this way: "Human nature with its powers as derived from Adam is now just itself, left to itself; this is how it is disordered."[165] Original sin is not a positive inclination to moral evil added to human nature following our first parents' sin. If original sin were, in fact, a positive inclination to evil, then God himself would be implicated in evil's cause as the one who inflicted this positive inclination in punishment for sin. Rather, original

York: Paulist Press, 1993); Servais Pinckaers, OP, "Reappropriating Aquinas's Account of the Passions," trans. Craig Steven Titus, in *Pinckaers Reader*, 273–87. Harak's book represents an admirable attempt to recover a Thomistic understanding of passion in moral action and character development. Unfortunately, it is hindered by several incorrect citations of Aquinas and a selective interpretation of the passages he cites. Pinckaers's essay purports only to be an initial offering. See also Diana Fritz Cates, *Aquinas on Emotions: A Religious-Ethical Inquiry* (Washington, D.C.: Georgetown University Press, 2009); Diana Fritz Cares, *Choosing to Feel: Virtue, Friendship, and Compassion for Friends* (South Bend, Ind.: University of Notre Dame Press, 1999); Paul Gondreau, *The Passions of Christ's Soul in the Theology of St. Thomas Aquinas* (Scranton, Penn.: University of Scranton Press, 2009); Robert Minder, *Thomas Aquinas on the Passions: A Study of Summa theologiae, 1a2ae 22–48* (Cambridge: Cambridge University Press, 2009); Nicholas Lombardo, OP, *The Logic of Desire: Aquinas on Emotion* (Washington, D.C.: The Catholic University of America Press, 2010).

163. *ST* I-II, q. 82, a. 1, co.; see also ad 2.

164. *ST* I-II, q. 82, a. 1, ad 1.

165. O'Brien, "Original Justice," in *Summa Theologiae*, ed. Gilby, 26:152. See also *ST* I-II, q. 82, a. 1, ad 1 and ad 3; a. 2, ad 2; a. 4, ad 1 and ad 3.

sin is the rupture of man's relationship with God and therefore the loss of his own integration. We were made to be in relationship with God; without that relationship we are left entirely to ourselves and to our own devices.

This has important consequences for Aquinas's view of fallen human nature. For example, while Thomas holds that man can still know truth without grace (but not without the divine light at work in his reason as mentioned earlier in this chapter), and while he can still work some particular goods, he can no longer achieve the complete good proportionate to his human nature due to the disordering and disintegration of the soul's powers.[166] This disintegration is properly called the "wounding of nature," where "all the powers of the soul are left, as it were, destitute of their proper order, whereby they are naturally directed to virtue; which destitution is called a wounding of nature."[167]

However, human nature retains some goodness even after original sin. Aquinas identifies three goods of human nature, even in the fallen state: "First, there are the principles of which nature is constituted, and the properties that flow from them, such as the powers of the soul, and so forth. Secondly, since man has from nature an inclination to virtue, as stated above ([I-II], q. 60, a. 1; q. 63, a. 1), this inclination to virtue is a good of nature. Thirdly, the gift of original justice, conferred on the whole human nature in the person of the first man, may be called a good of nature."[168] He eventually concludes that it is only the third good of nature, the gift of original justice, that is absolutely destroyed by original sin.

The first good, the principles of nature, is neither destroyed nor diminished. The principles of nature are determinative attributes of nature. To argue that they are destroyed would be to argue that nature itself is destroyed by sin, and we know this is not the case. We have retained our nature; we have retained the use of our faculties. The second good, however, the natural inclination to virtue, is diminished even if it is not destroyed. Our wounded inclination to virtue now requires healing grace (*gratia sanans*) for complete natural fulfillment.[169]

Virtue is the perfection of a power.[170] Thomas calls the inclination

---

166. See *ST* I-II, q. 109, aa. 2–3.
168. *ST* I-II, q. 85, a. 1.
170. See *ST* I-II, q. 55, a. 1.

167. *ST* I-II, q. 85, a. 5.
169. Ibid.

to virtue a "middle term" between the principles of rational nature and the perfection of those principles brought about by virtue.[171] He notes that "the good of nature, that is diminished by sin, is the natural inclination to virtue, which is befitting to man from the very fact that he is a rational being; for it is due to this that he performs actions in accord with reason, which is to act virtuously."[172] The human inclination to virtue is precisely the tendency in each of us to become fully human, the measure of which is determined by the very principles of our nature.[173] It should be asked: if the inclination to virtue is the midpoint between the principles of our nature and their fulfillment, and if those principles are undiminished by sin, how then is the inclination diminished?

Thomas responds by suggesting that diminution can be considered in two ways: either in reference to the root (the principles of human nature, that is, the powers of the soul) or in reference to those principles' ends (telê). The diminution cannot stem from the root, because the principles are not diminished by sin. Aquinas notes that if the root is diminished, then the human being is no longer rational but quasi-rational. If the root is completely destroyed, then fallen man is not rational at all and ceases to be man.[174]

The diminution of our inclination to virtue occurs in the second way, he writes, "in so far as an obstacle is placed against its attaining its term."[175] The diminution of the inclination to virtue can, moreover,

---

171. See *ST* I-II, q. 85, a. 2.

172. Ibid.

173. See O'Brien, "Fallen Nature," in *Summa Theologiae*, ed. Gilby, 26:156: "The principles of his [man's] nature, as is true of any reality, make man to be what he is. By the same token they include a direction towards the full realization of this way of being. Because he is human, man by his very nature is bent towards being fully human. This direction is called an inclination—or tendency to act towards the full realization of himself and the perfection of which he does not possess simply by existing. But the principles of his nature are the true index to what fulfillment of himself should be. Again, man is what he is through the principles of his nature. These principles themselves then bespeak of an inclination, an order to human perfection. Since virtue ensures that actions are in conformity to this order of nature, the principles also of themselves mean an inclination to virtue. Nature in its essential principles and in its bent to virtue, then, is not two distinct realities. The distinction is simply between the principles as establishing man in existence and as providing the spring for operations by which he will achieve completion."

174. See *ST* I-II, q. 85, a. 2.

175. Ibid.

be indefinite, "because obstacles can be placed indefinitely inasmuch as man can go on indefinitely adding sin to sin: and yet it [the inclination] cannot be destroyed entirely, because the root of this inclination always remains."[176] These obstacles are initially the result of the fact that our various powers are no longer directed by reason but are left to themselves.[177] But vices, which are habitual dispositions tending to more vicious actions, also become further obstacles.[178] When this conclusion is combined with Aquinas's insight that original sin is the privation of the harmony of the grace of original justice leading to disintegration, two connected conclusions are apparent.

First, original sin does not direct human nature to failure or imperfection. But rather, failure remains a possibility precisely because the very obstacle to our perfection is the multiplicity of conflicting ends available in the principles of human nature—the lower appetites can have ends at variance with the higher appetite. Deviation from our true and proper end is a genuine possibility in the principles of human nature itself, given free will. This is confirmed by the very definition of a sinful or vicious act as an act which does not conform to human reason, itself participating in the eternal law.[179]

For this study, it is important to understand that in Thomas's anthropology sexual delight (now a function of the fallen sensitive appetite) can impinge upon our higher pursuits if not tempered with the virtue of chastity. The next chapter will discuss this in more detail. Any consideration of virtue and natural law must include a consideration of the wounds of human nature caused by original sin. Similarly, any consideration of the great goods of love, sexuality, and marriage must not forget the difficulty fallen men and women have in integrating their desires with reason.

---

176. Ibid.   177. See *ST* I-II, q. 85, a. 3.
178. See *ST* I-II, q. 54, a. 3.

179. See *ST* I, q. 63, a. 1, in which Aquinas speaks about sin as deviation from the rectitude of nature. See also *ST* I-II, q. 71, a. 6, regarding human actions not in conformity with reason. In this reply to the fourth objection of this same article, Aquinas notes that what is sinful—contrary to eternal law and natural law—is contrary to reason because it is inordinate. Finally, see *ST* I-II, q. 85, a. 6, for a discussion on the natural corruptibility of man's composite human nature which, in turn, engenders a multiplicity ends for the various principles at work in the composite.

CONCLUSION

Thomas Aquinas developed a strong hylomorphic anthropology in which the body and soul are united in a composite human person. He insisted that this unity was immediate, that is, without the mediation of other souls or forms. In his view, the unity is so strong that one can legitimately insist that the soul needs the body just as much as the body needs the soul.

Moreover, Thomas provides us with a metaphysical understanding not only of substance in general but of individual substances. He calls individual substances "first substances." In the visible world, these first substances are concretized or individualized from other first substances through the composition of matter and form. Matter is specified and designated by accidental qualities; one member of a species differs from another materially. Species, on the other hand, are distinguished from one another in virtue of proper accidental qualities adhering to the form. One man may be taller than another, but both are capable of laughter, sorrow, and anger since these qualities stem from the substantial form: the human soul.

The Angelic Doctor located sexual difference among those individuating accidents adhering in matter. And though he followed Aristotle in assuming that women were "misbegotten males," his faith in the providence of God allowed him to make the initial steps toward sexual complementarity by insisting that the difference of sexes was part of God's providential plan for the human race. In Aquinas's anthropology sexual differences are individuating material attributes and so there is no sexual difference in the soul itself. Because of this, men and women share in a common human nature without separation from one another.

Aquinas does not address human personhood as such, though he says that personhood is the perfection of nature and the term applied to an individual (that is, a first substance) of a rational nature. Further, he leaves several questions unresolved in his treatment on personhood in God vis-à-vis personhood in men and women. For example, while he says that God is a person because he is incommunicable, he does not entirely explain what he means by incommunicability or how this might apply to human persons. Of course, incommunicability is a foundational point for Karol Wojtyła's understanding of the human person. It also remains to be seen what Thomas thinks of the relationship between men and women in the domestic life that he says is so necessary for the upbringing of human children. If sexual difference is only a material accident, how does it affect the complementarity of sexes in living life beyond sexual procreation? This is a question that will be addressed in chapter 7.

The key point of this chapter is that Thomas possessed a strong ontological understanding of human nature and human personhood. He combined this ontological view with the revelation that there is a provident creator who designed men and women for the purposes of the perfection of the universe. In addition, it is already beginning to be clear that Aquinas is not the naturalist theologian or philosopher that many of the manualists and twentieth-century moral theologians presumed he was.

Additionally, he was not unaware of the impact original sin had on the human composite. Since men and women are no longer beneficiaries of the nature-perfecting grace that Adam and Eve had in paradise, their passions are more capable of leading reason astray. Because of this wounding of nature, men and women experience sexual delight in a different way than Adam and Eve would have before the Fall. Indeed, before the Fall, Aquinas argues, they would have experienced the goodness of sexual pleasure in a way far more excellent than men and women do today. Since men and women now live with a fallen human condition, there is all the more reason for them to direct to reason those passions and delights inherent in their composition as body and soul. In the next chapter, we will see exactly how Aquinas proposes that this reality relates to the movement of love in the *Summa Theologiae.*

7

The Movement of Love in the *Summa Theologiae*

The focus of the previous chapter on the anthropology of Thomas Aquinas provided the foundation for an examination in this chapter (as well as the next) of the metaphysical notions of love and marriage in Aquinas's mature work, the *Summa Theologiae*. We continue to illustrate the fact that Thomas's anthropology is the implicit but necessary foundation for the spousal meaning of the body as articulated in Pope John Paul's *Theology of the Body*. The goal of this chapter is to show that Thomas situated love within the broad metaphysical framework of every being's attraction to the good. The importance which the Angelic Doctor ascribes to the *appetitus*, a being's inclination to the good, cannot be overstated. Just as John Paul argues that the spousal meaning of the body directs the human person out of himself to complete fulfillment in the gift of self, appetite is the phrase Thomas uses to describe the fact that all created beings are directed from nothingness out of themselves in the pursuit of perfection. Given man's fallen nature, this drive out of oneself is only properly ordered through the virtues, especially the virtues of prudence, temperance, and charity.

For these purposes, the chapter has three sections. The first section, on the metaphysical foundation of love, explores the notion that love is an attraction to the good and that there are different types of loves according to Aquinas, followed by an analysis of the role that nature plays in our attraction to the good. The second section focuses on the role of prudence and temperance in human love. Finally, the third section highlights the love of God, or the friendship with God, which is the theological virtue of charity.

THE METAPHYSICAL FOUNDATION OF LOVE

Love: Attraction to the Good

Thomas's thought on the good and our attraction to the good are foundational for understanding his theory of love. For Aquinas, as we have noted before, every agent acts for an end.[1] The end is that which is suitable to the agent's form: "Everything, insofar as it is in act, acts and tends towards that which is in accordance with its form."[2] In Aquinas's worldview, beings act in pursuit of the fullness of their form. He recognizes that created beings are imperfect.[3] It belongs to the form of a bird to have two wings and to fly. If a bird lacks either of these (or any of the other characteristics of what it means to be a bird), it is good inasmuch as it exists but it is not perfect. This is why God is God: he has no imperfections.[4]

Each natural thing has an "aptitude toward its natural form, that when it has it not it tends towards it; and when it has it, it is at rest therein."[5] Aquinas writes that "all desire their own perfection," and that which is desired by a being is desired because it is perfect *vis-à-vis* the agent in some respect or another.[6] This is why created beings are drawn outside of themselves. Their potencies are actualized only by other beings and ultimately by the supreme good, who is God. Aquinas notes that "in natural things, everything which, as such, naturally belongs to another, is principally and more strongly inclined to

---

1. See *ST* I-II, q. 1, a. 2.   2. *ST* I, q. 5, a. 5.
3. Ibid.
4. See *ST* I, q. 4, aa. 1–2; q. 6, aa. 1–2. Cf. *ST* I, q. 2, a. 3: "Now the maximum in any genus is the cause of all in that genus; as fire, which is the maximum of heat, is cause of all hot things. Therefore there must be also something which is to all beings the cause of their being, goodness, and every other perfection; and this we call God."
5. *ST* I, q. 19, a. 1.
6. See *ST* I, q. 5, a. 1.

that other to which it belongs, than towards itself."[7] Created beings
have a drive or tendency to the perfection of their natural form. In the
Summa Theologiae, Aquinas calls this tendency to perfection (to the
good) "appetite" (*appetitus*).[8] All things, even those without knowledge, have an appetite.[9]

For the Angelic Doctor, love is intrinsically bound to the appetite
for the good, for the fullness and perfection of one's being. He begins
his discussion of love in the *prima secundae* by grounding the notion
of love squarely in this drive of a being to the good: "Love is something pertaining to the appetite since good is the object of both."[10]
In the most basic sense, love is "the principle of movement towards
the end loved."[11] The word *love*, therefore, can be applied even to the
natural appetite since "the principle of this [natural] movement is the
appetitive subject's connaturalness with the thing to which it tends."[12]

Natural appetite means, first and foremost, the inclination each
thing has to "something like and suitable to the thing inclined."[13] The
natural appetite inclines each thing to something suitable to its natural form, to that which is connatural to it.[14] Aquinas says explicitly:
"Natural love is not only in the powers of the vegetal soul, but in all

---

7. *ST* I, q. 60, a. 5.   8. See *ST* I, q. 19, a. 1.

9. Ibid.

10. *ST* I-II, q. 26, a. 1. For other relevant exegeses on the inclination to the good
and love, see Jordan Aumann, "Thomistic Evaluation of Love and Charity," *Angelicum*
55 (1978): 533–41; David M. Gallagher, "The Will and Its Acts (Ia IIae, qq. 6–17)," in *The
Ethics of Aquinas*, ed. Stephen J. Pope (Washington, D.C.: Georgetown University Press,
2002), 70–73; Thomas Gilby, "Acting for a Purpose," in *Summa Theologiae*, ed. Gilby,
16:144–46; Robert Miner, *Thomas Aquinas on the Passions: A Study of* Summa Theologiae *1a2ae 22–48* (New York: Cambridge University Press, 2009), 126–32; Paul J. Wadell,
The Primacy of Love: An Introduction to the Ethics of Thomas Aquinas (Mahwah, N.J.:
Paulist Press, 1992), 36–43.

11. *ST* I-II, q. 26, a. 1. Robert Pasnau's overly analytical reading of Aquinas reveals its
limitations when he suggests that Aquinas's idea that love is a movement sounds rather mechanical (see *Thomas Aquinas on Human Nature*, 242). Following the lead of Josef
Pieper, Robert Miner suggests that Aquinas's use of the word *amor* in a variety of ways
reveals a fundamental dynamism between appetite and appetible object—see Miner,
Thomas Aquinas on the Passions, 118, citing Josef Pieper, *Faith, Hope, and Love* (San Francisco, Calif.: Ignatius Press, 1997), 146–47. It is my hope that my exegesis of Aquinas's
notion of love in the *Summa Theologiae* will serve as a helpful response to Pasnau's re-
mark.

12. Ibid.   13. *ST* I-II, q. 8, a. 1.

14. See *ST* I-II, q. 26, a. 1.

the soul's powers, and also in all the parts of the body, and universally in all things … since each thing has a connaturalness with that which is naturally suitable to it."[15] Elsewhere, he writes:

It is common to every nature to have some inclination; and this is its natural appetite or love. This inclination is found to exist differently in different natures; but in each according to its mode. Consequently, in the intellectual nature there is to be found a natural inclination coming from the will; in the sensitive nature, according to the sensitive appetite; but in a nature devoid of knowledge, only according to the tendency of the nature to something.[16]

Michael Sherwin notes that Aquinas's "method here is significant. By introducing rational love in the context of natural love, he is presenting rational love's relationship to cognition as part of a larger and more general dynamic. All appetitive principles of action presuppose knowledge. This is true even for non-rational creatures."[17] In Thomas's anthropology, appetite follows cognition: since "in order for a thing to be done for an end, some knowledge of the end is necessary."[18] Love requires knowledge. This is important. It means that "human action presupposes a voluntary receptivity to reality. At its most basic level, love is a response to the goodness of reality, a response to the real as it is or as it could be."[19]

Love is the principle of movement toward the end; appetite pursues an end in virtue of the fact that end is somehow connatural to the appetite. On the other hand, "the aptitude of the sensitive appetite or of the will to some good, that is to say, its very complacency in good [*complacentia boni*], is called sensitive love, or intellectual or rational love."[20] Michael Sherwin calls this complacency in the good "a pleasant affective affinity."[21] Aquinas delineates a threefold interaction between the appetite and the object loved (the appetible object).[22]

---

15. *ST* I-II, q. 26, a. 1, ad 3. See also *ST* II-II, q. 141, a. 1, ad 1: "Nature inclines everything to whatever is becoming to it. Wherefore man naturally desires pleasures that are becoming to him. Since, however, man as such is a rational being, it follows that those pleasures are becoming to man which are in accordance with reason."

16. *ST* I, q. 60, a. 1.

17. Sherwin, *By Knowledge and By Love*, 72.

18. *ST* I-II, q. 6, a. 1; cf. q. 15, a. 3. See also *SCG* II.23.

19. Sherwin, *By Knowledge and By Love*, 95.

20. *ST* I-II, q. 26, a. 1.

21. Sherwin, *By Knowledge and By Love*, 70.

22. See *ST* I II, q. 26, a. 2.

First, the appetible object gives the appetite "a certain adaptation to itself, which consists in complacency in that object; and from this follows movement towards the appetible object…. Accordingly, the first change wrought in the appetite by the appetible object is called love, and is nothing else than complacency [*complacentia*] in that object."[23] The appetible object introduces a pleasant affective affinity into the appetite. The soul's apprehension (whether sensitive or rational) recognizes something pleasing in the object, something which perfects the agent in one respect or another, and this produces a complacency in the object.[24] "From this complacency results a movement towards that same object, and this movement is desire; and lastly, there is rest which is joy."[25] There is a difference between sensitive love and rational or intellectual love, and this will be discussed further below, but here it is enough to note the relationship between the object loved and the appetite.[26] What separates the love of the will from all other loves is exactly free choice (*electionem*). Aquinas calls rational love, the love that is freely chosen, *dilectio*.[27]

Passion, Reason, and Will

Since Aquinas understands love as the appetitive movement of created being out of itself in search of the perfection of its form, it remains to be seen how man's free will and intellect affect this drive. This is to say, if man is a free rational animal as Aquinas says he is, then man is also free in some sense to determine what he loves, to determine that in which he believes he will find his perfection and fulfillment: whether it be another human person, or God, or some created good. To understand this further, it is now necessary to explore Aquinas's view of human love as a unique interaction between passion and freedom.

Strictly speaking, for Aquinas, sensitive love is the love that is a

---

23. Ibid.
24. See *ST* I-II, q. 27, a. 1.
25. *ST* I-II, q. 26, a. 2.
26. This is a marked difference from Aquinas's early work. In his commentary on Peter Lombard's *Sentences*, Thomas states that the form of the beloved actually moves into the appetite of the lover, and moves the appetite itself. Aquinas's mature thought sees the complacency (in which the lover's reason plays a role) as moving the appetite toward the beloved. For a history of the development of this theme in Aquinas's work, see Sherwin, *By Knowledge and By Love*, 64–81.
27. See *ST* I-II, q. 26, a. 3.

passion. In chapter 6, I noted that passions exist only in the sensitive appetite, as passions entail a corporeal transmutation. Only the sensitive appetite is affected by corporeal transmutation.[28] The sensitive appetite only knows individual objects, that a particular concrete being is blue, soft, etc. Reason, however, is able to abstract universal forms from particular conditions.[29]

Unlike animals, which are moved immediately by their passions, men and women are moved only when the superior intellectual appetite moves to the object following upon the apprehension of practical reason.[30] Love that is in the will is an intellectual love inasmuch as the intellectual appetite follows the reason of the subject himself.[31] Thomas writes, "in the intellectual appetite, love is a certain harmony of the appetite with that which is apprehended as suitable."[32]

The will loves that which is apprehended as good (the *bonum rationis*).[33] The Angelic Doctor admits that "sometimes the will tends to something which is apprehended as good, and yet is not really good."[34] Moreover, since in this life goods are complex, most beings are desirable and good in one respect but not in another. Chocolate may be desirable for its taste, but not for its effects on skin and weight. Thus, in reference to the goodness of an object, "there may a distinction according to the consideration of reason; so does it happen that one and the same thing is desired in way, and not desired in another."[35] An object may be suitable in one respect, but unsuitable in another. The reason and the will work in a tandem relationship in pursuit of their ends. The object of the will is the good, and therefore

---

28. See 204–9 above. Cf. *ST* I-II, q. 22, aa. 1 and 3. In a response to the objection that scripture speaks of love, joy, and anger in God and the angels, all of which are passions, Aquinas writes: "When love and joy and the like are ascribed to God or the angels, or to man in respect of his intellectual appetite, they signify simple acts of the will having like effects, but without passion" (*ST* I-II, q. 22, a. 3, ad 3; cf. q. 24, a. 3, ad 2).

29. See *ST* I, q. 85, a. 1; q. 79, a. 4. Cf. Simo Knuuttila, *Emotions in Ancient and Medieval Philosophy* (Oxford: Clarendon Press, 2004), 239–47, 251; Miner, *Thomas Aquinas on the Passions*, 19–41.

30. See *ST* I, q. 81, a. 3.   31. See *ST* I-II, q. 27, a. 2, ad 3.
32. *ST* I-II, q. 29, a. 1.

33. *ST* I-II, q. 8, a. 1 (emphasis added). Cf. *ST* I-II, q. 5, a. 8, ad 2; q. 6, a. 2, ad 1; q. 46, a. 5, ad 1; I, q. 19, a. 1; q. 82, a. 3.

34. *ST* I-II, q. 13, a. 5, ad 2.

35. *ST* I-II, q. 5, a. 8, ad 2. Cf. Sherwin, *By Knowledge and By Love*, 96–97.

the will moves all the powers of the soul to their proper acts.[36] The will commands the exercise of all the soul's powers, including the intellect.[37]

Nonetheless, the intellect plays its own role since, after all, the intellect presents the object of desire to the will which pursues the *bonum rationis* (the good as apprehended). The intellect thus determines or specifies the will's command.[38] Since the will is the principle of action and the power moving all others powers of the soul to exercise their respective acts, sin is in the will as its subject.[39] But because the will is determined by the apprehension of the intellect, the object that the will sinfully pursues also presupposes a deficiency in the intellect's apprehension. Thomas notes: "Since the object of the will is a good or an apparent good, it is never moved to an evil, unless that which is not good appear good in some respect to reason; so that the will would never tend to evil, unless there were ignorance or error in the reason."[40]

Sometimes ignorance is truly antecedent to the will, as when a person is really ignorant of knowledge he is not bound to know. Acting from this antecedent ignorance is not culpable.[41] Ignorance becomes the catalyst of sin only when it is chosen by will. In such a case, the will commands the intellect to remain in ignorance or in partial ignorance regarding the object of action. The good of sexual pleasure, for example, may be pursued but the will commands the reason away from considering the undesirability of intercourse outside

36. *ST* I-II, q. 9, a. 2.

37. See also *ST* I, q. 81, a. 4.

38. *ST* I-II, q. 9, a. 2. See *ST* I-II, q. 9, a. 2, ad 3: "The will moves the intellect as to the exercise of its act; since even the true itself which is the perfection of the intellect is included in the universal good as a particular good. But as to the determination of the act, which the act derives from the object, the intellect moves the will; since the good itself is apprehended under a special aspect as contained in the universal true. It is therefore evident that the same is not mover and moved in the same respect." Cf. *ST* I, q. 82, a. 4, co. and ad 1–2.

39. See *ST* I-II, q. 74, a. 1.

40. *ST* I-II, q. 77, a. 2. For detailed studies of the cause of evil as beyond the intention (*praeter intentionem*) of the will, see Stephen L. Brock, *Action and Conduct: Thomas Aquinas and the Theory of Action* (Edinburgh: T&T Clark, 1998), 216–42; Lawrence Dewan, "St. Thomas and the First Cause of Moral Evil," in *Wisdom, Law, and Virtue*, 186–96; Daniel Westberg, *Right Practical Reason*, 198–215.

41. See *ST* I-II, q. 6, a. 8.

of marriage. This ignorance is consequent upon an act of the will.[42] A man who simply chooses not to ask whether the merchandise he buys from the back of van in a city alley is stolen, even though he has a good sense that it is, is choosing to act from affected ignorance. Whereas the man who chooses not to consider the ramifications of extramarital sex in order to engage in the act with a woman he meets in the pub is acting from the ignorance of evil choice. This ignorance is caused either from passion (in this case a sensitive love that is actualized by sensuality, hormones, and perhaps alcohol, all corporeal transmutations) or perhaps even from a vice.[43] In either case, the chosen ignorance is disordered just as much as the action.[44] This is why elsewhere Aquinas writes that the "right inclination of the will is required antecedently for happiness, just as the arrow must take a right course in order to strike the target."[45] The will must be properly aligned to the true good.

In Aquinas's epistemology, something is apprehended as good and thus desirable in the relationship between the thing itself and its inherent goodness, on the one hand, and the disposition of the agent on the other.[46] The sensitive appetite, which is to say the passions, affect the disposition of the agent.[47] Whereas brute animals and human beings both have imaginations, only man is able to call upon his imagination at will. Fixation in the midst of passion, whichever passion, is a common experience among men and women in which a particular good becomes the focus of our attention to the exclusion of other goods. At other times, the sensitive appetite might be so intent on its object that the other powers of the soul are simply unable to be attentive to their own proper objects. The passions can thus distract the other powers.[48] Aquinas says persons often act contrary to their habitual knowledge, to what they know to be true and good, because "nothing prevents a thing which is known habitually from not

---

42. Ibid.

43. Vices are habitual dispositions to actions which are not befitting the agent's nature (see *ST* I-II, q. 71, a. 1). But it should still be noted that a person who sins through habit, or in this habitually acts from chosen ignorance, does so with a certain malice in Aquinas's view (see *ST* I-II, q. 78, a. 2).

44. See *ST* I-II, q. 74, a. 1, ad 2.
45. *ST* I-II, q. 4, a. 4, ad 2.
46. See *ST* I-II, q. 9, a. 2.
47. *ST* I-II, q. 9, a. 2. Cf. *ST* I-II, q. 10, a. 3.
48. See *ST* I-II, q. 77, a. 1.

being considered actually."[49] Even though a man knows adultery is wrong, generally, he may fail to apply this knowledge in a certain instance for any number of reasons. Perhaps he is lustful or has an impairing illness; perhaps because of drunkenness he is unable to see that the woman with whom he sleeps is not his wife.

More often than not, passions inhibit reason either by distraction, or by inclining reason to something contrary to the true good, or by some corporeal transmutation "the result of which is that the reason is somehow fettered so as not to exercise its act freely; even as sleep or drunkenness, on account of some change wrought on the body, fetters the use of reason.... Sometimes, when the passions are very intense, man loses his reason altogether: for many have gone out of their minds through excess of love or anger."[50] When emotions are intense, the heart beats quicker, adrenaline begins to flow in the body, and these biological changes (in Aquinas's language, corporeal transmutations) affect the reason. What is known habitually (that adultery is wrong) is unattended to in the heat of the moment.

While the imagination, at the command of reason, can present an object to the sensitive appetite, since the sensitive appetite depends on the body for its actualization it retains something of an independence from reason. Although the intellectual appetite must consent in order for man to act, nonetheless the sensitive appetite does not depend on the reason for its object when the object is presented by the body and not by the reason.[51] This is the difference between fantasy and reality. Even though the sensitive appetite is inclined to obey reason, the "condition or disposition of the body is not subject to the command of reason: and consequently in this respect, the movement of the sensitive appetite is hindered from being wholly subject to the command of reason."[52] Aquinas says that reason governs the sensitive appetite "not by a despotic supremacy, which is that of a master over his slave; but by a politic and royal supremacy, whereby the free are governed, who are not wholly subject to command."[53] In this life, we are often subject to unwanted thoughts, fantasies, and mental distractions that we ourselves do not initiate. They simply arise in our

---

49. *ST* I-II, q. 77, a. 2.
51. See *ST* I-II, q. 17, a. 7.
53. Ibid.

50. Ibid.
52. Ibid.

mind's eye. When we fixate on them, however, we are, in fact, choosing them.

Of course, in man's original state the passions were entirely subject to reason.[54] The passions are not themselves inherently sinful. They become so only inasmuch as they incline us toward action that is contrary to reason.[55] In this life, rational love requires the right ordering of our passions so that which we love, the persons we love, are loved for who they are and not entirely for passionate purposes. Our rational love must be rightly ordered and it must include passion. It is the whole person who loves. Jordan Aumann once wrote that "purely spiritual or volitional love without any resonance in the emotion of love is not a truly human love."[56]

Friendship and Concupiscence

Thomas says that rational love is properly divided into love of friendship (*amor amicitiae*) and love of concupiscence (*amor concupiscentia*).[57] Love is not divided against itself but rather the "the movement of love has a twofold tendency."[58] The first, the love of friendship, is the movement "towards the good which a man wishes to someone, to himself or to another."[59] The second, the love of concupiscence, are the goods he wishes for another.[60] That which is loved with *amor amicitiae* is loved for its own sake. That which is loved with *amor concupiscentiae* is loved secondarily and relative to something else, namely, the person, perhaps oneself, for which it is loved.[61]

Thomas will later cite the authority of Aristotle for his understanding of friendship: "According to the Philosopher, not every love

---

54. See *ST* I, q. 95, a. 2. Cf. *ST* III, q. 15, a. 4.

55. See *ST* I-II, q. 24, a. 4.

56. Aumann, "Thomistic Evaluation of Love and Charity," 540. Servais Pinckaers has also noted the need to reappropriate a proper understanding of passion in moral theology; see Pinckaers, "Reappropriating Aquinas's Account of the Passions," 273–87.

57. See *ST* I-II, q. 26, a. 4.

58. Ibid.

59. Ibid. See *ST* I-II, q. 26, a. 4, ad 1: "For a friend is, properly speaking, one to whom we wish good: while we are said to desire, what we wish for ourselves."

60. See *ST* I-II, q. 26, a. 4.

61. Ibid. See Aumann, "Thomistic Evaluation of Love and Charity," 542–46; Miner, *Thomas Aquinas on the Passions*, 122–26; Sherwin, *By Knowledge and By Love*, 74–77.

has the character of friendship, but that love to which is together with benevolence, when, to wit, we love someone so as to wish good to him."[62] He goes on to say that benevolence is not enough for friendship: "Neither does well-wishing suffice for friendship, for a certain mutual love is requisite, since friendship is between friend and friend: and this well-wishing is founded on some kind of communication."[63] Friendship is a certain communication of goodness between friends.

Since friendship requires communication between friends, *amor amicitiae* cannot be directed to irrational creatures.[64] We are unable to share good things with an irrational creature, which "is not competent, properly speaking, to possess good, this being proper to the rational creature which, through its free-will, is the master of its disposal of the good it possesses."[65] Moreover, friendship "is based on some fellowship of life; since *nothing is so proper to friendship as to live together*, as the Philosopher proves. Now irrational creatures can have no fellowship in human life which regulated by reason."[66] We can love irrational creatures not as friends but rather as goods directed to friendship. We can love them with *amor concupiscentiae*.

Aquinas notes that the difference between the love of things (*amor concupiscentiae*) and the love of persons (*amor amicitiae*) is this: "When we love a thing, by desiring it, we apprehend it as belonging to our well-being. In like manner when a man loves another with the love of friendship, he wills good to him, just as he wills good to himself: wherefore he apprehends him as his other self, in so far, to wit, as he wills good to him as to himself."[67] The Angelic Doctor makes the point that "the love which a man loves himself is the form and root of friendship."[68] The manner in which man loves himself will determine the character of his friendships.

---

62. *ST* II-II, q. 23, a. 1, citing Aristotle, *Nicomachean Ethics* VIII.2.1155b31. Unless otherwise noted, all English translations of this text are from *Nicomachean Ethics*, trans. Terence Irwin, 2nd ed. (Indianapolis, Ind.: Hackett, 1999).

63. *ST* II-II, q. 23, a. 1.   64. *ST* I, q. 20, a. 2, ad 3.

65. *ST* II-II, q. 25, a. 3.

66. Ibid. (emphasis added), citing Aristotle, *Nicomachean Ethics* VIII.5.1157b19.

67. *ST* I-II, q. 28, a. 1. Elsewhere, Aquinas qualifies this point. He notes, "We must hold that, properly speaking, a man is not a friend to himself, but something more than a friend, since friendship implies union.... Whereas a man is one with himself which is more than being united to another" (see *ST* II-II, q. 25, a. 4).

68. *ST* II-II, q. 25, a. 4.

Man's love for himself must be properly ordered. It is a fault to love one's self in a disordered way. "Those who love themselves are to be blamed, in so far as they love themselves as regards their sensitive nature, which they humor. This is not to love oneself truly according to one's rational nature, so as to desire for oneself the good things which pertain to the perfection of reason."[69] When self-love is dominated by the concupiscible appetite, not only do we love ourselves primarily as sensual beings, but friendship becomes more focused on pleasure and utility. "When friendship is based on usefulness or pleasure, a man does indeed wish his friend some good: and in this respect the character of friendship is preserved. But since he refers this good further to his own pleasure or use, the result is that friendship of the useful or pleasant, in so far as it is connected with love of concupiscence, loses the character of true friendship."[70]

Aquinas further clarifies this point when he speaks about ecstasy as an effect of love. Ecstasy, he says, "means to be placed outside of oneself."[71] He says that, on the one hand, ecstasy can sometimes be in the apprehensive power: when a person is raised above his comprehension and sensation to apprehend a higher knowledge or when a person's reason is overcome by violence or madness. But precisely because the appetite is also an outward movement, the appetite also experiences the ecstasy of love.

In the love of concupiscence the lover is carried out of himself but only in a certain sense, inasmuch "as not being satisfied with enjoying the good he has, he seeks to enjoy something out of himself. But since he seeks to have this extrinsic good for himself, he does not go out from himself simply, and this movement remains finally within him."[72] The concupiscent person's pursuits ultimately remain concerned only with himself. With the love of friendship, on the other hand, "a man's affection goes out from itself simply; because he wishes and does good to his friend, by caring and providing for him, for his sake."[73]

That love is a movement follows upon Aquinas's metaphysical principles and his anthropology, namely, on the relationship between

---

69. *ST* II-II, q. 25, a. 4, ad 3.
71. *ST* I-II, q. 28, a. 3.
73. Ibid.

70. *ST* I-II, q. 26, a. 4, ad 3.
72. Ibid.

the reason and the will, between truth and goodness. For Aquinas, the intellect creates a certain type of union between the knower and the known. The known is in the knower according to the mode of the knower.[74] There is also a union of the appetite, a union of love, which moves the lover to the beloved.[75] While the union of love can exist in different stages (whether the beloved is present or absent to the lover), what is clear is that for Aquinas the union of the lover with the beloved is real rather than notional. The union of love is with the beloved herself, it is not just a union to the idea of the beloved.[76]

Aquinas offers a distinction when the union of love is greater than the union of knowledge, that is, when it is better to love than to know.[77] It concerns the relative mode of comparison between the intellect and the will.

> When ... the thing in which there is good is nobler than the soul itself, in which is the idea understood; by comparison with such a thing, the will is higher than the intellect. But when the thing which is good is less noble than the soul, then even in comparison with that thing the intellect is higher than the will. Wherefore the love of God is better than the knowledge of God; but, on the contrary, the knowledge of corporeal things is better than the love thereof.[78]

Those things that are inferior to the soul are given simpler (and, hence, more noble) existence once they are known abstractly and simply by the intellect. Those things that are superior to the soul, however, cannot really be apprehended in the proper sense of the term. They can be deduced through cause-effect reasoning but the intellect cannot attain an understanding of their essence that would not in some way be less noble than as they exist in themselves.[79]

---

74. See *ST* I, q. 16, a. 1.   75. See *ST* I-II, q. 28, a. 1.
76. See *ST* I-II, q. 32, a. 3.

77. I am grateful to an insightful article written by Russell Hittinger on this topic. Hittinger fails to note the development of Aquinas's notion of love between the time he wrote his commentary on Peter Lombard's *Sentences* and the time he wrote the *Summa Theologiae* (discussed in Sherwin, *By Knowledge and By Love*, 96–97). However, he does provide an excellent explanation of Thomas's understanding of the relationship between knowledge and love. See Russell Hittinger, "When It Is More Excellent to Love Than to Know: The Other Side of Thomistic 'Realism,'" *Proceedings of the American Catholic Philosophical Association* 57 (1983): 171–79.

78. *ST* I, q. 82, a. 3.

79. Aquinas arrives at this same conclusion in his disputed questions on the truth,

Because the will is free, it is possible for it to love something inferior to the soul—to love it as an end in itself, and not as a means to a greater good. In doing so, love would go against reason which, in the union caused by knowledge, would possess the form of that thing more simply, and thus more nobly, than the thing itself. On the other hand, when we love that which the intellect cannot fully grasp, our love is noble since our beloved is nobler than the idea of our beloved. This is why it is degrading and blameworthy for a person to love a tree, a stone, or merely carnal pleasure: these things are beneath our nobility as rational creatures.

Happiness, for Aquinas, is that which every man and woman desires as their perfection, their end.[80] Although each person may differ in his opinion about what the ultimate end of life is, nonetheless every person naturally desires contentment and perfect fulfillment.[81] Thomas himself argues that some ends commonly pursued by people cannot be our final end. He picks wealth, honor, fame, glory, power, and pleasure as common examples of ends pursued that are ultimately unsatisfying.[82] Carnal pleasure will not bring us happiness because it is limited to the body and senses. I noted in chapter 6 that the senses are limited to the apprehension of singulars in Aquinas's anthropology. Singular goods participate in the ultimate and universal good.[83] No single carnal pleasure can fully satisfy the human person, as Aquinas reaffirms here, even though the body is required for perfect and complete happiness since soul and body are ordered to one another.[84] But neither can delight be our ultimate end, as (he says) "it results from the perfect good, the very essence of happiness … as its proper accident."[85] Delight is a consequence of perfect happiness. We delight in the good once it is possessed.

In Aquinas's metaphysics, happiness must be an operation precisely because the good is that which perfects, and that which perfects is that which is actualizes.[86] The final end of man must be an operation of man's most noble part, that which separates him from the

---

where he notes that "the intellect takes on the forms of things superior to the soul in a way inferior to that which they have in the things themselves." See *DV*, q. 22, a. 11.

80. See *ST* I-II, q. 1, aa. 1–2.
81. See *ST* I-II, q. 1, a. 7, co. and ad 2.
82. See *ST* I-II, q. 2, aa. 1–6.
83. See *ST* I-II, q. 1, a. 4, co. and ad 1.
84. See *ST* I-II, qq. 2 and 4, a. 6.
85. *ST* I-II, q. 2, a. 6; see q. 3, a. 4.
86. See *ST* I-II, q. 3, a. 2.

animals and makes him what he is: a rational animal. Thus, happiness is a good of the rational soul.[87] It is the operation of the speculative intellect, that part of our reason that contemplates reality and universal being.[88] Ultimately, in the Angelic Doctor's view, God is man's true last end. He is the supreme uncreated good in which all other created goods participate.[89] He argues that man can attain an imperfect happiness in this life by his own powers, but can only achieve perfect happiness with God through a supernatural and divine gift (that is, grace, discussed below).[90]

The goods that we pursue and love are subordinated to the highest good: God.[91] All other goods, all other loves, are true and right inasmuch as they direct us to the first good, God, and to love of him. Love must be properly ordered. For Aquinas, "virtue is the order or ordering of love ... because in us love is set in order by virtue."[92] From the Angelic Doctor's perspective, the sad truth about humanity is that the gift of freedom (of a rational appetite) and its accompanying drive to love coupled with man's intellectual capacities means that he is radically capable of selling himself short. He is capable of investing himself entirely in goods that, when not properly ordered to the supreme good, are beneath his dignity. Later Karol Wojtyła will refer to this as "disintegration." This is the perennial possibility of disintegration inherent in man's constitution. This is why love and the spousal meaning of the body require virtue and self-mastery.

87. See *ST* I-II, q. 2, a. 7.

88. See *ST* I-II, q. 3, a. 5. Aquinas also notes that the will plays a role in happiness inasmuch as it desires the ultimate good and takes delight once happiness is attained. However, happiness is not found in the operation of the will because that which is desired is present in the will already in the desire itself, inasmuch as that which is desired is conforming the will to itself. If happiness were an operation of the will, all men would be happy simply by desiring the good, and this is not the case (see *ST* I-II, q. 3, a. 4).

89. See *ST* I-II, q. 2, a. 8; q. 3, aa. 1 and 8.

90. See *ST* I-II, q. 5, aa. 1, 3, 5. The relationship of nature to the supernatural, of happiness to the beatific vision of God, was furiously debated in the twentieth century. The debate began with publication of Henri de Lubac's *Surnaturel* in 1946. See p. 271, note 231, for a more detailed discussion on the issues at play in this debate.

91. Aquinas says: "Those who sin turn from that in which their last end really consists: but they do not turn away from the intention of the last end, which intention they mistakenly seek in other things" (*ST* I-II, q. 1, a. 7, ad 1). Later in the *Summa*, he suggests that when a child comes to the age of reason, he is responsible for using his discretion to direct himself to his due end—God. See *ST* I-II, q. 89, a. 6, co. and ad 3.

92. *ST* I-II, q. 55, a. 1, ad 4.

VIRTUOUS LOVE

Love Is Prudent

The Angelic Doctor's presentation of the virtues in the *Summa* can be analyzed in a number of ways: the relationship between virtue and vice, the difference between acquired and infused virtue, or the necessity of the theological virtues for perfect happiness, to name just a few methods. In this chapter, I am concerned with virtue, inasmuch as virtue properly orders love. Given the relationship of love to reason and to the concupiscible appetite, it seems fitting, therefore, to explore the two virtues ascribed to these two principles: prudence and temperance. The virtue of justice will be of concern in the next chapter on Aquinas's view of marriage.

To understand prudence and virtue properly, it is necessary to understand what a virtue is for Aquinas. He defines virtue in two different ways. First, he says virtue is "a certain perfection of a power."[93] However, he also borrows and agrees with a definition of virtue common at the time: "Virtue is a good quality of the mind, by which we live righteously, of which no one can make bad use, which God works in us, without us."[94] Some powers, such as biological powers, are perfected in their activity (unless they are unhealthy) because they are naturally determined to a single object. However, some powers, such as the intellectual powers of man, are fundamentally indeterminate to concrete objects, even though they are determined to universal objects (for instance, the true and the good in the reason and the will, respectively). Intellectual powers can be determined to a wide variety of objects and to actions of varying goodness. We have seen that Aquinas's view of original sin is that man's intellectual powers are now disordered precisely because they are left to themselves and are, therefore, sometimes directed to conflicting goods or even false goods.

In Aquinas's view, man's powers are not destroyed by original sin but maintain an inclination to virtue, however difficult it may be to achieve that virtue.[95] The inclination to perfection is the middle term

---

93. See *ST* I-II, q. 55, a. 1.
94. *ST* I-II, q. 55, a. 5, obj. 1.
95. See *ST* I-II, q. 109, aa. 2–3; q. 60, a. 1; q. 63, a. 1; q. 85, a. 1.

between our powers and virtue because "the good of nature ... is the natural inclination to virtue, which is befitting to man from the very fact that he is a rational being; for it is due to this that he performs actions in accord with reason, which is to act virtuously."[96] This inclination in man is precisely his tendency to become fully human, the measure of which is determined by the principles of human nature.[97]

Even without additional grace, Aquinas believes that we can acquire virtue, although acquired virtue is fragile and precarious.[98] Simply put, the continued and repeated exercise of moral action produces a certain quality of the soul which he terms *habitus* (habit) or "a disposition whereby what which is disposed well or ill, and this, either in regard to itself or in regard to another."[99] A *habitus* can be acquired through a series of actions or it can be directly infused by God.[100] A habit is an interior ordering of a power to action.[101] Habits that order action in accordance with nature are virtues; habits that refer us to evil are vices.[102] A *habitus* "is a principle of progress and resourcefulness through full commitment."[103] According to Romanus Cessario: "*Habitus* supposes a conception of the human person as open to development and modification from both natural and divine

---

96. *ST* I-II, q. 85, a. 2.

97. See O'Brien, "Fallen Nature," 156: "The principle of his [man's] nature, as is true of any reality, makes man to be what he is. By the same token they include a direction towards the full realization of this way of being. Because he is a human, man by his very nature is bent towards being fully human. This direction is called an inclination—or tendency to act towards the full realization of himself and the perfection of which he does not possess simply by existing. But the principles of his nature are the index to what the fulfillment of himself should be. Again, man is what he is through the principles of his nature. These principles themselves then bespeak of an inclination, an order to human perfection. Since virtue ensures that actions are in conformity to this order of nature, the principles also of themselves mean an inclination to virtue. Nature in its essential principles and in its bent to virtue, then, is not two distinct realities. The distinction is simply between the principles as establishing man in existence and as providing the spring for operations by which he will achieve completion."

98. See *ST* I-II, q. 65, a. 2; q. 109, aa. 2–3 and 8. See Cessario, *Introduction*, 196–200.

99. *ST* I-II, q. 49, a. 1, citing Aristotle, *Metaphysics* V.20.1022b4.

100. See *ST* I-II, q. 51, aa. 2 and 4.   101. See *ST* I-II, q. 54, a. 2.

102. See *ST* I-II, q. 54, a. 3.

103. See Pinckaers, *Sources of Christian Ethics*, 225. See also ibid., 364: "Virtue is not a habitual way of acting, formed by the repetition of material acts and engendering in us a psychological mechanism. It is a personal capacity for action, the fruit of a series of fine actions, a power for progress and perfection."

causes."[104] Grace, our actions, and our sufferings all have a true effect on our personality.

Technically speaking, virtues are those habits that dispose us to do good. In this sense, then, Aquinas allows that there are such things as intellectual virtues (science, wisdom, understanding, and art), but that these are only virtues relatively speaking and not absolutely. An artist or a scientist, after all, may not be a morally good person.[105] Even the preeminent intellectual virtue of understanding whereby the speculative intellect is perfected in its consideration of truth itself (the very object of the intellect) is not enough to guarantee moral rectitude.[106] In addition to the possibility of passion overruling judgment, Aquinas says that concrete actions, the means to the fixed end of human nature, are manifold and infinite.[107] It is not enough to know truth itself, to know the good—we must be able to act and apply what we know to action.

The virtue of prudence is properly an intellectual virtue but it might be better understood as the virtue that bridges the intellectual virtues (and specifically the virtue of understanding) with right action.[108] Prudence perfects the practical reason (which makes concrete rather than speculative judgments). Aquinas defines prudence as "right reason about things to be done."[109] It is concerned primarily with the means to the ends apprehended by the speculative reason (both the ultimate end the person pursues and ends to action immediately considered).[110] This is why prudence is the most necessary of the four cardinal virtues.[111] It establishes the mean and measure of justice, fortitude, and temperance.[112]

By definition, prudence is the virtue whereby the multiplicity of means to any given end are discerned and chosen. But in Aquinas's

---

104. See Romanus Cessario, *The Moral Virtues and Theological Ethics*, 2nd ed. (South Bend, Ind.: University of Notre Dame Press, 2009), 36.

105. See *ST* I-II, q. 56, a. 3; cf. q. 58, a. 5.

106. *ST* I-II, q. 58, a. 5.

107. See *ST* I-II, q. 47, aa. 3 and 15; q. 49, a. 7.

108. See *ST* I-II, q. 57, a. 4, ad 1.

109. See *ST* I-II, q. 56, a. 3.

110. See *ST* I-II, q. 14, a. 2; q. 58, a. 5; II-II, q. 47, aa. 1–3.

111. See *ST* I-II, q. 57, a. 5; II-II, q. 47, a. 5, ad 3. Even the theological virtue of charity needs prudence; see Westberg, *Right Practical Reason*, 251.

112. See *ST* I-II, q. 64, a. 3; II-II, q. 50, a. 1, ad 1; q. 51, a. 2.

worldview, this does not mean that prudence is relativist or purely subjective. On the contrary, prudence is grounded in reality. He writes: "To prudence belongs not only the consideration of the reason, but also the application to action, which is the end of the practical reason."[113]

This is why understanding is needed for moral virtue.[114] We act based on our understanding of reality, on the one hand, and our experience on the other. Our experience is important in Aquinas's view. Past experience helps us to know what to expect from reality amid the infinite possible results from our actions. "It is because the infinite number of singulars cannot be comprehended by human reason, that *our counsels are uncertain* (Wis. 9:14). Nevertheless experience reduces the infinity of singulars to a certain number which occur as a general rule, and the knowledge of these suffices for human prudence."[115]

It is precisely in virtue's connection between the universal and the singular, epitomized in and catalyzed by the virtue of prudence, that frees Aquinas's virtue theory from mere abstraction. Servais Pinckaers writes: "Virtue cannot be reduced to a simple idea or proposition, however precise. It is a specific reality and is only revealed in the experience of action and life."[116] The focus on experience and the need for right experience is the reason, Pinckaers argues, that Aristotle insisted that the young should not study morality.[117]

113. *ST* II-II, q. 47, a. 3.

114. See *ST* I-II, q. 58, a. 5.

115. *ST* II-II, q. 47, a. 3, ad 2 (emphasis added). Several scholars over the last two decades have attempted to recover the role of prudence in reasoning about right human action and in natural law theory. These scholars have taken a decided position against the precept-oriented natural theory of philosophers like John Finnis and Germain Grisez. See, for example, Hall, *Narrative and Natural Law*; Daniel Mark Nelson, *The Priority of Prudence: Virtue and Natural Law in Thomas Aquinas and the Implications for Modern Ethics* (University Park: The Pennsylvania State University Press, 1991); Westberg, *Right Practical Reason*. These works are generally welcomed by many moral theologians for drawing attention to a fuller view of Aquinas's virtue theory and its relationship to natural law. However, they are not without their limitations. For a salient critique of these and other studies on Aquinas's virtue ethics, see Jean Porter, "Recent Studies in Aquinas's Virtue Ethic: A Review Essay," *Journal of Religious Studies* 26 (1998): 191–215. See also Romanus Cessario, "Moral Realism and the Natural Law," in his *Introduction to Moral Theology*, 52–99.

116. Pinckaers, "The Role of Virtue in Moral Theology," in *Pinckaers Reader*, 298–99.

117. See Aristotle, *Nicomachean Ethics* I.3.1095a1; Pinckaers, "The Role of Virtue in Moral Theology," 300–301.

Aquinas insists that in order to grow in prudence a person must not only grow in experience but must also be docile to learning from others. He must take counsel from prudent men and women.[118] With his emphasis on prudence, Thomas is insisting that morality is more than abiding by rules. The moral systems of casuistry so prominent from the seventeenth to the twentieth centuries represented an attempt to gain too much certitude in matters that are often too specific. One of the difficulties with the freedom of indifference described by Pinckaers is the reduced role not only of prudence but also the reduced emphasis on the authority of the community and one's elders in the formation of this virtue.

Early in his explicit treatment of prudence in the *secunda secundae*, Aquinas embraces the definition of Augustine: "*Prudence is love discerning aright that which helps from that which hinders us in tending to God*. Now love is said to discern because it moves the reason to discern."[119] This is an important observation. Prudence is not love "essentially" since love is in the will and prudence is a virtue of the practical intellect. However, inasmuch as the will commands the powers of the soul to exercise their act, the love in the will commands the act of prudence. According to one Thomist, here "we find in the very heart of the Thomistic intellect and will an *act* giving being to an *act*. The act of love in the appetite calls into being the act of knowledge in the intellect."[120]

It is not surprising then that Aquinas holds that "every sin is opposed to prudence."[121] The direct cause of every sin according to Aquinas is an affective adherence to a mutable good, an adherence which is contrary to the nature and dignity of man.[122] Such adherence develops from an inordinate self-love.[123] Precisely because pru-

---

118. See *ST* II-II, q. 47, a. 15; q. 49, a. 3. Even those who have divinely infused prudence know, at the very least, that they must prudently take the counsel of others (see *ST* II-II, q. 47, a. 14, ad 2).

119. *ST* II-II, q. 47, a. 1, ad 1 (emphasis added).

120. Charles O'Neil, *Imprudence in Aquinas* (Milwaukee, Wis.: Marquette University Press, 1955), 106. See especially 103–7 on the relationship of love and prudence in Aquinas; see also O'Neil, "Is Prudence Love?," *The Monist* 58 (1974): 119–39.

121. *ST* II-II, q. 55, a. 2, ad 3. Every vice is also contrary to prudence (see *ST* II-II, q. 119, a. 3, ad 3).

122. See *ST* I-II, q. 75, a. 1.

123. See *ST* I-II, q. 77, a. 4; cf. II-II, q. 153, a. 5, ad 3.

dence is about the means to the end loved, a defect concerning the end is the "worst of all."[124] In fact, the primary vice that Thomas believes resembles the virtue of prudence is a "prudence of the flesh" in which a man "looks upon carnal goods as the last end of his life," and so constructs an architecture of means to achieve those carnal goods.[125] This is self-love gone awry.

While prudence is the measure of the other cardinal virtues, prudence itself needs the other virtues, and perhaps especially the virtue of temperance. The many vices of imprudence arise from lust.[126] This is why Aquinas insists that the moral virtues are connected one to another through prudence.[127] Moral virtues protect the reason against inordinate passions that compromise judgment and inordinately affect love.[128]

Love Is Temperate

In Aquinas's moral theory, the virtue of temperance moderates the soul's appetite for "sensible and bodily goods."[129] To repeat: men and women have a sensitive appetite, which they have in common with brute animals. This sensitive appetite has concupiscible attractions to sensible and bodily goods, on the one hand, and flees (irascibly) from sensible and bodily evils.[130] The sensitive appetite, the locus of

---

124. See *ST* II-II, q. 47, a. 1, ad 3: "The worth of prudence consists not in thought merely, but in its application to action, which is the end of the practical reason. Wherefore if any defect occur in this, it is most contrary to prudence, since, the end being of most import in everything, it follows that a defect which touches the end is the worst of all."

125. See *ST* II-II, q. 55, a. 1; cf. ad 2: "The flesh is on account of the soul, as matter is on account of the form, and the instrument on account of the principal agent. Hence the flesh is loved lawfully, if it be directed to the good of the soul as its end. If, however, a man place his last end in a good of the flesh, his love will be inordinate and unlawful, and it is thus that prudence of the flesh is directed to the love of the flesh."

126. *ST* II-II, q. 54, a. 6. See also *ST* II-II, q. 54, a. 6, ad 3: "Carnal vices destroy the judgment of reason so much the more as they lead us away from reason." Cf. *ST* II-II, q. 153, a. 5, ad 1.

127. See *ST* I-II, q. 65, a. 1.

128. See *ST* II-II, q. 123, a. 12; q. 136, a. 1.

129. See *ST* II-II, q. 141, a. 3. For an analysis of Aquinas's understanding of the virtue of temperance, see Diana Fritz Cates, "The Virtue of Temperance (II IIae, qq. 141–170)," in *Ethics of Aquinas*, ed. Pope, 321–39; Cessario, *The Virtues*, 177–97; Pieper, *The Four Cardinal Virtues*, 143–206.

130. See *ST* I-II, q. 23, a. 1.

the passions in the soul, is the locus of virtue inasmuch as it is ordered to reason, or ought to be so but for the fallen state of man.

Aquinas argues that temperance must concern the greatest of pleasures, and, he says, these are the pleasures of touch. This is the case, he says, because "pleasure results from a natural operation, it is so much the greater according as it results from a more natural operation."[131] In this category, he locates pleasures of food, drink, and sexual activity.[132] These are the most pleasurable natural operations in man because they are consistent with the preservation of the individual and of the species.[133]

In fact, pleasure is so much a part of human life and flourishing that Aquinas considers it a vice absolutely "to reject pleasure to the extent of omitting things that are necessary for nature's preservation."[134] Since man shares these same pleasures and operations with animals, it is necessary that he experience them with the excellence proper to the rational person he is.[135] Immoderate pleasure, precisely because it concerns things lower than the simple and abstract objects of contemplation, can easily distract us from reason, divine law, and contemplation.[136]

The virtue of temperance moderates the passions according to the mean between excess and deficiency of pleasure.[137] This is why the virtue of prudence is so necessary. The mean shifts from situation to situation. What is the mean (and therefore what is virtuous) in one situation may be excessive or deficient in another situation.[138] The role of prudence is to discern the mean in every situation.[139] Temperance makes use of sensual pleasure "according to the demands

131. *ST* II-II, q. 141, a. 4.

132. See *ST* II-II, q. 141, aa. 4–5.

133. See *ST* II-II, q. 141, a. 5. Aquinas, however, also allows that temperance concerns unnecessary pleasures, provided those pleasures are not a hindrance to the body and to health (see *ST* II-II, q. 141, a. 6, ad 2). This is due to his anthropology which sees the body as necessary for the operations of the soul since even knowledge requires sense impressions in some way (cf. *ST* I, q. 78, a. 4; q. 80, aa. 6–8).

134. *ST* II-II, q. 142, a. 1.

135. See *ST* II-II, q. 142, a. 4; cf. q. 141, aa. 2–3.

136. See *ST* II-II, q. 142, a. 2, ad 1; a. 4; q. 141, a. 4.

137. See *ST* I-II, q. 59, a. 1. Cf. Aristotle, *Nicomachean Ethics* II.5.1105b28.

138. See *ST* I-II, q. 64, a. 1, ad 2; a. 2.

139. See *ST* I-II, q. 64, a. 3; q. 50, a. 1, ad 1; q. 51, a. 2.

of place and time, and in keeping with those among whom one dwells."[140] Because prudence determines the mean of temperance, as one author puts it, it is the habit "that assists persons in choosing how to feel."[141]

Since temperance is concerned primarily with food, drink, and sex, Aquinas treats abstinence, sobriety, and chastity as subjective parts of temperance. The virtue of chastity concerns matters relating to "venereal pleasures" and sexual intercourse.[142] Aquinas writes that "venereal pleasures are more impetuous, and are more oppressive on the reason than the pleasures of the palate: and therefore they are in greater need of chastisement and restraint, since if one consented to them this increases the force of concupiscence and weakens the strength of the mind."[143] Venereal pleasure is stronger than other pleasures precisely because it motivates man to a greater good: the preservation of the species. Furthermore, "the movement of the organs of generation is not subject to the command of reason, as are the movements of the other external members."[144] Because of original sin, Josef Pieper writes, "the human self is capable of throwing itself into disorder to the point of self-destruction."[145] Within sexual intercourse, the pleasure is so great "that the free act of reason in considering spiritual things is incompatible with the aforesaid pleasure."[146] Unrestrained venereal pleasures "work the greatest havoc in man's mind."[147] In fact, when a man finds himself overly distracted by carnal pleasures, he no longer seeks spiritual pleasures because they have become "distasteful to him."[148] Thomas says that venereal temptations are so strong that "of all a Christian's conflicts, the most difficult combats are those of chastity; wherein the fight is a daily one, but victory rare."[149]

The virtue of chastity disposes a person "to make moderate use of bodily members in accordance with the judgment of his reason

---

140. *ST* II-II, q. 142, a. 6, ad 2.

141. Cates, "The Virtue of Temperance," 325. Cf. *ST* II-II, q. 47, a. 7, ad 2–3; I-II, q. 15, a. 3; q. 57, a. 5.

142. See *ST* II-II, q. 151, aa. 1 and 4.   143. *ST* II-II, q. 151, a. 3, ad 2.

144. *ST* II-II, q. 151, a. 4.

145. Pieper, *The Four Cardinal Virtues*, 148.

146. *ST* II-II, q. 153, a. 2, ad 2.   147. *ST* II-II, q. 153, a. 1, ad 1.

148. *ST* II-II, q. 153, a. 5.   149. *ST* II-II, q. 154, a. 3, ad 1.

and the choice of his will."[150] Chastity orders venereal acts to be performed "in due manner and order."[151] Unlike his treatments of abstinence and sobriety, Aquinas omits any suggestion that the mean of chastity shifts according to circumstances.[152] Thomas argues, on the one hand, that venereal pleasure is not subject to the command of reason, but on the other, he says that chastity disposes us toward moderate use of bodily members according to the judgment of reason. Aquinas clarifies his position in a question on lust as to whether a venereal activity can exist without sinfulness—he says it can.[153] Yet, unlike the other pleasures of touch, Thomas suggests that venereal pleasure essentially impairs reason in the midst of the sexual act. In this way, it is not dissimilar to sleep.

Precisely because the reason is not able to moderate the experience of pleasure in the moment of sexual activity, the act of reason must be virtuous before it sets out to be interrupted by sex. This is why there is no talk of shifting circumstances for sexual pleasure. The mean of reason in regard to sexual activity is not contingent on accidental circumstances because, as Aquinas sees it, there is nothing about the circumstances or situation that can moderate the overpowering nature of venereal pleasure. Engaging in the sexual act, like engaging in sleep or in taking food, must be proportioned to the order of reason, which directs things to their end.[154] Since "it is no sin if one, by the dictate of reason, makes use of certain things in a fitting manner and order for the end to which they were adapted, provided this end be something truly good.... The preservation of the nature of the human species is very great good ... [and] the use of venereal acts [is] directed to the preservation of the whole human race."[155]

Throughout the treatise on temperance, the mean for sexual activity is to engage in venereal acts primarily for procreation. The vice of lust stems from a repeated intention to enjoy venereal pleasures

---

150. *ST* II-II, q. 151, a. 1, ad 1. Given that Aquinas uses the phrase *"delectationes venerae"* throughout the treatise on chastity, it is certain that here, when he uses the term "bodily members," he means the sexual organs.

151. *ST* II-II, q. 153, a. 2.

152. I am grateful to Cates for pointing this out. See Cates, "The Virtue of Temperance," 333.

153. *ST* II-II, q. 153, a. 1, ad 2.   154. See *ST* II-II, q. 141, a. 6.

155. *ST* II-II, q. 153, a. 2.

alone without an intention for procreation.[156] As Aquinas sees it, venereal acts are properly used in accordance with reason, and reason dictates that they be used for their purpose, which is procreation. The vice of lust and its acts is the use of the sexual organs contrary to reason, which is contrary to their purpose, for the sake of venereal pleasure alone.[157] Aquinas holds that the sexual act for procreation is legitimate only within the marital relationship in which the offspring will receive the best upbringing.[158]

I will say more on Aquinas's view of marriage in chapter 8. Presently, I am concerned only with the virtues of prudence and temperance in their relationship with love. In this light, it makes sense that the treatise on temperance is not much concerned with the proper relationship between man and woman, husband and wife. The virtue of temperance is concerned only with the person's passions and their moderation according to reason: "From the very fact that a man holds [*tenet se*] to that which is in accord with reason, he is said to contain himself [*se tenere*]."[159] Although he may not use this term, self-possession is certainly a goal of Aquinas's virtue theory and this means being in control of one's concupiscible passions. Pieper writes: "Temperance is selfless self-preservation. Intemperance is self-destruction through the selfish degradation of the powers which aim at self-preservation."[160]

It is a common mistake to view the virtue of temperance as a sort of repression of sexuality, as if Thomas seeks to govern all passion and feeling through the rubric of a cold and hard Aristotelian logic disguised as moderating reason.[161] Nothing could be further from the truth. For Aquinas, the virtue brings tranquility and joy to the soul, not a conflicted battle of repression.[162] In fact, this is the difference between the continent person and the temperate person. The continent person experiences the vehement passions in the sensitive ap-

156. *ST* II-II, q. 154, a. 11, ad 3.   157. See *ST* II-II, q. 153, aa. 3–4.
158. See *ST* II-II, q. 154, a. 2.   159. *ST* II-II, q. 155, a. 1, ad 1.
160. Pieper, *The Four Cardinal Virtues*, 148.
161. Pasnau, following Martha Nussbaum's theory of emotion, states that Aquinas has a relatively negative view of the passions. See Pasnau, *Thomas Aquinas on Human Nature*, 262–64. Cf. Martha Nussbaum, *Love's Knowledge: Essays on Philosophy and Literature* (New York: Oxford University Press, 1990).
162. See *ST* II-II, q. 141, a. 2, ad 2.

petite, which he must continually struggle to moderate.[163] It is precisely because the passions are rightly ordered that they were not suppressed in the paradise of Adam and Eve. This is why Aquinas says that sexual pleasure was even greater then than it is now.[164] The temperate person experiences delight in food, in drink, and in sexual activity in a way fitting to the dignity, beauty, and honor of the human person.[165]

CHARITY: THE FRIENDSHIP OF GOD

Grace and Nature

No discussion of the topic of love in the *Summa Theologiae* is complete without an exegesis of Thomas's conception of the theological virtue of charity. For Thomas, the theological virtue of charity is a certain friendship with God.[166] As we have seen, every act of the will is preceded by an act of the intellect because the will is a rational appetite. While the will tends to the good, it is the good apprehended by reason (the *bonum rationis*).[167] For its part, the intellect has by nature an understanding (*intellectus*) of first principles (such as the principle of non-contradiction and that whole is greater than a part) that are simply understood without deductive argumentation.[168] All movement in the human person is the result of the interaction between these two faculties: intellect and will.

However, to avoid an infinite regress of interaction (the intellect specifying the will and the will exercising the intellect), Aquinas says there is an exterior mover who is above human nature that puts the process into act.[169] In his treatise on grace, for example, he notes: "Man is master of his acts and of his willing or not willing, because of his deliberate reason, which can be bent on one side or another. And although he is master of his deliberating or not deliberating, yet this can only be by a previous deliberation; and since it cannot go on to

---

163. See Cates, "The Virtue of Temperance," 323, and Cates, *Aquinas on the Emotions.*
164. See *ST* I, q. 98, a. 2, ad 3.   165. See *ST* II-II, q. 141, a. 2, ad 3.
166. See *ST* II-II, q. 23, a. 1.
167. *ST* I, q. 19, a. 1; q. 80, a. 2; q. 82, a. 1; I-II, q. 8, a. 1; q. 13, a. 5, ad 2.
168. See *ST* I, q. 79, a. 8.
169. See *ST* I, q. 2, a. 3; q. 82, a. 4, ad 3; I-II, q. 9, a. 4; q. 17, a. 5, ad 3.

infinity, we must come at length to this, that man's free-will is moved by an extrinsic principle, which is above the human mind, to wit by God."[170] This is why Thomas can say that God's agency remains present even to our fallen nature, even though without grace we can have no direct experience or knowledge of it.[171] He is the Prime Mover and formal cause of the intellect and will.

In the very first question of his treatise of grace, Aquinas writes that man knows whatever he knows through God's own efficient causality, which brings the intellect to act in the first place and gives it its form as an intellectual power.[172] The form God bestows on human understanding (an intelligible light, the Angelic Doctor calls it) is sufficient "for knowing certain intelligible things, viz., those we can come to know through the senses."[173] For higher things, however, the human intellect needs "a stronger light, viz., the light of faith or prophecy which is called the *light of grace*."[174] In the will, too, in all that we pursue we are pursuing God, who is the supreme good, whether we are conscious of this fact or not. God is the end (*telos*) of all created beings, the supreme good is that which is all satisfying for which every individual longs.[175]

The difficulty is that because of God's infinite greatness and the vast expanse between him and mankind, man is unable to know, without divine assistance, anything more about God other than that he exists and that he is the first cause.[176] A particular man can come to this knowledge through the natural light of his reason only after a long life of philosophical reasoning and, even then, not without some error in his thinking.[177]

If the vision of God is the *telos* of man, and if the vision of God surpasses all human powers, can man achieve his happiness?[178] Thomas says that any happiness that man can achieve in this life on his own

---

170. *ST* I-II, q. 109, a. 2, ad 1.

171. See *ST* I, q. 8, a. 3; cf. ad 3: "No other perfection, except grace, added to substance, renders God present in anything as the object known and loved; therefore only grace constitutes a special mode of God's existence in things."

172. See *ST* I-II, q. 109, a. 1.   173. Ibid.

174. Ibid. (emphasis added).

175. See *ST* I-II, q. 1, aa. 4 and 6; q. 3, a. 8; q. 34, a. 3.

176. See *ST* I, q. 13, a. 12.   177. *See ST* I, q. 1, a. 1; II-II, q. 2, a. 4.

178. See *ST* I, q. 12, a. 4; I-II, q. 3, a. 8.

power is necessarily imperfect.[179] However, because the beatific vision of God is our *telos*, our nature has a natural receptivity to the grace of God, which alone can bring about true and perfect happiness: "The beatific vision and knowledge are to some extent above [*supra*] the nature of the rational soul, inasmuch as it cannot reach it of its own strength; but in another way it is in accordance with [*secundum*] its nature, inasmuch as it is capable of it [*capax eius*] by nature, having been made in the likeness of God.... But the uncreated knowledge is in every way above [*supra*] the nature of the human soul."[180] Elsewhere in the *Summa*, he clarifies that, yes, "the reason and will are naturally directed to God, inasmuch as He is the beginning and end of nature, but in proportion to nature. But the reason and will, according to their nature, are not sufficiently directed to Him in so far as he is the object of supernatural happiness."[181]

So it seems, in Aquinas's view, that "God ordained human nature to attain the end of eternal life, not by its own strength, but by the help of grace."[182] Nevertheless, we are not permitted to conclude that God is bound to offer grace to every human person. His will cannot be forced by our actions or preparations. Grace is an entirely gratuitous gift from God.[183] In this life, we can only know with certainty that we have received grace if we receive a special revelation from God confirming the fact. Otherwise, we must live with mere conjecture that we are receiving the grace of God through certain known

---

179. See *ST* I-II, q. 5, a. 7.

180. *ST* III, q. 9, a. 2, ad 3. This is a theme repeated throughout the *Summa Theologiae*. See *ST* I, q. 62, a. 6, ad 1: "As grace comes of God's will alone, so likewise does the nature of the angel: and God's will ordained nature for grace, so did it ordain the various degrees of nature to the various degrees of grace"; q. 95, a. 1, s.c.: "Man and angel are both ordained to grace"; I-II, q. 113, a. 10: "In certain miraculous works it is found that the form introduced is beyond the natural power of such matter, as in the resurrection of the dead, life is above the natural power of such a body. And thus the justification of the ungodly is not miraculous, because the soul is naturally capable of grace; since from its having been made to the likeness of God, it is fit to receive God by grace." Cf. *De malo*, q. 2, a. 11: "As the sun pours light into air, so God pours grace into the soul. And grace is indeed superior to the nature of the soul, and yet there is in the nature of the soul and any rational creature an aptitude to receive grace, and the grace received strengthens the soul to perform requisite acts."

181. *ST* I-II, q. 62, a. 1, ad 3.

182. *ST* I-II, q. 114, a. 2, ad 1.

183. See *ST* I, q. 19, a. 3; I-II, q. 112, aa. 1–3.

facts—among other things, if we delight in God, despise worldly things, and are not conscious of having committed a mortal sin.[184]

In Aquinas's theological anthropology, grace exists in the soul as a sort of quality.[185] Thomas wants to be clear. Grace does not effect a substantial change in the soul. Rather it is a substantial quality. If grace were its own substantial form, it would inherently alter the substance of nature. This would constitute a most extreme discontinuity between the human nature of the pagan and the believer.[186] Grace does not normally move the soul as if by efficient causality. God does not force a man or woman to accept grace. Rather, grace acts on the human person formally.[187] This is a recurrent theme when Aquinas speaks about charity and the other theological and infused virtues.

Grace, which heals and elevates human nature, is more than a disposition added to the powers of the soul to reach out for the divine; it is in the very essence of the soul itself: "For as man in his intellectual power participates in the divine knowledge through the virtue of faith, and in his power the will participates in the divine love through the virtue of charity, so also in the nature of the soul does he participate in the divine nature, after the manner of a likeness, through a certain regeneration or re-creation."[188] Grace creates a new relationship between the rational creature and his Lord and God—"friendship with God." This is the theological virtue of charity.[189]

Charity: The Love Ordering All Loves

The relationship with God, brought about through grace, corresponds to the pursuit of man's supernatural happiness.[190] Aquinas concludes: "Hence it is necessary for man to receive from God some additional principles, whereby he may be directed to supernatural happiness.... Such like principles are called *theological virtues*; first, because their object is God ... secondly, because they are infused in us by God alone; thirdly, because these virtues are not made to known to us, save by Divine revelation, contained in Holy Writ."[191]

---

184. See *ST* I-II, q. 112, a. 5.

185. *ST* I-II, q. 110, a. 2.

186. See *ST* I-II, q. 110, a. 2, ad 2.

187. See *ST* I-II, q. 110, a. 2, ad 1.

188. See *ST* I-II, q. 110, a. 4.

189. See *ST* I, q. 38, a. 1; q. 43, a. 3; III, q. 23, a. 3.

190. *ST* I-II, q. 62, a. 1.

191. Ibid (emphasis added). For excellent exegeses on the theological virtue of char-

The three theological virtues—faith, hope, and love—are principles added to the reason and the will. In Thomas's theological system, they respect human nature: "First, as regards the intellect, man receives certain supernatural principles, which are held by means of a Divine light: these are the articles of faith.—Secondly, the will directed to this end, both as to the movement of intention, which tends to that end as something attainable—and this pertains to hope—and as to a certain spiritual union, whereby the will is, so to speak, transformed into that end—and this belongs to charity."[192] Since Aquinas insists that grace works with nature, he also insists that although the three theological virtues are infused in the human soul together, their acts are distinct. And in the order of generation, the act of faith precedes that of hope, which, in turn, precedes the act of charity. This is the case because "the movement of the appetite cannot tend to anything, either by hoping or loving, unless that thing be apprehended by the sense or by the intellect."[193] For this reason, the virtues of faith and hope can exist when charity is lost (by mortal sin), although they will be lifeless, but charity can never exist in this life without faith and hope.[194]

The theological virtue of faith is not only an intellectual exercise. The assent given to the articles of faith is not the intellectual assent of science; rather, it is an intellectual assent commanded by the will.[195] It is the lack of absolute clarity that separates opinion and belief from scientific reasoning. Unlike angelic substances, who know truths simply and intuitively, the human person must come to know truth through a process of reasoning. This process cannot regress *ad infinitum* but is always grounded on the self-evident first principles of understanding, which are then verified and further illumined.[196] Science is "derived from self-evident and therefore seen principles."[197] When, however, the scientific reasoning process falters precisely be-

ity and the infused moral virtues, see Cessario, *Moral Virtues*, 94–125; Cessario, *The Virtues*, 61–95; Eberhard Schockenhoff, "The Theological Virtue of Charity (IIa IIae, qq. 23–46)," in *Ethics of Aquinas*, ed. Pope, 244–58.

192. *ST* I-II, q. 62, a. 3. Aquinas appeals to 1 Cor 13:13 in I-II, q. 62, a. 4, s.c., for the list of the three theological virtues.

193. *ST* I-II, q. 62, a. 4.   194. See *ST* I-II, q. 65, aa. 4–5.
195. *ST* II-II, q. 2, a. 9.   196. See *ST* I, q. 79, a. 8.
197. *ST* II-II, q. 1, a. 5.

cause of lack of clarity, the will is necessarily engaged: "It is proper to the believer to think with assent: so that the act of believing is distinguished from all other acts of the intellect, which are about the true or the false."[198] Thus the act of belief elicited by the theological virtue of faith is meritorious because it is an "act of the intellect assenting to the Divine truth at the command of the will moved by the grace of God, so that it is subject to the free-will in relation to God."[199] Therefore, it seems that the grace bestowed upon the believer is not only the light of faith but a grace that moves and shapes a corresponding inclination of the will.

This inclination is a sort of "inward instinct" given by grace: "The believer has sufficient motive for believing, for he is moved by the authority of Divine teaching confirmed by miracles, and, what is more, by the inward instinct of the Divine invitation [*interiori instinctu Dei invitantis*]."[200] In another place, he writes rather plainly: "Some act of the will is required before faith, but not an act of the will quickened by charity. This latter act presupposed faith, because the will cannot tend to God with perfect love, unless the intellect possess right faith about him."[201] In fact, what distinguishes living faith from lifeless faith is precisely whether faith lives quickened by charity.

The object of faith, the first truth, "is directed to the object of the will, i.e., the good, as to its end: and this good which is the end of faith, viz., the Divine Good, is the proper object of charity. Therefore, charity is called the form of faith in so far as the act of faith is perfected and formed by charity." Indeed, "the distinction of living from lifeless faith is in respect of something pertaining to the will, i.e. charity, and not in respect of something pertaining to the intellect."[202] This is why Aquinas insists that with respect to their acts, faith necessarily precedes hope and charity, but, with regard to perfection, charity precedes both faith and hope.[203] Again, the will only tends to a good as apprehended.

---

198. *ST* II-II, q. 2, a. 1.   199. *ST* II-II, q. 2, a. 9.
200. *ST* II-II, q. 2, a. 9, ad 3.   201. *ST* II-II, q. 4, a. 7, ad 5.
202. *ST* II-II, q. 4, a. 4. In a response to an objection, Aquinas makes the point that "when living faith becomes lifeless, faith is not changed, but its subject, the soul, which at one time has faith without charity, and at another time, with charity" (ad 4).
203. See *ST* II-II, q. 62, a. 5; cf. q. 23, a. 8.

In a grand movement of grace, God not only introduces the light of faith but gives the human person the ability, through an interior instinct, to assent to faith. This assent is then quickened and formed by the virtue of charity. The infusion of faith with charity confronts us with the true grandeur of Aquinas's vision. Namely, "faith works by love."[204] Placing this wonderful truth along side the notion that charity is friendship with God and we have an even more beautiful picture of God's plan. Not only does the revealing God raise our minds to share in his own self-understanding through the light of faith, but he also gives us fellowship with him in his divine nature.

Thomas explicitly disagrees with Peter Lombard, who he understood to teach that the theological virtue of charity was caused by the Holy Spirit dwelling in the mind and causing the movement of love without any intermediary habit. If that were the case, Aquinas argues, then the movement of charity would not be a movement of the person's will. It would not be voluntary but rather a forced movement from an extrinsic power.[205] The same is true, he continues, if the Holy Spirit were moving the will as an instrument. According to the Angelic Doctor:

No act is perfectly produced by an active power, unless it be connatural to that power by reason of some form whereby it is inclined to the end appointed to it by Him; and in this He ordereth all things sweetly [Wis 8:1].... it is most necessary that, for us to perform the act of charity, there should be in us some habitual form superadded to the natural power, inclining that power to the act of charity, and causing it to act with ease and pleasure.[206]

This form superadded to the power of the will is part and parcel of grace that becomes a certain quality of the soul.

As I mentioned earlier, in Aquinas's view, charity differs from hope in this respect. Hope tends to God as something attainable, whereas charity effects both a spiritual union with God, who is our supreme end, and a transformation in him.[207] This is only possible by an elevation of the man's natural powers through some superadded form. It is not difficult to see why Aquinas says that charity is the most excellent of all virtues since it "attains God Himself that it may rest in Him,

---

204. *ST* II-II, q. 23, a. 6, ad 2.
206. Ibid.

205. See *ST* II-II, q. 23, a. 2.
207. See *ST* I-II, q. 62, a. 3.

but not that something may accrue to us from Him."[208] The infusion of grace as superadded forms means that Aquinas's view of grace is not extrinsicist.[209]

This is also why Thomas says that without charity there can be no true and perfect virtue, as only imperfect virtue is possible without grace. Virtue is ordered to the good, and the good is primarily an end. In Aquinas's worldview, an end is twofold: last end and proximate end, the latter ideally being ordered to the former. The proximate end, in his system, is not wholly subsumed into the ultimate end. The proximate end retains its own character. Hence, he writes, "If ... we take virtue as being ordered to some particular end, then we may speak of virtue being where there is no charity, in so far as it is directed to some particular good.... If ... this particular good be a true good, for instance the welfare of the state, or the like, it will indeed be a true virtue, imperfect, however unless it be referred to the final and perfect good."[210]

Since the good is an end, this translates to an ultimate universal good (which is God) and also to particular goods. Aquinas concludes: "Accordingly it is evident that simply true virtue is that which is directed to man's principal good; thus also the Philosopher says that virtue is the disposition of a perfect thing to that which is best: and in this way no true virtue is possible without charity."[211] He goes on to say that an imperfect virtue is possible inasmuch as it may be

208. *ST* II-II, q. 23, a. 6.

209. See Cessario, *Introduction*, 200.

210. *ST* II-II, q. 23, a. 7. It should be noted here that even though Aquinas cites Augustine in this article, he disagrees with Augustine on this point. Augustine held that no virtue was possible whatsoever without the theological virtue of charity. Augustine believed only in a strict dichotomy between sinful self-love and charity, thus any act that was not motivated by charity was necessarily motivated by sinful self-love (see Mahoney, *Making of Moral Theology*, 37–71). Aquinas disagrees in this article by pointing to the possibility that true proximate ends (which tend to the universal end) can be pursued in a stable manner for the good of the individual and of the community. For further discussion, see Schockenhoff, "The Theological Virtue of Charity," 250–51. For a contemporary attempt to articulate the Augustinian position as Thomas's own position, see Thomas M. Osborne, "The Augustinianism of Thomas Aquinas's Moral Theory," *The Thomist* 67 (2003): 279–305. For a more traditional explanation of Aquinas's view of virtue without charity, see Brian Shanley, "Aquinas on Pagan Virtue," *The Thomist* 63 (1999): 553–77.

211. *ST* II-II, q. 23, a. 7, citing Aristotle, *Physics* VII.3.247a1.

directed to a particular end provided that end be a true good and not a false good. But "it is charity which directs the acts of all other virtues to the last end, and which, consequently, also gives the form to all other acts of virtue: and it is precisely in this sense that charity is called the form of the virtues."[212]

In Aquinas's virtue theory, those virtues acquired through habituation are imperfect because they are *not explicitly* directed to divine reason.[213] When prudence, justice, temperance, and fortitude are acquired by habituation, they are concerned primarily with right reason of human affairs directing those affairs to the good of the individual and the good of the community (even though these goods participate in the divine good).[214] This is why Thomas says that there are infused virtues which accompany the theological virtues: "The theological virtues direct us sufficiently to our supernatural end, inchoately: i.e., to God Himself immediately. But the soul needs further to be perfected by infused virtues in regard to other things, yet in relation to God."[215] With grace, we must learn to love God in all of our actions *explicitly*.

The primary difference between infused and acquired virtues is this: "those infused moral virtues, whereby men behave well in respect of their being fellow-citizens with the saints, and of the household of God [Eph 2:19], differ from the acquired virtues, whereby man behaves well in respect of human affairs."[216] The infused virtues go hand-in-hand with the theological virtue of charity: they cannot exist in the human soul without charity and charity cannot exist without them.[217] When charity is lost because of mortal sin, which is to say when a single action undertaken with sufficient reflection and full consent is a grave violation against God's love, the infused virtues are lost. (Although, because they are acquired by habituation, acquired virtues require repeated behavior to reverse.)[218] Charity, the

---

212. *ST* II-II, q. 23, a. 8. Charity is the mother of all virtues (see ad 3).

213. See *ST* I-II, q. 63, a. 2; cf. q. 65, a. 2.

214. See *ST* I-II, q. 63, a. 4; q. 61, a. 5, co. and ad 4.

215. *ST* I-II, q. 63, a. 3, ad 2.   216. *ST* I-II, q. 63, a. 4.

217. See *ST* I-II, q. 65, aa. 2–3.

218. See *ST* I-II, q. 63, a. 2, ad 2. For a more detailed study of the infused virtues see Cessario, *Moral Virtues*, 102–25; Michael Sherwin, "Infused Virtue and the Effects of Acquired Vice: A Test Case for the Thomistic Theory of Infused Cardinal Virtues," *The Thomist* 73 (2009): 29–52.

love of God at work in the human person, is the love that orders men and women, and all the activities of their life, to the ultimate end: God himself.

Thomas spends twelve articles addressing the loves that are commanded or ordered by charity other than the love of God.[219] These are not different loves. The theological virtue of charity is one virtue interiorly but is differentiated in different acts.[220] We are to love our neighbor but not the guilt of their sin; to love angels but not demons; to love ourselves but not irrational creatures. Any "love" for irrational creatures or for demons is not for their own sake, but for our own sake or for God's glory.[221] In the end, Thomas concludes that there are four objects that ought to be loved with the theological virtue of charity. Primarily, there is God, the principle of object of the virtue. We should love God above all else.[222]

Secondly are those things which partake in the happiness of God: angels and men. Man loves himself because charity is the love of God and all that partakes of God, which includes us.[223] A man loves his neighbor for the same reason, namely that all men and women are made in the image of God and partake in God to some degree.[224] But a man is not to sacrifice his spiritual beatitude, his love of God, for his neighbor, even if to keep his neighbor free from sin.[225]

A person does not love every other with equal intensity out of charity, for man loves his neighbor inasmuch as he or she is proximate to God himself (who is the principal object of charity). Those neighbors closer to God rightly receive more intense love from a man infused with charity than whose are not.[226] There is also an order of charity in regard to natural relationships. Man should love his parents with a greater dignity but his children with greater priority, because of the differing sorts of relationships to his kin.[227] He should love his wife with greater passion but his parents with greater respect.[228]

---

219. See *ST* II-II, q. 25. 220. See *ST* II-II, q. 23, a. 5, co. and ad 2.
221. See *ST*, II-II, q. 25, a. 11, co. 222. See *ST* II-II, q. 25, a. 12; q. 26, aa. 1–3.
223. *ST* II-II, q. 25, a. 4. Aquinas says that sinners and the wicked are not blamed because they love themselves, but because they love themselves wrongly. They are too much in love with the carnal aspect of their human nature. See *ST* II-II, q. 25, a. 4, ad 3; a. 7.
224. See *ST* II-II, q. 25, a. 1; q. 44, a. 2. 225. *ST* II-II, q. 26, a. 4.
226. See *ST* II-II, q. 26, a. 6. 227. See *ST* II-II, q. 26, aa. 8–9.
228. See *ST* II-II, q. 26, aa. 10–11.

Finally, man loves his body because it participates in a kind of overflow of happiness from man's participation in God. Man loves his body because it was created by God, but he does not love the effects wrought in it by original sin.[229] The love of the body is beneath the love of persons even when ordered by the theological virtue of charity because the body participates in happiness secondarily from the soul, which participates in happiness primarily. This follows from Aquinas's own anthropology discussed in chapter 6, in which the body is ordered to the goods of the soul and receives from the soul its form. Thus our love for our body must fall behind our love for God and our love for our neighbor, even to the point of suffering bodily harm for the good of our neighbor or for ourselves in spiritual matters.[230]

CONCLUSION

Thomas Aquinas's understanding of love as a movement toward the good combines with his understanding of the good as perfecting of limited and imperfect creatures to give a decisive metaphysical bent to his theology of love. Like other created beings, men and women go out of themselves by nature in order to seek the perfection that other beings can provide (and, ultimately, that only God can give). Ideally, reason must come to govern our appetites if we are to make prudent choices of which goods to pursue and in what manner: a man loves his wife in a certain manner that is different than the manner in which he loves other persons.

For men and women to proceed through life in a way that maintains their own human dignity as rational creatures created in the image of God, they must learn to love rightly. Their loves must be properly ordered according to the dignity of their human nature. This is made all the more difficult by the possibility of the concupiscible and irascible appetites pursuing their own ends apart from reason, especially since original sin has wounded the natural harmony between body and soul, reason and emotion.

---

229. See *ST* II-II, q. 25, a. 5.
230. See *ST* II-II, q. 26, a. 4, ad 2; a. 5, co. and ad 2.

Virtue orders love. Prudence orders love by establishing the *ratio* behind behavior, affection, and the manifestation of love so that a person loves appropriately in every situation he finds himself. Temperance combines with prudence to order the passions which ought to accompany love so that they do not overtake that which is most human: man's reason. When man loves rationally and appropriately, he loves passionately and most humanly.

However, on their own, prudence and temperance order love only within the confines of human achievement: within the family and within society. But man is made for more. He is made for eternal life with his creator, who fulfills this destiny only by gratuitous gift. The gift of grace brings not only knowledge by faith of our ultimate end and hope in attaining that, but it also brings charity which unites the will to God in a love that creates a friendship in every sense of the word: communion and mutual benevolence. This new friendship with God puts man on a new horizon, in which every aspect of his life is oriented explicitly to the ultimate end that is God. Charity creates its own order of love between man and God, man and his family, man and his neighbors, and, finally, man and his body. Thus with charity we receive the infused virtues. New supernatural principles are superadded upon our natural principles of the intellect, will, and sensitive appetite in order to orient all of our actions and thoughts to God, who is the supreme good that rightly orders all other activity and perfects all deficiency.[231]

---

231. Henri de Lubac's *Surnaturel* was followed in 1965 by two works clarifying the issues raised in 1946. There were translated into English in the late 1960s. See Henri de Lubac, *Surnaturel: Etudes Historiques* (Paris: Aubier, 1946); Henri de Lubac, *The Mystery of the Supernatural* (London: Chapman, 1967); Henri de Lubac, *Augustinianism and Modern Theology* (London: Chapman, 1969). It is no understatement to assert that the distinction between grace and nature is at work in many, if not most, twentieth-century disputes in Catholic moral theology. For a history of this debate, see Stephen Duffy, *The Graced Horizon: Nature and Grace in Modern Catholic Thought* (Collegeville, Minn.: Liturgical Press, 1992); Fergus Kerr, *After Aquinas: Versions of Thomism* (Oxford: Blackwell), 134-48; Mahoney, *Making of Moral Theology*, 72-115.

For a sympathetic reading of de Lubac's work see Paul McPartlan, *Sacrament of Salvation: An Introduction to Eucharistic Ecclesiology* (N.Y.: T&T Clark, 1995), 45-60. Thorough scholastic analyses are offered by Denis Bradley, *Aquinas on the Twofold Human Good: Reason and Human Happiness in Aquinas's Moral Science* (Washington, D.C.: The Catholic University of America Press, 1997) and Lawrence Feingold, *The Natural Desire to See God: According to St. Thomas and His Interpreters* (Washington, D.C.: The Catholic University of America Press, 2004).

The traces of Thomistic support for Pope John Paul II's notion of the spousal meaning of the body should now be coming into view. As we saw in earlier chapters of this study, the pope never abandoned wholesale the Thomistic education he received. Even though his *Theology of the Body* is explicitly a biblical anthropology, Thomas's metaphysics, anthropology, and philosophy were also informed by his faith in God. It should not be surprising that what John Paul isolated as a scriptural theme—that man's existence is only truly fulfilled with the sincere gift of himself to another—can be located in Aquinas's *Summa Theologiae* even though the Angelic Doctor is not here explicitly commenting on scripture (although he was a scriptural commentator).[232]

There is yet another critical piece in this puzzle. As we have seen, the catalyst for *Theology of the Body* was Pope Paul VI's encyclical *Humanae Vitae*. John Paul argued that the spousal meaning of the body is typified most commonly in this life in the marriage of man and woman. Therefore, to complete our analysis of Aquinas's contribution to the spousal meaning of the body, it is necessary in the next chapter to analyze Aquinas's understanding of marriage and the conjugal act.

232. Another study might explore the prevalence of love as movement and love as ecstasy in Aquinas's scriptural commentaries. This study has limited itself to the *Summa Theologiae* as its primary source.

8

Marriage and the Conjugal Act according to Thomas Aquinas

Thus far we have considered the impact that Thomas's view of the human person as a composite of body and soul has had on the other relevant aspects of his understanding of human life. We have also focused on his notion of love as a movement out of one person to another and the ways in which this movement is properly ordered by virtue. Both of these have connections to the spousal meaning of the body (the relation of body and soul, along with the outward movement of love), which will be made more clear in this chapter. We now turn to an exegesis of Aquinas's understanding of marriage. In his mature work, Thomas argued that marriage is the greatest of friendships. We will see that the Angelic Doctor articulates a notion of self-offering and self-gift of spouses in marriage, a self-giving that builds the foundation for the domestic society of the family.

Given the importance that he places on the hylomorphic unity of the human person, it is important that any treatment of Aquinas's view of marriage explore his consideration of sexual difference within that marital relationship. This is a vital point when serving as an ambassador of Aquinas to a modern audience: while Aquinas was a product of his cultural milieu, he was not an advocate of the absolute subjection of women to men. Aquinas thinks that marriage is a sort of mutual self-offering, he must therefore allow for the equal dignity of spouses. In short, marriage is true friendship that moves beyond sexual relations to establish a domestic society.

We will be able to explore how this complete self-offering in friendship of one spouse to another is rendered in Aquinas's view of the conjugal act. This will show clearly the way in which Aquinas's conception of marriage and the conjugal act support both the position offered by John Paul in *Theology of the Body* and the inseparability of the unitive and procreative as an expression of the spousal meaning of the body.

Admittedly, any scholar of the *Summa Theologiae* interested in Thomas's thought on marriage will be able to glean very little information from it about Aquinas's mature thought on the relationship between husband and wife. The Angelic Doctor treats the life and nature of Christ along with the sacraments in the *tertia pars* of the *Summa*. It is likely that he began writing this final portion of his *magnum opus* during the last year of his life, while he was regent in Naples.[1] Unfortunately for the disciples of Aquinas, on December 6, 1273, while celebrating Mass, Aquinas had a mystical experience which his companion Reginald could only describe as an "astonishing transformation" (*fuit mira mutatione commotus*), and after which Aquinas simply said he could write no more.[2] He died three months later on March 7, 1274.[3]

Later, his disciples completed the questions of the *tertia pars* by adding a *supplementum*. These questions were lifted verbatim from parallel passages of Aquinas's earliest work, his commentary on Peter Lombard's *Sentences*.[4] Aquinas's treatment of marriage in the *supplementum*, therefore, is not entirely indicative of his mature thought. For an accurate understanding of Aquinas's mature thought, we must turn to other works from the later years of the Angelic Doctor's life, principally the *Summa contra Gentiles*, which was completed by 1267 at the latest.[5]

Here we will work from the presumption that unless Thomas ex-

1. See Torrell, *Saint Thomas Aquinas*, 1:261–62.
2. Ibid., 1:289.   3. Ibid., 1:293.
4. See Jean-Pierre Torrell, OP, *Aquinas's Summa: Background, Structure, and Reception* (Washington, D.C.: The Catholic University of America Press, 2004), 62.
5. See Torrell, *Saint Thomas Aquinas*, 1:101–2.

plicitly modified his position on marriage in a later work, then the *supplementum* of the *Summa Theologiae* represents his settled convictions. Even though he never wrote an extended treatise on marriage, he devoted several chapters to marriage in the *Summa contra Gentiles*. There, he does, in fact, broaden his view of marriage. He also mentions matrimony briefly in other mature works, including the *secunda pars* and *tertia pars* of the *Summa Theologiae*. There is no other way for a scholar of Aquinas to proceed than to assume that had the Angelic Doctor changed his thinking on certain aspects of marriage, he would have at least hinted at it in the *Summa contra Gentiles* or in his other works, even before he had the opportunity to rework his thought fully in a completed *Summa Theologiae*.

Indeed, Aquinas's understanding of marriage and his arguments in favor of monogamy and the indissolubility of the marital bond did develop and mature in his later years. This development is evident in the differences between the treatise on marriage in the *supplementum* and his writing in the *Summa contra Gentiles*. Of particular importance is the fact that Aquinas came to understand marriage as the greatest of friendships between human beings. As we shall see, this conclusion then strengthens his arguments in favor of monogamy and marital indissolubility, and it further supports the notion of marriage as a privileged expression of the love of friendship, which brings the lover and the beloved into a union. It consequently provides the perfect conclusion for our study, because it lays the clear foundation for the work of Pope John Paul II.

MARRIAGE AS THE
GREATEST FRIENDSHIP

The Nature and Role of Women according to Thomas

Numerous studies have detailed the development of thinking—theological, canonical, and cultural—on marriage during the Middle Ages. During the eleventh and twelfth centuries especially, the church became the standard bearer for understanding marriage as a union between two equally consenting persons.[6] There are inherent difficulties

6. See, e.g., Antti Arjava, ed., *Consent and Coercion to Sex and Marriage in Ancient and Medieval Societies* (Washington, D.C.: Dumbarton Oaks Research Library and Collection,

in attempting to reconstruct the social status of women in any historical era. Historian Glenn Olsen notes that

assessing a "status" typically involves evaluating a large number of not necessarily commensurate and always changing factors simultaneously. The status of
an individual, let alone of some large category as "women," depends on a host
of factors. These range from age and class through economic circumstances to
the possession of various forms of personal freedom. Even if specified in the
medieval sources, these have inevitably to be ranked by some scale of values,
either our own or a composite coming from the period under study.[7]

Yet it would be purposefully neglectful to ignore that Thomas had a
certain view of women that is no longer held by most scholars.

Previously, we explored Aquinas's anthropology, highlighting the
importance of the relationship between the body and soul in the human person. We also briefly explored Aquinas's understanding of sexual difference, and the fact that it serves the purpose of propagating
the species. We have not, however, discussed in depth how Thomas
understood the relationship between men and women in the *Summa
Theologiae*. Even though he holds that men and women are not different in their souls (the seat of the *imago Dei*), since the human person
is a body-soul composite, the differences of the sexes must be considered in their relationship to one another. In fact, Aquinas's consideration of the relationship between man and woman centers on the purpose of this specific difference between the two. Kristin Popik notes:
"Sexual differentiation is ordained to generation.... Thus it is to the ac-

---

1993), esp. part 3; Judith Evans Grubbs, *Law and Family in Late Antiquity: The Emperor
Constantine's Marriage Legislation* (New York: Oxford University Press, 2000), 183–93;
James A. Brundage, *Law, Sex, and Christian Society in Medieval Europe* (Chicago: The University of Chicago Press, 1987), 188–89; James Brundage, "The Paradox of Sexual Equality
in the Early Middle Ages," in *Shifting Frontiers in Late Antiquity*, eds. Ralph W. Mathisen
and Hagith S. Sivan (Brookfield, Vt.: Variorum, 1996), 256–64; Charles J. Reid, Jr., *Power over the Body, Equality in the Family: Rights and Domestic Relations in Medieval Canon
Law* (Grand Rapids, Mich.: Eerdmans, 2004), 37–44; Edward Schillebeeckx, OP, *Marriage: Human Reality and Saving Mystery*, trans. N. D. Smith (New York: Sheed and Ward,
1967), 287–303.

7. Glenn W. Olsen, "Marriage in Barbarian Kingdom and Christian Court: Fifth
through Eleventh Centuries," in *Christian Marriage: A Historical Study*, ed. Olsen (New
York: Crossroad, 2001), 150. Historian Georges Duby repeatedly acknowledges these
sorts of difficulties in his work on the history of marriage in the Middle Ages. See
Georges Duby, *Love and Marriage in the Middle Ages*, trans. Jane Dunnett (Chicago: The
University of Chicago Press, 1994).

tivity of generation, to the roles which males and females play in generation that Aquinas looks in order to determine the nature of masculinity and femininity and how they are related to each other."[8]

Following Aristotelian biology, Aquinas believed that the male provides the active agent in procreation that works on the female's passive material to form the child.[9] Since in Aristotelian-Thomistic metaphysics it is a greater good to be in act than to be passive, masculinity is thought to be superior to femininity. Femininity is inferior precisely because of its passivity in relation to the masculine and also because the female comes into existence through a defect in a particular case (even though her birth serves God's divine purpose): the male gamete fails to reproduce its likeness with a male child.[10] Throughout the *Summa Theologiae*, Aquinas presumes that the male sex is nobler than the female sex. He says fathers should be loved more than mothers because they are the active principles of our generation.[11] When speaking of Christ's incarnation, he takes it for granted that the male sex is superior.[12] And this is true across all animal species. This is the reason, Thomas says, that only males were used in the holocaust sacrifices of the Old Testament.[13]

Since the differences are bodily and not spiritual, the passivity of the body translates to a general physical weakness according to Aquinas. But this bodily weakness affects the soul of the human composite. Thus, Aquinas (following Aristotle) asserts that women are generally weaker and less persevering than men.[14] Weakness of body yields a weakness of soul. This is why women have a greater need for the virtue of sobriety: "In women there is not sufficient strength of mind to resist concupiscence."[15] They are at greater risk for allowing their appetites

8. Kristin Popik, "The Philosophy of Woman of St. Thomas Aquinas, Part One: The Nature of Woman," *Faith and Reason* 4, no. 4 (Winter 1978): 26. See also Kristin Popik, "The Philosophy of Woman of St. Thomas Aquinas, Part Two: The Role of Woman," *Faith and Reason* 5, no. 1 (Spring 1979): 12–42. Popik's study is a thorough exegesis of all of Aquinas's writings on the nature of woman. The following pages of my own study are indebted to Popik's work. See also Allen, *Concept of Woman*, 1:385–412.

9. See ST I, q. 92, a. 1; q. 98, a. 2; q. 118, aa. 1–2; III, q. 31, a. 5. Cf. Aristotle, *On the Generation of Animals* I.20.728b21–35.

10. See ST I, q. 92, a. 1, ad 1; Cf. Aristotle, *On the Generation of Animals* II.3.737a28.

11. See ST II-II, q. 26, a. 10.   12. See ST III, q. 31, a. 4, obj. 1 and ad 1.

13. See ST I-II, q. 102, a. 3, ad 9.

14. See ST II-II, q. 138, a. 1, ad 1. Cf. Aristotle, *Nicomachean Ethics* VII.7.1150b15.

15. ST II-II, q. 149, a. 4.

to run rampant since their bodies (and thus their minds) are weaker.[16] Because of this, Aquinas repeats that man's reason is superior to that of woman, at least in this life.[17] Indeed, "in matters pertaining to the soul woman does not differ from man as to the thing (for sometimes a woman is found to be better than many men as regards the soul)."[18]

Even though the Angelic Doctor speaks of the inferiority of women to men in general terms, there are instances where he suggests that in individual cases a woman may be better. In fact, any individual woman may be stronger and more reasonable than any individual man. In the very same response to an objection when he speaks of the weakness of women, he mentions another possibility. He writes:

Accordingly, since woman, as regards the body, has a weak temperament, the result is that for the most part, whatever she holds to, she holds to it weakly; although in rare case the opposite occurs, according to Proverbs 31:10, Who shall find a valiant woman? And since small and weak things are accounted as though they are not, the Philosopher speaks of women as though they had not the firm judgment of reason, although the contrary happens in some women.[19]

In the *tertia pars*, he explicitly identifies Mary Magdalene as an example of a uniquely strong woman.[20] In other areas of his mature work, he identifies Mary and the Samaritan woman as examples of uniquely strong women.[21]

In various parts of the *Summa*, Aquinas makes comments about the disposition of the body in the activity of the soul. For example, he

---

16. See *ST* II-II, q. 156, co. and ad 1.

17. See *ST* II-II, q. 70, a. 3; q. 177, a. 2; q. 182, a. 4.

18. *ST*, Supp., q. 39, a. 1, co. Cf. Aquinas, *Scriptum super Libros Sententiarum Magistri Petri Lombardi* IV, d. 25, q. 2, a. 2, qua. 1, ad 4. Christopher Roberts draws an appropriate conclusion: "On Aquinas's premises, it follows that sexual difference is part of our natural existence without which we cannot be human, but sexual difference is also not sufficient to make us human and it does not in itself enable or bring us to our supernatural, beatific destinies. Our ultimate destiny is, according to Aquinas, something first and foremost enjoyed by the contemplative soul, which is where the *imago Dei* exists. Beatitude or eschatological fulfillment is a gift of grace bestowed on the soul by God" C. Roberts, *Creation and Covenant: The Significance of Sexual Difference in the Moral Theology of Marriage* (N.Y.: T&T Clark, 2007), 202–3.

19. *ST* II-II, q. 156, a. 1, ad 1.   20. See *ST* III, q. 55, a. 1, ad 1.

21. On this aspect of Aquinas's work, see Popik, "The Philosophy of Woman of St. Thomas Aquinas, Part One," 46–51.

writes that one person may understand something better than another because of the body's disposition or because of its better health.[22] He says that some men may be less persevering because of the "softness" (effeminacy) of their bodies.[23] Some women may grow in the virtue of sobriety and find themselves stronger than some men.[24] Grace is also a great equalizer, available to all who receive it.[25] In another work contemporaneous with the *Summa Theologiae*, Aquinas even suggests that women surrounded by theoretical and speculative discussion grow in understanding, strength, and virtue more than other women and even other men outside of these circles.[26] Popik concludes that these passages from Aquinas indicate that the "inferiority [of women] is not so great as to be impossible of being overcome with a bit of practice, by cultural factors, and by education."[27]

Aquinas's conclusions about the relationship between men and women will naturally have an impact on his understanding of the marital relationship. Throughout his career, Thomas viewed marriage as a freely chosen common society in which men and women played differing roles. This society, however, is characterized by a friendship between men and women.

Marriage in the *Supplementum* to the *Summa Theologiae*

The material of the *supplementum* to the *Summa Theologiae*, culled from Aquinas's commentary on Peter Lombard's *Sentences*, was written at the dawn of his academic life. In the *supplementum*, Thomas begins his treatment of marriage by arguing that it is natural. It is not natural because it is absolutely necessary (as the upward motion of fire is necessary). Matrimony is a matter of free will, and nothing happens with absolute necessary in matters of the will.[28] Rather, marriage

22. See *ST* I, q. 85, a. 7.
23. See *ST* II-II, q. 138, a. 1.
24. See *ST* II-II, q. 149, a. 4.
25. See, e.g., *ST* III, q. 72, a. 8, co. and ad 3.
26. See Aquinas, *In Evangelius S. Ioannis Commentarium* IV, lec. 10, v. 10, no. 598. An English translation of this passage is available: *Commentary on the Gospel of St. John, Part I*, trans. James A. Weisheipl, OP, and Fabian R. Larcher, OP (Albany, N.Y.: Magi Books, 1980), 246. I am grateful Popik for calling attention to this passage. Cf. Popik, "The Philosophy of Woman of St. Thomas Aquinas, Part One," 46–47.
27. Popik, "The Philosophy of Woman of St. Thomas Aquinas, Part One," 47.
28. See *ST*, Supp., q. 41, a. 1 (cf. *In IV Sententiarum*, d. 26, q. 1, a. 1). For excellent

is natural, Aquinas says, in the same way as virtue is natural. This is to say, nature inclines man to marriage, even though he must still freely choose it. For Aquinas, marriage is connatural for two reasons—the principal and secondary ends of matrimony.[29]

The "principal end" of marriage is "the good of offspring. For nature intends not only the begetting of offspring, but also [their] education and development until [they] reach the perfect state of man as man, and that is the state of virtue."[30] And this, he asserts, requires a stable tie between the man and a "definite" woman.[31] The secondary end is "the mutual services which married persons render one another in household matters."[32] Natural reason, therefore, directs man to this "society of man and woman which consists in matrimony."[33] Marriage is the bond between the man and the woman.[34]

---

summaries of Aquinas's understanding of marriage, see Angela McKay, "Aquinas on the End of Marriage," in *Human Fertility: Where Faith and Science Meet*, eds. Richard J. Fehring and Theresa Notare (Milwaukee, Wis.: Marquette University Press, 2008), 53–70; Roberts, *Creation and Covenant*, 99–109. I am especially grateful for McKay's study, which concerns the development of Aquinas's thought on marriage.

29. See *ST*, Supp., q. 41, a. 1 (cf. *In IV Sententiarum*, d. 26, q. 1, a. 1).

30. Ibid. That procreation includes the education and nutrition of children is not a position unique to Thomas. See Augustine, *De Genesi ad litteram* IX, chap. 7.

31. Ibid.

32. Ibid. In the section below, it will be shown that Thomas's thought on the relationship between the primary and secondary ends of marriage changes slightly in the *Summa contra Gentiles*. For an excellent study of Aquinas's thought on the two ends of marriage, see Guy de Broglie, SJ, "La conception thomiste des deux finalités du mariage," *Doctor Communis* 30 (1974): 3–41.

33. *ST*, Supp., q. 41, a. 1 (cf. *In IV Sententiarum*, d. 26, q. 1, a. 1). In the very next article, Aquinas argues that matrimony is not commanded since the contemplation of God is the highest activity a person can undertake. True and undivided contemplation cannot tolerate the distraction with worldly affairs that marriage requires. Since every society is best served by each person accomplishing his task for the common good, as long as there are married couples who serve the common good by procreation and education of offspring, some persons may renounce marriage for the common good by contemplating God (see *ST*, Supp., q. 41, a. 2). Cf. *In IV Sententiarum*, d. 26, q. 1, a. 2. See also Pinckaers, *Sources*, 433 and 442–47; Reid, *Power over the Body*, 78. This is one of the few instances in which Thomas disagrees with Augustine. Augustine held that the necessity of procreation differed according to the eras of salvation history. After the resurrection of Christ, he believed, celibacy was always preferable to marriage and there was no longer a strict need for procreation. See, e.g., Augustine, *De scanta virginitate*, §9. Cf. Paul Ramsey, "Human Sexuality in the History of Redemption," *Journal of Religious Ethics* 16 (1988): 56–88.

34. See *ST*, Supp., q. 48, a. 1.

That marriage is primarily directed to the begetting of children is important for Aquinas's understanding of marriage in other ways. For example, it is because the marital bond leads to children that Aquinas says that marriage existed before original sin. In fact, Aquinas held that because of its necessity for procreation, marriage was an office of nature before it was a sacrament.[35] The sacrament of matrimony adds a sacred quality to the natural institution of marriage inasmuch as the sacrament affords both the grace of indivisibility between the partners and the nature of a sign of Christ's love for the church.[36] To be clear, Aquinas insists that the sacramental quality of marriage is its most excellent feature (since grace surpasses nature), but the intention for offspring is the most essential defining characteristic of this union.[37]

It is important to note that for Thomas, procreation includes not only the biological generation of children, but also their education and upbringing until the child reaches "the perfect state of man as man, and that is the state of virtue."[38] Education requires time and a community of persons. This is why the all-important inclusion of education with procreation means also that even early in Aquinas's thought, the secondary end of mutual cooperation is directed to and included in the primary end. The education of the children is that "to which as its end is directed the entire communion of works that exists between man and wife as united in marriage, since parents lay up for their children (2 Cor. 12:14); so that the offspring like a principal end includes another, as it were, secondary end."[39]

In the *supplementum*, Aquinas shows how these two ends prohibit certain forms of unions, specifically polygamy and concubinage. Polygyny does not hinder the primary end if a man has several wives since, Aquinas believes, "one man is sufficient to get children of several wives, *and* to rear the children born of them."[40] Yet, having many wives hinders the secondary ends inasmuch as it creates discord in

35. See *ST*, Supp., q. 42, a. 2. Cf. *In IV Sententiarum*, d. 26, q. 2, a. 2.
36. See *ST*, Supp., q. 49, a. 2, co. and ads 4 and 7. Cf. *In IV Sententiarum*, d. 31, q. 1, a. 2.
37. See *ST*, Supp., q. 49, a. 3. Cf. *In IV Sententiarum*, d. 31, q. 1, a. 3.
38. *ST*, Supp., q. 41, a. 1. Cf. *In IV Sententiarum*, d. 26, q. 1, a. 1.
39. *ST*, Supp., q. 49, a. 2, ad 1. Cf. *In IV Sententiarum*, d. 31, q. 1, a. 2.
40. *ST*, Supp., q. 65, a. 1 (emphasis added). Cf. *In IV Sententiarum*, d. 33, q. 1, a. 1.

the conjugal society and, therefore, jeopardizes the mutual benef-
icence of the partners.[41] However, the Angelic Doctor insists that
polyandry is violation of the principal end of marriage. If a woman
has several husbands, the paternity of the children will be questionable and human beings are concerned mostly with the good of their
own offspring rather than somebody else's.[42] Having a concubine,
and indeed engaging in sexual intercourse outside of marriage, likewise jeopardizes the primary end of marriage since the education of
offspring requires the stable union of man and woman.[43]

Additionally, Thomas argues that the union between man and
woman must naturally be enduring because educating children in virtue requires the parents' care "for a long time."[44] In fact, Aquinas suggests that this education continues throughout a parent's lifetime.[45]
Yet, in the very next article, he will insist that inseparability in marriage is a secondary precept of natural law (or the secondary intention of nature) and not a primary one (primary intention). Aquinas's
delineation between primary and secondary precepts of natural law
(that is, intentions of nature) and how these precepts may be dis-
pensed is instructive:

A dispensation from a precept of the law of nature is sometimes found in the
lower causes, and in this way a dispensation may bear upon the secondary
precepts of the natural law, but not on the first precepts because these are always existent as it were, as stated above [cf. *ST*, Supp., q. 65, a. 1] in reference
to the plurality of wives [which goes against the secondary end of marriage
but not the primary end].... But sometimes this reason is found in the higher causes, and then a dispensation may be given by God even from the first
precepts of the natural law, for the sake of signifying or showing some Divine mystery, as instanced in the dispensation vouchsafed to Abraham in the
slaying of his innocent son. Such dispensations, however, are not granted to
all generally, but to certain individual persons, as also happens in regard to
miracles.[46]

41. *ST*, Supp., q. 65, a. 1.

42. See *ST*, Supp., q. 65, a. 1, ad 8. Cf. *In IV Sententiarum*, d. 33, q. 1, a. 1.

43. See *ST*, Supp., q. 65, a. 3; q. 65, a. 5. Cf. *In IV Sententiarum*, d. 33, q. 1, a. 3, qua. 1
and 3.

44. *ST*, Supp., q. 41, a. 1, ad 2. Cf. *In IV Sententiarum*, d. 26, q. 1, a. 1.

45. *ST*, Supp., q. 67, a. 1. Cf. *In IV Sententiarum*, d. 33, q. 2, a. 1.

46. *ST*, Supp., q. 67, a. 2. Cf. *In IV Sententiarum*, d. 33, q. 2, a. 2, qua. 1.

This, in turn, allows Aquinas to explain how it is possible that spouses might separate, and, indeed, have separated in the past.

He begins by noting that if indissolubility is a primary precept of nature then only a divine cause could dispense a couple from marriage.[47] But, he says, indissolubility is a secondary precept because it "is not directed to the good of the offspring, which is the principal end of marriage, except in so far as parents have to provide for their children for their whole life, by due preparation of those things that are necessary in life. Now this preparation does not pertain to the first intention of nature, in respect of which all things are common."[48] Therefore, he says, dispensations from indissolubility can be granted by causes other than God himself such as the Mosaic or ecclesial law.

Aquinas admits that in the fallen state, divorce is permitted (and here, he follows Jesus Christ's only explicit teaching on marriage). This, however, does not negate the fact that inseparability is naturally part of matrimony, even if only secondarily.[49] While indissolubility is a second intention of nature it "belongs to its [marriage's] first intention as a sacrament of the Church. Hence, from the moment it was made a sacrament of the Church, as long as it remains such it cannot be a matter of dispensation, except perhaps by the second kind of dispensation [a divine dispensation]."[50] It is the grace of Christ in the sacrament that restores indissolubility. While these passages may give the impression that Aquinas was less than convinced of the indissolubility of marriage, it is important to recall his purpose here: to explain the historical instances of dispensation from this natural norm.

The early Aquinas saw marriage as "a particular kind of companionship pertaining to that common action [of offspring and mutual services]"—indeed, as a society.[51] Every society needs a head, and Aquinas repeatedly says the husband is the head of the family in the management of the household.[52] But there is a division of labor in the

47. ST, Supp., q. 67, a. 2.
48. Ibid.
49. See ST, Supp., q. 67, a. 1, ads 1 and 2. Cf. In IV Sententiarum, d. 33, q. 2, a. 1.
50. ST, Supp., q. 67, a. 2, ad 3. Cf. In IV Sententiarum, d. 33, q. 2, a. 2, qua. 1.
51. ST, Supp., q. 43, a. 3, ad 3. Cf. In IV Sententiarum, d. 26, a. 1; d. 27, q. 2, a. 2; ST, Supp., q. 41, a. 1.
52. See ST, Supp., q. 44, a. 2, ad 1; q. 52, a. 3, ad 3; q. 67, a. 6, ad 1. Cf. In IV Sententiarum, d. 27, q. 1, a. 1, qua. 2; d. 36, a. 3; d. 33, q. 2, a. 3, qua. 1.

household management just as there is a division of roles in the marital act. The two are equal in this act, says Aquinas, even if he still holds that the man is more noble in his part than the woman, because, as he sees it, it is more noble to be active than passive. He writes: "Although the father ranks above the mother, the mother has more to do with the offspring than the father has.... Wherefore the mother has a closer relation to the nature of marriage than the father has."[53] Elsewhere, he writes that slavery is an impediment to marriage precisely because marriage involves an equal debt of both parties to the other, which is not the case between slave and master.[54] He writes that the husband is subject to his wife in the generative act, and that she has a claim on his body for this purpose.[55]

Even though the man may be the head of the family, the Angelic Doctor cautions that the "head in its own capacity is bound to the members."[56] In the parts of the Summa Theologiae that are more mature than the supplementum, it becomes clear that Aquinas sees man's governance over the family as political rather than despotic. The man must treat his wife with respect, especially in the marital act, neither demeaning her nor treating her as an object of lust to satisfy his wanton pleasure.[57] In fact, Aquinas says that one of the graces contained in the sacrament of matrimony is the grace for the man to relate to his wife in the marital act in a becoming manner.[58]

Aquinas did modify some elements of his understanding of marriage later in his life. Angela McKay astutely notes that his early defense of monogamy and indissolubility "is an attempt to derive these requirements strictly from the two activities that men and women share.... One who reads the text from the Commentary on the Sentences in isolation might well think that Aquinas believed that marriage could be justified only by procreation and the other necessities of life."[59] McKay notes that the Aristotelian notion of imperfect friendship, friendship of utility, revolves around shared activity and is very

53. ST, Supp., q. 44, a. 2, ad 1. Cf. In IV Sententiarum, d. 27, q. 1, a. 1, qua. 2.
54. See ST, Supp., q. 52, a. 1, ad 1. Cf. In IV Sententiarum, d. 36, a. 1.
55. See ST, Supp., q. 52, a. 3; q. 64, a. 1. Cf. In IV Sententiarum, d. 36, a. 3.
56. ST, Supp., q. 64, a. 5, ad 4. Cf. In IV Sententiarum, d. 33, q. 1, a. 3, qua. 3.
57. See ST, Supp., q. 49, a. 6, co. and ad 1. Cf. In IV Sententiarum, d. 31, q. 2, a. 3.
58. See ST, Supp., q. 42, a. 3. Cf. In IV Sententiarum, d. 26, q. 2, a. 3.
59. McKay, "Aquinas on the End of Marriage," 63–64.

fragile. Once the activity is no longer shared, the mutual benefits no longer received, the friendship dissipates.[60] She asks: "If divorce ... is unlawful only because of the time that the upbringing of children requires, then why should it not be licit for those spouses who are infertile or whose children have died to divorce?"[61] In the *Commentary on the Sentences*, Aquinas never discusses the character of the relationship between the man and the woman, the nature of their companionship. In the *Summa contra Gentiles*, however, he fills this lacuna in his thought.

Marriage in the *Summa contra Gentiles*

Aquinas's presentation of marriage in the *Summa contra Gentiles* has many of the same elements of his earlier teaching presented in the *supplementum* of the *Summa Theologiae* but it differs in two important respects. First, as McKay has already noted, Aquinas is more concerned with the character of the relationship, moving "beyond the 'ends' of marriage he offered in the *Sentences* ... to introduce more 'personalistic' considerations."[62] Specifically, in this *Summa*, Thomas presents marriage as the greatest of friendships and explores the ramifications for such a statement. Secondly, the Angelic Doctor more closely unites the generation of offspring with their upbringing.

In the *Summa contra Gentiles*, Aquinas presents marriage as friendship. In his treatment, he offers allusions and sometimes direct reference to Aristotle's *Nicomachean Ethics*. For example, in one place he writes: "The greater that friendship is, the more solid and long-lasting will it be. Now, there seems to be the greatest friendship [*maxima amicitia*] between husband and wife, for they are united not only in the act of fleshly union, which produces a certain gentle association [*suavem societatem*] even among beasts, but also in the partnership of the whole range of domestic activity."[63] Aquinas's understanding of friendship (largely dependent on Aristotle) is found in the *secunda pars* of the *Summa Theologiae*, which I discussed in chapter 7. Presently, it is sufficient to note that Aristotle believed that greater or

---

60. See ibid., 56–58. Cf. Aristotle, *Nicomachean Ethics* VIII.3, VIII.6, IX.12.
61. McKay, "Aquinas on the End of Marriage," 64.
62. Ibid.
63. See, e.g., *SCG* III.123, no. 6.

more complete friendships were more durable, and that friendships based solely on utility or pleasure dissolve once the friend is no longer useful or pleasant.[64]

Aristotle argued that all friendship, whether the imperfect friendships of utility and pleasure or the complete friendship of virtue between good people, involves a shared activity between the friends. He writes: "Whatever someone [regards as] his being, or the end for which he chooses to be alive, that is the activity he wishes to pursue in his friend's company."[65] The shared activity of rearing children forms the basis for the natural friendship between man and woman in Aristotle's thinking:

The friendship of man and woman also seems to be natural. For human beings form couples more naturally than they form cities, to the extent that the household is prior to the city, and more necessary, and childbearing is shared more widely among the animals. For the other animals, the community goes only as far as childbearing. Human beings, however, share a household not only for childbearing, but also for the benefits in their life. For the difference between them implies that their functions are divided, with different ones for the man and the woman; hence each supplies the other's needs by contributing a special function to the common good. For this reason their friendship seems to include both utility and pleasure.[66]

So it seems that Aristotle held that all marriages consist at least in the friendship of utility or pleasure, which he has said, is easily dissolved. He is careful to include the possibility that husband and wife may have a complete or perfect friendship (the virtuous friendship) "if they are decent."[67] Complete friendship requires the friends to be good and virtuous.[68]

It seems that in the *Summa contra Gentiles*, Aquinas not only borrows Aristotle's sense of friendship to describe the relationship of husband and wife, but he also insists that this friendship goes beyond mere utility and pleasure to virtuous friendship. Thus, he notes that friendship is characterized by equality and specifically cites Aristo-

---

64. See, e.g., *Nicomachean Ethics* VIII.3 for Aristotle's treatment on the different types of friendships.

65. Aristotle, *Nicomachean Ethics* IX.12.

66. Aristotle, *Nicomachean Ethics* VIII.12.

67. Ibid.

68. See *Nicomachean Ethics* VIII.3.

tle.[69] One of Aquinas's mature arguments against polygamy is precisely Aristotle's point that true and complete friendship is not possible with many people simultaneously.[70] It is precisely because the friendship is complete and virtuous that marriage should be indissoluble.[71] Moreover, the indissolubility is important so that their love for one another will be more faithful.[72] In the *Summa contra Gentiles*, as McKay notes, "what Aquinas' remarks seem to demonstrate is an increasing awareness that marriage consists not merely in sharing activities, but also about sharing those activities in a highly specific context, namely in the context of complete friendship."[73]

In addition, Aquinas works in the *Summa contra Gentiles* to connect more firmly the generation of offspring with their upbringing, which further strengthens his arguments for the indissolubility of marriage. Aquinas explicitly ties upbringing to the teleology of the semen itself by insisting that this teleology would be "frustrated" if the emission of semen allows for generation without upbringing. The generation of offspring includes production of, nutrition for, and upbringing of offspring. He writes that seminal emission without being ordered to nutrition and upbringing would be contrary to the good of man.[74]

In Thomas's view, generation is a natural act directed toward the common good: the good of the species, the good of the state, and the good of the church.[75] Hence, Aquinas says that "disorders connected with the act of generation are not only opposed to natural instinct, but are also transgressions of divine and human laws. Hence, a greater sin results from a disorder in this area than in regard to the use of food or other things of that kind."[76] This is also why he says that fornication is a very serious sin: it is contrary to the natural good. He even asserts that "after the sin of homicide whereby a human nature

69. See *SCG* III.124, no. 4. Cf. *Nicomachean Ethics* VIII.5.1158a1: "Friendship is said to be equality. And this is true above all in the friendship of good people."

70. Cf. *SCG* III.124, no. 5. Cf. *Nicomachean Ethics* VIII.6.

71. See *SCG* III.123, no. 6.

72. See *SCG* III.123, no. 8. Aquinas uses friendship to buttress his arguments against marriage within consanguine family lines by insisting that friendship should be expanded throughout the world and this is accomplished by persons marrying (and thus developing friendships with) persons from outside their family of origin (see *SCG* III.125, no. 6).

73. McKay, "Aquinas on the End of Marriage," 69.

74. See *SCG* III.122, no. 6.   75. See *SCG* III.123, no. 7; IV.78, no. 2.

76. *SCG* III.123, no. 7.

already in existence is destroyed, this type of sin appears to take next place, for by it the generation of human nature is precluded."[77]

Given the importance of upbringing, Aquinas repeats many of the same arguments he made in the *supplementum* about the necessity for an indissoluble relationship in which the father remains with the mother to assist in this task. He writes that women cannot raise children alone since they cannot provide for themselves and are not strong enough to issue the corrections necessary in the children's education in the virtue of prudence.[78] Elements from both the commentary on Lombard's *Sentences* and the *Summa contra Gentiles* appear in the completed parts of the *Summa Theologiae*. Although Aquinas only mentions marriage briefly in these portions of the *Summa Theologiae*, what he does write is instructive for his settled view of marriage.

Marriage in the *Summa Theologiae*

In the most detailed article on marriage in the *secunda pars*, Aquinas repeats many of his earlier positions about marriage. The article states that the primary purpose of marriage is the generation and education of children, and this lifelong task requires the man and the woman to live in a mutual bond. Marriage is between a definite man and a definite woman and is directed to the common good of the human race.[79] In the *tertia pars*, he includes an additional notion to the form of marriage—the union of souls. He writes: "Now the form of matrimony consists in a certain inseparable union of souls, by which husband and wife are pledged by a bond of mutual affection that cannot be sundered. And the end of matrimony is the begetting and upbringing of children: the first of which is attained by conjugal intercourse; the second by the other duties of husband and wife, by which they help one another in rearing their children."[80]

Though Aquinas acknowledges that some women are more intel-

---

77. *SCG* III.122, no. 9.

78. *SCG* III.122, nos. 7–8. No doubt in the Middle Ages this was at least partially true, since women had very little access to the public square. Moreover, the certitude of a man's offspring would be impossible if the separation of men and women were routinely acceptable (cf. *SCG* III.123, no. 5).

79. See *ST* II-II, q. 154, a. 2.

80. *ST* III, q. 29, a. 2.

ligent, stronger, and more virtuous than some men, when he speaks of the structural role of society and the family, he assumes that masculinity is superior to femininity. Following Aristotle's notion that man is a social being, Aquinas writes that all human beings are inclined to live in common. The difficulty with common life is that individuals are also inclined to their own good. Thus, the Angelic Doctor writes, "a social life cannot exist among a number of people unless under the presidency of one to look after the common good; for many, as such, seek many things, whereas one attends only to one. Wherefore the Philosopher says, in the beginning of the *Politics*, that wherever many things are directed to one, we shall always find one at the head directing them."[81] He goes on to say that any person who is given knowledge and virtue receives these gifts "to the benefit of others."[82]

In the *secunda pars*, Aquinas reasserts that the family is itself a society in which there are varying roles.[83] Since he believes that men are physically stronger and more virtuous than women, it is natural for the man to be the one who governs the family and to direct it to the common good.[84] This relative inequality of male and female bodies would have existed in the state of innocence.[85] And this natural subjection of wife to husband would have existed then too.[86] This subjection became more rigorous after sin inasmuch as now, Aquinas says, she "has to obey her husband's will even against her own."[87]

It is true that in various places throughout the *Summa Theologiae*, Thomas compares woman to man as a lower reason to a higher reason, with the lower requiring the direction of the higher.[88] Aquinas is, however, also clear that the rule of husband over wife is not a despotic governance but an economic or civil one. Despotic rule is characterized by a servile subjection in which the ruler governs others for his own benefit. Economic or civil rule (political rule) is a government for the good of all.[89] The woman is not the slave of the man.[90]

Yet, when Aquinas speaks of the differences between the role

81. *ST* I, q. 96, a. 4.
82. Ibid.
83. See *ST* I-II, q. 105, a. 4.
84. See *ST* I, q. 92, a. 1, ad 2.
85. See *ST* I, q. 96, a. 3.
86. See *ST* I, q. 96, a. 4.
87. *ST* II-II, q. 164, a. 2, ad 1.
88. See *ST* I, q. 79, a. 9; I-II, q. 74, a. 7; II-II, q. 182, a. 4.
89. See *ST* I, q. 92, a. 1, ad 2; cf. q. 96, a. 4.
90. See *ST* I, q. 92, a. 3.

of slaves and the role of women in the home, it can seem as if he is equating the two. After noting that the members of the household are concerned with "everyday actions directed to the necessities of life," he states:

Now the preservation of man's life may be considered from two points of view. First, from the point of view of the individual, i.e., in so far as man preserves his individuality: and for the purpose of the preservation of life, considered from this standpoint, man has at his service external goods, by means of which he provides himself with food and clothing and other such necessities of life: in the handling of which he has need of servants. Secondly, man's life is preserved from the point of view of the species, by means of generation, for which purpose man needs a wife, that she may bear him children.[91]

The distinction between the two follows precisely the difference between despotic and political rule. Despotic rule seeks only the good of the ruler, while political rule seeks the good of all. Popik observes that Aquinas "is distinguishing, not equating, the positions of slave and woman. The slave fulfills needs which pertain to the individual good of the man, and the woman is needed for generation, which is not ordered to his good but to the good of the species.... The woman does not merely supply the man with some personal needs of his as a slave does; he needs her in order to generate offspring, which is for her good as much as for his."[92] Moreover, unlike a slave, which is commonly considered property, a wife is not a man's possession in Aquinas's thought. Committing adultery with a married woman is not equivalent to theft.[93]

In the *Summa Theologiae*, Thomas understands that there is a certain equality in marriage between the husband and wife. For example, in the treatise on justice, when Aquinas distinguishes between relationships of persons in justice, he sets marriage apart as a unique arrangement. The relationship between two men subject to the state is characterized by justice, simply speaking. But when a person "belongs" to another there is a different form of justice. Thus, a child be-

91. *ST* I-II, q. 105, a. 4.
92. Popik, "The Philosophy of Woman of St. Thomas Aquinas, Part Two," 20.
93. See *ST* II-II, q. 66, a. 3; q. 118, a. 2.

longs to his father, and the father, therefore, has paternal rights over his son. A master has dominative rights over his slaves. In these two relationships, there is no strict justice between the two since one party is not considered civilly equal to the other: the son is not equal to his father and the slave is not equal to his master. However, there is a sort of equal domestic justice between husband and wife that differs from the subservient relationship of children and slaves to the head of the household.[94] It is not a strict civic justice since women, in Aquinas's worldview, have no role in the public square.[95]

This is why when he considers the sin of adultery, even though he considers it as a sin against lust in the treatise on temperance, Thomas's explanation of adultery gives the distinct impression that it is also a sin against justice. He writes that it is a "twofold offense against chastity and the good of human procreation."[96] By uniting with a woman not joined to him, a husband harms the upbringing of his own children. By uniting with another's woman, he harms the upbringing of another's children. And, Aquinas says, the same is true for adulterous women just as much as adulterous men. Adultery breaks the good faith between the spouses.[97]

Within the marriage, man and woman have different but equally necessary roles. The woman is concerned with the begetting of children and the "community of works pertaining to family life."[98] While she is "subject to her husband in matters relating to the family life, so it belongs to the husband to provide the necessaries of that life."[99] The man is to have a certain "solicitude" for his wife and his children.[100] In a work contemporaneous with the *Summa Theologiae*, his *Commentary on Aristotle's Politics*, the Angelic Doctor notes that the woman is directly responsible for the management of the interior life of the family. For example, she is "concerned with the preservation of the household wealth which the man acquires."[101] In his *Commentary*

94. *ST* II-II, q. 57, a. 4.

95. See Popik, "The Philosophy of Woman of St. Thomas Aquinas, Part Two," 20–21, 32.

96. *ST* II-II, q. 154, a. 8.

97. See *ST* II-II, q. 154, a. 8, ad 2.

98. *ST* II-II, q. 164, a. 2.

99. Ibid.

100. See *ST* II-II, q. 186, a. 4.

101. Popik, "The Philosophy of Woman of St. Thomas Aquinas, Part Two," 25, citing Aquinas, *Commentary on Aristotle's Politics* III.2, no. 376.

on the Ethics, he says that the wife is concerned with domestic operations.[102] Popik's conclusion is forceful: "The fact that the woman is subject to her husband in household affairs does not mean that she is without authority in the home.... Aquinas likens the husband's and wife's rule of the family to aristocratic rule, in which each of them has responsibility over matters pertaining to them both. Although she is ultimately subject to her husband's direction, the wife is the manager of all the internal affairs of the household."[103]

Aquinas allows a great deal of freedom for wives within the family. Even though he continues the convention of publicly prohibiting women from teaching (which he inherits from Paul's letters, among other places), he allows (and even insists) that they teach within their home.[104] A wife's subjection to her husband is only in matters relating to the household. She is a free person with regard to her own affairs. For example, she can freely assent to the faith without her husband's permission since this does not concern the management of the home.[105] Yet she is not allowed to take a religious vow or to take any oaths, since these can interfere with her management of the household.[106] The same is true of her administration of money within the home. Aquinas says that she is free to give alms from the household money if she has the "express or presumed consent of her husband."[107] With the exception of her dowry (which is given for the management of the family), she is free to give from her own money and property without her husband's consent, although Thomas says she "should be moderate, lest through giving too much she impoverish her husband."[108] This suggests that Aquinas understands that the property and money which the spouses earn are shared by the household.

---

102. See Popik, "The Philosophy of Woman of St. Thomas Aquinas, Part Two," 25, citing Aquinas, *Commentary on Aristotle's Nicomachean Ethics* VIII.12, no. 1721.

103. Popik, "The Philosophy of Woman of St. Thomas Aquinas, Part Two," 25.

104. See *ST* III, q. 55, a. 1, ad 3; q. 67, a. 4, ad 1.

105. See *ST* II-II, q. 10, a. 12, ad 1.

106. See *ST* II-II, q. 88, a. 8, co. and ad 3; q. 89, a. 9, ad 3. On the biblical warrants for Aquinas's teaching, see Lisa Sowle Cahill, *Between the Sexes: Foundations for a Christian Ethics of Sexuality* (Phila.: Fortress Press, 1985), 114–18.

107. *ST* II-II, q. 32, a. 8, ad 2.

108. Ibid.

From our present vantage point, that Aquinas accepted (yet tempered) Aristotle's conception of woman as a "defective male," severely limited the public role of women and made women subject to men in matters of the household can appear quite negative. Yet, in spite of his cultural milieu, he held for equality between the spouses. While the equality of roles may be disputed by contemporary standards, Thomas did hold that both spouses must be equal in their self-offering in marriage. No human person could be forced either to marry or to renounce marriage.[109] Aquinas held that wives were able not only to manage the affairs of the household and their husband's money (with only his presumed consent), they could keep their own wealth and money, managing it as they see fit (provided it does not interfere with the life of the home).[110]

Very importantly, as Popik observes, Aquinas never says explicitly that women as a group of persons are subject to men.[111] In fact, he takes for granted that widows are under the authority of no man.[112] Elsewhere, Aquinas makes no distinction between boys and girls and their freedom (after they reach the age of reason) in professing religious vows, without their father's consent on the matter.[113] Unlike slaves, who are not free in their person, men and women can dispose of themselves any way they like without their father's approval.[114] In Aquinas's view, a girl was under the protection of her father lest she fall into a wanton and promiscuous lifestyle, which would bring shame on her family.[115] This is the distinguishing characteristic of seduction: it is the robbing of a woman's virginity, which, in Aquinas's

---

109. See *ST* II-II, q. 104, a. 5.

110. See *ST* II-II, q. 32, a. 8.

111. See Popik, "The Philosophy of Woman of St. Thomas Aquinas, Part Two," 35–36.

112. See, e.g., *ST* II-II, q. 65, a. 4, obj. 2 and ad 2.

113. See *ST* II-II, q. 88, a. 9; q. 189, a. 9.

114. *ST* II-II, q. 88, a. 8. However, it is true that Aquinas uses a girl's subjection to her father as analogous example to explain a person's relationship to his superior (*ST* II-II, q. 88, a. 8, ad 3). In this example, he writes, "no vow of a religious stands without the consent of his superior, as neither does the vow of a girl while in her father's house without his consent." Clearly, Aquinas means here to insist that a girl under her father's rule cannot vow anything without her father's consent. Yet in the very next article, once she reaches the age of reason, Aquinas is clear: the girl, just as much as her brother, can give herself over to religion.

115. See *ST* II-II, q. 154, a. 6, co.

milieu, rendered her incapable of marriage.[116] Yet, it is precisely this defining of women only in relation to the men of their lives that puts many contemporary moral theologians ill at ease.[117]

In her magisterial study on women in philosophy and theology, *The Concept of Woman*, Prudence Allen identifies several theories of sexual identity at work in the history of Western philosophy and theology. She identifies Aristotle as the founder of a view she calls sexual polarity, the idea that men and women are not only significantly different from one another but that women are inferior to men. His theory was based entirely on his biology and embryology—the idea of woman's material inferiority. She writes: "Aristotle chose to isolate what he believed was woman's contribution to generation and then, upon that idea, to develop an account of the differences between the sexes in a wide range of other aspects of human life. This pattern of isolating a single factor in women's biological nature is common in sex-polarity arguments."[118]

Regarding Aquinas's own conception of sexual identity, Allen is much more favorable, without denying his limitations. She notes that "while Thomas was misled by Aristotle in the adoption of his rationale for philosophical differences between women and men, he was correctly led by Aristotle towards the goal of presenting a philosophy of the person as an integrated, unified existent."[119] Moreover, she writes, "Thomas partially opened the door to a philosophy of sex complementarity on the highest of level of existence [namely, in heaven and in resurrected glory]."[120] She expresses her hope that this opening could one day lead to a Thomistic theology of sexual complementarity without the Aristotelian conclusions based on a faulty biology.[121]

---

116. Ibid.

117. See, e.g., Kari Elizabeth Borresen, *Subordination and Equivalence: The Nature and Role of Woman in Augustine and Thomas Aquinas* (Kampen: Kok Pharos, 1981), 253. Yet, one must be careful to judge Aquinas from the standards of the twenty-first century, especially given thirteenth-century social conditions and lack of a public role for women.

118. Allen, *The Concept of Woman*, 126.

119. Ibid., 411. Of course, Aristotle himself did not have a concept of personhood. Human beings are individuated by their matter and form, potency and act. See Joseph Torchia, "Aristotle: The Human Composite," in Torchia, *Exploring Personhood*, 71–95.

120. Allen, *The Concept of Woman*, 411.

121. See ibid., 412.

Popik similarly notes that Aquinas's theory of "the inferiority of woman is solidly based on the Aristotelian biological theory of femininity as passivity, as defective in comparison with masculine activity and perfection. Without this foundation, the only ground of woman's inferiority for St. Thomas is her physical weakness and a few scriptural passages, which are clearly used only as supportive arguments in his writings."[122] She admires the fact that in spite of Aquinas's cultural milieu, his Aristotelian formation, and the scriptural precedent, that Thomas was able to argue as he does for any sort of equality between the two sexes.[123] Jean Porter also recognizes Aquinas's qualified assertion of the equality of the sexes: both created in the image of God.[124] Lisa Sowle Cahill also praises Aquinas for identifying marriage as a certain friendship between the spouses, which incorporates the sexual act.[125]

In the preceding, I have argued that Thomas's view of marriage is nuanced enough to include not only sexual differentiation (which he must concede given his strict hylomorphism), but also elements of equality, self-offering, and the union of souls. In particular, the idea that the union of souls is the form of marriage has special importance when discussing the spousal meaning of the body, which (as I noted in chapter 5) is communicated in the sacrament of marriage through marital consent and the conjugal act. Marriage has both a formal and a material element even in Aquinas's thought. The material element is the conjugal act rightly ordered.

---

122. Popik, "The Philosophy of Woman, Part Two," 37.

123. See ibid., 36–39.

124. Jean Porter, *Natural and Divine Law: Reclaiming the Tradition for Christian Ethics* (Grand Rapids, Mich.: Eerdmans, 1999), 211.

125. See Cahill, *Between the Sexes*, 118–19: "If the thought of Thomas about men and women, marriage, and sex does not always escape the strictures of a medieval outlook, I think we can hardly regard his failure as greater or more culpable than the idealization of individual freedom and glorification of sex, equally unbiblical, that often accompany the modern view of what is natural and fulfilling for humans.... His most valuable and original contribution to a Christian theology and ethics of sexuality is his insight that marital commitment is a profound form of friendship, intensified by physical expression."

THE CONJUGAL ACT
ACCORDING TO THOMAS AQUINAS

The Conjugal Act in the *Summa Theologiae*

It seems the Angelic Doctor understood the importance of the conjugal act not just for procreation but also for the marital relationship itself. The conjugal act signifies not only the goods of marriage but also the very union of the spouses' souls. In chapter 7, I analyzed Aquinas's view of temperance and chastity. In this chapter, I am more concerned with his understanding of sex within marriage. First, I want to review some of the basic observations about chastity from chapter 7. There, I noted that in Thomas's moral theory, the virtue of temperance moderates the concupiscible pleasures of touch, those greatest of sensual pleasures for the human person.[126] Temperance and the other virtues associated with it (sobriety, abstinence, and chastity) moderate these pleasures according to the mean between excess and deficiency.[127] Chastity is important in Aquinas's view since the pleasures associated with sexual intercourse are so great "that the free act of reason in considering spiritual things is incompatible with the aforesaid pleasure."[128]

The virtue of chastity disposes a person to make use of the sexual act in accordance with reason and in a due manner.[129] Reason directs all things to their end. And the end of the generative organs are just that: generation.[130] It precisely because of this that Aquinas insists that engaging in the sexual act is not sinful but can be truly good, even meritorious, if it is engaged in according to reason (that is, directed to the procreation and upbringing of offspring).[131] In Aquinas's view, the pleasures associated with sexual intercourse are not evil. They overcome reason not because they were created to do so but because of the punishment due to original sin: "That venereal concupiscence and pleasure are not subject to the command and moderation of reason, is due to the punishment of the first sin, inas-

126. See *ST* II-II, q. 151, a. 4.   127. See *ST* I-II, q. 59, a. 1.
128. *ST* II-II, q. 153, a. 2, ad 2.
129. See *ST* II-II, q. 151, a. 1, ad 1; q. 153, a. 2.
130. See *ST* II-II, q. 141, a. 6; q. 154, a. 11, ad 3.
131. See *ST* II-II, q. 154, a. 1, ad 2; a. 2.

much as the reason, for rebelling against God, deserved that its body should rebel against it."[132] The lustful person is one who habitually prefers these pleasures over and against the intention to procreate.[133]

The carnal union is very important in Aquinas's conception of marriage, since it is this union that separates a person's love of his spouse from the love he has for his parents.[134] Still, precisely because sexual intercourse in our fallen condition entails such vehement pleasure that overpowers reason, it is possible that even an act of intercourse within marriage may be at least venially sinful.[135] Despite this fact, the marital act can be meritorious as well if engaged in for the right reasons.[136]

Even though reason distinguishes the human person from other animals, Aquinas is not against its temporary impairment for a greater good, such as sleep or procreation.[137] As Thomas sees it, there must be some goods associated with marriage, which, he says, "excuse" or "rightly order" the marital act and its accompanying pleasure as well as the necessity of sharing one's possessions with another for a lifetime.[138] Following Augustine's lead, although he does not acknowledge him here, the Angelic Doctor identifies three goods: offspring, fidelity, and the sacrament.[139] These goods are not extrinsic factors that make the marital act good and so rightly order marriage from the outside. They are, in fact, goods intrinsic and essential to the nature

132. *ST* II-II, q. 153, a. 1, ad 2.

133. See *ST* II-II, q. 153, aa. 3–4; q. 154, a. 11, ad 3.

134. See *ST* II-II, q. 26, a. 11.

135. See *ST* II-II, q. 41, a. 4. Here Thomas supports the view established by Augustine that marital sex is at least venially sinful if pursued merely for the sake of satisfying concupiscence. Similarly, if a spouse requests the satisfaction of the marriage debt beyond reasonable measure, it is venially sinful. See Augustine, *De bono coniugali*, chaps. 6–9.

136. *ST* II-II, q. 41, a. 4.

137. See, e.g., *ST* II-II, q. 153, a. 1, ad 2. As I noted in the previous chapter, this is exactly why Aquinas condemns drunkenness, which he defines as the immoderate use of alcohol and its intoxicating effects beyond what is necessary for health (*ST* II-II, q. 149, a. 1; a. 3; q. 150, a. 1).

138. See *ST*, Supp., q. 49, a. 1. Cf. *In IV Sententiarum*, d. 31, q. 1, a. 1.

139. See *ST*, Supp., q. 49, a. 2. Cf. *In IV Sententiarum*, d. 31, q. 1, a. 2. For a summary on Augustine's view of marriage, see Mackin, *The Marital Sacrament*, 190–231; Glenn W. Olsen, "Progeny, Faithfulness, Sacred Bond: Marriage in the Age of Augustine," in *Christian Marriage*, ed. Olsen, 101–45; Roberts, *Creation and Covenant*, 39–78.

of marriage.[140] These three goods are the reasons why the marital act is not always sinful in Aquinas's view.[141] This is why the marital act itself does not corrupt virtue: the temporary overwhelming of reason does not instill a vicious habit if the act is engaged in rightly and in rational order (which is to say within marriage and primarily for the purposes of procreation).[142]

Although marriage provides the faculty or authority for sexual intercourse, the marital act is not itself essential for the marital union.[143] For Thomas, the consent between two persons is the most important element in establishing the marriage, but this consent includes a consent to carnal union. He writes:

> The consent that makes a marriage is a consent to marriage, because the proper effect of the will is the thing willed. Wherefore, according as carnal intercourse stands in relation to marriage, so far is the consent that causes marriage a consent to carnal intercourse.... Marriage is not essentially the carnal union itself, but a certain joining together of husband and wife ordained to carnal intercourse, and a further consequent union between husband and wife, in so far as they each receive power over the other in reference to carnal intercourse, which joining together is called the nuptial bond.[144]

---

140. See *ST*, Supp., q. 49, a. 1, ad 2. Cf. *In IV Sententiarum*, d. 31, q. 1, a. 1.

141. See *ST*, Supp., q. 41, a. 3; q. 49, a. 4. Cf. *In IV Sententiarum*, d. 27, q. 1, a. 3; d. 31, q. 2, a. 1.

142. See *ST*, Supp., q. 41, a. 3, ad 6; q. 49, a. 4, ads 1 and 3. Cf. *In IV Sententiarum*, d. 27, q. 1, a. 3.; d. 31, q. 2, a. 1.

143. See *ST*, Supp., q. 42, a. 4: "Integrity is twofold. One regards the primal perfection consisting in the very essence of a thing; the other regards the secondary perfection consisting in operation. Since then carnal intercourse is an operation or use of marriage which gives the faculty for that intercourse, it follows that carnal intercourse belongs to the latter, and not to the former integrity of marriage." Cf. *In IV Sententiarum*, d. 26, q. 2, a. 4. In the early Middle Ages, theologians and canonists debated the relationship between consent and consummation. By the time of Aquinas's writing the opinion was relatively settled that consent was essential but that consummation ratified the consent. See Brundage, *Law, Sex, and Christian Society*, 229–42; Schillebeeckx, *Marriage*, 287–302. From a theological perspective, both sides wanted to protect the virginity of Mary, on the one hand, and the reality of the marriage between her and Joseph on the other. This is why Aquinas offers that wonderful phrase in the *tertia pars* mentioned above when discussing that unique marriage: "The form of matrimony consists in a certain inseparable union of souls, by which husband and wife are pledged by a bond of mutual affection that cannot be sundered" (*ST* III, q. 29, a. 2).

144. *ST*, Supp., q. 48, a. 1. Cf. *In IV Sententiarum*, d. 28, a. 4.

The consent orders the couple to intercourse and orders intercourse rightly within the union that bears the goodness of offspring, fidelity, and the sacrament. And in his own language, Aquinas says that carnal intercourse actually signifies each of these three goods of marriage. Clearly, intercourse signifies offspring since this is its biological end, yet it also signifies the fidelity of consent. In fact, he writes that "nothing is more expressly significant of consent than carnal intercourse."[145] Finally, carnal intercourse signifies the indissolubility of the union brought about by the sacramental grace, which is itself a sign of Christ's union with his church.[146]

The Marriage Debt, Union, and Procreation

In a passage cited above, Aquinas wrote that the consent of marriage includes a power over each other's body. Each spouse gives to the other authority over his or her body in the marital act, directing it to procreation (the natural end of the procreative organs). Like other medieval theologians, Aquinas understands this mutual right and responsibility as the "marriage debt" each owes to the other.[147] The marriage debt is another aspect of fidelity that is proper to the relationship: "Just as the marriage promise means that neither party is to have intercourse with a third party, so does it require that they should mutually pay the marriage debt. The latter is indeed the chief of the two since it follows from the power which each receives over the other. Consequently both these things pertain to faith [that is, fidelity]."[148]

The husband and the wife are equal in responsibility to "pay the debt," which is to offer their bodies to the other.[149] However, because Aquinas recognizes differences between the husband and wife, and because he believes the man is the stronger principle of the relation-

145. *ST*, Supp., q. 46, a. 2. Cf. *In IV Sententiarum*, d. 28, a. 2.

146. See *ST*, Supp., q. 42, a. 4, ad 2; cf. a. 1, ads 4–5 and *In IV Sententiarum*, d. 26, q. 2, aa. 1 and 4.

147. I am grateful to Paul Gondreau for suggesting the importance of the marital debt in a personalist reading of Thomas's moral theory. See Gondreau, "The 'Inseparable Connection,'" 758–60.

148. *ST*, Supp., q. 49, a. 2, ad 3. Cf. *In IV Sententiarum*, d. 26, q. 2, a. 2.

149. See *ST*, Supp., q. 64, aa. 1 and 5. Cf. *In IV Sententiarum*, d. 32, a. 1; a. 5, qua. 1. For a more detailed review of the concept of the marriage debt in the medieval period, see Noonan, *Contraception*, 285, 357–58; and Brundage, *Law, Sex and Society*, 359–60.

ship, he indicates that there are differences in how the husband and
wife communicate their desire for the other. Thus, for example, the
man must not be modest in asking for his wife to "pay the debt." He
must explicitly ask. The wife need not respond when he only hints of
his wishes.[150] Yet because Aquinas believes women to be more modest, he expects the husband to be much more intuitive and to respond
to his wife even if she makes only subtle indications of her desires.[151]

The equality of authority of the spouses over each other's bodies in
marriage is so pronounced in Aquinas's view that he prohibits a slave
from marrying a master since the slave is not free in offering her body
to her husband.[152] Elsewhere, Thomas writes that the inability to engage in the act of coitus (which is quite different than sterility or infertility) can render a marriage invalid precisely because one of the spouses cannot offer his or her body to the other.[153] To the objection that the
marital act is not essential to marriage, Aquinas responds: "Although
the act of carnal copulation is not essential to marriage, ability to fulfill
the act is essential, because marriage gives each of the married parties
power over the other's body in relation to marital intercourse."[154] It is
important to note, though, that a spouse may reject the other's requests
for the marital act for legitimate reasons of health.[155] What is clear,
however, is that even though the conjugal act is teleologically ordered
per se to the procreation and the education of children, Thomas did not
believe that if a particular conjugal act happened not to produce a child
that the act was therefore sinful. In fact, his writing on the marital debt
suggests a secondary, if not equal, use of the conjugal act: the expression of honesty and fidelity in the marriage.

In the *supplementum*, Thomas writes: "The end which nature in-

---

150. See *ST*, Supp., q. 64, a. 5, ad 2. Cf. *In IV Sententiarum*, d. 32, a. 5, qua. 1.

151. See *ST*, Supp., q. 64, a. 2. Cf. *In IV Sententiarum*, d. 32, a. 2, qua. 1.

152. See *ST*, Supp., q. 52, a. 1. Cf. *In IV Sententiarum*, d. 36, a. 1.

153. See *ST*, Supp., q. 58, a. 1. Cf. *In IV Sententiarum*, d. 34, a. 1.

154. *ST*, Supp., q. 58, a. 1, ad 2. Cf. *In IV Sententiarum*, d. 34, a. 2.

155. See *ST*, Supp., q. 64, a. 1, ads 2 and 3. Cf. *In IV Sententiarum*, d. 32, a. 1. In these
passages, Aquinas speaks only of the husband rejecting his wife because of his health
or some other legitimate reason that prevents him from engaging in the conjugal act.
However, there is nothing presented here nor elsewhere that would suggest his use of
the husband's rejection is anything more than an example. Aquinas nowhere denies this
same freedom to wives.

tends in sexual union is the begetting and rearing of the offspring; and that this good might be sought after, it attached pleasure to the union.... Accordingly to make use of sexual intercourse on account of its inherent pleasure, without reference to the end for which nature intended it, is to act against nature, as also is it if intercourse be not such as may fittingly be directed to that end."[156] Later, in the *Summa contra Gentiles*, Aquinas notes:

It is evident that ... every emission of semen, in such a way that generation cannot follow, is contrary to the good of man. And if this be done deliberately, it must be a sin. Now, I am speaking of a way from which, in itself [*secundum se*], generation could not result: such would be any emission of semen apart from the natural union of male and female. For which reason, sins of this type are called contrary to nature [*contra naturem*]. But, if by accident [*per accidens*] generation cannot result from the emission of semen, then this is not a reason for it being against nature, or a sin; as for instance, if the woman happens to be sterile.[157]

Here, Aquinas distinguishes those venereal acts which are *contra naturem* from those conjugal acts which are in themselves procreative but which are in particular instance *per accidens* non-procreative for a circumstantial reason (for example, the sterility of the woman).

John Noonan has suggested that this later development represents a change in Aquinas's position.[158] However, even in the *supplementum*, Aquinas suggests that it is not sinful to engage in intercourse even if procreation is not the result. Acknowledging Aquinas's view that the pleasure concomitant with the marital act is not in itself sinful— though its vehemence is the result of original sin—it is interesting to note what he says about the marital goods and how they "excuse" this pleasure in the marital act:

Just as the marriage goods, in so far as they consist in a habit, make a marriage honest and holy, so too, in so far as they are in the actual intention, they make the marriage act honest, as regards those two marriage goods which relate to the marriage act. Hence when married persons come together for the purpose of begetting children, or of paying the debt to one another

---

156. *ST*, Supp., q. 64, a. 3. Cf. *In IV Sententiarum*, d. 32, a. 3.
157. *SCG* III.122.
158. See Noonan, *Contraception*, 242.

(which pertains to faith), they are wholly excused from sin. . . . Consequently there are only two ways in which married persons can come together without any sin at all, namely in order to have offspring, and in order to pay the debt; otherwise it is always at least a venial sin.[159]

Here, Aquinas makes it clear that there are two ways in which a couple avoids venial sin in engaging in the marital act: the intention to beget children and the intention to pay the debt. The larger issue at work here, of course, is the concept that any act of sexual intercourse between husband and wife might be a venial sin. Yet I believe there are other passages in the *supplementum* that help clarify Aquinas's reasoning here. They concern the relation of the marriage debt to the sin of lust.

Thomas insists that the marriage act may become vicious if the motivation is lust. The gravity of the sin of lust, whether it be venial or mortal, is measured by the presence of the marriage goods in the intention of the spouse. And in these passages, Aquinas universally references the husband in his examples as the one prone to lust.[160] Thus he writes: "If the motive be lust, yet not excluding the marriage blessings, namely that he [the husband] would by no means be willing to go to another woman, it is a venial sin; while if he exclude the marriage blessings, so as to be disposed to act in like manner with any woman, it is a mortal sin."[161] A man who sins mortally with lust is willing to satisfy his sexual needs with any woman, it just so happens that he has a wife ready at hand.

Later, Aquinas clarifies his position in regards to the sinfulness of lust. The lustful man seeks the pleasure itself without any intention to satisfy the marital debt or to generate offspring. The difference is the attention he pays to the fidelity he owes his wife:

If pleasure [in the marital act] be sought in such a way as to exclude the honesty of marriage, so that, to wit, it is not as a wife but as a woman that a man treats his wife, and that he is ready to use her in the same way if she were not his wife, it is a mortal sin; wherefore such a man is said to be too ardent a

159. *ST*, Supp., q. 49, a. 5. Cf. *In IV Sententiarum*, d. 32, q. 2, a. 2.
160. I note that even though in Aquinas's view it is women who are more in need of sobriety, it is men who are consistently identified in his treatises on lust.
161. *ST*, Supp., q. 41, a. 4. Cf. *In IV Sententiarum*, d. 26, q. 1, a. 4.

lover of his wife, because his ardor carries him away from the goods of marriage. If, however, he seeks pleasure within the bonds of marriage, so that it would not be sought in another than his wife, it is a venial sin.[162]

This explains why Thomas also asserts that "if a man intends by the marriage act to prevent fornication in his wife, it is no sin, because this is a kind of payment of the debt that comes under the good of faith. But if he intends to avoid fornication in himself, then there is a certain superfluity, and accordingly there is a venial sin."[163] Aquinas wants to keep the motives of the husband (and, by extension, the wife) free from lust in order to prevent the spouses from using one another merely for the satisfaction of sexual desire. In fact, Thomas departs from the theological norm of his day by insisting that even if a man seeks pleasure primarily, provided he seeks it within the bounds of marriage—procreation and fidelity—it is only a venial sin, not a mortal one.[164]

The marital debt gives each spouse power over the other's body. Aquinas never used the notion of self-gift in his treatment on marriage. The theology of gift is a contemporary development in moral theology.[165] However, I suggest that his understanding of the marital debt in the *supplementum*, which he never corrects or modifies in his mature work, is comparable to the idea that the spouses give their bodies over to the other in the marriage consent.

While Aquinas uses terms such as authority and power, he clarifies his meaning. The spouses must be equally free in the consent to marriage and so equal in giving their bodies over to the other. They

162. *ST*, Supp., q. 49, a. 6. Cf. *In IV Sententiarum*, d. 31, q. 2, a. 3.

163. *ST*, Supp., q. 49, a. 5, ad 2.

164. See *ST*, Supp., q. 49, a. 6. See Ronald Lawler, Joseph Boyle, and William E. May, *Catholic Sexual Ethics: A Summary, Explanation, and Defense*, 2nd ed. (Huntington, Ind.: Our Sunday Visitor Press, 1998), 61–63. For a history of the pursuit of marital sex for the sake of avoiding the sin of fornication, see Brundage, *Law, Sex, and Christian Society*, 282–84; Noonan, *Contraception*, 343–45.

165. Brian Johnstone has offered a brief history of the development of the theology of the gift. See Brian V. Johnstone, "The Ethics of the Gift According to Aquinas, Derrida, and Marion," *Australian eJournal of Theology* 3 (2004). In this very helpful article, Johnstone offers a historical narrative of the development of the subject-object distinction. Furthermore, he offers an exegesis of Aquinas's understanding of gift by looking at the treatises on the Holy Spirit and grace in the *Summa Theologiae*.

must be capable of equally rendering the marriage debt. Furthermore, the fact that the husband cannot make use of his wife's body for lustful purposes suggests something different than these terms convey to modern ears. While both the husband and the wife can explicitly request "payment" of this debt, they cannot do so for lustful purposes. Finally, the natural structure of the act itself, when respected, further prevents lust from overwhelming them. For the nature of the act in itself tends to procreation even if *per accidens* a particular marital act does not beget any children. Only if such a *per accidens* non-procreative conjugal act is used for "its inherent pleasure, without reference to the end for which nature intended it" then it is a sinful act because it reveals a primary motive of lust and not fidelity or the payment of the marriage debt.[166]

I agree with Paul Gondreau's argument that Thomas's sexual theory must be interpreted in light of his hylomorphic anthropology. Procreation is the primary end of marriage in Aquinas's view because the generation and education of offspring is what separates the relationship of husband and wife from every other personal relationship.[167] Gondreau isolates the connection with hylomorphism: "Just as human nature cannot be defined in abstraction from the bodily (i.e., animal) dimension, so neither can we abstract the bodily, procreative dimension from the nuptial, symbolic meaning of our sexuality."[168] The love of marriage is specified by its expression in the marital act.[169]

Gondreau has drawn an interesting conclusion from Aquinas's notion that the form of matrimony consists in the union of souls.

---

166. See *ST*, Supp., q. 64, a. 3. Cf. *In IV Sententiarum*, d. 32, a. 3.

167. See *ST*, Supp., q. 49, a. 3. Cf. *In IV Senteniarium*, d. 31, q. 1, a. 3. See Gondreau, "'Inseparable Connection,'" 760. Gondreau shows here that Raymond of Peñafort, Aquinas's elder in the Dominican Order, had already made this observation. Cf. Raymond of Peñafort, *Summa on Marriage* II.3. An English translation of this text is available: Raymond of Peñafort, *Summa on Marriage*, trans. Pierre Payer (Toronto: Pontifical Institute of Medieval Studies, 2005), 20.

168. Ibid.

169. Regarding the marriage of Mary and Joseph, Aquinas argues that their marriage was perfect in its form (the essential union of souls) but only partly in the exercise of marriage (the procreation and upbringing of children). Although they never consummated their marriage, nevertheless their marriage was exercised in the upbringing of the child Jesus. See *ST* III, q. 29, a. 2.

While it may be anachronistic to say that Thomas had a concept of the "unitive" aspect of the conjugal act and of marriage, Gondreau argues, I think correctly, that the unitive dimension of marriage is this union of souls of which Aquinas speaks. The union of souls is not an afterthought in Aquinas's view. Precisely because the unitive represents the inseparable union of souls, it "expresses human sexuality's participation in the rational, in what is highest and noblest in us. The personalist [unitive] dimension raises our procreative animality, as it were, to the properly human."[170] Gondreau further concludes that since, in Aristotelian-Thomistic metaphysics, the form is the principle of unity between matter and form (just as the soul is the principle of unity between body and soul), this explains why married couples seek, first, union with one another before they seek children together.

Throughout his writings on marriage, Aquinas, like Augustine, routinely insists that the procreation of offspring includes not only their biological generation but also their education and upbringing. Thomas routinely insists that human children are not like animal young. They require a unique form of care and education. On this account, Aquinas elaborates numerous qualities of married life: monogamy, fidelity, parental solicitude for children, and indissolubility. The domestic society that mother and father create is the society in which their children will be raised. Gondreau draws the conclusion: "We do not just 'produce babies' like animals.... Rather, we first enter into a communion of personal spousal love, from which the begetting of human children flows, followed by the welcoming of these children into this same communion of love, into a family."[171]

One of the last moral textbooks written before the close of the Second Vatican Council made this same point:

Sometimes the primary ends are referred to by modern writers as the biological and social ends, while the secondary ends are called personalist. However, in contrasting personalist values with biological and social values one should not make the mistake of imagining that procreation and rearing of children are not personalist values, too, or that the so-called personalist values do not contribute to the biological and social ends. Procreation is not

170. Gondreau, "'Inseparable Connection,'" 761. Cf. *ST* III, q. 29, a. 2.
171. Gondreau, "'Inseparable Connection,'" 762.

just a continuation of the race or the nation. It is inherently a continuation and fulfillment of the persons of husband and wife also. Parenthood may well be, and in fact frequently is, the highest of the personalist values in a given marriage which is *de facto* fruitful.[172]

The conclusion of this section serves to directly rebut those contemporary moral theologians who insist that Thomas's sexual theory is overly dependent on the physical structures of nature and hence too concerned with the teleological structure of the sexual act.[173] A Thomistic anthropology is unable to separate the physical from the spiritual. Respecting the naturally procreative structure of the sexual act guarantees and protects its unitive and personalist dimension from motivations unworthy of human dignity. Respecting the unitive and personalist dimension guarantees that procreation is more than simply biological.

This is precisely why Aquinas's anthropology lends itself to the notion of a spousal meaning of the body. Since the human person is a body-soul composite, the body is not simply the soul's biological or physiological tool. As I showed in chapter 6 of this study, the body and soul mutually implicate each other in action and in thought. I also noted in that chapter that the body and soul composite that is man must, like all created being, come out of himself in order to find complete perfection in another (and, ultimately, in the other: God). Only God is complete perfection in himself. Nowhere in man's natural existence is this more apparent than in the sexual act itself, which requires a person of the opposite sex for teleological perfection. Without these admittedly basic insights along with Aquinas's notions of love and virtue, which I presented in chapter 7, and his understanding of marriage as a union of souls and highest friendship, Thomas's sexual ethic could be construed as physicalist. As it stands, however, Aqui-

172. John C. Ford and Gerald Kelly, *Contemporary Moral Theology*, vol. 2: *Marriage Questions* (Cork: Mercier Press, 1963), 49.

173. See, e.g., Charles E. Curran, *Contemporary Problems in Moral Theology* (Notre Dame, Ind.: Fides, 1970), 106; Charles Curran, *A New Look at Christian Morality* (Fides, 1970); Josef Fuchs, *Moral Demands and Personal Obligations* (Washington, D.C.: Georgetown University Press, 1993), 31; Richard M. Gula, *Reason Informed by Faith: Foundation of Catholic Morality* (New York: Paulist Press, 1989), 223–28. For a terse response to these theologians, see William E. May, *An Introduction to Moral Theology*, 2nd ed. (Huntington, Ind.: Our Sunday Visitor Press, 2003), 80–84.

nas's view of marriage, much of which depends on Augustine's teaching, offers a robust Aristotelian hylomorphic framework in which we can understand what it means to say that the body speaks a language. Because men and women are created composite beings with bodies and souls, *both* elements reach out to another for perfection—both the body and the soul are searching for perfection, and thus the human person as a whole is searching for perfection. The movement of love is a movement not only of the soul but also of the body, since the soul and body are two principles of the human composite. And this reaching out to the other (with both body and soul), the hallmark of John Paul's spousal meaning of the body, being manifest in marriage means that in spite of apparent inequalities of sexual roles, Aquinas's argument required him to insist upon not only the equality of the spouses in the self-offering of marriage (an offering which included the rendering of the marital debt) but also to insist upon the view that the conjugal act was a visible or material manifestation of this union.

CONCLUSION

It is certainly true that some of Thomas's perspective on women is at odds with contemporary values. Yet in spite of his cultural milieu and his respect for Aristotelian biology, the Angelic Doctor made extraordinary steps in his theory of marriage and the conjugal act. He agreed that men were the head of the household, for which he had not only cultural custom but biblical warrant on his side, but he nonetheless insisted that there was a definite equality between husband and wife. He even established that there is a certain domestic justice between the two. Moreover, he insisted that a wife's freedom must be respected, while both husband and wife are subject to the common good of the household.

There was a definite development in Thomas's thinking on the nature of marriage. Early in his life, he was not sure how to characterize the nature of the relationship between husband and wife. As a result, he seemingly settled for the lowest caliber of friendship in Aristotle's view: a friendship of utility based on a shared activity, which was the procreation and education of children. Later in his life, however, he began to see marriage as the supreme form of friendship between human beings. Building on Aristotle's own understanding of perfect friendship, Aquinas was able to make a more appealing argument for the indissolubility of monogamous marriage in the *Summa contra Gentiles*.

Finally, we have seen that Thomas's view of the conjugal act need not be interpreted in a strictly physicalist way, as some have argued in the past. In fact, it is not too difficult to see his understanding of the marital debt through the same lens of the gift of self that Karol Wojtyła and others have written about. Equally important is the ramifications Aquinas's hylomorphic anthropology has for his understanding of the conjugal act. The material and the immaterial cannot be separated in this life, nor can the procreative and the unitive aspects of the conjugal act. The body is implicated in the love between man and woman. This is a central tenet of John Paul's *Theology of the Body*: the body communicates the person, and it communicates love.

Conclusion

My goal in this book has been to show the rich metaphysical foundation that Thomas Aquinas's anthropology provides for the spousal meaning of the body as articulated by Pope John Paul II in his *Theology of the Body* catecheses. My hope is that by articulating Aquinas's anthropology and his understanding of marriage alongside that of John Paul II, it is now easier to see how the thought of these two thinkers can be mutually enriching. This is shown first in the clear influence of Aquinas on the early thought of Wojtyła, exemplified in his firm loyalty to the theological method of Aquinas as demonstrated at the beginning of his academic career and never abandoned by him even as he turned increasingly to phenomenology in the 1970s. Secondly, we have seen how *Theology of the Body*, which offers a biblical and experiential anthropology, can supplement Aquinas's thought. It is critical to understanding Wojtyła and to appreciating the opportunity afforded in this synthesis of his work with Aquinas to note that the Wojtyła never rejected the value of natural theology and metaphysical theory. On the contrary, he consistently affirmed the need for Thomistic metaphysics to distinguish moral good from evil.

In this study, I have argued that elements of John Paul's spousal meaning of the body can be found in the mature thought of Aquinas. Furthermore, I have read *Theology of the Body* as a development in the twentieth-century debate on marriage and contraception. A principal element of that debate, I have suggested, is the relationship between the category of personhood and the category of human nature. I have also shown that early in his academic career, Wojtyła recognized the deficiency of purely academic or speculative theology in reaching the faithful. In some ways, his entire life was devoted to the task of connecting the speculative and the practical, the dogmatic and the experiential, the objective and the subjective. *Theology of the Body* was by no means the pinnacle of his life's work, as he would serve as pope for another twenty-one years after these catechetical talks. Nonetheless, it represents a remarkable project of defending, and perhaps rearticulating, the church's sexual ethic.

This background helps to explain why the pope never explicitly explains the ontological foundation which he presumes in *Theology of the Body*. When he studied for the priesthood, Wojtyła had the benefit of a basic scholastic education, common at the time, in which he learned Thomistic metaphysics (although he later admitted how difficult the subject was for him). His early academic work indicates a thorough assimilation of Thomistic categories. Yet by the time he penned the manuscript for the book that eventually became the *Theology of the Body* catecheses, he was convinced that a more experiential and phenomenological approach would be most effective in articulating the norms of sexual morality.

While he did not abandon his own background, there is a real possibility that at least some, if not many, readers of these catecheses do not have the benefit of the same scholastic education in metaphysics which John Paul received and which he presumed in his work. Without an ontological foundation supporting the anthropology John Paul presents, it is easy to miss the fact that he is not simply speaking metaphorically or lyrically. He is not romanticizing the body or marriage.

Thomas's hylomorphic theory gives philosophical credence to what in *Theology of the Body* is primarily a biblical anthropology. That the spousal meaning of the body entails an intrinsic urge to the other and the freedom to love the other rightly is compatible with Aquinas's worldview is evident from the following points. First, like Wojtyła, Aquinas holds for a strict unity between body and soul. The human person is not constituted by either principle alone but by both. Second, Aquinas agrees that all created being is inherently driven out of itself in search of complete perfection. Third, this movement, called love, must be properly ordered, and this ordering is the chief characteristic of virtue. Without virtue, in Thomas's moral theory, man dissipates into a creature pursuing disparate ends with no guidance from reason.

Fourth, marriage as the highest form of friendship entails a free exchange of consent, which includes the voluntary offering of one's body to the other. Finally, because of the hylomorphic unity of the human person, the conjugal act involves not only a biological aspect (procreation) but also a personalist aspect (paying the marital debt, fidelity, and education of offspring). The fact that Aquinas, like Augustine, routinely includes the education of offspring with procreation as the primary end of marriage and advocates a teleological importance for sexual pleasure (reasonably enjoyed) suggests that he himself was not entirely convinced that biological necessity (procreation) was the only use for the conjugal act. Indeed, paying the marital debt as an expression of fidelity is another good use of the act in Aquinas's view. The conjugal act might be considered to express the very union of souls that Aquinas came to believe marriage is.

However, it is my considered opinion that there are weaknesses in both Aquinas's presentation and in *Theology of the Body*. Aquinas did not offer a view of the experience of human consciousness or a full explanation of human personhood (though he did offer a modified version of Boethius's definition of the person). Consciousness and human personhood did not become overriding issues until the modern period. Similarly, Thomas did not provide a detailed view of the conjugal act as an expression of the fidelity and unity between spouses, but the fact that he asserted that either an intention to procreate or to pay the marital debt was sufficient to avoid sin in marital sex suggests he would be open to the idea.

The emphasis Aquinas places on the marital debt as an expression of conjugal fidelity, along with his appreciation of sexual pleasure and his admission that not every conjugal act is procreative, suggests that he was struggling to develop a richer understanding of conjugal intercourse than the one he had inherited. It is in these areas that I see the principles necessary to develop a Thomistic spousal meaning of the body. In my view, his limitations in developing a personalist reading of sexual intimacy to complement his sexual ethic and his understanding of marriage are strictly the result of his historical and cultural milieu. I believe that Karol Wojtyła, in a decidedly different historical setting, resolves many of the deficiencies in Aquinas's presentation.

Karol Wojtyła's anthropology, especially what he presented in the *Theology of the Body* catecheses, can serve to ameliorate or even correct these deficiencies in Aquinas's thought. His focus on human consciousness and the human person as a subject has brought greater clarity to theological discourse, especially surrounding sexual ethics. Moreover, in a post-Cartesian modernity, his insistence on the importance of the body offers a holistic view of men and women and their relationship with one another. Yet, as he states throughout his *corpus*, the objectivity of the body is itself necessary but insufficient to understand the uniqueness or originality of every human person. The biblical anthropology he offers moves beyond (yet does not reject) the anthropology of Aquinas.[1]

1. The focus of this book has been the pre-pontifical published work of Karol Wojtyła leading up to *Theology of the Body*. In this period of his life, Wojtyła was less concerned about the differing roles of men and women in the family, in the church, and in the world. However, the anthropology of *Theology of the Body*, which sees the human person's uniqueness going deeper than his somatic constitution, is present in *Mulieris Dignitatem*. In that letter he expands his argument that men and women are called to a *communio personarum* by explicitly connecting their communion and relationship with each other with the communion of the divine persons of the Trinity. See, for example, *MD*, pars. 7–10. Here John Paul further elaborates his anthropology by incorporating the Trinitarian dynamism of truth and love within the communion of the divine persons. He is able then to highlight the vocations unique to men and women (who make their own self-gift to each other and to God) without a dependence on the physical differences between them. " I am convinced John Paul intended to speak analogously about the similarities of the Divine *communio personarum* and the human *communio personarum*. He says as much: "*The image and likeness of God in man*, created as man and woman (in the analogy that can be presumed between Creator and creature)" (*MD*, par. 7). Later, he writes: "For biblical Revelation says that, while man's 'likeness' to God is true, the '*non-likeness*' which separates the whole of creation from the Creator is *still more essentially true*" (ibid., par. 8). The insistence upon analogy does not lessen the importance of John Paul's conclusions. It confirms that faith moves beyond reason. John Paul insists on this point when he speaks about the relationship of men and women as the *communio personarum* (ibid., par. 7). By calling the reader's attention to theological analogy, I want simply to highlight the differences between human persons and divine persons. Somatic sexual difference is, after all, from God just as much as the call the *communio personarum*. An anthropology from above raises the dignity of the human body and sexual difference by clarifying their true purpose in the light of faith. Without an element from below, an anthropology from above runs the risk of reducing the body's participation in that *communio personarum* which characterizes humanity, and especially marriage. Yet without the witness of faith, an anthropology from below can easily fall into sexual prejudice and gender stereotyping. For a slightly different interpretation of this, see John Grabowski, "Mutual Submission and Trinitarian Self-Giving," *Angelicum* 74 (1997): 489–512.

Given the importance that the body has for both thinkers, the role of sexual difference can and should be further developed based on their thought. Aquinas, on the one hand, follows through with the logical conclusions of his hylomorphism but was limited by the scientific conclusions he inherited from Aristotle. In *Theology of the Body*, on the other hand, the pope asserts that the spousal meaning of the body is experienced differently by men and women, yet he also insists their somatic constitution is more important than the fact that they are male and female. *Theology of the Body* could have been strengthened had the pope further explored exactly how the spousal meaning of the body differs for men and women.

While it can be argued that Aquinas was prejudicial or mistaken in the roles he assigned mothers and fathers in the family, it is certainly true that he was interested in articulating the structures that a family needs for its survival and the propagation and education of children. Since John Paul does not spend time explaining the differences between men and women adequately in *Theology of the Body*, he does not spend time addressing the structure of the family. Although he discusses procreation and parenthood as manifestations of the spousal meaning of the body, he never discusses children, their role in the family, and the parents' obligations to them.[2] Reading *Theology of the Body* in line with the tradition that came before it, especially on this point, can bring clarity to the pope's articulation of the spousal meaning of the body as the gift of self, manifest in marriage especially in the conjugal act, but not exclusively so.

In his early academic career, Wojtyła was more focused on emphasizing Thomas's thought as he looked for a way to connect faith and doctrine to lived experience. I have argued that in the 1970s he made a much more intentional shift to phenomenology because he did not think that teleology-based ethic alone was effective in articulating Christian moral norms. Is his phenomenology simply a matter of "window-dressing" for traditional teleological arguments, or was he truly attempting to offer a new philosophical *ratio* for Christian morality?

It is arguable that (at least initially) he was not sure of his own

---

2. In his later pontifical writings, however, the family and children become more prominent. See, for example, *MD*, pars. 18–19, and *FC*, pars. 13–14.

project. I noted in the third chapter of this book that during the 1970 colloquium at the University of Cracow on *The Acting Person*, Wojtyła flatly stated that he was not trying to combine Thomism with phenomenology. Indeed, he thought such a combination was impossible. Yet, in the introduction to the 1979 English edition of *The Acting Person*, a translation that I noted has been criticized for rendering explicitly Thomistic terms and concepts in incomprehensible ways, he writes that this is exactly what he was trying to do: combine phenomenology with Thomism. Whether that project can be successful remains to be seen. But at the end of his life he was adamant that the church simply cannot proceed in the twenty-first century without the metaphysical ontology of Aquinas, lest, in his words, "we end up in a vacuum."[3]

Theology of the Body is extraordinarily popular, especially in catechetical and parochial settings. Yet it is my belief that these catecheses must be interpreted according to their own genesis, which was a manuscript furthering the conversation on questions of marriage and contraception. In this light, they should be read in continuity rather than in isolation from Wojtyła's earlier work. I believe this hermeneutic would take readers and commentators back to the very anthropology and metaphysics offered by Aquinas in which Wojtyła was trained.

It has been over thirty years since Pope John Paul II began delivering in his Wednesday audiences the material that became known as *Theology of the Body*. With the passage of time, perhaps the salient insights the pope articulated in that work will increasingly be the subject of academic dialogue and scrutiny, especially through the lens of the theological tradition preceding Wojtyła. In that way, the pope's work will be strengthened and refined for generations yet to come. My hope is that this study will contribute to that important project.

---

3. See John Paul II, *Memory and Identity*, 12: "If we wish to speak rationally about good and evil, we have to return to Saint Thomas Aquinas, that is, to the philosophy of being. With the phenomenological method, for example, we can study the experiences of morality, religion, or simply what it is to be human, and draw from them a significant enrichment of our knowledge. Yet we must not forget that all these analyses implicitly presuppose the reality of the Absolute Being and also the reality of being human, that is, being a creature. If we do not set up from such 'realist' presuppositions, we end up in vacuum."

Bibliography

Adams, Marilyn McCord. "The Structure of Ockham's Moral Theory." In *The Context of Casuistry*, edited by James F. Keenan and Thomas A. Shannon, 25–52. Washington, D.C.: Georgetown University Press, 1995.

———. *William Ockham*. South Bend, Ind.: University of Notre Dame Press, 1987.

Allen, Prudence, RSM. *The Concept of Woman: The Aristotelian Revolution 750 BC– AD 1250*. Montreal: Eden Press, 1985.

Arjava, Antti, ed. *Consent and Coercion to Sex and Marriage in Ancient and Medieval Societies*. Washington, D.C.: Dumbarton Oaks Research Library and Collection, 1993.

Aquinas, Thomas. *Commentarium super Ioannem*. Edited by Raphaelis Cai. 5th ed. Turin: Marrietti, 1972. Translated by James A. Weisheipl and Fabian R. Larcher as *Commentary on the Gospel of St. John*. Albany, N.Y.: Magi Books, 1980.

———. *Opusculum de ente et essentia*. Turin: Marrietti, 1948. Translated by Armand Maurer as *On Being and Essence*. Toronto: Pontifical Institute of Medieval Studies, 1949.

———. *Quaestiones disputatae de malo*. Opera Omnia 23. Rome: Commisio Leonina, 1996. Translated by Richard Regan and edited by Brian Davies as *On Evil*. Oxford: Oxford University Press, 2003.

———. *Quaestiones disputatae de veritate*. Opera Omnia 22 A–C. Rome: Editori di San Tommaso, 1972–76. Translated by Robert W. Mulligan, James V. McGlynn, and R. W. Schmidt as *On Truth*. 3 vols. Indianapolis, Ind.: Hackett, 1995.

———. *Scriptum super libros sententiarum magistri Petri Lombardi Episcopi Parisiensis*. Edited by Mandonnet. 2 vols. Paris: Lethielleux, 1929–47.

———. *Summa contra Gentiles*. Opera Omnia 13–15. Rome: Riccardi Garroni, 1918–30. Translated by A. C. Pegis, J. F. Anderson, V. J. Bourke, and C. J. O'Neil as *Summa contra gentiles*. 4 vols. South Bend, Ind.: University of Notre Dame Press, 1975.

———. *Summa Theologiae*. Torino: Edizioni San Paolo, 1962. Translated by the Fathers of the English Dominican Province as *Summa theologiae*. Allen, Tex.: Christian Classics, 1981.

———. *Summa Theologiae*. Edited by Thomas Gilby, OP. 61 vols. Translated by the Blackfriars. New York: McGraw-Hill, 1964.

Aristotle. *The Complete Works of Aristotle: The Revised Oxford Translation*. Edited by Jonathan Barnes. 2 vols. Princeton, N.J.: Princeton University Press, 1984.

———. *Nicomachean Ethics*. Translated by Terence Irwin. 2nd ed. Indianapolis, Ind.: Hackett, 1999.

Asci, Donald P. *The Conjugal Act as a Personal Act*. San Francisco, Calif.: Ignatius Press, 2002.

Ashley, Benedict, OP. *Theologies of the Body: Humanist and Christian*. Braintree, Mass.: The Pope John Center, 1985.

Augustine. *De bono coniugali*. PL 40.

———. *De Genesi ad Litteram*. PL 34.

———. *De nuptiis et concupiscentia*. PL 44.

Aumann, Jordan, OP. "Thomistic Evaluation of Love and Charity." *Angelicum* 55 (1978): 533–41.

Austriaco, Nicanor, OP. "Immediate Hominization from the Systems Perspectives." *National Catholic Bioethics Quarterly* 4 (2004): 719–38.

Baruzi, Jean. *Saint Jean de la Croix et le problem de l'experience mystique*. Paris: Felix Alcan, 1924.

Berman, Harold J. *Law and Revolution: The Formation of the Western Legal Tradition*. Cambridge, Mass.: Harvard University Press, 1983.

Blazynski, George. *John Paul II: A Man from Krakow*. London: Weidenfeld and Nicholson, 1979.

Borresen, Kari Elisabeth. *Subordination and Equivalence: The Nature and Role of Woman in Augustine and Thomas Aquinas*. Kampen: Kok Pharos, 1995.

Boyle, Leonard. *The Setting of the* Summa theologiae *of Saint Thomas*. Toronto: The Pontifical Institute of Medieval Studies, 1982.

Bradley, Denis. *Aquinas on the Twofold Human Good: Reason and Human Happiness in Aquinas's Moral Science*. Washington, D.C.: The Catholic University of America Press, 1997.

Brock, Stephen L. *Action and Conduct: Thomas Aquinas and the Theory of Action*. Edinburgh: T&T Clark, 1998.

Brown, Montague. "Aquinas on the Resurrection of the Body." *The Thomist* 56 (1992): 165–207.

Brundage, James A. *Law, Sex, and Christian Society in Medieval Europe*. Chicago: The University of Chicago Press, 1987.

———. "The Paradox of Sexual Equality in the Early Middle Ages." In *Shifting Frontiers in Late Antiquity*, edited by Ralph W. Mathisen and Hagith S. Sivan, 256–64. Brookfield, Vt.: Variorum, 1996.

Buttiglione, Rocco. *Karol Wojtyła: The Thought of the Man Who Became Pope John Paul II*. Translated by Paolo Guietti and Francesca Murphy. Grand Rapids, Mich.: Eerdmans, 1997.

Cahill, Lisa Sowle. *Between the Sexes: Foundations for a Christian Ethics of Sexuality*. Philadelphia: Fortress Press, 1985.

———. "Catholic Sexual Ethics and the Dignity of Person: A Double Message." *Theological Studies* 50 (1989): 120–50.

————. *Sex, Gender, and Christian Ethics.* Cambridge: Cambridge University Press, 1996.

Cahill, Lisa Sowle, John Garvey, and T. Frank Kennedy, SJ. *Sexuality and the U.S. Catholic Church: Crisis and Renewal.* New York: Crossroad, 2006.

Callan, Charles J., OP. *Moral Theology: A Complete Course Based on St. Thomas Aquinas and the Best Modern Authorities.* 2 vols. New York: Joseph F. Wagner, 1929.

Cates, Diana Fritz. *Choosing to Feel: Virtue, Friendship, and Compassion for Friends.* Notre Dame, Ind.: University of Notre Dame Press, 1997.

————. *Aquinas on the Emotions: A Religious-Ethical Inquiry.* Washington, D.C.: Georgetown University Press, 2009.

————. "The Virtue of Temperance (II IIae, qq. 141–170)." In *The Ethics of Aquinas,* edited by Pope, 321–39.

Cessario, Romanus, OP. *Introduction to Moral Theology.* Washington, D.C.: The Catholic University of America Press, 2001.

————. *The Virtues, or The Examined Life.* New York: Continuum, 2002.

————. *A Short History of Thomism.* Washington, D.C.: The Catholic University of America Press, 2005.

————. *The Moral Virtues and Theological Ethics.* 2nd ed. South Bend, Ind.: University of Notre Dame Press, 2009.

Cloutier, David. "Heaven Is a Place on Earth? Analyzing the Popularity of Pope John Paul II's Theology of the Body." In *Sexuality and the U.S. Catholic Church: Crisis and Renewal,* edited by Cahill et al., 18–31.

Codex Iuris Canonici. Translated by Edward N. Peters as *The 1917 Pio-Benedictine Code of Canon Law in English Translation with Extensive Scholarly Apparatus.* San Francisco, Calif.: Ignatius Press, 2001.

Cortest, Luis. *The Disfigured Face: Traditional Natural Law and Its Encounter with Modernity.* New York: Fordham University Press, 2008.

Council of Trent. *Decreta Super Reformatione.* July 15, 1563. In *Decrees of the Ecumenical Councils,* translated by Tanner, 2:744–53.

Cowburn, John. *Personalism and Scholasticism.* Milwaukee, Wis.: Marquette University Press, 2005.

Cracow Diocesan Commisison on *Humanae Vitae.* "Les fondements de la doctrine de l'Eglise concernant les principles de la vie conjugale." *Analecta Cracoviensia* 1 (1969): 194–230. English translation in *Nova et Vetera* (*English Edition*) 10 (2012): 321–59.

Crosby, John F. "The Personalism of John Paul II as the Basis of His Approach to the Teaching of 'Humanae vitae.'" *Anthropotes* 5 (1989): 48–49.

————. *The Selfhood of the Human Person.* Washington, D.C.: The Catholic University of America Press, 1996.

Crowe, Michael Bertram. *The Changing Profile of the Natural Law.* The Hague: Nijhoff 1977.

Curran, Charles E. "Christian Marriage and Family Planning." *Jubilee* 12 (August 1964): 8–13.

————, ed. *Contraception: Authority and Dissent.* New York: Herder and Herder, 1969.

―――. "Natural Law and Contemporary Moral Theology." In *Contraception*, 151–75.

―――. *Contemporary Problems in Moral Theology*. Notre Dame, Ind.: Fides, 1970.

―――. *A New Look at Christian Morality*. South Bend, Ind.: Fides, 1970.

―――. *The Moral Theology of Pope John Paul II*. Washington, D.C.: Georgetown University Press, 2005.

Curran, Charles, et al. "Statement by Catholic Theologians, Washington, D.C., July 30, 1968." In *Readings in Moral Theology*, no. 8: *Dialogue about Catholic Sexual Teaching*, edited by Charles Curran and Richard A. McCormick. New York: Paulist Press, 1993.

Curran, Charles, Robert E. Hunt, et al. *Dissent in and for the Church: Theologians and "Humanae Vitae."* New York: Sheed and Ward, 1969.

Dale, Richard C. *The Problem of the Rational Soul in the Thirteenth Century*. Leiden: Brill, 1995.

Dauphinais, Michael, and Matthew Levering, eds. *John Paul II and St. Thomas Aquinas*. Naples, Fla.: Sapientia Press, 2006.

De Broglie, Guy, SJ. "La conception thomiste des deux finalités du marriage." *Doctor Communis* 30 (1974): 3–41.

De Haro, Ramón García. *Marriage and Family in the Documents of the Magisterium: A Course in the Theology of Marriage*. Translated by William E. May. San Francisco, Calif.: Ignatius Press, 1995.

De Lubac, Henri, SJ. *Surnaturel: Etudes historiques*. Paris: Aubier, 1946.

―――. *The Mystery of the Supernatural*. Translated by Rosemary Sheed. London: Chapman, 1967.

―――. *Augustinianism and Modern Theology*. Translated by Lancelot Sheppard. London: Chapman, 1969.

Dewan, Lawrence, OP. *Wisdom, Law, and Virtue: Essays in Thomistic Ethics*. New York: Fordham University Press, 2007.

―――. "Jean Porter on Natural Law: Thomistic Notes." In *Wisdom, Law, and Virtue*, 242–68.

―――. "St. Thomas and Moral Taxonomy." In *Wisdom, Law, and Virtue*, 444–77.

―――. "St. Thomas, Metaphysics, and Human Dignity." In *Wisdom, Law, and Virtue*, 58–67.

―――. "St. Thomas, the Common Good, and the Love of Persons." In *Wisdom, Law, and Virtue*, 271–78.

Doms, Herbert. *The Meaning of Marriage*. Translated by George Sayer. New York: Sheed and Ward, 1939.

Donceel, Joseph. "Abortion: Mediate v. Immediate Animation." *Continuum* 4 (1967): 167–71.

―――. "Immediate Animation and Delayed Hominization." *Theological Studies* 31 (1970): 76–105.

Donohoo, Lawrence J., OP. "The Nature and Grace of *Sacra Doctrina* in St. Thomas's *Super Boetium de Trinitate*." *The Thomist* 63 (1999): 343–401.

Duby, Georges. *Love and Marriage in the Middle Ages*. Translated by Jane Dunnett. Chicago: University of Chicago Press, 1994.

Duffy, Stephen J. *The Graced Horizon: Nature and Grace in Modern Catholic Thought.* Collegeville, Minn.: The Liturgical Press, 1992.

———. *The Dynamics of Grace.* Collegeville, Minn.: The Liturgical Press, 1993.

Duhamel, Joseph S. "The Time Has Come (Book Review)." *America* 108 (April 27, 1963): 210.

Dulles, Avery, SJ. *Magisterium: Teacher and Guardian of the Faith.* Naples, Fla.: Sapientia Press, 2007.

Durbin, Paul T. "Appendix 6: St. Thomas and the History of Theories of Knowledge." In Aquinas, *Summa Theologiae*, edited by Gilby, 12:181–84.

———. "Appendix 7: Naïve Realism." In Aquinas, *Summa Theologiae*, edited by Gilby, 12:185–87.

East, Edward M. *Mankind at the Crossroads.* New York: Charles Scribner's Sons, 1923.

Emery, Gilles, OP. "The Unity of Man, Body and Soul in St. Thomas Aquinas." In Emery, *Trinity, Church, and the Human Person: Thomistic Essays*, 209–35. Naples, Fla.: Sapientia Press, 2007.

———. *The Trinity in Aquinas.* Washington, D.C.: The Catholic University of America Press, 2008.

———. *The Trinitarian Theology of St. Thomas Aquinas.* Translated by Francesca Murphy. Oxford: Oxford University Press, 2010.

Farrelly, M. John. *Predestination, Grace, and Free Will.* London: Burns and Oates, 1964.

Feingold, Lawrence. *The Natural Desire to See God: According to St. Thomas and His Interpreters.* Washington, D.C.: The Catholic University of America Press, 2004.

Ford, John C., and Gerald Kelly. *Contemporary Moral Theology.* Westminster, Md.: The Newman Press, 1964.

Fourth Lateran Council. *De Confessione Facienda.* November 30, 1215. In *Decrees of the Ecumenical Councils*, translated by Tanner, 245.

———. *De Concilis Provincialibus.* November 30, 1215. In *Decrees of the Ecumenical Councils*, translated by Tanner, 236–37.

———. *De Instructione Ordinandorum.* November 30, 1215. In *Decrees of the Ecumenical Councils*, translated by Tanner, 248.

Fuchs, Joseph. *Moral Demands and Personal Obligations.* Translated by Brian McNeil. Washington, D.C.: Georgetown University Press, 1993.

Gallagher, David M. "The Will and Its Acts (Ia IIae, qq. 6–17)." In *The Ethics of Aquinas*, edited by Pope, 70–73.

Gallagher, John. "Magisterial Teachings from 1918 to the Present." In *Human Sexuality and Personhood, Proceedings of the Workshop for the Hierarchies of the United States and Canada Sponsored by the Pope John Center Through a Grant from the Knights of Columbus.* Braintree, Mass.: Pope John Center, 1990.

———. *Time Past, Time Future: An Historical Study of Catholic Moral Theology.* New York: Paulist Press, 1990.

Gibbons, William J., SJ. "Antifertility Drugs and Morality." *America* 98 (1957): 346–48.

Gilby, Thomas. "Appendix 1: Acting for a Purpose." In Aquinas, *Summa Theologiae*, edited by Gilby, 16:144–46.

———. "Appendix 5: The Vision of God." In Aquinas, *Summa Theologiae*, edited by Gilby, 16:153–55.

Gondreau, Paul. "The 'Inseparable Connection' between Procreation and Unitive Love (*Humanae Vitae*, §12) and Thomistic Hylemorphic Anthropology." *Nova et Vetera (English Edition)* 6 (2008): 731–64.

Grabowski, John S. "Mutual Submission and Trinitarian Self-Giving." *Angelicum* 74 (1997): 489–512.

———. "Person or Nature? Rival Personalisms in 20th Century Catholic Sexual Ethics." *Studia Moralia* 35 (1997): 283–312.

———. *Sex and Virtue: An Introduction to Catholic Sexual Ethics*. Washington, D.C.: The Catholic University of America Press, 2003.

Gregory of Nyssa. *De hominis opificio*. PG 44.

Grubbs, Judith Evans. *Law and Family in Late Antiquity: The Emperor Constantine's Marriage Legislation*. New York: Oxford University Press, 2000.

Gula, Richard M. *Reason Informed by Faith: Foundations of Catholic Morality*. New York: Paulist Press, 1989.

Gury, Jean. "Azor." In *Dictionnaire de Théologie Catholique*, edited by Émile Amann, vol. 1. Paris: Letouzey et Ané, 1930.

Hall, Pamela. *Narrative and Natural Law: An Interpretation of Thomistic Ethics*. South Bend, Ind.: University of Notre Dame Press, 1994.

Hanigan, James P. *What Are They Saying about Sexual Morality?* New York: Paulist Press, 1982.

Harak, Simon, SJ. *Virtuous Passions: The Formation of Christian Character*. New York: Paulist Press, 1993.

Häring, Bernard. *The Law of Christ: Moral Theology for Priests and Laity*. 3 vols. Translated by Edwin G. Kaiser. Paramus, N.J.: Newman Books, 1961–66.

———. "Statement in the *National Catholic Reporter*." *National Catholic Reporter*, August 7, 1968.

———. "The Inseparability of the Unitive-Procreative Functions of the Marital Act." In *Contraception: Authority and Dissent*, edited by Curran, 176–92.

Heaney, Stephen J. "Aquinas and the Presence of the Human Rational Soul in the Early Embryo." *The Thomist* 56 (1992): 19–48.

Hildebrand, Dietrich von. *Marriage*. New York: Longmans, Green, and Company, 1942.

———. *In Defense of Purity: An Analysis of the Catholic Ideals of Purity and Virginity*. Baltimore, Md.: Helicon Press, 1962.

———. *The Encyclical* Humanae Vitae—*A Sign of Contradiction: An Essay on Birth Control and Catholic Conscience*. Chicago: Franciscan Herald Press, 1969.

Hollander, Samuel. *The Economics of Robert Malthus*. Toronto: University of Toronto Press, 1997.

Horgan, John, ed. Humanae Vitae: *The Encyclical and the Statements of the National Hierarchies*. Dublin, Ireland: Irish University Press, 1972.

Hoyt, Robert, ed. *The Birth Control Debate: The Interim History from the Pages of* The National Catholic Reporter. Kansas City, Mo.: National Catholic Reporter Publishing, 1968.

Huber, Paulette, AdPPS. *The Teachings of Pius XII on Marriage and the Family*. PhD diss., The Catholic University of America, 1950.

Hünermann, Peter. "The Final Weeks of the Council." In *History of Vatican II*, edited by Guiseppe Alberigo and Joseph A. Komonchak, 5:363–484. 5 vols. Maryknoll, N.Y.: Orbis, 1995–2003.

Ide, Pascal. "Une théologie du don: les occurrences de *Gaudium et spes*, n. 24, §3 chez Jean-Paul II." *Anthropotes* 17 (2001): 149–78; 313–44.

Janssens, Louis. "L'inhibition de l'ovulation est-elle moralement licite?" *Ephemerides Theologicae Lovanienses* 34 (1958): 357–60.

———. "Morale conjugale et progesogènes." *Ephemerides Theologicae Lovanienses* 39 (1963): 787–826.

———. "Considerations on *Humanae Vitae*." *Louvain Studies* 2 (1969): 231–53.

Jensen, Steven. *Good and Evil Actions: A Journey through Saint Thomas Aquinas*. Washington, D.C.: The Catholic University of America Press, 2010.

Jonsen, Albert R., and Stephen Toulmin. *The Abuse of Casuistry: A History of Moral Reasoning*. Berkeley: University of California Press, 1988.

Joyce, Mary Rosera. *Love Responds to Life: The Challenge of Humanae Vitae*. Kenosha, Wis.: Prow, 1971.

John Chrysostom. *Homiliae in Genesis*. PG 25.

John Paul II, Pope. *Original Unity of Man and Woman: Catechesis on the Book of Genesis*. Boston: Pauline Books and Media, 1981.

———. *Familiaris Consortio*. Apostolic Exhortation of November 22, 1981. *AAS* 74 (1982): 81–191. Vatican translation found in Boston: Pauline Books and Media, 1981.

———. *Blessed Are the Pure of Heart: Catechesis on the Sermon on the Mount and the Writings of St. Paul*. Boston: Pauline Books and Media, 1983.

———. *Reflections on "Humanae Vitae": Conjugal Morality and Spirituality*. Boston: Pauline Books and Media, 1984.

———. *The Theology of Marriage and Celibacy: Catechesis on Marriage and Celibacy in the Light of the Resurrection of the Body*. Boston: Pauline Books and Media, 1986.

———. *Mulieris Dignitatem*. Apostolic Letter of August 15, 1988. *AAS* 80 (1988): 1653–1729. Vatican translation found in Boston: Pauline Books and Media, 1988.

———. *Veritatis Splendor*. Encyclical Letter of August 6, 1993. *AAS* 85 (1993): 1133–1228. Vatican translation found in Boston: Pauline Books and Media, 1993.

———. *Crossing the Threshold of Hope*. Edited by Vittorio Messori. Translated by Jenny McPhee and Martha McPhee. New York: Alfred A. Knopf, 1994.

———. *Gratissimam Sane*. Apostolic Letter of February 2, 1994. *AAS* 86 (1994): 868–925. Vatican translation found in Boston: Pauline Books and Media, 1994.

———. *Evangelium Vitae*. Encyclical Letter of March 25, 1995. *AAS* 87 (1995): 401–522. Vatican translation found in Boston: Pauline Books and Media, 1995.

———. "Letter to Women." Apostolic Letter of June 29, 1995. *AAS* 87 (1995): 803–12. Vatican translation found in Boston: Pauline Books and Media, 1995.

———. *The Theology of the Body: Human Love in the Divine Plan*. Boston: Pauline Books and Media, 1997.

———. *Memory and Identity: Conversations at the Dawn of a Millenium.* New York: Rizzoli, 2005.

———. *Man and Woman He Created Them: A Theology of the Body.* Translated by Michael Waldstein. Boston: Pauline Books and Media, 2006.

John Paul II, Pope, and André Frossard. *Be Not Afraid! Pope John Paul II Speaks Out on His Life, His Beliefs, and His Inspiring Vision for Humanity.* Translated by J. R. Foster. New York: St. Martin's Press, 1984.

Johnstone, Brian V. "The Ethics of the Gift According to Aquinas, Derrida, and Marion." *Australian eJournal of Theology* 3 (2004).

Kaiser, Robert Blair. *The Politics of Sex and Religion.* Kansas City, Mo.: Leaven Press, 1985.

Käppelli, Thomas, OP, and Antione Dondaine, OP, eds. *Monumenta Ordinis Fratrum Praedicatorum historica.* Vol. 20 of *Capitulorum Provincialium Provinciae Romanae* (1243–1244). Rome: Institutum Historicum Fratrum Praedicatorum, 1941.

Kaufmann, Philip S. *Why You Can Disagree and Remain a Faithful Catholic.* Rev. ed. New York: Crossroad, 1995.

Kaveny, Cathleen. "What Women Want: 'Buffy,' the Pope, and the New Feminists." *Commonweal* 130, no. 19 (November 7, 2003): 18–24.

———. "The 'New' Feminism? John Paul II and the 1912 Encyclopedia." *Commonweal* 135, no. 6 (March 28, 2008): 8.

Kelly, Gerald, SJ. "Confusion: Contraception and 'The Pill.'" *Theology Digest* 12 (1964): 123–30.

Kerr, Fergus, OP. *After Aquinas: Versions of Thomism.* Oxford: Blackwell, 2002.

———. *Twentieth-Century Catholic Theologians: From Neoscholasticism to Nuptial Mysticism.* Oxford: Blackwell, 2007.

Knuuttila, Simon. *Emotions in Ancient and Medieval Philosophy.* Oxford: Clarendon Press, 2004.

Kupczak, Jaroslaw, OP. *Destined for Liberty: The Human Person in the Philosophy of Karol Wojtyła/Pope John Paul II.* Washington, D.C.: The Catholic University of America Press, 2000.

———. *Gift and Communion: John Paul II's Theology of the Body.* Washington, D.C.: The Catholic University of America Press, 2014.

Kwasniewski, Peter. "St. Thomas, Exstasis, and Union with the Beloved." *The Thomist* 61 (1997): 587–603.

Labourdette, Michael, OP. "La foi théologale et la connaissance mystique d'apès S. Jean de la Crois." *Revue Thomiste* 42 (1937): 16–57.

Lawler, Ronald, Joseph Boyle, and William E. May. *Catholic Sexual Ethics: A Summary, Explanation, and Defense.* 2nd ed. Huntington, Ind.: Our Sunday Visitor Press, 1998.

Levering, Matthew. *Predestination: Biblical and Theological Paths.* Oxford: Oxford University Press, 2011.

Liebard, Odile M., ed. *Love and Sexuality.* Wilmington, N.C.: McGrath, 1978.

Lombard, Peter. *Sententiarum libri quattuor.* PL 192.

Long, Steven A. "Obediential Potency, Human Knowledge, and the Natural Desire for God." *International Philosophical Quarterly* 37 (1997): 45–63.

———. *The Teleological Grammar of the Moral Act*. Naples, Fla.: Sapientia Press, 2007.

———. "The False Theory Undergirding Condomistic Exceptionalism: A Response to William F. Murphy, Jr. and Rev. Martin Rhonheimer." *The National Catholic Bioethics Quarterly* 8 (2008): 709–32.

Lynch, John, SJ. "Another Moral Aspect of Fertility Control." *Linacre Quarterly* 20 (1953): 120–22.

———. "Fertility Control and the Moral Law." *Linacre Quarterly* 20 (1953): 83–89.

———. "Progestational Steroids: Some Moral Problems." *Linacre Quarterly* 25 (1958): 93–99.

———. "Notes on Moral Theology." *Theological Studies* 23 (1962): 233–65.

———. "The Time Has Come (Book Review)." *Marriage* 45 (June 1963): 16–17.

———. "Notes on Moral Theology: The Oral Contraceptives." *Theological Studies* 25 (1964): 237–49.

Mackin, Theodore, SJ. *The Marital Sacrament*. New York: Paulist Press, 1989.

Mahoney, John. *The Making of Moral Theology: A Study of the Roman Catholic Tradition*. Oxford: Clarendon Press, 1987.

Malinski, Mieczyslaw. *Pope John Paul II: The Life of Karol Wojtyła*. Translated by P. S. Falla. New York: Seabury Press, 1979.

Malthus, Thomas R. *An Essay on the Principle of Population*. New York: Oxford University Press, 1993.

Mann, J. A. "Personalism." In *The New Catholic Encyclopedia*, edited by Bernard L. Marthaler, 11:172. New York: McGraw-Hill, 1967.

Mattison, William. "'When they rise from the dead, they neither marry nor are given to marriage': Marriage and Sexuality, Eschatology, and the Nuptial Meaning of the Body in Pope John Paul II's Theology of the Body." In *Sexuality and the U.S. Catholic Church*, edited by Cahill et al., 32–51.

May, William E. *Contraception: "Humanae Vitae" and Catholic Moral Thought*. Chicago: Franciscan Herald Press, 1984.

———. *An Introduction to Moral Theology*. 2nd ed. Huntington, Ind.: Our Sunday Visitor Press, 2003.

McAleer, Graham. *Ecstatic Morality and Sexual Politics: A Catholic and Antitotalitarian Theory of the Body*. New York: Fordham University Press, 2005.

McCarthy, David Matzko. *Sex and Love in the Home*. Rev. ed. London: SCM Press, 2004.

McClory, Robert. *Turning Point: The Inside Story of the Papal Birth Control Commission, and How Humanae Vitae Changed the Life of Patty Crowly and the Future of the Church*. New York: Crossroad, 1995.

McCool, Gerald A., SJ. *Catholic Theology in the Nineteenth Century*. New York: Seabury Press, 1977.

———. *The Neo-Thomists*. Milwaukee, Wis.: Marquette University Press, 1994.

McCormick, Richard A. "Notes on Moral Theology." *Theological Studies* 29 (1968): 732–41.

McDonnell, Kevin. "Does William of Ockham Have a Theory of Natural Law?" *Franciscan Studies* 34 (1974): 383–92.

McKay, Angela. "Aquinas on the End of Marriage." In *Human Fertility: Where Faith and Science Meet*, edited by Richard J. Fehring and Theresa Notare. Milwaukee, Wis.: Marquette University Press, 2008.

McNeil, John T. *A History of the Care of Souls*. New York: Harper, 1951.

McNeil, John T., and Helena M. Gamer, eds. *Medieval Handbooks of Penance: A Translation of the Principal* Libri Poenitentiales *and Selections from Related Documents*. New York: Columbia University Press, 1938.

McPartlan, Paul. *Sacrament of Salvation: An Introduction to Eucharistic Ecclesiology*. New York: T&T Clark, 1995.

Meeks, Wayne A. *The Origins of Christian Morality: The First Two Centuries*. New Haven, Conn.: Yale University Press, 1993.

Migne, J.-P., ed. *Patrologiae cursus completus. Series latina.* 220 vols. Paris, 1844–64.

———, ed. *Patrologiae cursus completus. Series graeca.* 161 vols. Paris, 1857–66.

Minder, Robert. *Thomas Aquinas on the Passions: A Study of* Summa Theologiae *1a2ae 22–48*. New York: Cambridge University Press, 2009.

Mullady, Brian Thomas. *The Meaning of the Term "Moral" in St. Thomas Aquinas*. Vatican City: Libreria Editrice Vaticana, 1986.

Murphy, William F., Jr. "Developments in Thomistic Action Theory: Developments toward a Greater Consensus." *The National Catholic Bioethics Quarterly* 8 (2008): 505–28.

Nelson, Daniel Mark. *The Priority of Prudence: Virtue and Natural Law in Thomas Aquinas and the Implications for Modern Ethics*. University Park: Pennsylvania State University Press, 1991.

Noonan, John T. *Contraception: A History of Its Treatment by the Catholic Theologians and Canonists*. Cambridge, Mass.: Harvard University Press, 1986.

———. *A Church That Can and Cannot Change: The Development of Catholic Moral Teaching*. South Bend, Ind.: University of Notre Dame Press, 2005.

Nussbaum, Martha. *Love's Knowledge: Essays on Philosophy and Literature*. New York: Oxford University Press, 1990.

O'Brien, Thomas C. "Appendix Eight: Original Justice." In Aquinas, *Summa Theologiae*, edited by Gilby, 26:144–53.

———. "Appendix Nine: Fallen Nature." In Aquinas, *Summa Theologiae*, edited by Gilby, 26:154–59.

O'Connell, Francis J., CSSR. "The Contraceptive Pill." *American Ecclesiastical Review* 137 (1953): 48–59.

———. *Outlines of Moral Theology*. Milwaukee, Wis.: Bruce Publishing, 1953.

———. "Is Contraception Intrinsically Wrong?" *American Ecclesiastical Review* 150 (1964): 434–39.

Olsen, Glenn W., ed. *Christian Marriage: A Historical Study*. New York: Crossroad, 2001.

———. "Marriage in Barbarian Kingdom and Christian Court: Fifth through Eleventh Centuries." In *Christian Marriage*, 146–212.

———. "Progeny, Faithfulness, Sacred Bond: Marriage in the Age of Augustine." In *Christian Marriage*, 101–45.

O'Neil, Charles. *Imprudence in Aquinas*. Milwaukee, Wis.: Marquette University Press, 1955.

———. "Is Prudence Love?" *The Monist* 58 (1974): 119–39.

O'Reilly, Michael. "Conjugal Chastity in Pope Wojtyła." PhD diss., The Pontifical University of St. Thomas, 2007.

Osborne, Thomas M. "The Augustinianism of Thomas Aquinas's Moral Theory." *The Thomist* 67 (2003): 279–305.

Pantin, William A. *The English Church in the Fourteenth Century.* South Bend, Ind.: University of Notre Dame Press, 1962.

Pasnau, Robert. *Thomas Aquinas and Human Nature: A Philosophical Study of Summa theologiae Ia 75–89.* New York: Cambridge University Press, 2002.

Paul VI, Pope. *Humanae Vitae.* Encyclical Letter of June 25, 1968. *AAS* 60 (1968): 481–503. English translation from Boston: Pauline Books and Media, 1968.

Pegis, Anton C. *St. Thomas and the Problem of the Soul in the Thirteenth Century.* Toronto: St. Michael's College, 1934.

———. "The Separated Soul and Its Nature in St. Thomas." In *St. Thomas Aquinas 1274–1974 Commemorative Studies*, edited by Armand Maurer, 1:131–58. Toronto: Pontifical Institute of Medieval Studies, 1974.

Peifer, John F. *The Concept in Thomism.* New York: Bookman Associates, 1952.

Peterson, William. *Malthus: Founder of Modern Demonrgaphy.* 2nd ed. Piscataway, N.J.: Transaction Publishers, 1988.

Pieper, Josef. *The Four Cardinal Virtues.* South Bend, Ind.: University of Notre Dame Press, 1965.

Pilsner, Joseph. *The Specification of Human Actions in St. Thomas Aquinas.* New York: Oxford University Press, 2006.

Pinckaers, Servais, OP. *The Sources of Christian Ethics.* Translated by Mary Thomas Noble, OP. Washington, D.C.: The Catholic University of America Press, 1995.

———. *The Pinckaers Reader: Renewing Thomistic Moral Theology.* Edited by John Berkman and Craig Steven Titus. Washington, D.C.: The Catholic University of America Press, 2005.

———. "Aquinas on Nature and the Supernatural." In *The Pinckaers Reader*, 359–68.

———. "Beatitude and the Beatitudes in Aquinas's *Summa theologiae*." In *The Pinckaers Reader*, 115–29.

———. "Conscience and the Christian Tradition." In *The Pinckaers Reader*, 321–41.

———. "A Historical Perspective on Intrinsically Evil Acts." In *The Pinckaers Reader*, 185–235.

———. "Morality and the Movement of the Holy Spirit." In *The Pinckaers Reader*, 385–95.

———. "Reappropriating Aquinas's Account of the Passions." In *The Pinckaers Reader*, 273–87.

———. "The Role of Virtue in Moral Theology." In *The Pinckaers Reader*, 288–303.

Pius XI, Pope. *Casti Connubii.* Encyclical Letter of December 31, 1930. *AAS* 22 (1930): 539–92. Translated in Liebard, *Love and Sexuality*, 23–70.

Pius XII, Pope. "Address to the Italian Medical-Biological Union of St. Luke." November 12, 1944. In Liebard, *Love and Sexuality*, 84–95.

———. "Address to Midwives." October 29, 1951. *AAS* 43 (1951): 850–70. Translated in Liebard, *Love and Sexuality*, 101–22.

————. "Address to the Second World Congress on Fertility and Sterility." May 19, 1956. *AAS* 48 (1956): 468–74. Translated in Liebard, *Love and Sexuality,* 173–79.

————. "Address to the Seventh International Hematological Congress (12 September 1958)." *AAS* 50 (1958): 732–40. Translated in Liebard, *Love and Sexuality,* 234–43.

————. *Dear Newlyweds: Pope Pius XII Speaks to Young Couples.* Kansas City, Mo.: Sarto House, 2001.

Plé, Albert. *Chastity and the Affective Life.* Translated by Marie-Claude Thompson. New York: Herder and Herder, 1966.

Pope, Stephen J., ed. *The Ethics of Aquinas.* Washington, D.C.: Georgetown University Press, 2002.

Popik, Kristen. "The Philosophy of Woman of St. Thomas Aquinas, Part One: The Nature of Woman." *Faith and Reason* 4, no. 4 (Winter 1978): 16–56.

————. "The Philosophy of Woman of St. Thomas Aquinas, Part Two: The Role of Woman." *Faith and Reason* 5, no. 1 (Spring 1979): 12–42.

Porter, Jean, ed. *Pope and Pill: More Documentation on the Birth Regulation Debate.* Baltimore, Md.: Helicon Press, 1969.

————. "Recent Studies in Aquinas's Virtue Ethic: A Review Essay." *The Journal of Religious Studies* 26 (1998): 191–215.

————. *Natural and Divine Law: Reclaiming the Tradition for Christian Ethics.* Grand Rapids, Mich.: Eerdmans, 1999.

————. *Nature as Reason: A Thomistic Theory of the Natural Law.* Grand Rapids, Mich.: Eerdmans, 2005.

————. "A Response to Martin Rhonheimer," *Studies in Christian Ethics* 19 (2006): 379–95.

Pyle, Leo, ed. *The Pill and Birth Regulation.* Baltimore, Md.: Helicon Press, 1964.

Quay, Paul. "Contraception and Conjugal Love." *Theological Studies* 22 (1961): 18–40.

Rahner, Karl, SJ. *Theological Investigations.* 23 vols. New York: Crossroad, 1961–79.

————. "On the Relationship between Nature and Grace." In *Theological Investigations,* 1:297–318. New York: Crossroad, 1961.

————. *Foundations of the Christian Faith: An Introduction to the Idea of Christianity.* Translated by William V. Dych. New York: Crossroad, 1985.

Ratzinger, Joseph. *Eschatology: Death and Eternal Life.* Translated by Michael Waldstein. 2nd ed. Washington, D.C.: The Catholic University of America Press, 2007.

Raymond of Peñafort. *Summa on Marriage.* Translated by Pierre Payer. Toronto: Pontifical Institute of Medieval Studies, 2005.

Reid, Charles J., Jr. *Power Over the Body, Equality in the Family: Rights and Domestic Relations in Medieval Canon Law.* Grand Rapids, Mich.: Eerdmans, 2004.

Renard, Henri. "The Functions of Intellect and Will in the Act of Free Choice." *Modern Schoolman* 24 (1947): 85–92.

Reuss, J. M. "Eheliche Hingabe und Zeugung: Ein Diskussionsbeitrag zu einem differenzierten Problem." *Tubinger Theologische Quartalschrift* 143 (1963): 454–76.

Rhonheimer, Martin. *Natural Law and Practical Reason: A Thomistic View of Moral Autonomy*. Translated by Gerald Malsbary. New York: Fordham University Press, 2000.

———. "Reply to Jean Porter." *Studies in Christian Ethics* 19 (2006): 397–402.

———. Review of *Nature as Reason: A Thomistic View of the Theory of the Natural Law* by Jean Porter. *Studies in Christian Ethics* 19 (2006): 357–78.

Richard of St. Victor. *De Trinitate*. PL 196.

Roberts, Christopher C. *Creation and Covenant: The Significance of Sexual Difference in the Moral Theology of Marriage*. New York: T&T Clark, 2007.

Rock, John. "We Can End the Battle over Birth Control." *Good Housekeeping* (July 1961): 44–45, 107–9.

———. *The Time Has Come: A Catholic Doctor's Proposals to End the Battle over Birth Control*. New York: Alfred A. Knopf, 1963.

Routhier, Gilles. "Finishing the Work Begun: The Trying Experience of the Fourth Period." In *History of Vatican II*, edited by Guiseppe Alberigo and Joseph A. Komonchak, translated by Matthew J. O'Connell, 5:49–184. 5 vols. Washington, D.C.: The Catholic University of America Press, 2006.

Rowland, Tracey. "Natural Law: From Neo-Thomism to Nuptial Mysticism." *Communio* 35 (2008): 374–96.

Sabetti, Aloysio, SJ, and Timotheo Barrett, SJ. *Compendium theologiae moralis*. Edited by Daniel F. Creeden, SJ. 34th ed. New York: Frederick Pustet, 1939.

Scheler, Max. *Formalism in Ethics and Non-Formal Ethics of Values*. Translated by Manfred S. Frings and Roger L. Funk. Evanston, Ill.: Northwestern University Press, 1973.

Schemenauer, Kevin. *Conjugal Love and Procreation: Dietrich Von Hildebrand's Superabundant Integration*. Lanham, Md.: Lexington Books, 2011.

Schillebeeckx, Edward, OP. *Marriage: Human Reality and Saving Mystery*. Translated by N. D. Smith. New York: Sheed and Ward, 1967.

Schmitz, Kenneth L. *At the Center of the Human Drama: The Philosophical Anthropology of Karol Wojtyła/John Paul II*. Washington, D.C.: The Catholic University of America Press, 2000.

Schockenhoff, Eberhard. "The Theological Virtue of Charity (IIa IIae, qq. 23–46)." In *Ethics of Aquinas*, edited by Pope, 244–58.

Schu, Walter J. *The Splendor of Love: John Paul II's Vision of Marriage and the Family*. New Hope, Ky.: New Hope Publications, 2002.

Selling, Joseph. *The Reaction to Humanae Vitae: A Study in Special and Fundamental Theology*. PhD diss., The Catholic University of America, 1973.

Shanley, Brian. "Aquinas on Pagan Virtue." *The Thomist* 63 (1999): 553–77.

Shannon, William H. *The Lively Debate: Response to Humanae Vitae*. New York: Sheed & Ward, 1970.

Sherwin, Michael, OP. *By Knowledge and By Love: Charity and Knowledge in the Moral Theology of St. Thomas Aquinas*. Washington, D.C.: The Catholic University of America Press, 2005.

———. "Infused Virtue and the Effects of Acquired Vice: A Test Case for the Thomistic Theory of Infused Cardinal Virtues." *The Thomist* 73 (2009): 29–52.

Shivanandan, Mary. *Crossing the Threshold of Love: A New Vision of Marriage in the Light of John Paul II's Anthropology.* Washington, D.C.: The Catholic University of America Press, 1999.

Sieve, Benjamin. "A New Anti-Fertility Movement." *Science* 116 (October 10, 1952): 373–85.

Smith, David Woodruff. "Mind and Body." *The Cambridge Companion to Husserl.* Edited by Barry Smith and David Woodruff Smith. Cambridge: Cambridge University Press, 1995. 323–393.

Smith, Janet E. *Humanae Vitae: A Generation Later.* Washington, D.C.: The Catholic University of America Press, 1991.

Snoeck, André. "Fecundation inibée et morale Catholique." *Nouvelle Revue Theologique* 75 (1953): 690–702.

Spezzano, Daria. *The Glory of God's Grace: Deificiation According to St. Thomas Aquinas.* Washington, D.C.: The Catholic University of America Press, 2015.

Spinello, Richard A. *The Genius of John Paul II: The Great Pope's Moral Vision.* New York: Sheed and Ward, 2007.

Stump, Eleanor. *Aquinas.* New York: Routledge, 2005.

Szulc, Tad. *Pope John Paul II: The Biography.* New York: Scribner, 1995.

Tanner, Norman P., ed. *Decrees of the Ecumenical Councils.* 2 vols. Washington, D.C.: Georgetown University Press, 1990.

Taylor, Charles. *A Secular Age.* Cambridge: Belknap Press of Harvard University Press, 2007.

Torchia, Joseph, OP. *Exploring Personhood: An Introduction to the Philosophy of Human Nature.* New York: Rowman and Littlefield, 2008.

Torrell, Jean-Pierre, OP. *Saint Thomas Aquinas.* 2 vols. Translated by Robert Royal. Washington, D.C.: The Catholic University of America Press, 1996, 2003.

———. *Aquinas's Summa: Background, Structure, and Reception.* Washington, D.C.: The Catholic University of America Press, 2004.

Trewavas, Antony. "Malthus Foiled Again and Again." *Nature* 418 (August 8, 2002): 668–70.

Tugwell, Simon, OP. "Introduction to the Life and Work of Thomas Aqiunas." In *Albert and Thomas: Selected Writings,* edited by Simon Tugwell, OP. New York: Paulist Press, 1988.

Valsecchi, Ambrogio. *Controversy: The Birth Control Debate 1958–1968.* Translated by Dorothy White. Washington, D.C.: Corpus Books, 1985.

Van der Mark, W., OP. "Vruchtbaarheidsreheling. Poging tot antwoord op een nog open vraag." *Tijdschrift voor Theologie* 3 (1963): 379–413.

Vatican Council I. *De Fide Catholica.* April 24, 1870. In *Decrees of the Ecumenical Councils,* translated by Tanner, 2:804–11.

Vatican Council II. *Gaudium et Spes.* December 7, 1965. *AAS* 58 (1966): 1025–1115. In *Decrees of the Ecumenical Councils,* translated by Tanner, 2:1069–1135.

Waddell, Paul J. *The Primacy of Love: An Introduction to the Ethics of Thomas Aquinas.* New York: Paulist Press, 1992.

Waldstein, Michael. "The Project of a New English Translation of John Paul II's *Theology of the Body* on Its 20th and 25th Anniversary." *Communio* 31 (2004): 345–51.

———. "John Paul II: A Thomist Rooted in St. John of the Cross." *Faith & Reason* 30 (2005): 195–218.

———. "Introduction." In *John Paul II, Man and Woman He Created Them: A Theology of the Body*, translated by Michael Waldstein, 1–128. Boston: Pauline Books and Media, 2006.

Wallace, William. "Nature and Human Nature as the Norm of Medical Ethics." In *Catholic Perspectives on Medical Morals*, edited by Edmund D. Pelligrino, John P. Langan, and John C. Harvey, 23–52. Dordrecht: Kluwer, 1989.

Wéber, Edouard-Henri. *La person humaine au XIIIe siècle: L'avènement chez les Maîtres parisiens de l'acception modern de l'homme*. Paris: J. Vrin, 1991.

Weigel, George. *Witness to Hope: The Biography of Pope John Paul II*. New York: Harper Collins, 1999.

———. *The End and the Beginning: Pope John Paul II—The Victory Freedom, The Last Years, The Legacy*. New York: Image Books, 2011.

Weisheipl, James A. "Thomism." In *The New Catholic Encyclopedia*, edited by Bernard L. Marthaler, 14:126. New York: McGraw-Hill, 1967.

West, Christopher. *Theology of the Body Explained: A Commentary on John Paul II's: Man and Woman He Created Them*. Rev. ed. Boston: Pauline Books and Media, 2007.

Westberg, Daniel. *Right Practical Reason: Aristotle, Action, and Prudence in Aquinas*. Oxford: Clarendon Press, 1994.

William of Ockham. *Super quattuor sententiarum subtilissimae quaestiones*. Opera theologica 1–4. St. Bonaventure, N.Y.: Franciscan Institute, 1967–80.

Williams, George Hunston. *The Mind of John Paul II: Origins of His Thought and Action*. New York: Seabury Press, 1981.

Witham, Larry. *Curran vs. Catholic University: A Study of Authority and Freedom in Conflict*. Riverdale, Md.: Edington-Rand, 1991.

Wojtyła, Karol. "Crisis in Morality." In *Crisis in Morality: The Vatican Speaks Out*, 1–7. Washington, D.C.: United States Catholic Conference, 1969.

———. "The Intentional Act and the Human Act, that is, Act and Experience." *Analecta Husserliana* 5 (1976): 269–80.

———. *En esprit et en vérité: Recueil de texts 1949–1978*. Translated and edited by Gwendoline Jarcyk. Paris: Le Cenutrion, 1978.

———. "Abécédaure éthique." In *En esprit et vérité*, 103–59.

———. "Fruitful and Responsible Love." In Wojtyła, *Fruitful and Responsible Love with Contributions*, 12–34. New York: Seabury Press, 1979.

———. *Faith according to Saint John of the Cross*. Translated by Jordan Aumann, OP. San Francisco, Calif.: Ignatius Press, 1981.

———. *Max Scheler y la etica Cristiana*. Translated into Spanish by Gonzolo Haya. Madrid: Biblioteca de Autores Cristianos, 1982.

———. *Wykłady lubelskie*. Lublin: Wydawnictwo Towarzystwa Naukowego Katolickiego Uniwersytetu Lubelskiego, 1986. A German translation is available: *Erizehung zur Liebe*. Munchen: Wilhelm Heyne Verlag, 1981.

———. *Love and Responsibility*. Translated by H. T. Willets. San Francisco, Calif.: Ignatius Press, 1991.

———. *Person and Community: Selected Essays.* Translated and edited by Teresa Sandok. New York: Peter Lang, 1993.

———. "Ethics and Moral Theology." In *Person and Community,* 101–6.

———. "Human Nature as the Basis of Ethical Formation." In *Person and Community,* 95–99.

———. "In Search of the Basis of Perfectionism in Ethics." In *Person and Community,* 45–56.

———. "On the Directive or Subservient Role of Reason in Ethics in the Philosophy of Thomas Aquinas, David Hume, and Immanuel Kant." In *Person and Community,* 57–72.

———. "On the Metaphysical and Phenomenological Basis of the Moral Norm in the Philosophy of Thomas Aquinas and Max Scheler." In *Person and Community,* 73–94.

———. "Participation or Alienation?" In *Person and Community,* 197–207.

———. "The Person: Subject and Community." In *Person and Community,* 219–61.

———. "The Personal Structure of Self-Determination." In *Person and Community,* 187–95.

———. "The Problem of Catholic Sexual Ethics: Reflections and Postulates." In *Person and Community,* 279–99.

———. "The Problem of Experience in Ethics." In *Person and Community,* 107–27.

———. "The Problem of the Constitution of Culture through Human Praxis." In *Person and Community,* 263–75.

———. "The Problem of the Separation of Experience from Act in Ethics in the Philosophy of Immanuel Kant and Max Scheler." In *Person and Community,* 23–44.

———. "The Problem of the Theory of Morality." In *Person and Community,* 129–61.

———. "The Problem of the Will in the Analysis of the Ethical Act." In *Person and Community,* 3–22.

———. "Subjectivity and the Irreducible in the Human Being." In *Person and Community,* 209–17.

———. "The Teaching of the Encyclical 'Humanae Vitae' on Love: An Analysis of the Text." In *Person and Community,* 301–14.

———. "Thomistic Personalism." In *Person and Community,* 165–75.

———. *The Acting Person.* Translated by Andrzej Potocki. Boston: D. Reidel Publishing Company, 1999.

———. *El don del amor: escritos sobre la familia.* Translated by Antonio Esquivias and Rafael Mora. 2nd ed. Madrid: Ediciones Palabra, 2001.

———. "La experiencia religiosa de la pureza." In *El don del amor,* 69–81.

———. "La verdad de la Encíclica 'Humanae vitae.'" In *El don del amor,* 185–99.

———. "The Anthropological Vision of *Humanae Vitae*" Translated by William E. May. *Nova et Vetera* 7 (2009): 231–50.

Wojtyła, Karol, et al. "The Foundations of the Church's Doctrine Concerning the Principles of Conjugal Live: A Memorandum Composed by a Group of Moral Theologians from Krakow." Translated by Thérése Scarpelli Cory. *Nova et Vetera* 10 (2012): 321–59.

Zalba, Marcelino, SJ. "Casus de usu artificii contraceptive." *Periodica de re morali, canonica et liturgica* 51 (1962): 140–85.

Index

Abelard, Peter, 2n2

Acting Person, The (Wojtyła), 5–6, 116–23, 145–51, 314

action and agency, human: Aristotle and Wojtyła's view of, 107, 118; disintegrated, 151; dynamism of, 146–48; language of the body and, 184–87; natural instincts, 148–49; self-mastery, 191–93; two experiences of, 146. *See also* conjugal act

adultery, 163, 181, 187, 194, 290–91

Aeterni Patris (Leo XIII), 37–38

Albert the Great, 24

Allen, Prudence, 294

An Evaluation of the Possibility of Constructing a Christian Ethics on the Basis of the System of Max Scheler (Wojtyła), 98–103

Anglican Communion, 47–48

"Anthropological Vision of *Humanae Vitae*, The" (Wojtyła), 156–58

Aquinas, Saint Thomas: action, theory of, 146; career and work of, 15–16; conflict over teachings of, 24–25; faith, understanding of, 96–97; goodness and being, connection between, 110; influence of, 2; John Paul II and, 1, 5–7, 10, 166; John Paul's theology of the body catacheses and, 309–11; Leo XIII's revival of the teaching of, 37–38; Lombard's *Sentences*, commentary on, 239n26; manualists's departure from the theology of, 44; moral theology, synthesis of, 16–22; mystical experience and death of, 219n106, 274; Raymond of Peñafort, response to, 14; renewed interest in, 7; Scheler and, at-

tempt to bring into dialogue, 150n137; sexual identity, conception of, 294–95; supplement to the *Summa Theologica*, 220n106; weaknesses in the presentation by, 311; the will, approach to, 19–22, 104–5, 107–8, 223–25, 228n159, 238–42, 247–50, 254, 260–61, 264–66, 298; Wojtyła's description of the philosophy of, 111n103; Wojtyła's shift in tone regarding, 114–15

Aquinas on love, 235–36, 270–71; attraction to the good, 236–39; friendship and concupiscence, 244–46; grace and nature, 260–63; happiness and the proper ordering of love, 246–49; passion, reason, and will, 239–44; the theological virtues, 263–70; the virtue of charity, 260–70; the virtue of prudence, 250–55; the virtue of temperance, 255–60

Aquinas on marriage and the conjugal act, 259, 273–75, 307–8; the conjugal act in the *Summa Theologiae*, 296–99; the marriage debt, union, and procreation, 299–307; marriage in the *Summa contra Gentiles*, 285–88; marriage in the *Summa Theologiae*, 288–96; marriage in the *Supplementum* to the *Summa Theologiae*, 279–85; women, nature and role of, 275–79

Aquinas's anthropology, 198–99, 233–34; the body and knowledge, 209–13; man as composite of body and soul, 199–204, 306–7; original innocence and original sin, 226–32; personhood, 214–19; powers of a soul united to a body, 204–9;

Paul VI *(cont.)*
the papal commission on contraception, 73; *Humanae Vitae*, 6, 79–90, 152–60, 163, 188–93; *modi* submitted to the Second Vatican Council, 69–70; papal commission on contraception, 68
Pecci, Gioacchino, 37
penitentials, the, 13–14
periodic continence, 65–68, 84, 158, 193
Perone, Giovanni, 36
personalism: Aquinas on the person, 214–19; birth control debate, emergence in, 62–64; in *Humanae Vitae*, 80, 82–83; marriage, value of, 51; the personalistic norm, 128–30, 139–40, 142; Pius XII on, 57; religion and purity, connection between, 141–42; rise of, 4–5; sexual ethics and, 137–40; understanding of marriage based on, shift to, 51–55; of Wojtyła, 5–6, 112–22
"Personal Structure of Self-Determination, The" (Wojtyła), 124
phenomenology: ontology and, Wojtyła's effort to synthesize, 111–14, 117; Thomism and, question of combining, 314; Wojtyła's first major study of, 102
physicalism, 3–5; in the birth control debate, 63–65, 74; exterior principles of action and, 30–31; failure to incorporate the personalistic norm, 139; in *Humanae Vitae*, 89–90; in the language of Pius XI, 50
Pieper, Josef, 257
Pinckaers, Servais: Aquinas's theory of beatitude, 18, 22–23; freedom of indifference, 254; manualists as descendants of Ockham, 11; manualist tradition, critique of, 41, 43; moral and mystical theology, separation between, 32; on Ockham, 26, 28–31; on the pedagogy of the Society of Jesus, 33–35; on virtue, 253
Pius XI, 48–51, 65, 65n95
Pius XII, 56–57, 61–62, 65
Plato, 24, 209–11
Popik, Kristin, 276–77, 279, 290, 292–93, 295
Porter, Jean, 295
"Problem of Catholic Sexual Ethics, The" (Wojtyła), 115–16, 137–40
"Problem of Experience in Ethics, The" (Wojtyła), 123–24
"Problem of Scientific Ethics, The" (Wojtyła), 108

"Problem of the Theory of Morality, The" (Wojtyła), 123–24
procreation: education and upbringing of children included in, 281, 287–88, 305; legitimation of the sexual act, Aquinas on, 259, 300–304; natural instinct for reproduction, 148–49; natural law and, 190–91; as order of nature in marriage, 136–37; as primary end of marriage, 139–40; responsible parenthood and, 153–54; sexual difference for Aquinas in, 277; sexual ethics and, 3–4; the spousal meaning of the body and, 172. *See also* birth control
Protestant Reformation, 32–33
prudence, 235, 250–57, 268, 271, 288
purity, 141–43, 166n12, 178

Quay, Paul, 64

Ratzinger, Joseph, 199n1
Raymond of Peñafort, 14–15
reason: importance of for Aquinas, 225–26; passion and, 239–44; procreation and, 296–98; superiority of male for Aquinas, 278, 289; Wojtyła's trust in, 108–9
redemption, 178–83, 187
Redemptor Hominis (John Paul II), 167n15
"Religious Experience of Purity, The" (Wojtyła), 141–43, 145
Richard of St. Victor, 217
Riedmatten, Henri de, 73
Roberts, Christopher, 278n18
Rock, John, 46, 64–67
Roman Rota, 55–56
Routhier, Gilles, 69
Różycki, Ignacy, 94n6, 98n22

Sabetti, Aloysio, 42
sacramentality, principle of, 175n49
Sapieha, Cardinal Adam, 93
Scheler, Max, 98–102, 104–8, 117, 150n137
Schmitz, Kenneth, 104n57, 121, 150n134
scholasticism, 2–3, 31–33, 36, 95
Schu, Walter J., 129, 184–85n96
Scotus, John Duns, 25
Second Vatican Council. *See* Vatican Council II
self-determination: Ockham's view of, 28–29; relationship with God and, 168;